ALSO BY UCADIA

Pactum De Singularis Caelum
Pactum De Singularis Christus
Pactum De Singularis Islam
Pactum De Singularis Spiritus

Maxims of Divine Law
Maxims of Natural Law
Maxims of Cognitive Law
Maxims of Bioethics Law
Maxims of Ecclesiastical Law
Maxims of Positive Law
Maxims of Sovereign Law
Maxims of Fiduciary Law
Maxims of Administrative Law
Maxims of Economic Law
Maxims of Monetary Law
Maxims of Civil Law
Maxims of Criminal Law
Maxims of Education Law
Maxims of Food & Drugs Law
Maxims of Urban Law
Maxims of Company Law
Maxims of Technology Law
Maxims of Trade & Intellectual Property Law
Maxims of Security Law
Maxims of Military Law
Maxims of International Law

MISSALE CHRISTUS

TERTIUS

Proper of Sacraments, Rites and Prayers

Official English First Edition

By

UCADIA

Published by Ucadia Books Company, a Delaware stock corporation (File Number 6779670)
901 N Market St #705 Wilmington Delaware 19801.
First edition.

ISBN 978-1-64419-068-5

Pactum De Singularis Caelum
Covenant of One Heaven

Article 134 (Supreme Sacred Gifts & Rites)

Supreme Sacred Gifts and Rites of Heaven shall be the customary rules, standards and procedures whereby the Thirty-Three (33) Sacred Gifts of Heaven are properly administered and dispensed by qualified and authorised persons, in accord with the most sacred Covenant.

"**Missal of Christ**" (*Missale Christus*) shall be the original and primary sacred text containing the necessary rubrics, canons, sacramentaries, votives, invocations, instructions and orders for the proper conduct and proceeding of Sacred Liturgy of the Universal Rites of One Christ. The conduct of all sacramentaries concerning the thirty-three Sacraments and Extra-Sacramental Rites and Rubrics of Heaven shall be in accord with the Missal of Christ (Missale Christus).

Pactum De Singularis Christus
Covenant of One Christ

Article 14 (Missale Christus)

Universal Ecclesia of One Christ shall fulfil its sanctifying function through the Sacred Liturgy, being the rightful exercise of the presbyterial function entrusted to it by Christ. Within the Sacred Liturgy, the sanctification of humanity is perfected through visible signs and effected in a competent manner proper to each sign. Through the Sacred Liturgy, the worship of God and the Divine Creator of Heaven and Earth is conducted by the united Members of the Living Body of One Christ.

In accord with Article 134 (*Supreme Sacred Gifts and Rites*) of the most sacred Covenant *Pactum De Singularis Caelum*, The Missal of Christ (*Missale Christus*) shall be the original and primary sacred text containing the necessary rubrics, canons, sacramentaries, votives, invocations, instructions and orders for the proper conduct and proceeding of Sacred Liturgy of the Universal Rites of One Christ.

The conduct of all Sacramentals and Extra-Sacramentals of Heaven is in accord with the Missal of Christ (*Missale Christus*).

The Missal of Christ (*Missale Christus*) shall be divided into three (3) sacred books:-

(i) Proper of Life & Mysteries; and

(ii) Proper of Days of Heroes & Saints; and

(iii) Proper of Sacraments, Rites & Prayers.

MISSALE CHRISTUS

TERTIUS

PROPER OF SACRAMENTS, RITES & PRAYERS

CONTENTS

Title I – Holy Sacraments & Rites of Universal Ecclesia

I.I – DIVINE NATURE & PURPOSE OF SACRAMENTS

Divine Nature & Purpose of Sacraments

1. Revealed through authentic Christian faith is an immutable fact that each and every human being is simultaneously a spiritual being as well as a mental and physical being. Christ himself revealed this truth through his life, death and resurrection; and that our existence does not simply end with the physical death of our body; and that our purpose of being does not rest solely upon the experiences, wants or desires of everyday life.

Instead, Jesus Christ reveals to all people of all times and places that it is our ultimate destiny to be reconciled unto our ultimate Divine Creator - through care of our spiritual well being as much as our mental and physical well being. Moreover, despite our weaknesses and transgressions, no one be condemned or eternally cursed by Our Heavenly Creator; as all are granted the unmerited gifts of Divine Love, Divine Mercy and Divine Forgiveness. Furthermore, it is a tenet of Christian faith that our Divine Father entrusts to us through Christ the necessary gifts to nourish and protect our spiritual well being on our journey.

This is the primary reason and purpose of the Holy Sacraments as defended and honoured by those that follow the teachings of Christ above the lesser words of men and women that: *Through the Holy Spirit, the Divine Father with the Son, aided by the Grace of Mother Mary and all the saints and martyrs, bestows the offer of the extraordinary gifts of the Holy Sacraments upon each and every man, woman and child, and therefore the capacity to be reconciled with God, in fulfilment of the presence of the Kingdom of Heaven upon the Earth.*

Thus, the Holy Sacraments are not merely an expression of faith for Christians, but an essential element of existence itself. For without such Divine Grace, it follows that because of our human limitations it would be impossible to be reconciled to God by our own accord; or united with our Divine self by prayer and piety alone; or fully at peace with one another purely upon a virtuous and exemplary life.

Sacredness of Christian Life, Intention and Action

2. A true Christian is one who recognises the spark of the Divine in all things and the intrinsic sacredness of all life, intention and action. Thus, as Christ revealed the universal importance of free will and choice, so the Holy Sacraments are a Divine Gift that through the Holy Spirit illuminates the lives, minds and actions of the People of God.

An authentic Christian is one who openly embraces the intrinsic sacredness of Life, Intention and Action by bearing true witness to the Good News by serving the real needs of others as the Living

Embodiment of Christ.

It follows then that the intention behind each action is as important as the action itself as a demonstration of thanks and respect to God and the Divine Creator; and a profession of faith in God that the whole of life is sacred, not merely a narrow aspect of life such as conception or nativity or death. Indeed, to a true Christian, the celebration of the Eucharist through Mass is a high celebration of Divine Mercy, but not the only example of weekly or daily devotion. In the preparation of meals; and in the travel to and from destinations; and in the conduct of work or study; and in the interaction with others especially those less fortunate, are all manifest signs of an authentic Christian Life through the Holy Sacraments.

3. The word sacrament comes from the Latin word *sacramentum* being a composite word from the root *sacro/sacer* meaning "consecrate, dedicate, devote; or sacred, holy" and *mentum* meaning "a memorial, or instrument or event of intention, mind, intellect, judgement or reasoning". Origin and nature of the word Sacrament

Therefore, a sacrament by definition is an intended sacred memorial, or instrument or event (or all of these elements).

When such elements are officially defined and combined, they are often described as a *rite* or *rites* that are then required to be followed, usually in a precise manner, by one who is then duly authorised to perform such rites.

When the words associated with a sacrament are officially defined and combined, then such words are usually described as the *formula*, being precise phrases in combination with certain actions that form the rite.

4. All valid Sacraments share the same essential elements, being: General Character of Sacraments

(i) A defined structure in liturgy of at least one or more separate and deliberate Acts, themselves divided into smaller Parts representing completed Moments being sacred instances of units of time-space-location; and

(ii) One or more roles for authorised Persons known as Celebrant(s) officiating some or all of the Acts; and

(iii) One or more roles for Persons known as Participant(s) or Supplicants(s) who participate under the guidance of the Celebrant(s) in some or all of the Acts; and

(iv) One or more roles for Persons known as Observant(s) who witness the celebration of the Sacrament and validate it as a Sacred Event; and

(v) The memorialisation of the celebration of the Sacrament as a Sacred Event through some produced instrument representing a Record of the (Sacred) Event.

Source of valid Sacraments

5. All valid sacraments are those said to be derived from the Love, Mercy and Forgiveness of God and the Divine Creator through authentic Revelation. Therefore, valid sacraments are never formed by men alone; and certainly never genuinely formed by doctrine, but by the Revelation and the inspired instruction of the Holy Spirit.

Because all valid Sacraments are derived from God and the Divine Creator through authentic Revelation, the deeper knowledge and understanding of the Magisterium of Christ as expressed within the Good News of Holy Scripture is a living progression and cannot ever be properly concluded as fixed and immutable.

It is the height of arrogance, absurdity and error for men and women to suppose that God speaks to his people only when it is deemed doctrinally expedient. It is not for men to decide when God speaks, but entirely up to the Divine Creator whom he chooses to be his servants.

Therefore, while the Universal Ecclesia of Christ is able to declare the certainty, immutability and authenticity of the Good News, it is forbidden by the very words of Christ and the Apostles to close its heart to the continual revelations of the gift of the Holy Spirit in seeing more deeply and hearing more clearly.

Consecrated Persons as Instruments of Divine Grace not cause of it

6. As all sacraments by tradition involve one or more acts, or intentions, or formal rituals as prescribed by authentic and sacred liturgical works, a common error is to wrongly conclude that consecrated persons in administering a sacrament are the cause of it, rather than merely being an instrument of Divine Grace.

It is because of the inherit limitations and weaknesses of the human mind that men and women deliberately or inadvertently interpose their own moral judgements for those of God and the Divine Creator. Yet Christ himself warned his disciples against such hubris and supreme arrogance as demonstrated by the doctors of the law during those times.

An unmistakable characteristic of those who claim to be pious and yet are in opposition to the true Revelations of Christ through the authentic message of the Good News is that they readily impose themselves between Heaven and Earth as false gods. In contrast, a true servant of a calling to consecrated and clerical life in Christ, is one who constantly remains present to the fact that they are merely instruments of Divine Grace and not the cause of it.

7. While there have been periods of relative stability in what the faithful have interpreted through Revelation to be the authentic Holy Sacraments, it has not been an entirely static process, but one gained from deep contemplation, respect and evolution of spirit. Revelation and the Sacraments

The understanding of the Holy Sacraments today were not delivered fully formed through Sacred Scripture, but were discerned and revealed by the Holy Spirit over generations of faithful.

The Holy Spirit is an extraordinary teacher, whereby even the most protracted disputes may be overcome in the mutual acceptance of the fundamental truth of such Holy Sacraments as Baptism. This in itself is living proof of the ever evolving character of the Sacraments, even if the rubrics and formula of certain rites have not changed for extended periods of time.

8. In previous ages, when faced with the obstinate inflexibility of doctrines and laws concerning sacraments clearly in error and contradicting the Magisterium of Christ, certain Christians and Jews have reacted to such misguided behaviour by rationalising sacraments as optional, compared to the mandatory faith in the Good News of the Crucified and Risen Christ. Necessity of valid Sacraments

Thus, the obsessively narrow and punitive nature of some scholars and clergy has weakened and confused the very framework of Divinely ordained sacraments they claimed to protect; and weakened their universality among the faithful.

Christ himself is unequivocal concerning the authentic sacraments being vital signs and means to express and strengthen the bonds of love, knowledge, devotion and mercy between God and the Divine Creator of Heaven and Earth and the entire community of humanity.

Therefore, the clarity concerning the authentic nature of holy sacraments and their presence in the lives of all Christians is seen as a vital necessity and not a choice or option of authentic Christian faith.

I.II – SACRAMENTS, TRANSGRESSIONS & SIN

1. It is an ultimate tenet of Christian Faith that Christ suffered and died so that the sins of the world be forgiven. Christ himself made clear this as a key purpose for his arrival and return. Similarly, the most ancient records of the prophets and revelations of Heaven before Christ have Sacraments, Transgressions & Sin

given witness to a time that the notion of sin would be banished from the Earth forever.

Therefore, to speak most plainly, either Christ did fulfil his word or not. The existence of Sacred Liturgy and the presence of the most Holy Sacraments testifies to the most fundamental Christian belief that Christ entirely fulfilled his Divine Mission. Furthermore, every true Christian is called to demonstrate their faith to the words of Christ in testifying to this fact, that Christ did vanquish sin and the impediments between humanity and the Divine Creator of all existence.

Why then does the word "sin" still persist so prominently in previous lesser liturgies and the writings of men and women seeking to apply their interpretations to the words of Christ and God? Is it because wicked and evil acts have persisted throughout each generation? Or is it because no word could be found to substitute the notion of sin? Or has a persistent sign of lingering doubt existed for generations midst some of those entrusted by Christ to be his reliable representatives on Earth?

Free will and the capacity to transgress Divine Law

2. The Divine Creator in all aspects fully comprehends the consequences of free-will and that each and every person has the capacity to choose to do good or ill against their neighbour and themselves. Thus, Christ was fully aware of the capacity of future generations to still participate in vile and wicked behaviour against the hopes and dreams of the Divine Creator of all Existence.

Instead, Christ made clear a pillar of true Christianity is the end of the use of spiritual impediments as a weapon, in the same manner that the scribes, pharisees, lawyers, moneylenders, bankers and leaders did at his time.

Through the use of equivalent words to sin at the time of Christ, ancient and corrupt elites did use the notion of spiritual impediments to presume certain ethnicities, communities and people were inherently unable to possess certain property or rights, or travel to certain locations, or work in certain occupations. In other words, a claimed "Divinely Ordained" underclass of people, less than fully human.

At the time of Christ, wicked and vile priests had conspired with moneylenders and bankers to invent a form of "spiritual accounting" whereby transgressions represented both a spiritual and temporal debt and graces or indulgences represented a form of spiritual and temporal credit. Thus money was corrupted from being a means of exchange to being a means of cursing the very people that use it and perpetuating a system of perpetual financial enslavement, all with the approval and conspiracy of corrupt priests and teachers of law.

3. The words and actions of Christ are unambiguous and incapable of reasoned confusion concerning the fate of the notion of and use of Sin. His life, suffering, death, resurrection and return is a manifest sign of the vanquishing and elimination of the notion of Sin. To be a follower of Christ is to trust that he has completely banished forever the most wicked concept of Original Sin; and that Christ has vanquished all concepts and notions of inherited spiritual impediments that have been used to justify permanent underclasses of poor and debt slaves; and that Christ has ended any spiritual legitimacy or validity ascribed to ancient vile and perverse notions of using monetary and legal systems to somehow "monetise" sin.

Christ ending the notion of sin and manipulation of spiritual impediments

Indeed, there is ample evidence to suggest that the most vile and heretical notions of using spiritual impediments as a means of profiting from the misery of people via corrupted legal and financial systems have resurfaced again in certain societies and places through growing generations of nihilists, against the very teachings and commands of Christ. These people are the enemy of Heaven and Earth and hide as liberals or conservatives, priests and judges, bankers and leaders; and believe in nothing but their own greatness and narcissistic existence. They are always most dangerous to the future of humanity precisely because they see themselves as gods and care nothing for others.

4. The oldest forms of Christian Liturgy and expressions of faith of Christ give witness to the truth that the Unification of the Living Body of Christ as the Universal Ecclesia of Christ represents a new Heaven and a new Earth and fulfilment of the Kingdom of Heaven upon the Earth and the vanquishing of all notions and use of Sin.

Transgression & Forbiddence to use word Sin

In accord with Article 29 (*Divine Mercy, Remedy & Redemption*) of the most sacred Covenant *Pactum De Singularis Caelum*, the term and use of the word "Sin" is forbidden, reprobate, suppressed and never to be revived. Instead, the word and the equivalent concept of "**Transgression**" is be used to define mistake, fault, concept, default, fraud, profanity, tyranny and impiety.

Whilst references and honour to historic and canonical texts and scripture are permitted the continued use of the word in Sacred Liturgy in historic context, all teachings, lessons, education and interpretation as to present and future events and the reference to "sin" is absolutely forbidden to be continued and an offence against the Living Body of One Christ.

I.III – SACRAMENTS, PERSONS & RIGHTS

1. By their inherit nature, all Sacraments concern Persons and certain Rights, Powers, Authorities, Privileges, Qualities and Characters ascribed to them. In respect of Sacraments and of Law, there sometimes exists confusion between the notion of Persons compared to Beings. Sacraments, Persons & Rights

The Maxims of Divine Law teach us that a "**Being**" is the embodiment of the Divine in temporal form, possessing certain independent computational abilities. In contrast, a "**Person**" is a form of Sacred Circumscribed Space enclosing certain characteristics and appearances as to the identity of one or more Beings, formed through a valid entry, registration and record within a Roll in accord with the most sacred Covenant *Pactum De Singularis Caelum*.

Thus, as Beings exist in Space, the effect of Sacraments upon Persons necessarily affects their state of Being. Yet whilst Beings and Persons remain intimately linked, it must always be remembered they are important and distinct notions.

2. The significance of the true understanding of the notion and nature of Persons is born out by one of the most important Holy Sacraments of the Universal Ecclesia of One Christ in the form of the Rite of Baptism. Christ, Persons & Rite of Baptism

The Rite of Baptism is historically viewed as the "gateway to the sacraments". From the very beginning of the faith it has been understood that "through baptism people are freed from any spiritual impediment; and are reborn as children of God; and are indelibly connected to Christ as part of his Living Body as the Universal Ecclesia".

Of all the Sacraments and Rites, it is the Rite of Baptism that Christ remains insistent is key. The full power and revelation of this significance is only borne out by more deeply comprehending the context at the time.

At the time of Christ, an evil empire and philosophy ruled the world whereby a very small group of elites saw themselves as "living gods" with virtually unlimited rights, while the rest of humanity were seen as less than human. To maintain such nihilistic perversions, these elites corrupted ecclesiastical, civil and financial laws so that a man or woman not born to rare privilege was less than human as an Inferior Person.

God sees everything and Christ fully comprehended this perversion against the laws of Heaven and Earth. Christ knew that a Person can only be created by ecclesiastical acts. Thus the Rite of Baptism was the rite giving life to a new form of Person – a True Person free of any claimed spiritual impediment, or debts or inferiority to any one else.

3. To ignore the fundamental purpose of the Rite of Baptism of Christ in forming a True Person unblemished and with the full rights and dignities of Heaven, is to ignore one of the singular miracles of Christ and the presence of the embodiment of the Divine Creator on Earth.

Christ ending the notion of Inferior Persons and Slaves

The Christian Rite of Baptism ends any notion of Divinely ordained slavery, or class of inferior persons, or inherited spiritual or financial impediments, or a lack rights or dignities.

Only the most wicked generations of nihilists hiding in the garments of clergy, or judges, or scribes or pharisees or lawyers could possibly seek to diminish and hide this Mission of Christ. No Person is unloved by God. No Person is less in the eyes of God. No Person is condemned by God.

I.IV – CONSEQUENCES OF VANQUISH & ELIMINATION OF SIN

1. In accord with Article 29 (*Divine Mercy, Remedy & Redemption*) of the most sacred Covenant *Pactum De Singularis Caelum*, there are seven (7) levels of Transgression. The higher the level of Transgression, the more serious the transgression:-

Consequences of Vanquish and Elimination of Sin

(i) Mistake or Error; and

(ii) Fault (Delict); and

(iii) Contempt (Profanity); and

(iv) Default (Delinquency); and

(v) Fraud (Perfidy); and

(vi) Tyranny; and

(vii) Impiety.

2. Upon giving authentic witness to the vanquishing of Sin by Christ and the definition of Transgression, the concept of Salvation is fulfilled and satisfied and therefore can no longer be applied, or taught as a future aspiration. Instead, the Living Body of One Christ shall honour Divine Mercy and Divine Love in the form of Redemption and Credit, underwritten by the good character, behaviour and actions of people, in accord with the rules as defined by the most sacred Covenants *Pactum De Singularis Caelum* and *Pactum De Singularis Christus*.

Redemption and Salvation

Any ecclesiastical, civil, secret or private forms of law that seek to perpetuate the notion of the salvation of transgressions as the recovery or claim of debt; and of the treatment of people as wrecked upon the sea, or other admiralty and maritime concepts, shall be rendered null and void from the beginning and a Transgression of Delinquency, Profanity and Perfidy against God and the Divine Creator of all Existence and all Heaven and Earth.

3. Upon giving authentic witness to the vanquishing of Sin by Christ and the satisfaction of Salvation, all forms of money, finance and assets based upon the "monetisation of sin" or the "salvaging of debt or sin" are morally repugnant, profane, sacrilegious and to be conclusively and absolutely suppressed and never to be revived. Any monetary system or financial system based upon the claimed spiritual, or ecclesiastical, or moral bankruptcy of communities, or nations is absolutely and completely immoral, unlawful, illegal and null and void from the beginning, having no force or effect.

Credit and Debt and Sacraments

Any financial system or monetary system based upon liens against the people, or their persons or names or souls is morally repugnant, profane, sacrilegious and to be conclusively and absolutely suppressed and never to be revived, having no force or power or effect in law. Furthermore, the monetisation of birth certificates is absolutely prohibited.

Any body, fraternity, company, person, institute, society or entity that seeks to perpetuate the notion of the "Monetisation of Sin", or global or national bankruptcies, or "monetisation of birth certificates", or liens or other condemnations against the people shall have their rights, property, powers and authorities rendered null and void from the beginning and shall have recorded and memorialised the fact of their Transgression of Delinquency, Profanity and Perfidy against God and the Divine Creator of all Existence and all Heaven and Earth.

4. It is strictly forbidden to use any of the Holy Sacraments or any person holding Sacred Office to participate in any rite or practise concerning gold or silver held in reserves, or bars, or such places having any sacredness whatsoever.

Holy Sacraments forbidden to be used to bless, sanctify or recognise gold or silver reserves

The use of Gold or Silver in any form as the basis of underwriting currencies or assets or any financial instruments is an abomination and an affront against all forms of spiritual law and the laws of Christ and the Divine Creator; and against the only true spiritual currencies permitted to be used including Supreme Credo (Credits), Gold Credo (Credits) and Silver Credo (Credits).

Any persistent practice or ceremony that seeks to perpetuate or invoke that Gold or Silver in any way be a spiritual store of souls or any spiritual energy shall have no legitimacy, force or effect; and shall be an immediate cause for that person or persons to be stripped of Sacred Office, declared an apostate and to suffer the fate of interdiction.

5. The perpetuation of any concepts concerning Allodial Title or any other rights claimed indirectly upon the alleged spiritual impediments of others, especially if argued under the wicked, vile and banished notion of Original Sin, is an abomination and an affront against all forms of spiritual law and the laws of Christ and the Divine Creator; and against the rights prescribed within the most sacred Covenant *Pactum De Singularis Caelum*.

Holy Sacraments forbidden to be used to condone, perpetuate or support corrupt practices.

Any persistent practice or ceremony that seeks to perpetuate the promotion of an elite holding claim to greater rights under alleged spiritual laws, to the detriment of others who they claim are spiritually impaired shall have no legitimacy, force or effect; and shall be an immediate cause for that person or persons to be stripped of Sacred Office, declared an apostate and to suffer the fate of interdiction.

I.V – HOLY SACRAMENTS OF UNIVERSAL ECCLESIA

1. **Holy Sacraments of God** and the *Testament of Light* of Christ and the Holy Spirit are perpetually entrusted through the most sacred covenant *Pactum De Singularis Caelum* unto the Universal Ecclesia of One Christ as the Living Body of Christ.

Holy Sacraments of Universal Ecclesia

The Thirty Three (33) valid sacraments of *Summa Sacramenta* are authentically deposited in trust by God and the Divine Creator of all Heaven and Earth, through Christ and the work of the Holy Spirit, to the Universal Ecclesia of One Christ in accord with the *Authenticus Depositum Fidei* (Authentic Deposit of Trust).

2. As visible actions of Christ and his Ecclesia united as one insoluble Body, the valid sacraments of *Summa Sacramenta* are the signs and means to express and strengthen the bonds of love, knowledge, devotion and mercy between God and the Divine Creator of Heaven and Earth and the entire community of humanity.

Purpose of Summa Sacramenta

Accordingly, in the celebration of the sacraments, the sacred ministers and other members of the united Christian and Jewish family must use the greatest veneration and necessary diligence.

3. A valid and authentic Sacrament is a distinct and related set of Temporal and Divine Actions forming a significant moment of unity:-

Nature of Valid and Authentic Sacrament

(i) Temporal Actions as a *rite* or *rites*, following in a precise manner according to a set *formula*, some intended sacred memorial, instrument or event (or all of these elements); and

(ii) Divine Actions derived from the Love, Mercy and Grace of the Divine Creator through authentic revelation, in harmony with right intentioned Temporal Actions.

4. All valid sacraments are those said to be derived from Heaven and the Divine Creator through authentic Revelation. Valid sacraments are never formed by temporal beings alone; and certainly never genuinely formed by doctrine, but by the Revelation and the inspired instruction of the most sacred Covenant *Pactum De Singularis Caelum*, the sacred Covenant *Pactum De Singularis Christus* and related covenants and sacred texts. Source of valid Sacraments

5. All valid sacraments firstly owe their name according to the Divine Actions and Gifts associated with them and not by the Temporal Actions that may be associated. Thus Temporal Actions associated with a valid sacrament are more appropriately classified as a *rite* or *rites* of a sacrament. Name of valid Sacraments

6. A Sacrament not properly conferred in accord with the sacred Covenant *Pactum De Singularis Christus* has no ecclesiastic power nor effect in law and is invalid *ab initio* (from the beginning). Only authorised persons may validly confer a Sacrament of Heaven properly through the role of Celebrant, possessing the Right *Ius Divinum Sacramentum* as the Divine Right to grant and impart Holy Sacraments:- Conferral of valid Sacraments

(i) Only persons properly consecrated and ordained into Holy Orders or invested into office holding a Right derived from *Ius Divinum Magisterium* or *Ius Divinum Visium* or *Ius Divinum Oratorium* in accord with the most sacred Covenant *Pactum De Singularis Caelum* and the sacred Covenant *Pactum De Singularis Christus* possesses the powers and authority to confer and administer these sacraments under Extraordinary Conditions; and

(ii) Only persons properly invested into office holding the Right of *Ius Divinum Administratum*, *Ius Divinum Officium* or *Ius Divinum Imperium* in accord with the most sacred Covenant *Pactum De Singularis Caelum* and the sacred Covenant *Pactum De Singularis Christus* possesses the powers and authority to confer and administer these sacraments under Ordinary Conditions.

Sacred ministers cannot deny the sacraments to those who seek them at appropriate times and who are properly disposed, and are not prohibited by law from receiving them. All ministers have a sacred duty to take care that those who seek the sacraments are prepared to receive them by proper instruction and are attentive to the norms issued by competent authority.

In celebrating the sacraments, only those things required for the validity of the sacrament must be observed; accordingly, no one is to add, omit, or alter anything in them on one's own authority.

The minister is to seek nothing for the administration of the sacraments beyond the offerings defined by competent authority, always taking care that the needy are not deprived of the assistance of the sacraments because of poverty.

7. All valid sacred rites, also known as rituals, customs and acts are derived from the thirty three (33) valid sacraments of One Heaven. A valid ritual, custom or act derived from one of the thirty (33) valid sacraments and expressed ecclesiastically may be said to be on the "ecclesiastical side" of the law:- Character of Summa Sacramenta

(i) Seven (7) are known as the Key Sacraments, also known as the Keys of Heaven or simply The Keys being Recognition, Purification, Invocation, Obligation, Delegation, Satisfaction and Resolution; and

(ii) Fourteen (14) are known as the Cardinal Sacraments or The Ways being Sanctification, Sustentation, Unification, Amalgamation, Authentication, Absolution, Volition, Vocation, Testification, Compassion, Conscription, Convocation, Authorisation and Elucidation; and

(iii) Twelve (12) are known as the Apostolic Life Sacraments or the The Means being Inspiration, Resurrection, Incarnation, Confirmation, Illumination, Exultation, Glorification, Divination, Visitation, Salvation, Emancipation and Veneration.

I.VI – KEY SACRAMENTS

1. **Key Sacraments**, also known as *Clavem Sacramenta*, also known as "The Keys" are seven (7) of the thirty three (33) sacred rites of the supremely sacred Covenant *Pactum De Singularis Caelum* instituted by the Divine Creator and entrusted to the Society of One Heaven and all associated valid entities being Recognition, Purification, Invocation, Obligation, Delegation, Satisfaction and Resolution. The seven Clavem Sacramenta are:- Key Sacraments

(i) "***Ritus Sacramentum Recognosco***" be the Divine Right of the Key Sacrament of Recognition; and

(ii) "***Ritus Sacramentum Purificatio***" be the Divine Right of the Key Sacrament of Purification; and

(iii) "***Ritus Sacramentum Invocatio***" be the Divine Right of the Key Sacrament of Invocation; and

(iv) "***Ritus Sacramentum Obligatio***" be the Divine Right of the Key Sacrament of Obligation; and

(v) "***Ritus Sacramentum Delegatio***" be the Divine Right of the Key Sacrament of Delegation (Trust); and

(vi) "***Ritus Sacramentum Satisfactio***" be the Divine Right of the Key Sacrament of Satisfaction; and

(vii) "***Ritus Sacramentum Resolutio***" be the Divine Right of the Key Sacrament of Resolution.

2. The Key Sacraments of Heaven are a manifest symbol of the plenary authority of the Society and the sacred Covenant Pactum De Singularis Caelum, exemplified by the expression *potestas clavium* or simply the "Power of the Keys". Power of the Keys

3. Since the Key Sacraments are the same for every occasion and every Homo Sapien, whether living or deceased, it is only for the supreme authority of the one true apostolic Universal Ecclesia of One Christ to approve or define the requirements for their validity and what pertains to their licit celebration, administration, and reception and to the order to be observed in their celebration. Authority to define requirements

I.VII – CARDINAL SACRAMENTS

1. **Cardinal Sacraments** also known as *Cardinalis Sacramenta*, also known as "The Ways" are fourteen (14) of the thirty-three (33) sacred rites of the supremely sacred Covenant *Pactum De Singularis Caelum* instituted by the Divine Creator and entrusted to the Society of One Heaven and all associated valid entities being: Sanctification, Sustentation, Amalgamation (Union), Unification (Matrimony), Authentication (Record), Absolution (Confession), Volition (Oath), Vocation (Vow), Testification, Compassion (Mercy), Conscription (Binding), Convocation, Authorisation and Elucidation (Enlightenment):- Cardinal Sacraments

(i) "***Ritus Sacramentum Sanctificatio***" be the Divine Right of the Cardinal Sacrament of Sanctification; and

(ii) "***Ritus Sacramentum Sustentatio***" be the Divine Right of the Cardinal Sacrament of Sustentation; and

(iii) "***Ritus Sacramentum Amalgamatio***" be the Divine Right of the Cardinal Sacrament of Amalgamation (Union); and

(iv) "***Ritus Sacramentum Unificatio***" be the Divine Right of the Cardinal Sacrament of Unification (Matrimony); and

(v) "***Ritus Sacramentum Authentico***" be the Divine Right of the Cardinal Sacrament of Authentication (Record); and

(vi) "***Ritus Sacramentum Absolutio***" be the Divine Right of the Cardinal Sacrament of Absolution (Confession); and

(vii) "***Ritus Sacramentum Volitio***" be the Divine Right of the Cardinal Sacrament of Volition (Oath); and

(viii) "***Ritus Sacramentum Vocatio***" be the Divine Right of the Cardinal Sacrament of Vocation (Vow); and

(ix) "***Ritus Sacramentum Testificatio***" be the Divine Right of the Cardinal Sacrament of Testification; and

(x) "***Ritus Sacramentum Compassio***" be the Divine Right of the Cardinal Sacrament of Compassion (Mercy); and

(xi) "***Ritus Sacramentum Conscripto***" be the Divine Right of the Cardinal Sacrament of Conscription (Binding); and

(xii) "***Ritus Sacramentum Convocatio***" be the Divine Right of the Cardinal Sacrament of Convocation; and

(xiii) "***Ritus Sacramentum Auctoriso***" be the Divine Right of the Cardinal Sacrament of Authorisation; and

(xiv) "***Ritus Sacramentum Elucidato***" be the Divine Right of the Cardinal Sacrament of Elucidation (Enlightenment).

2. As ways, points, junctures and hinges for the actions of the Divine Creator and One Heaven, the Cardinal Sacraments are signs and gifts which express and strengthen the society and effect the sanctification of a community and thus contribute in the greatest way to establish, strengthen, and manifest spiritual unity.

Ways, Points, Junctures & Hinges

3. Since the Cardinal Sacraments are the same for every valid religion and Society, it is only for the supreme authority of the one true apostolic Universal Ecclesia of One Christ to approve or define the requirements for their validity and what pertains to their licit celebration, administration, and reception and to the order to be observed in their celebration.

Authority to define requirements

I.VIII – APOSTOLIC LIFE SACRAMENTS

Apostolic Life Sacraments

1. **Apostolic Life Sacraments**, also known as *Sacramenta Vitae Apostolicae*, also known as "The Means" are the twelve (12) of the thirty-three (33) sacred rites *of the supremely sacred Covenant Pactum De Singularis Caelum* instituted by the Divine Creator and entrusted to the Society of One Heaven and all associated valid entities being: Inspiration (Annunciation), Resurrection (Baptism), Incarnation (Christening), Confirmation (First Communion), Illumination, Exultation, Glorification, Divination, Visitation, Salvation, Emancipation and Veneration:-

   (i) "***Ritus Sacramentum Inspiratio***" be the Divine Right of the Apostolic Life Sacrament of Inspiration (Annunciation); and

   (ii) "***Ritus Sacramentum Resurrectio***" be the Divine Right of the Apostolic Life Sacrament of Resurrection (Baptism); and

   (iii) "***Ritus Sacramentum Incarnatio***" be the Divine Right of the Apostolic Life Sacrament of Incarnation (Christening); and

   (iv) "**Ritus Sacramentum Confirmatio**" be the Divine Right of the Apostolic Life Sacrament of Confirmation (First Communion); and

   (v) "***Ritus Sacramentum Illuminatio***" be the Divine Right of the Apostolic Life Sacrament of Illumination; and

   (vi) "***Ritus Sacramentum Exultatio***" be the Divine Right of the Apostolic Life Sacrament of Exultation; and

   (vii) "***Ritus Sacramentum Glorificatio***" be the Divine Right of the Apostolic Life Sacrament of Glorification; and

   (viii) "***Ritus Sacramentum Divinatio***" be the Divine Right of the Apostolic Life Sacrament of Divination; and

   (ix) "***Ritus Sacramentum Visitatio***" be the Divine Right of the Apostolic Life Sacrament of Visitation; and

   (x) "***Ritus Sacramentum Salvatio***" be the Divine Right of the Apostolic Life Sacrament of Salvation; and

   (xi) "***Ritus Sacramentum Emancipatio***" be the Divine Right of the Apostolic Life Sacrament of Emancipation (Unbinding) of any and all debts and obligations and reverence of funerary celebrations; and

(xii) "***Ritus Sacramentum Veneratio***" be the Divine Right of the Apostolic Life Sacrament of Veneration.

2. All Living and Departed Members of the Universal Ecclesia of One Christ are entitled to receive the full benefits of all twelve (12) Life Sacraments, whether living or deceased either upon the anniversaries prescribed for the conferral of a sacrament or upon proof of majority and competency for the specific Life Sacraments of Kommoinos, Adventus, Genius, Perfectus and Sapientia. A member who has not first received the prior Life Sacrament, cannot be admitted validly to receiving the subsequent sacrament. Conferral of Life Sacraments

3. As actions of the Divine Creator and One Heaven the Life Sacraments are signs and means which express and strengthen faith, render worship to the Divine and effect the sanctification of humanity and thus contribute in the greatest way to establish, strengthen, and manifest ecclesiastical unity. Accordingly, in the celebration of the sacraments the sacred ministers and the other members of the faithful must use the greatest veneration and necessary diligence. Authority to define requirements

I.IX – UNIVERSAL RITES

1. **Universal Ecclesia of One Christ** fulfils its sanctifying function through the *Sacred Liturgy*, being the rightful exercise of the presbyterial function entrusted to it by Christ. Within the Sacred Liturgy, the sanctification of humanity is perfected through visible signs and effected in a competent manner proper to each sign. Through the Sacred Liturgy, the worship of God and the Divine Creator of Heaven and Earth is conducted by the united Members of the Living Body of One Christ. The Missal of Christ (*Missale Christus*) are the Universal Rites defining the necessary rubrics, canons, votives, invocations, instructions and orders for the proper conduct and proceeding of Sacred Liturgy of the Universal Rites of One Christ. Universal Rites

2. "The following forms of Universal Rites are recognised and subject to the present sacred Liturgy, including (but not limited to):- Recognised Forms of Universal Rites

(i) "**Dedication**" being a form of Rite for the consecration of places, buildings, monuments and structures; and

(ii) "**Restoration**" being a form of Rite for the reconsecration of a place, building, monument or structure to its original sacred state; and

(iii) "**Reformation**" being a form of Rite for the restoring of a cleric state of office to a sacred state; and

(iv) "**Blessing**" being a form of Rite for invoking Divine assistance, favour, approval or protection; and

(v) "**Expulsion**" being a form of Rite for the driving out of a particular spirit or presence from Sacred Circumscribed Space; and

(vi) "**Nullification**" being a form of Rite for making legally and lawfully invalid a previous agreement or right; and

(vii) "**Deconsecration**" being a form of Rite for the removal of the consecrated and sacred state and function of a place, building, monument or structure; and

(viii) "**Secularisation**" being a form of Rite for the removal of the clerical authority of a person previously ordained; and

(ix) "**Exorcism**" being a form of Rite for the enforced removal, arrest or custody of one or more spirits in breach of the rules governing Sacred Circumscribed Space and the laws of Divine Trust, Mind and Spirit; and

(x) "**Inquisition**" being a form of Rite for the formal investigation into the truth and efficacy of some matter; and

(xi) "**Dispensation**" being a form of Rite for the granting of permission to do or perform an act not otherwise permitted, or to omit doing something otherwise enjoined; and

(xii) "**Abrogation**" being a form of Rite for the repealing by authority of some legislative act; and

(xiii) "**Ordination**" being a form of Rite for the consecration of a qualified candidate for the clerical state; and

(xiv) "**Inauguration**" being a form of Rite for the inducting into office with solemnity a person elected to high civil office; and

(xv) "**Sanction**" being a form of Rite for the enforced censuring, restriction or punishment of a person holding or occupying an office, in response to a demonstrated and proven act of maladministration or malfeasance; and

(xvi) "**Coronation**" being a form of Extra-Sacramental Rite for the solemn sacred ceremonial investiture of a person into sovereign office and the formation of a new sacred sovereign trust between the people and the new sovereign; and

(xvii) "**Investiture**" being a form of Rite for the solemn sacred acceptance of a person into office that involves the formation of a new trust involving the transfer and vesting of one or more Ecclesiastical or Sovereign or Official Rights.

I.X – CUSTOMARY RITES

1. **Divine Mercy and Respect** dictates that the faithful be accorded the privilege of honouring tradition and custom, where such rites do not contravene such Universal Laws prohibiting actual or simulated blood sacrifice, cursing or profanities. Thus, Members who hold affinity to one or more Traditional and Customary Rites as recognised by the sacred Covenant *Pactum De Singularis Christus* are free to continue the service and proceeding of certain registered and approved customary rites. Customary Rites

   However, rites that are not registered or approved may not be practised; and rites that are contrary to the norms and principles of the sacred Covenant *Pactum De Singularis Christus* are reprobate, forbidden and to be suppressed.

2. All Christian communities that honour tradition and custom, respecting Sacred Scripture and acknowledging the call for unity of the Living Body of Christ are welcome to enter into a lasting communion that dignifies such trust in God and the Divine Creator of all Existence and Heaven and Earth by ensuring the retention of traditional and customary titles, rights, ceremonies, churches and heritage under a solemn oath and vow that the entirety of the Living Body of Christ shall seek to protect and preserve such tradition and custom now and forever more. Traditions & Customary Rites of Christianity

   The present most sacred liturgy recognises the dignity and honour of the following Traditional and Customary Rites as eligible for communion and unity with the one true Living Body of Christ in the celebration of the Proper of Sacraments, Rites and Prayers of the Universal Ecclesia, whilst honouring their traditions and customs, being:

   (i) Roman (Catholic) Rite; and

   (ii) Latin (Catholic) Rite; and

   (iii) Anglican Rite; and

   (iv) Byzantine Rite; and

   (v) Chaldean Rite; and

   (vi) Armenian Rite; and

(vii) Antiochene Rite; and

(viii) Alexandrian Rite; and

(ix) Catholic Episcopal and Evangelical Rite; and

(x) Baptist Rite; and

(xi) Lutheran Rite; and

(xii) Methodist Rite; and

(xiii) Presbyterian Rite; and

(xiv) Pentecostal Rite; and

(xv) Evangelical Rite; and

(xvi) Scottish Rite; and

(xvii) Russian Orthodox Rite; and

(xviii) Greek Orthodox Rite; and

(xix) Romanian Orthodox Rite; and

(xx) Serbian Orthodox Rite; and

(xxi) Bulgarian Orthodox Rite; and

(xxii) Macedonian Orthodox Rite; and

(xxiii) Belarus Orthodox Rite; and

(xxiv) Georgian Orthodox Rite; and

(xxv) Ukranian Orthodox Rite; and

(xxvi) Ethiopian Orthodox Rite; and

(xxvii) Coptic Orthodox Rite; and

(xxviii) Armenian Orthodox Rite; and

(xxix) Syriac Orthodox Rite; and

(xxx) Eritrean Orthodox Rite; and

(xxxi) Latter Day Rite.

3. All Jewish communities that honour tradition and custom, respecting Sacred Scripture and acknowledging the call for unity of the Living Body of Christ are welcome to enter into a lasting communion that dignifies such trust in God and the Divine Creator of all Existence and

Traditions & Customary Rites of Judaism

Heaven and Earth by ensuring the retention of traditional and customary titles, rights, ceremonies, synagogues and heritage under a solemn oath and vow that the entirety of the Living Body of Christ shall seek to protect and preserve such tradition and custom now and forever more.

The present most sacred liturgy recognises the dignity and honour of the following Traditional and Customary Rites as eligible for communion and unity with the one true Living Body of Christ, being:

(i) Orthodox Rite; and

(ii) Conservative Rite; and

(iii) Reformed Rite.

Title II – Sacrament of Recognition

II.I – SACRAMENT OF RECOGNITION

1. Recognition (*Ritus Sacramentum Recognosco*) is the first of the seven (7) Key Sacraments, also known as the Keys of Heaven. The Sacrament of Recognition is the Key that unlocks the Virtue of Respect being the gift of unmerited Divine Gift of Grace and Favour of the Divine Creator of All. It is a necessary presence with all other valid Sacraments and Rites.

Sacrament of Recognition (Ritus Sacramentum Recognosco)

The Sacrament of Recognition is granted and conferred in accordance with the most sacred Covenants *Pactum De Singularis Caelum*, *Pactum De Singularis Christus*, and *Missale Christus* and associated approved liturgy.

2. The Divine Purpose of the Sacrament of Recognition is to assist persons in establishing a firm and clear respect of both their inner thoughts and mind and of the outer world around them. Thus, the Sacrament of Recognition is the formal observance and respect of a person, object or concept through its proper classification and estimation.

Divine Purpose of the Sacrament of Recognition

Recognition (and therefore Respect), is the foundation Living Virtue as all other virtues depend first upon the firm foundation of respect. Without self-respect, there can be no respect of others. Without respect of the world, there can be no self-respect.

3. There are only two (2) valid and licit forms for the Sacrament of Recognition as defined by the most sacred *Missale Christus* and associated approved liturgy being General and Ordinary :-

Forms of the Sacrament of Recognition

(i) "**General Recognition**" is when the Sacrament of Recognition is bestowed as part of the proper performance of the sign of the cross upon the body; or the bow of the head or genuflect of the knee before a consecrated symbol of the cross; and

(ii) "**Ordinary Recognition**" is when the Sacrament of Recognition is bestowed at the commencement of a formal Rite, through the proper performance of the sign of the cross upon the body; and the oration of suitable words in sacred Recognition of the Universal Mystery of Divine Nature.

II.II – DIVINE ACTION OF RECOGNITION

1. The Divine Action of *Recognition* is the supernatural effect of receiving the sanctifying essence of unmerited favour in the sight of

Divine Grace and Action of

the Divine Creator, otherwise known as Divine Grace. The Divine Action of Recognition is necessarily present in all authentic Rites and Sacraments. Recognition

2. *Recognition* is a wholly Divine and unmerited action, warranted by God and the Divine Creator. It is not an action effected within the temporal realm, nor can it be equated to physical terms or constructs. Understanding of Divine Action of Recognition

Recognition is the first and necessary Divine Gift and Sacrament to enable all others. Without Recognition there can be no certainty of sight or knowledge or intention of any other Rite or Sacrament.

The true nature of merit is not that a man or woman or soul be more or less worthy, but that no human being nor spirit can demand or claim the sight or favour of the Divine. The paradox of free will is that every being possesses the capacity to turn away and not recognise what is present. Furthermore, no being possesses the right to demand of another that they recognise and see anything against their free will. Existence itself depends upon the immutable truth of universal free will.

Thus, the supernatural sacrament of Recognition must be given freely upon the intention of God and the Divine Creator – hence the authentic action of Recognition is always by definition unmerited.

II.III – CONDITIONS OF SACRAMENT OF RECOGNITION

1. The Key Sacrament of Recognition is bestowed automatically when the three conditions for Ordinary or General Recognition are properly present, namely: Conditions of Sacrament of Recognition

   (i) *Intention* is the will of the mind to perform a deliberate action of identification and reverence; and

   (ii) *Conception* is the state of conscious mind, aware of both the intention to perform an act of identification and reverence with the Universal Ecclesia and its doctrines and wisdom; and

   (iii) *Action* as the act of performing a physical action of making the sign of the cross, or vocalising the appropriate sacred words of identification, or submission before the Divine Creator and Heaven.

2. The Sacrament of Recognition on its own carries no separate formal rites, nor requirement for the presence of consecrated and authorised persons for its administration. No formal rites

Title III – Sacrament of Purification

III.I – SACRAMENT OF PURIFICATION

1. **Purification (*Ritus Sacramentum Purificatio*) is the second of the seven (7) Key Sacraments**, also known as the Keys of Heaven. The Sacrament of Purification is the Key that unlocks the Living Virtue of Honesty (and Truth).

Sacrament of Purification (Ritus Sacramentum Purificatio)

The Sacrament of Purification may also be granted and conferred on its own in accordance with the most sacred Covenants *Pactum De Singularis Caelum*, *Pactum De Singularis Christus* and associated approved liturgy.

2. The Divine Purpose of the Sacrament of Purification is firstly to aid to clear and cleanse the mind from the temporary presence of negative, confusing or distracting thoughts, in order to help better focus attention and intention toward some sacred purpose. Secondly, Purification exists to prepare physical objects and bodies to receive other sacraments by dissolving any negative bonds, previous uses or intentions, or applications. Thus Purification is a necessary action in the preparing of sacramentals and the body of a priest before the ceremony of Mass.

Divine Purpose of the Sacrament of Purification

Purification does not exist as a form of "antidote" to an opposing construct known as impurities or impure thoughts. Such mental constructs give a wide margin for subjective interpretation and promote obsessive negative critique on temporary states of behaviour, in direct contradistinction to the purpose of Purification.

3. There are only two (2) valid and licit forms for the Sacrament of Purification as defined by the most sacred *Missale Christus* and associated approved liturgy being General and Ordinary:-

Forms of the Sacrament of Purification

(i) "**General Purification**" is when the Sacrament of Purification is bestowed automatically as part of the proper performance of duties by a person entrusted to act as a fiduciary or agent; and

(ii) "**Ordinary Purification**" is when the Sacrament of Purification is bestowed automatically as an element of a formal sacramental ritual performed by properly consecrated and ordained clergy.

III.II – DIVINE GRACE & ACTION OF PURIFICATION

1. The Divine Grace and Action of *Purification* is the supernatural effect of being cleansed of any imperfection and impediments that would otherwise hinder or negatively affect the ministration of liturgical rites

Divine Grace and Action of Purification

and duties, or the receiving of authentic sacraments, or the conduct of personal prayer and reflection.

Given that the very nature of the mystery of the Holy Sacraments is the receiving of certain Divine and Supernatural gifts or imprints of character, it follows that a potential recipient of such Divine and Supernatural gifts must be suitably respectfully prepared.

It also follows that a manifest lack of proper preparation, excluding those circumstances and conditions of need that preclude adequate preparation, can result in an impediment to the effect of certain Holy Sacraments and Rites, whether or not the presence of such an impediment is stated at the time.

2. The necessary actions associated with the conditions of receiving Purification within a proper Rite of the Universal Ecclesia are by definition intended to impose some degree of temporary discomfort, reflecting a satifactory level of submission and sacrifice associated with the relevant Sacrament and Rite.

Sacrifice & Suffering and Purification

Significantly, it is not however the intention to inflict forms of great pain or suffering upon those seeking the relevant Sacrament and Rite. Thus a complete absence of any form of discomfort or sacrifice, negates any possible manifestation of reasonable submission or purgation. Similarly, an overbearing or even sadistic level of discomfort, or pain or suffering also negates the efficacy of the relevant Sacrament and Rite.

3. *Purification* is a wholly Divine and unmerited action, warranted by God and the Divine Creator. It is not an action effected within the temporal realm, nor can it be equated to physical terms or constructs.

Understanding of action and Divine Grace of Purification

A person does not purify themselves, but supplicates their physical and mental being through earnest preparation, intention, sacrifice, suffering and actions in the faith of receiving the Divine Grace and Supernatural Action of Purification.

4. Except for the Sacrament of Recognition, the Divine Grace and Supernatural Action of *Purification* is central to the proper effect and ministration of all subsequent Rites and Sacraments.

Divine Grace and Action of Sacrament of Purification

However, the specific methods and actions associated with Purification differ according to the specific nature and circumstance of each valid and proper Sacrament and Rite.

Prior to the conduct of Ordinary Mass, participants are encouraged to fast from any form of consumption of meat or alcohol for a period of not less than eight hours.

Prior to the conduct of Sacraments and Rites that carry the imprint of a certain sacred and permanent character, participants are expected to fast from excessive consumption of alcohol or sugar; and remain celibate for a period of not less than fourteen days.

III.III – CONDITIONS OF SACRAMENT OF PURIFICATION

1. The Key Sacrament of Purification is bestowed automatically when the conditions for Ordinary or General Purification are properly present, namely: Conditions of Sacrament of Purification

(i) *Intention* is the clear action of mind to strongly desire to be purified; and

(ii) *Submission* is both the mental and physical action of humiliating oneself before the Divine and clearing the mind of all distracting traces of ego, self importance, negative emotions; and

(iii) *Purgation* as one or more physical actions of cleansing, including (but not limited to) cleaning the body, cleaning a room or place, abstinence, fasting, silence, isolation and deep meditative prayer.

2. The Sacrament of Purification on its own carries no separate formal rites on its own, nor mandatory requirement for the presence of consecrated and authorised persons for its administration. No formal rites

Title IV – Sacrament of Invocation

IV.I – SACRAMENT OF INVOCATION

1. Invocation (*Ritus Sacramentum Invocatio*) is the third of the seven (7) Key Sacraments, also known as the Keys of Heaven. The Sacrament of Invocation shall be granted and conferred in accordance with the most sacred Covenants *Pactum De Singularis Caelum*, *Pactum De Singularis Christus*, and *Missale Christus* and associated approved liturgy. Sacrament of Invocation (Ritus Sacramentum Invocatio)

2. Invocation by its very definition means "to vocalise some call for assistance; or the presence; or manifestation of one or more divine beings". Thus the positive vocal expression of such a call or entreaty or prayer is fundamental to the operative function of any proper Invocation. When it is not vocalised, an Invocation is properly defined as a Meditation. Invocation

   All communication to the *Angelorum Systemata* (Angelic Systems) of Angels, Saints and Beloved of Heaven by living Members of One Heaven shall be by Invocation in accord with the most sacred Covenant *Pactum De Singularis Caelum*. The methods, rules and standards of proper Invocation are defined by the most sacred Covenant *Pactum De Singularis Caelum* and associated covenants and no other. All properly conferred Invocation shall be received, recorded and acknowledged by the *Angelorum Systemata* (Angelic Systems) of One Heaven.

   An Invocation may be memorialised in writing as witness to the event. However, any such memorandum or certificate is always dependent upon the action of the said Invocation first being spoken.

   A proper Invocation may stand alone, or may represent part of a more complex series of ritual or events. When an Invocation is made from the use of some formula of words in prose, or sung or spoken, then it shall be known more formally as an Incantation. However, when a proper Invocation stands alone and involves the use of free form and self selection of words by the one making the Invocation, then it shall be known simply as an Invocation.

3. Seven types of Invocation or Meditation (non-vocalised Invocation) are recognised being *Adoration, Blessing, Intervention, Intercession, Confession, Lamentation* and *Thanksgiving*:- Characteristics of Invocation

   (i) "**Adoration**" is recognised as the type of Invocation or Meditation used for giving honour and praise to a higher spiritual presence; and

   (ii) "**Blessing**" is recognised as the type of Invocation or

Meditation used to summons an authentic spiritual presence to another, often consonant with the act of consecration and the ritual of anointing; and

(iii) "**Intervention**" is recognised as the type of Invocation or Meditation used for directly summonsing the presence of spirits or asking something for one's self; and

(iv) "**Intercession**" is recognised as the type of Invocation or Meditation used for asking something for others; and

(v) "**Confession**" is recognised as the type of Invocation or Meditation used for the atonement and repentance of wrongdoing and the asking of forgiveness; and

(vi) "**Lamentation**" is recognised as the type of Invocation or Meditation used for crying in distress and asking for vindication; and

(vii) "**Thanksgiving**" is recognised as the type of Invocation or Meditation used for offering gratitude.

IV.II – DIVINE GRACE & ACTION OF INVOCATION

1. The Divine Grace and Action of *Invocation* is the supernatural effect of vocalising some call for assistance; or the presence; or manifestation of one or more divine beings. Divine Grace and Action of Invocation

2. Invocation is a wholly Divine and unmerited action, warranted by God and the Divine Creator. It is not an action effected within the temporal realm, nor can it be equated to physical terms or constructs. Understanding of action and Divine Grace of Invocation

3. The Divine Grace and Supernatural Action of Invocation is central to the proper effect of Divine Communciation as Invocation is the primary means of communication with and between the Angels, Saints and Beloved of the *Angelorum Systemata* (Angelic Systems) of Heaven. Divine Grace and Action of Sacrament of Invocation

IV.III – CONDITIONS OF SACRAMENT OF INVOCATION

1. While the genuine Intention of a proper Invocation or Meditation (non-vocalised Invocation) is in itself the most important element of a valid Invocation, the following elements are recognised as the optimum structure for a valid Invocation being Identification, Petition and Affirmation:- The fundamental elements of valid Invocation

   (i) *Identification* is the identity of the person or group in whose name the Invocation is directed; and

(ii) *Petition* is the body of the Invocation itself; and

(iii) *Affirmation* is the offering and affirmation of the one who makes the Invocation as their commitment to the positivity of Intention and the truth of Petition.

Reprobate, Profane and Repugnant forms of Invocation

2. In accord with the most sacred Covenant *Pactum De Singularis Caelum*, an Invocation shall be reprobate, profane, repugnant and therefore invalid and improper and rejected by the Angels, Saints and Beloved of the *Angelorum Systemata* (Angelic Systems) of Heaven:-

(i) If it is deliberately harmful, negative or malevolent in its intent, design or inference; or

(ii) If it is deliberately dishonest, deceptive or perfidious in its intent, design or inference; or

(iii) If it is frivolous, or profane or disrespectful in its intent, or tone, or design or inference; or

(iv) If it is irrational, or unreasonable or illogical in its intent, or tone, or design or inference; or

(v) If it is motivated or driven by hate, greed, jealously, anger or lust; or

(vi) If it is motivated or driven by an attempt to shift blame or avoid accepting self-responsibility; or

(vii) If it is motivated or driven by a desire, or wish, or worship of money or abundant material wealth.

Title V – Sacrament of Obligation

V.I – SACRAMENT OF OBLIGATION

1. **Obligation (*Ritus Sacramentum Obligatio*) is the fourth of the seven (7) Key Sacraments**, also known as the Keys of Heaven. The Sacrament of Obligation is the Key that unlocks the Living Virtue of Commitment and Fortitude. Sacrament of Obligation (Ritus Sacramentum Obligatio)

   The Sacrament of Obligation may also be granted and conferred on its own in accordance with the most sacred Covenants *Pactum De Singularis Caelum*, *Pactum De Singularis Christus*, and *Missale Christus* and associated approved liturgy.

2. The purpose of the sacrament of Obligation is the formal recognition and celebration of entrusting to the Divine Creator through a solemn consensual covenant certain promises which one or more persons bind themselves to honour and uphold. Divine Purpose of the Sacrament of Obligation

3. There are only two (2) valid and licit forms for the Sacrament of Obligation as defined by the most sacred *Missale Christus* and associated approved liturgy being General and Ordinary:- Forms of the Sacrament of Obligation

   (i) "**General Obligation**" is when the Sacrament of Obligation is bestowed automatically as part of the proper formation of a Binding relation in association with a promise, or pledge, or agreement or security, or surety or bond; and

   (ii) "**Ordinary Obligation**" is when the Sacrament of Obligation is bestowed automatically as an element of a formal sacramental ritual performed by properly consecrated and ordained clergy.

V.II – DIVINE GRACE & ACTION OF OBLIGATION

1. The Divine Grace and Action of *Obligation* is the supernatural effect of personal and willing sacrifice and commitment to performance of one or more duties being recognised in Heaven. Divine Grace and Action of Obligation

2. Obligation is a wholly Divine and unmerited action, warranted by God and the Divine Creator. It is not an action effected within the temporal realm, nor can it be equated to physical terms or constructs. Understanding of action and Divine Grace of Obligation

3. The Divine Grace and Supernatural Action of Obligation is central to the proper effect of all subsequent Sacraments imparting a permanent character. Divine Grace and Action of Sacrament of Obligation

   Without a personal willingness and expression of some sacrifice and commitment to performance of one or more duties, the imparting of such supernatural characteristics will necessarily be impeded.

This is because any valid and legitimate Office under Heaven necessarily demands a certain level of self discipline, self sacrifice and performance of duty. Thus, the presence of the Holy Sacrament of Obligation is essential to imparting any such characteristics.

V.III – CONDITIONS OF SACRAMENT OF OBLIGATION

1. The Key Sacrament of Obligation is bestowed automatically when the conditions for Ordinary or General Obligation are properly present, namely: Conditions of Sacrament of Obligation

(i) *Intention* is the establishment of the willingness of a person, free from coercion or mental reservation, to undertake one or more duties; and

(ii) *Consideration* is the terms whereby one or more duties are to be performed; and

(iii) *Acceptation* is the formal acceptance of the terms of such duties and performance.

2. The Sacrament of Obligation on its own carries no formal rites, nor requirement for the presence of consecrated and authorised persons for its administration. No formal rites

Title VI – Sacrament of Delegation

VI.I – SACRAMENT OF DELEGATION

1. Delegation (*Ritus Sacramentum Delegatio*) is the fifth of the seven (7) Key Sacraments, also known as the Keys of Heaven. The Sacrament of Delegation is the Key that unlocks the Living Virtue of Trust and Faith.

Sacrament of Delegation (Ritus Sacramentum Delegatio)

The Sacrament of Delegation may also be granted and conferred on its own in accordance with the most sacred Covenants *Pactum De Singularis Caelum*, *Pactum De Singularis Christus*, and *Missale Christus* and associated approved liturgy.

2. The purpose of the Sacrament of Delegation is the formal recognition and blessing of a relationship and agreement whereby certain Form, Rights and Obligations are lawfully delegated to the control of one or more Persons as fiduciaries for the benefit of one or more other Persons.

Divine Purpose of the Sacrament of Delegation

3. There are only two (2) valid and licit forms for the Sacrament of Delegation as defined by the most sacred *Missale Christus* and associated approved liturgy being General and Ordinary:-

Forms of the Sacrament of Delegation

(i) "**General Delegation**" is when the Sacrament of Delegation is bestowed automatically as part of the proper formation of a Trust relation in the making of a true Oath and one or more Vows and then accepting such Oath to form the positions of Trustor and Trustee in relation; and

(ii) "**Ordinary Delegation**" is when the Sacrament of Delegation is bestowed automatically as an element of a formal sacramental ritual performed by properly consecrated and ordained clergy.

VI.II – DIVINE GRACE & ACTION OF DELEGATION

1. The Divine Grace and Action of *Delegation* is the supernatural effect of bestowing one or more rights, authorities or powers from Heaven; and from a higher Office to a lower Office.

Divine Grace and Action of Delegation

No authority or rights or power may be claimed or bestowed or enacted from any Office in any temporal or Divine realm without first the presence of the Divine Grace and Action of *Delegation*.

2. *Delegation* is a wholly Divine and unmerited action, warranted by God and the Divine Creator. It is not an action effected within the temporal realm, nor can it be equated to physical terms or constructs.

Understanding Divine Grace of Delegation

3. The Divine Grace and Supernatural Action of Delegation is central to the proper effect of the function of every and any legitimate and valid Office and source of power and authority within every temporal and spiritual realm.

Divine Grace and Action of Sacrament of Delegation

All rights, powers and authority associated with any Office must first be delegated from the Divine according to the proper conditions of such rights, powers and authority, through the Divine Grace and Action of *Delegation*.

VI.III – CONDITIONS OF SACRAMENT OF DELEGATION

1. The Key Sacrament of Delegation is bestowed automatically when the conditions for Ordinary or General Delegation are properly present, namely:

Conditions of Sacrament of Delegation

(i) *Authorisation* is the establishment of one or more clear purpose for the bestowing of one or more rights, powers or authorities; and the specific source in valid and legitimate law of such authorisation; and

(ii) *Limitation* as the act of demonstrating the limits and conditions of authority to be bestowed; and

(iii) *Benefication* as the act of receiving the benefit of the right, power or authority in sacred trust.

2. The Sacrament of Delegation on its own carries no formal rites, nor requirement for the presence of consecrated and authorised persons for its administration.

No formal rites

Title VII – Sacrament of Satisfaction

VII.I – SACRAMENT OF SATISFACTION

1. **Satisfaction (*Ritus Sacramentum Satisfactio*) is the sixth of the seven (7) Key Sacraments**, also known as the Keys of Heaven. Sacrament of Satisfaction (Ritus Sacramentum Satisfactio)

   The Sacrament of Satisfaction may also be granted and conferred on its own in accordance with the most sacred Covenants *Pactum De Singularis Caelum*, *Pactum De Singularis Christus*, and *Missale Christus* and associated approved liturgy.

2. The purpose of the sacrament of Satisfaction is the formal recognition of the fulfilment and completion of any outstanding conditions and terms of an agreement recognised as possessing sacred value and importance. Divine Purpose of the Sacrament of Satisfaction

3. There are only two (2) valid and licit forms for the Sacrament of Satisfaction as defined by the most sacred *Missale Christus* and associated approved liturgy being General and Ordinary:- Forms of the Sacrament of Satisfaction

   (i) "**General Satisfaction**" is when the Sacrament of Satisfaction is bestowed automatically as part of the noble and pious forgiveness of debts, the proper settlement and closure of accounts, the zeroing of balances and the provision of proper proof of such fiduciary obligations; and

   (ii) "**Ordinary Satisfaction**" is when the Sacrament of Satisfaction is bestowed automatically as an element of a formal sacramental ritual performed by properly consecrated and ordained clergy.

VII.II – DIVINE GRACE & ACTION OF SATISFACTION

1. The Divine Grace and Action of *Satisfaction* is the supernatural effect of recognition of the fulfilment and completion of any outstanding conditions and terms of an obligation recognised as possessing sacred value and importance. Divine Grace and Action of Satisfaction

2. *Satisfaction* is a wholly Divine and unmerited action, warranted by God and the Divine Creator. It is not an action effected within the temporal realm, nor can it be equated to physical terms or constructs. Understanding of action and Divine Grace of Satisfaction

3. The Divine Grace and Supernatural Action of *Satisfaction* is central to the proper effect of properly concluding sacred obligations with respect, dignity and honour. Divine Grace and Action of Sacrament of Satisfaction

VII.III – CONDITIONS OF SACRAMENT OF SATISFACTION

1. The Key Sacrament of Satisfaction is bestowed automatically when the conditions for Ordinary or General Satisfaction are properly present: Conditions of Sacrament of Satisfaction

    (i) *Identification* is the identification of the sacred obligation that is satisfied; and

    (ii) *Verification* is the verification and conformation of satisfaction; and

    (iii) *Gratification* is the grace, merit, gratitude and esteem granted in honouring the satisfaction of one or more sacred obligations.

2. The Sacrament of Recognition on its own carries no formal rites, nor requirement for the presence of consecrated and authorised persons for its administration. No formal rites

Title VIII – Sacrament of Resolution

VIII.I – SACRAMENT OF RESOLUTION

1. Resolution (*Ritus Sacramentum Resolutio*) is the seventh of the seven (7) Key Sacraments, also known as the Keys of Heaven. — Sacrament of Resolution (Ritus Sacramentum Resolutio)

   The Sacrament of Resolution may also be granted and conferred on its own in accordance with the most sacred Covenants *Pactum De Singularis Caelum*, *Pactum De Singularis Christus*, and *Missale Christus* and associated approved liturgy.

2. The purpose of the Sacrament of Resolution is the formal recognition of agreed decisions, determinations and solutions as both a conclusion as well as progression of one or more subsequent events. — Divine Purpose of the Sacrament of Resolution

3. There are only two (2) valid and licit forms for the Sacrament of Resolution as defined by the most sacred *Missale Christus* and associated approved liturgy being General and Ordinary:- — Forms of the Sacrament of Resolution

   (i) "**General Resolution**" is when the Sacrament of Resolution is bestowed automatically as part of the proper conduct and intention of two or more persons in respect of a formal proposal of solution; and

   (ii) "**Ordinary Resolution**" is when the Sacrament of Resolution is bestowed automatically as an element of a formal sacramental ritual performed by properly consecrated and ordained clergy.

VIII.II – DIVINE GRACE & ACTION OF RESOLUTION

1. The Divine Grace and Action of *Resolution* is the supernatural effect of recognition of agreed decisions, determinations or solutions as both a conclusion or progression of events. — Divine Grace and Action of Resolution

   All judgements, rulings, commands, orders and sentences depend upon the Divine Grace and Action of *Resolution.*

2. *Resolution* is a wholly Divine and unmerited action, warranted by God and the Divine Creator. It is not an action effected within the temporal realm, nor can it be equated to physical terms or constructs. — Understanding of action and Divine Grace of Resolution

3. The Divine Grace and Supernatural Action of *Resolution* is central to the proper effect of all judgements, rulings, commands, orders and conclusions not otherwise satisfied by the Sacrament of Satisfaction. — Divine Grace and Action of Sacrament of Resolution

VIII.III – CONDITIONS OF SACRAMENT OF RESOLUTION

Conditions of Sacrament of Resolution

1. The Key Sacrament of Resolution is bestowed automatically when the conditions for Ordinary or General Resolution are properly present:
   - (i) *Identification* is the identification of the item or matter to be resolved; and
   - (ii) *Authorisation* is the properly delegated authority, right or power to resolve by conclusion; and
   - (iii) *Conclusion* is the action and decision issued under the Sacrament of Resolution.

No formal rites

2. The Sacrament of Resolution on its own carries no formal rites, nor requirement for the presence of consecrated and authorised persons for its administration.

Title IX – Sacrament of Sanctification & Rite of Consecration

IX.I – SACRAMENT OF SANCTIFICATION

1. Sanctification (*Ritus Sacramentum Sanctificatio*) and Rite of Consecration is the first of the fourteen (14) Cardinal Sacraments, also known as the Ways of Heaven. *Sacrament of Sanctification (Ritus Sacramentum Sanctificatio)*

   The Sacrament of Sanctification and Rite of Consecration may also be granted and conferred on its own in accordance with the most sacred Covenant *Pactum De Singularis Caelum*, *Pactum De Singularis Christus*, and *Missale Christus* and associated approved liturgy.

2. The purpose of the Sacrament of Sanctification is the solemn dedication to Divine purpose and service of a particular person, place, object or thing, thus the formation of *Sacred Circumscribed Space*. Only the Rite of Consecration properly conferred creates Sacred Circumscribed Space. *Sanctification*

3. Sacred Circumscribed Space is a uniquely recorded enclosure and dimension of Ucadia Sacred Space-Day-Time as prescribed by the most sacred Covenant *Pactum De Singularis Caelum*. Only those duly authorised and legitimate Ucadian Bodies, Ucadian Societies, Ucadian States, Ucadian Persons and Ucadian Companies, or those bodies, persons or corporations granted limited Rights under Convention and Treaty are permitted to record, register, keep and maintain Sacred Circumscribed Space. *Sacred Circumscribed Space*

4. The Universal Ecclesia of Christ having been granted certain Rights of Ecclesiastical and Sovereign Dominion by the Divine Creator of all Existence and all Heaven and Earth, reserves its absolute Rights to assert, declare, affirm, avow, enforce and defend its Divine and Natural Rights to record, register, keep and maintain Sacred Circumscribed Space, by any and every lawful means necessary. *Authority of Universal Ecclesia and Sacred Circumscribed Space*

5. All proper, valid and legitimate Sacred Circumscribed Space is clearly and uniquely named dimension of Ucadia Space-Day-Time, whereby: *Elements of valid Sacred Circumscribed Space*

   (i) Such Sacred Circumscribed Space is properly defined, consistent with the most sacred Covenant *Pactum De Singularis Caelum*; and

   (ii) The specific Sacred Circumscribed Space is able to properly define its origin to a higher jurisdiction of Sacred Circumscribed Space, also identified by a proper eighteen digit and character number and identifier; and

(iii) The specific Sacred Circumscribed Space was either formed in accord with the most sacred Covenant Pactum De Singularis Caelum, or associated Covenants and Charters, or by one or more properly dispensed sacraments of the thirty three *Summa Sacramenta*; and

(iv) The Sacred Circumscribed Space does not contradict or usurp any previous proper, valid and legitimate existing Sacred Circumscribed Space.

6. Any claimed space, close, place, region, zone, precinct or any other type of enclosure formed by edict, or statute or sacrament that is in conflict with the most sacred Covenants *Pactum De Singularis Caelum* and *Pactum De Singularis Christus*, shall be invalid, illegitimate and null and void ab initio (from the beginning), having no force or effect or Rights in law.

Space created by falsity or error

7. Any and all Enclosure Acts issued by any parliaments, monarchs or bodies; and all subsequent, dependent and related Statutes, including but not limited to all fraudulent, perfidious, false and deceptive documents purported to be of an earlier age in relation to the claimed enclosure of certain lands, spaces, closes, fields, places, regions, zones, precincts, territories, dominions and estates are hereby disavowed as morally repugnant, profane, sacrilegious, heretical and contrary to the Rule of Law, Christian teachings, Civilised Society, Divine Law, Natural Law and are therefore invalid, illegitimate and null and void ab initio (from the beginning), having no force or effect or Rights in law.

Unilateral acts of enclosure false and morally repugnant

8. All Measurement and Standards of Sacred Circumscribed Space shall always be in accord with the most sacred Covenant *Pactum De Singularis Caelum*, associated covenants and charters and the present sacred Liturgy. All other forms of measurement and standards shall be null and void, unlawful and illegal, having no force or effect, unless the non-Ucadian and foreign body, or foreign society, or foreign person or foreign corporation has a Convention or Treaty with the Universal Ecclesia of One Christ.

Measurement and Standards of Sacred Circumscribed Space

9. By Divine Mandate and Authority, the Universal Ecclesia of One Christ shall form, maintain and keep in custody the following sixteen types of Registers of Sacred Circumscribed Space, including (but not limited to):

Character of Sacred Circumscribed Space

(i) *Land* (including all names, places and words also used to define Land) as a fixed and circumscribed piece of ground and earth of one Acre or more in surface area and then measured from the centre of the planet to the centre point of the surface area; and

(ii) *Forest* as a fixed and circumscribed piece of ground and earth of ten Acres or more in surface area that is preserved or reclaimed wilderness, natural habitat, untouched and uncultivated for agriculture; and

(iii) *Island* (including all names, places and words also used to define Island) as a fixed and continuous piece of ground and earth, larger than twelve Acres in surface area; and circumscribed by water; and

(iv) *Sea* (including all names, places and words also used to define not land) as a fixed and continuous area of open water, larger than twelve thousand Acres in surface area; and circumscribed by at least two or more Islands and at least one other Sea; and

(v) *Air* (including all names, places and words also used to define neither land nor water) as a fixed and circumscribed piece of space between Land and the outer reaches of the atmosphere of a planet; and

(vi) *Divine Person* as movable circumscribed space inhabited by the spirit of one or more Divine Beings; and

(vii) *True (Natural) Person* as movable circumscribed space inhabited by the physical and living biological body of one or more Homo Sapiens; and

(viii) *Superior (Legal) Person* as movable circumscribed space inhabited by the legal construct of a legal body (estate) possessing one more more rights to property; and

(ix) *Instrument* as fixed circumscribed space formed within the bounds of a physical or digital document, whereby the entry of the identity of a legal body or rights or event or other elements exist; and

(x) *Object* as fixed circumscribed space inhabited by an object; and

(xi) *Office* as a fixed or movable circumscribed space inhabited by a Person; and

(xii) *Place* as a fixed circumscribed space inhabited by two or more Persons; and

(xiii) *Network* as a digital circumscribed space of networked computers, inhabited by Persons as Network Users; and

(xiv) Internet as a digital circumscribed space, inhabited by Persons as Users; and

(xv) *Domain* (also Web Domain) as a digital circumscribed space of web information, inhabited by Persons as Network Users; and

(xvi) *Database* as a digital circumscribed space of digital information, inhabited by Persons as Database Users or Application Users.

10. Sacred Circumscribed Space is by logic and definition the space enveloping and surrounding an element; and its domain of existence. It is therefore a gross error to presume that Sacred Circumscribed Space is the element itself.

Sacred Circumscribed Space is space not the element within the space

11. Any and all claimed Sacred Circumscribed Space held as Allodial Title or Peculiar Title (as a Peculiarity) and therefore claimed to be owned absolutely, free of any claim is hereby disavowed as an absurdity and abomination before all Heaven and Earth; and is condemned as a profound sacrilege, heresy, profanity, morally repugnant, perfidious and deliberately false, having no force or effect in law. Furthermore, every Member of the Universal Ecclesia of One Christ is empowered by *Sacred Writ*, to pursue any, every and all means to ensure any and all records of such profanity, sacrilege, heresy and abomination before all Heaven and Earth is expunged, removed, withdrawn, determined, extinguished and abolished, including any and all false presumptions of claiming such false rights under covenants as "chosen people" or blood heritage or any other falsity.

Allodial or Peculiar Title as Abomination

12. There are only four (4) valid and licit forms for the Rite of Consecration as defined by the most sacred *Missale Christus* and associated approved liturgy being General, Dedicatory, Ordinary and Extraordinary:-

Forms of the Rite of Consecration

(i) "**General Consecration Rite**" is when the Sacrament of Sanctification is imparted through the authority and character of Holy Orders of one who is properly ordained, to then solemnly dedicate to Divine purpose and service a particular person, place, object or thing and the formation of Sacred Circumscribed Space. For example, General Consecration is the implicit form of the sacrament as an element of all Apostolic Life Sacraments; and

(ii) "**Dedicatory Consecration Rite**" is when the Sacrament of Sanctification is imparted through the authority and character of Holy Orders of one who is propertly ordained, to then solemnly dedicate a place, object or thing, already generally consecrated (already created as Sacred Circumscribed Space) and set it apart for religious purposes; and

(iii) "**Ordinary Consecration Rite**", also known as Holy Orders, is when the Sacrament of Sanctification is permanently imprinted upon the character of willing, qualified and competent candidates, to be set apart as Clergy and dedicated in life and service to the Evangelisation of the Paschal Mystery of Christ; and the Sacred Scripture; and the most sacred unity and fulfilment of the Good News; and the pastoral care of the people through the continual performance of heroic acts of virtue; and the gift of the religious rites and ceremonies of the Living Body of Christ; and

(iv) "**Extraordinary Consecration Rite**", also known as Holy Writ, is when the Sacrament of Sanctification is bestowed by and through the authority of the Supreme Patriarch; or through the authorised and licit actions of specifically commissioned and competent clergy to perform certain solemn rites and actions of Invocation, Incantation, Officium, Testification, Dispensation, Veneration, Sanction and Unction.

IX.II – DIVINE GRACE & ACTION OF SANCTIFICATION

1. The Divine Grace and Action of *Sanctification* is the supernatural effect of creating Sacred Circumscribed Space. Divine Grace and Action of Sanctification

2. *Sanctification* is a wholly Divine and unmerited action, warranted by God and the Divine Creator. It is not an action effected within the temporal realm, nor can it be equated to physical terms or constructs. Understanding of action and Divine Grace of Sanctification

3. The Divine Grace and Supernatural Action of *Sanctification* is central to the proper effect of Sacred Circumscribed Space and any and all forms of valid form associated with one or more records. Divine Grace and Action of Sacrament of Sanctification

   In the absence of the Divine Grace and Supernatural Action of *Sanctification* there can be no legitimate form or record of Land, Forest, Island, Sea, Air, Person, Instrument, Object, Office, Place, Network, Internet, Domain or Database.

IX.III – RITE OF CONSECRATION

1. The Rite of Consecration is implicit as an element of all Life Sacraments and may not be conducted as a replacement or alternate sacrament to an established Sacrament identified as possessing the quality of consecration. Rite of Consecration

Methods of Consecration and Other Sacraments

2. Whereas the Sacrament of Consecration is equivalent to the creation and formation of Sacred Circumscribed Space, all other forms of Consecration are present within other individual sacraments and rites:-

(i) The *Sacrament of Resurrection and Rite of Baptism* creates Sacred Circumscribed Space around a Human Being forming a valid Person; and

(ii) The *Sacrament of Incarnation and Rite of Christening* creates Sacred Circumscribed Space around a Human Being or Person to form a wholly Christian Person; and

(iii) The *Sacrament of Unification and Rite of Matrimony* is one of only three Sacraments that are capable of creating the Sacred Circumscribed Space of a Divine Person, formed from the proper union of a male and female Person; and

(iv) The *Rite of Ordination* is the second of three temporal rites that are capable of creating the Sacred Circumscribed Space of a Divine Person, formed from the perfection of holy orders, oaths and vows; and

(v) The *Rite of Coronation* is the third of three temporal rites capable of creating the Sacred Circumscribed Space of a Divine Person, formed from the perfection of sacred sovereign orders, oaths and vows; and

(vi) The *Sacrament of Amalgamation and Rite of Union* is the Sacrament that creates the Sacred Circumscribed Space of Superior and Legal Persons; and

(vii) The *Sacrament of Authentication and Rite of Record* is the Sacrament that creates the Sacred Circumscribed Space of Instruments of Trust, Title, Estates and Property; and

(viii) The *Sacrament of Convocation and Rite of Convention* is the Sacrament that creates the Sacred Circumscribed Space of places of sanctuary, law and administrative authority; and

(ix) The *Rite of Dedication* is the rite that creates dedicated places of ecclesiastical, clerical or administrative significance; and

(x) The *Rite of Blessing* is the rite that creates Sacred Circumscribed Space around objects such as Sacred Vestments, Sacred Perennial Objects, Sacred Seasonal Objects and Sacred Consumable Objects.

Title X – Sacrament of Sustentation & Rite of Eucharist

X.I – SACRAMENT OF SUSTENTATION

1. Sustentation (*Ritus Sacramentum Sustentatio*) and Rite of Eucharist is the second of the fourteen (14) Cardinal Sacraments, also known as the Ways of Heaven. Sacrament of Sustentation (Ritus Sacramentum Sustentatio)

The Sacrament of Sustentation and Rite of Eucharist is the embodiment of the Spirit of the Paschal Mystery of Christ Risen, whereby God and the Divine Creator of all Existence personified as Christ chooses willingly to be the instrument of Divine Mercy, Forgiveness and Joy for all who have lived and all who will ever live, now and into the future forever.

The Sacrament is granted and conferred in accordance with the most sacred Covenants *Pactum De Singularis Caelum*, *Pactum De Singularis Christus*, and *Missale Christus* and associated approved liturgy.

2. The celebration of the most Holy Eucharist is rightly central to the Christian and Jewish experience as a plenary union in Christ in the form of the one true Holy Apostolic Universal Ecclesia and therefore is fundamental to the human experience of all Christians and Jews. Divine Purpose of the Sacrament of Sustentation and Rite of Eucharist

In the celebration of the most sacred Rite of the Eucharist, the united members of the Living Body of Christ remember not only the consent and acceptance of the Holy Spirit to be made flesh and blood, but to then suffer the uncertainties and doubt and emotions of human experience, and furthermore to freely sacrifice himself as the Testament of the Lamb, as the one true Christ Risen, so that all men and women and his church are freed from sin, from condemnation and are forever redeemed and saved.

While Customary and Traditional Rites are free to honour the Eucharist from the perspective of the ritual of bread and wine representing the embodiment of the self-sacrifice of Christ through the Cross and the sign of spiritual nourishment, it is also necessary to express the entirety of the Paschal teaching and not merely its beginning, middle or end.

The celebration of the Eucharist in simple and visible signs of unleavened bread, water and wine, is as much the wedding feast in celebration of the matrimony of Christ with his Church and the perpetual presence of the Holy Spirit, as it is a symbol of self-sacrifice and a symbol of renewal.

Great care and diligence must be taken therefore in the formation of

Eucharistic Celebration in the form of Mass, that the entirety of the Eucharist is properly respected.

3. There exists only one form of the Sacrament of Sustentation.

Form of the Sacrament of Sustentation

4. No higher order life form including but not limited to any Homo Sapien, animal or non-hydro carbon higher order life form may be harmed or injured in any way by any celebration of the Rite of Eucharist. For the proper and sacred celebration of the most holy Eucharist is in honouring the self-sacrifice of Christ and the votive offering of those willing to dedicate an element of Self-Sacrifice through self discipline, mercy, frugality and simplicity for the benefit of others.

Forbiddance of any harm associated with Rite of Eucharist

Any form of sacrifice of animals or any form of higher order life is an abomination against all united Heaven and Earth; and a profound sacrilege and act of contempt against God and the Divine Creator of all Existence, Christ and the Holy Spirit; and a disgrace against the name of every Angel, Saint, Spirit and Demon.

X.II – DIVINE GRACE AND ACTION OF SUSTENTATION

1. The Divine Grace and Action of *Sustentation* is the supernatural effect of transformation of the Eucharist into the living presence of Christ as the Bread of Life and the embodiment of the sacrifice of the Crucified and Living Christ.

Divine Grace and Action of Sustentation

2. *Sustentation* is a wholly Divine and unmerited action, warranted by God and the Divine Creator. It is not an action effected within the temporal realm, nor can it be equated to physical terms or constructs.

Understanding of action and Divine Grace of Sustentation

3. The Divine Grace and Supernatural Action of *Sustentation* is central to the proper effect of the Holy Rite of Eucharist. Such supernatural presence and grace is made manifest *first* by the suitable qualification of the recipient; and *second* by the proper authority of one administering the sacrament; and *third* by the constituent parts and order that must be established in order to effect the sacrament.

Divine Grace and Action of Sacrament of Sustentation

In accord with sacred liturgy, in the absence of one or more of these central requisits, no legitimate manifestation of such Divine Grace and Action can occur.

X.III – RITE OF EUCHARIST

1. The Holy Rite of the Blessed Eucharist represents the constituent parts and their order that must be established in order to effect the

Rite of Eucharist

Divine and Supernatural Sacrament of Sustentation.

3. There are only two valid and licit forms for the Rite of Holy Eucharist as defined by associated approved liturgy being *Ordinary* and *Extraordinary*: Forms of Rite of Holy Eucharist

(i) *Ordinary Rite* is conferred by a competent minister possessing Holy Orders through the Liturgy of the Eucharist and Holy Mass; and

(ii) *Extraordinary Rite* is conferred by a competent minister possessing Holy Orders as part of the Sacrament of Salvation and Rite of Reconciliation, or Sacrament of Emancipation and Funerary Rites without Mass, or as an optional element of the Rite of Reformation, or Rite of Investiture or Rite of Coronation.

X.IV – ELEMENTS OF RITE OF HOLY EUCHARIST

1. Elements of the Rite of Holy Eucharist are those constituent parts that must be established in order to effect the Holy Sacrament and manifest the Divine Grace and Action of Transfiguration. Elements of Rite of Holy Eucharist

2. The Proper and Essential Order of Elements of the Rite of Holy Eucharist are reflected within the Liturgy of the Eucharist, namely:- Order of Elements of Rite of Holy Eucharist

(i) Offertory Antiphon; and

(ii) Presentation of the Offering; and

(iii) Preface; and

(iv) Eucharistic Prayer; and

(v) Acclamation; and

(vi) Doxology; and

(vii) Christs' Prayer; and

(viii) Sign of Peace; and

(ix) Breaking of the Bread; and

(x) Holy Communion; and

(xi) Communion Antiphon; and

(xii) Prayer of Thanksgiving; and

(xiii) Promise of the People; and

(xiv) Concluding Blessing.

X.V – CONDITIONS OF RITE OF HOLY EUCHARIST

Conditions of Rite of Holy Eucharist

1. Conditions of the Rite of Eucharist are those requisite qualifications and contingencies permitted in the proper ministration of the Rite. There shall exist only two possible Conditions for the ministration of Rite of Holy Eucharist being *Universal* and *Special*:-

   (i) *Universal* are the Conditions that apply to all forms and circumstances of the Rite of Eucharist; and

   (ii) *Special* are the Conditions that apply to forms and circumstances of the Rite of Eucharist other than through the Liturgy of the Eucharist and as part of specific Sacraments and Rites such as the Sacrament of Salvation and Rite of Reconciliation, or Sacrament of Emancipation and Funerary Rites without Mass, or as an optional element of the Rite of Reformation, or Rite of Investiture or Rite of Coronation.

Impediments to Participating in Rite of Holy Eucharist and receiving Holy Communion

2. A baptised person shall be impeded from participating in a Rite of Holy Eucharist and receiving Holy Communion:-

   (i) If the person is actively subject to the imposition or declaration of the penalty of excommunication or interdiction by an authorised clerical body; or

   (ii) If the person has been found culpable by a competent forum of law of a manifestly grave, wicked or perverse offence, yet the person in question remains obstinate in refusing to accept any responsibility or demonstrate genuine remorse or any attempt of confession and the Sacrament of Absolution; or

   (iii) If the person is conscious of committing a manifestly grave, wicked or perverse offence, yet has made the decision at the time not to accept personal responsibility, nor experience any form of genuine remorse, or seek the Rite of Confession and Sacrament of Absolution.

Ordained Minister not to act as Prosecutor or Judge

3. Other than impediments identified and published by a competent forum of law or authorised clerical body, all other impediments that would otherwise prevent a person from participating in the Rite of Holy Eucharist and receiving Holy Communion are a matter between the conscience of the person in question and the Divine Creator.

   An ordained minister must not under any circumstances seek to interpose themselves between Christ and the Divine Creator and members of the People of God in deciding who is worthy or not worthy to participate in the Rite of Holy Eucharist and receive Holy Communion.

Any ordained minister that succumbs to acting in a manner of prosecutor or judge in denying a person to participate in the Rite of Holy Eucharist and receive Holy Communion, even if they claim to have good reason to suspect such a person is genuinely impeded, shall be culpable themselves of a grave offence against Heaven, causing a temporary impediment to their own clerical powers.

4. *Universal Conditions* for the conferral of the Rite of Holy Eucharist apply to all forms and circumstances of the Rite:- Universal Conditions

(i) Every baptised person of a denomination of the Universal Ecclesia of One Christ, not otherwise impeded, is capable and permitted to participate in the Rite of Holy Eucharist and receive Holy Communion; and

(ii) A person who is to participate in the Rite of Holy Eucharist and receive Holy Communion is to make a genuine attempt to abstain from meat and excessive consumption of alcohol for at least eight hours before holy communion; and

(iii) A person who is to participate in the Rite of Holy Eucharist and receive Holy Communion is to abstain for at least one hour before holy communion from any food and drink, except for only water and medicine; and

(iv) The elderly, the infirm, and those who care for them can participate in the Rite of Holy Eucharist and receive Holy Communion even if they have eaten something within the preceding hour; and

(v) An ordained priest who celebrates the Most Holy Eucharist two or three times on the same day can consume some food and drink before the second or third celebration even if there is less than one hour between them; and

(vi) After being initiated into the Most Holy Eucharist, each of the faithful is obliged to participate in the Rite of Holy Eucharist and receive Holy Communion a minimum of once a year (at Easter), but preferably at least once every ninety days.

5. *Special Conditions* for the conferral of the Rite of Holy Eucharist as part of a Sacrament and Rite or special Rite are to be incorporated to the Sacrament or Rite in question. Special Conditions

X.VI – MINISTER OF RITE OF HOLY EUCHARIST

Minister of Rite of Holy Eucharist

1. A minister ordained to Holy Orders, not otherwise impeded, is the only person and Sacred Office permitted to confer the Sacrament of Sustentation and the Rite of Holy Eucharist:-

    (i) An ordained minister is not permitted to celebrate the Eucharist more than once a day except in cases where the law and necessity permits; and

    (ii) An ordained minister may concelebrate the Rite of Holy Eucharist through the Liturgy of the Eucharist and Mass with other ordained ministers, especially with ministers of different denominations of the Universal Ecclesia of One Christ; and

    (iii) An ordained minister is free to celebrate the Rite of Eucharist individually, however, but not while a concelebration is taking place in the same church or oratory; and

    (iv) It is expressly forbidden for clerical authorities of different denominations of the Universal Ecclesia of One Christ to deny the concelebration of the Liturgy of the Eucharist and Mass between ministers of different denominations, unless such exceptional circumstances exist concerning a Sacred Place or Feast Day or unique celebration of a particular denomination; and

    (v) It is for ordained ministers alone to offer prayers, especially the eucharistic prayer, or to perform actions during the Liturgy of the Eucharist that are proper to the celebrant; and

    (vi) Except for a just and reasonable cause, an ordained minister is not permitted to celebrate the Eucharist more than once a day except in cases where the law permits; and

    (vii) Except for a just and reasonable cause, a priest is not to celebrate the Rite of Eucharist without the participation of at least some member of the faithful present.

Title XI – Sacrament of Amalgamation & Rite of Union

XI.I – SACRAMENT OF AMALGAMATION

1. Amalgamation (*Ritus Sacramentum Amalgamatio*) and Rite of Union is the third of the fourteen (14) Cardinal Sacraments, also known as the Ways of Heaven.

Sacrament of Amalgamation (Ritus Sacramentum Amalgamatio)

The Sacrament of Amalgamation and Rite of Union is granted and conferred in accordance with the most sacred Covenants *Pactum De Singularis Caelum*, *Pactum De Singularis Christus*, and *Missale Christus* and associated approved liturgy.

2. Amalgamation is granted and administered when two or more parties come together of their own free will, without mental reservation, with at least one binding promise or acceptance of obligation under a Rite of Oath or Rite of Vow.

Divine Purpose of the Sacrament of Amalgamation

A binding promise or acceptance of obligation under a Rite of Oath or Rite of Vow is a sacred act, governed first by Divine Law and then only by lesser forms of laws such as Positive Law.

Thus, as a sacred act, the amalgamation of two or more purposes for a common purpose must be administered by sacred rite and custom, then underpinning any secular laws of a given society.

No society has the moral authority to enforce a binding promise or acceptance of obligation unless the laws of such a society first recognise the sacred and solemn nature of the act itself.

XI.II – DIVINE GRACE & ACTION OF AMALGAMATION

1. The Divine Grace and Action of *Amalgamation* is the supernatural effect of granting binding and enforceable effect to the conditions of a solemn promise or acceptance of obligation.

Divine Grace and Action of Amalgamation

2. *Amalgamation* is a wholly Divine and unmerited action, warranted by the God and the Divine Creator. It is not an action effected within the temporal realm, nor can it be equated to physical terms or constructs.

Understanding of action and Divine Grace of Amalgamation

3. The Divine Grace and Supernatural Action of *Amalgamation* is central to the proper effect of the Holy Rite of Union. Such supernatural presence and grace is made manifest *first* by the suitable qualification of the recipient; and *second* by the proper authority of one administering the sacrament; and *third* by the constituent parts and order that must be established in order to effect the sacrament.

Divine Grace and Action of Sacrament of Amalgamation

In accord with sacred liturgy, in the absence of one or more of these central requisites, no legitimate manifestation of such Divine Grace and Action can occur.

XI.III – RITE OF UNION

1. The Holy Rite of Union represents the constituent parts and their order that must be established in order to effect the Divine and Supernatural Sacrament of Amalgamation. In the absence of one or more of these central requisites, no legitimate manifestation or imprint of such Divine Grace and Action of Amalgamation can occur. Rite of Union

2. There are only six (6) valid and licit forms for the Rite of Union as defined by the most sacred *Missale Christus* and associated approved liturgy being Ecclesial, Political, Fraternal, Corporate, Civil and Mutual:- Forms of the Rite of Union

   (i) "**Ecclesial Union**" is when the Sacrament of Amalgamation is imparted through the Rite and Act of Ordination and the receiving of Holy Orders; and

   (ii) "**Political Union**" is when the Sacrament of Amalgamation is imparted through the Rite and Act of Inauguration of a democratically elected Leader; and

   (iii) "**Fraternal Union**" is when the Sacrament of Amalgamation is imparted through the Act of Investiture between a person installed into office as a member of a fraternal and official body; and

   (iv) "**Corporate Union**" is when the Sacrament of Amalgamation is imparted through the Act of Incorporation of an Association; and

   (v) "**Civil Union**" is when the Sacrament of Amalgamation is imparted through the Act of Recordation to two (2) consenting adults; and

   (vi) "**Mutual Union**" is when the Sacrament of Amalgamation is imparted through the Registration of a mutual agreement between two (2) or more parties.

XI.IV – ELEMENTS OF RITE OF UNION

1. Elements of the Rite of Union are those constituent parts that must be established in order to effect the Holy Sacrament and manifest the Divine Grace and Action of Amalgamation. Elements of Rite of Union

2. An *Obligation* means a sacred duty whereby one or more parties as *Obligants* are bound to act or refrain from acting. An Obligation thus Obligation

shall impose on the *Obligor* a duty to perform and shall at the same time create a corresponding right to demand performance by the *Obligee* to whom the performance is to be tendered.

4. *Performance* means the accomplishment of a promise, a covenant or other obligation of a Union, according to its terms. Performance

5. A *Condition* shall mean a declaration or provision that shall make the existence of a Right dependent on the occurrence of an event. Condition

6. As an enforceable act, a Union must meet eight (8) key elements being authorisation, comprehension, intention, consideration, obligation, negotiation, acceptation and registration:- Order of Elements of Rite of Union

(i) *Authorisation* means a party must first have the legal and moral authority to enter into a Union; and

(ii) *Comprehension* means each party must demonstrate a clear level of understanding as to entering into a Union; and

(iii) *Intention* means each party must intend to enter into a Union; and

(iv) *Consideration* means there must be something of substance on offer as part of the Union; and

(v) *Obligation* means there must be at least one promise associated with a sacred duty; and

(vi) *Negotiation* means there must be a meeting of minds negotiated before a Union is accepted; and

(vii) *Acceptation* means there must be evidence that the Union was accepted and thus the terms enforceable; and

(viii) *Registration* means the Union Instrument as well as the key information was duly registered and recorded in a valid and proper Register of Union.

7. A Union shall not be legally and morally enforceable unless in writing as an Instrument then registered and recorded in a proper Register. At a minimum, the Register shall take note of:- Registration of Union Instrument

(i) The names, addresses and details of the parties of the Union, including witnesses and any guarantors or insurers; and

(ii) The specific obligations of the Union, including any dates and amounts or measures; and

(iii) The value and nature of the considerations of the Union; and

(iv) The agreed penalties for breach and the agreed time frames and terms of remedy.

XI.V – CONDITIONS OF RITE OF UNION

1. Conditions of the Rite of Union are those requisite qualifications and contingencies permitted in the proper ministration and effect of the particular forms of the Rite. Conditions of Rite of Union

2. The Conditions for the Rite of Ecclesial Union shall be subject to the same conditions as the Rite of Ordination. Ecclesial Conditions

3. The Conditions for the Rite of Sovereign Union shall be subject to the same conditions as the Rite of Coronation. Sovereign Conditions

4. The Conditions for the Rite of Political Union shall be subject to the same conditions as the Rite of Inauguration. Political Conditions

5. The Conditions for the Rite of Fraternal Union shall be subject to the same conditions as the Rite of Investiture. Fraternal Conditions

6. The Conditions for the Rite of Corporate Union shall be subject to the same conditions as an Act of Incorporation, consistent with the present sacred Liturgy. Corporate Conditions

7. *Civil Union* shall be granted and administered when a couple of the same gender or a man and woman upon reaching majority choose and consent of their own free will to validate their union through a registration and covenant of trust in accordance with the most sacred Covenant *Pactum De Singularis Caelum* and associated approved liturgy: Civil Conditions

   (i) While a man or a woman may enter into more than one Union consecutively and never concurrently, a man and a woman may only be bestowed once the Sacrament of Unification through the Rite of Holy Matrimony; and

   (ii) When a man and woman are bestowed with the Sacrament of Unification they also receive the Sacrament of Amalgamation; and

   (iii) If the Sacrament of Union is approved to be bestowed upon a same sex couple, in recognition of their right to civil equality, the ceremony is forbidden to be performed within the main body of a Sacred Place of Worship; and

   (iv) Any civil or lesser body that seeks to attack, undermine, denigrate the absolute moral authority of the Universal Ecclesia of One Christ or the Holy Society of One Islam or the Sacred Society of One Spirit in such matters, or to contort words and phrases to imply a delinquency of duty and obligation to protect the Sacraments and Civil Equality is culpable of the most grievous transgressions.

8. The Conditions for the Rite of Mutual Union shall be subject to the same conditions as the definition of Consensus and Agreements defined by Ucadian Law and associated Charters and Instruments. Mutual Conditions

XI.VI – IMPEDIMENTS TO UNION

1. Only authorised persons may validly and legitimately administer the Rite of Union: Minister of Rite of Union

(i) Only persons properly ordained as a Minister or invested into office holding *Magisterium* or *Visium* possesses the powers and authority to confer and administer the Rite of Union under Extraordinary Conditions; and

(ii) Only persons properly invested into office holding *Administratum*, *Officium* or *Imperium* possesses the powers and authority to administer the Rite of Union under Ordinary Conditions.

2. A Breach is any breaking of peace or violation of a term or condition, or Right of either Party, or any obligation, engagement or duty, either by commission or omission, whether knowing or unknowing, in relation to any valid Agreement in accord with these including, but not limited to any:- Breach of Agreement

(i) Breach of Promise being a violation of any promise; or

(ii) Breach of Duty being any violation or omission of a legal or moral duty and more particularly the neglect or failure to fulfil in a just and proper manner the duties of an office, agency or fiduciary capacity; or

(iii) Breach of Trust being any act done by a person holding fiduciary responsibility in relation to a trust or office and more particularly the wrongful omission by a trustee of an act required by the terms of the trust, or wrong misappropriation by a trustee of any fund or property that had been lawfully committed to him in a fiduciary capacity; or

(iv) Breach of Warranty being the failure or falsehood of an affirmative promise or statement in writing, or the non-performance of an executor stipulation; or Breach of Agreement being any failure without legal excuse to perform any promise that forms the entirety or part of the present Agreement, whether anticipatory, or constructive or continuing, or unequivocal.

3. All alleged Breaches shall be defined as either *Minor* or *Material* (Major), whereby:- Minor Breach and Material Breach

(i) A *Minor Breach* is any alleged Breach that technically violates one or more Terms and Conditions of the Agreement, but does not destroy the inherent Trust or Value and therefore the Duties and Obligations of the Agreement and is possible to be cured by the offending Party within a reasonable period of time; and

(ii) A *Material Breach*, also known as Major Breach or Fundamental Breach is any alleged Breach as specified within the Terms and Conditions or any other unnamed condition of such a serious nature that unless it is immediately cured by the offending Party, then such alleged Breach is likely to destroy the inherit Trust and Value of the Agreement.

4. A failure to cure any alleged Breach within the Time Limit prescribed and the waiving of the right to appeal to Arbitration shall place the offending Party in Default. Default is therefore any failure to fulfil an Obligation prescribed by any valid Agreement in accord with the most sacred Covenant *Pactum De Singularis Caelum* and present liturgy after every reasonable opportunity in Good Faith has been presented to the offending Party to remedy and cure the alleged Breach. Default

A Party that is in Default of any valid Agreement automatically accepts they are delinquent in honour and integrity and therefore waives all rights to sue or cross-claim or claim of legal excuse in any legal proceedings or litigation in respect of the particular Agreement.

Title XII – Sacrament of Unification & Rite of Matrimony

XII.I – SACRAMENT OF UNIFICATION

1. Unification (*Ritus Sacramentum Unificatio*) and Rite of Matrimony is the fourth of the fourteen (14) Cardinal Sacraments, also known as the Ways of Heaven.

   Sacrament of Unification (Ritus Sacramentum Unificatio)

   The Sacrament of Unification and Rite of Matrimony is granted and conferred in accordance with the most sacred Covenants *Pactum De Singularis Caelum*, *Pactum De Singularis Christus*, and *Missale Christus* and associated approved liturgy.

2. The Sacrament of Unification and Rite of Matrimony is granted and administered when a man and a woman upon reaching majority choose and consent of their own free will to sanctify their union through a registered divine matrimonial covenant in accordance with the most sacred Covenants *Pactum De Singularis Caelum*, *Pactum De Singularis Christus* and associated approved liturgy. The Sacrament of Unification and Rite of Matrimony may only be bestowed once.

   Divine Purpose of the Sacrament of Unification

3. There exists only one form of the Sacrament of Unification and Rite of Matrimony being Sacred and Irrevocable Unification. Therefore, as the Sacrament is a Sacred and Irrevocable Event, producing a Supreme Sacred Record in Heaven and upon the Earth, no properly conferred Sacrament of Unification can be withdrawn, or annulled or dissolved.

   Form of the Sacrament of Unification

   However, upon such circumstances of separation or death, one who has been bestowed the Sacrament of Unification is permitted to formalise a new Union through the Sacrament of Amalgamation and Rite of Union. Thus, the act of Divorce only applies to civil unions and the Sacrament of Amalgamation and never to Unification.

   Furthermore, the transgression of Adultery only applies to both perpetrators equally culpable of acts of sexual extramarital affairs whilst one or the other or both are still publicly and legally being bound to another through the Sacrament of Unification or Sacrament of Amalgamation. The application of unequal punishment based on gender, or capital punishment in any form for the delict of Adultery is morally repugnant, profane, sacrilegious, forbidden, reprobate and to be suppressed now and forever.

XII.II – DIVINE GRACE AND ACTION OF UNIFICATION

1. The Divine Grace and Action of *Unification* is the supernatural effect of the proper ministration of the Rite of Matrimony with the transformation of the Spirit of two persons recognised as becoming

   Divine Grace and Action of Unification

one in the halls and records of Heaven.

2. *Unification* is a wholly Divine and unmerited action, warranted by God and the Divine Creator. It is not an action effected within the temporal realm, nor can it be equated to physical terms or constructs. Understanding of action and Divine Grace of Unification

3. The Divine Grace and Supernatural Action of Unification is central to the proper effect of the Holy Rite of Matrimony. Such supernatural presence and grace is made manifest *first* by the suitable qualification of the recipient; and *second* by the proper authority of one administering the sacrament; and *third* by the constituent parts and order that must be established in order to effect the sacrament. Divine Grace and Action of Sacrament of Unification

In accord with sacred liturgy, in the absence of one or more of these central requisites, no legitimate manifestation of such Divine Grace and Action can occur.

XII.III – RITE OF MATRIMONY

1. The Holy Rite of Matrimony represents the constituent parts and their order that must be established in order to effect the Divine and Supernatural Sacrament of Unification. In the absence of one or more of these central requisites, no legitimate manifestation or imprint of the Divine Grace and Action of Unification can occur. Rite of Matrimony

2. There are only two (2) valid and licit forms for the Rite of Matrimony as defined by the most sacred *Missale Christus* and associated approved liturgy being Ordinary and Extraordinary: Form of the Rite of Matrimony

   (i) "**Ordinary Rite of Matrimony**" is conferred by a competent minister as the second section (Liturgy of Christian Life) of Holy Mass; and

   (ii) "**Extraordinary Rite of Matrimony**" is conferred by a competent minister as a separate rite and celebration on its own.

XII.IV – ELEMENTS OF RITE OF MATRIMONY

1. Elements of the Rite of Matrimony are those constituent parts that must be established and conferred in the proper order to effect the Divine and Supernatural Action of Unification. Elements of Rite of Matrimony

2. The main Order of Elements of the Rite of Matrimony are: Order of Elements

   (i) Petition; and

   (ii) Inquisition; and

(iii) Purification; and

(iv) Obligation; and

(v) Dedication (Blessing of Rings); and

(vi) Vocation; and

(vii) Unification.

3. In respect of Holy Matrimony and the Rite of Union: Matrimony and Union

(i) Matrimony comprises two Sacraments, the Sacrament of Union and the Holy Sacrament of Matrimony; and

(ii) However, the Sacrament of Union also imparted with the Holy Sacrament of Matrimony only applies to the consecration of the temporal state of Union recognised civilly; and

(iii) Upon such circumstances of separation or death, one who has been bestowed the Sacrament of Matrimony is permitted to formalise a new Union through the Sacrament of Union as such an action does not affect the permanent and irrevocable Divine Record of Holy Matrimony; and

(iv) Thus, the act of Divorce only applies to civil unions and the Sacrament of Union and never to the Holy Sacrament of Matrimony; and

(v) As the act of Divorce only applies to civil unions and not to the Sacrament of Holy Matrimony, no one may be denied receiving other Sacrament on the basis of Divorce; and

(vi) Furthermore, the transgression of Adultery only applies to both perpetrators equally culpable of acts of sexual extramarital affairs whilst one or the other or both are still publicly and legally being bound to another through the Sacrament of Matrimony or Sacrament of Union; and

(vii) The application of unequal punishment based on gender, or capital punishment in any form for the delict of Adultery is morally repugnant, profane, sacrilegious, forbidden, reprobate and to be suppressed now and forever.

XII.V – CONDITIONS OF RITE OF MATRIMONY

1. There exists only one form of the Sacrament of Matrimony being Sacred and Irrevocable Matrimony. Therefore, as the Sacrament of Matrimony is a Sacred and Irrevocable Event, producing a Supreme Conditions of Rite of Matrimony

Sacred Record in Heaven and upon the Earth, no properly conferred Sacrament of Matrimony can be withdrawn, or annulled or dissolved:

(i) The Divine Gift of the Sacrament of Unification and Rite of Holy Matrimony may only be bestowed between a naturally borne Man and a Woman. All other forms of Union may be blessed and respected through the Rite of Civil Union; and

(ii) A Man or Woman may only receive the Divine Gift of the Sacrament of Unification and Rite of Holy Matrimony once in their life; and

(iii) A Man or Woman must have reached the age of eighteen years to receive the Divine Gift of the Sacrament of Unification and Rite of Holy Matrimony; and

(iv) Both the Man and Woman seeking the Divine Gift of the Sacrament of Unification and Rite of Holy Matrimony must be baptised and not otherwise impeded from receiving the Rite of Holy Eucharist; and

(v) Both the Man and Woman must come of their own free will, without mental reservation, or reason to believe there is something impeding the legitimacy of such an act.

XII.VI – MINISTER OF RITE OF MATRIMONY

1. Only persons properly ordained as a Minister or invested into office holding *Magisterium* or *Visium* possesses the powers and authority to confer and administer the Rite of Matrimony. Minister of Rite of Matrimony

XII.VII – ORDINARY RITE OF MATRIMONY

1. The *Ordinary Rite of Matrimony* shall be as follows: Ordinary Rite of Matrimony

LITURGY OF CHRISTIAN LIFE

Liturgy of Christian Life

PETITION

Matrimony
Petition

CELEBRANT

(To all assembled)

I call upon those who seek to make their solemn petition today in the name of Christ our Saviour to now come forward and make their presence and prayer known.

(The bride and groom come forward)

CELEBRANT

What is it you ask in the name of the Father and of the Son and of the Holy Spirit?

BRIDE AND GROOM

Matrimony.

CELEBRANT

(To bride and groom)

The Sacrament of Unification that you ask to receive through the Rite of Holy Matrimony is a supremely sacred and solemn gift and obligation.

It is the sacred foundation of our community and society that ensures children may be raised in a loving and united family; and that through the support, guidance and intercession of all the angels and saints, a husband and wife may continue to grow and experience a deeper and richer life together.

The Rite of Holy Matrimony as instituted by Christ himself is a manifest sign of unity with Heaven; and with one another through the mystery of two people becoming a greater singular spiritual presence in the eyes of all Heaven and Earth.

As a consequence, the Sacrament of Unification through the Rite of Holy Matrimony may only be imparted once to a man or woman in their lifetime as it imprints a permanent character of Divine unity.

Even if the challenges and trials of life may seek to conspire to try to break such unity, in Heaven what is promised cannot be broken; and what is made cannot be unmade.

Knowing then the significance and obligation of what you ask, and the inquiry that must be first made as to your qualification, intentions and faithfulness, is the Rite of Holy Matrimony of the Universal Ecclesia what you truly seek?

BRIDE AND GROOM

Yes.

INQUISITION

CELEBRANT

(To bride and groom)

To proceed with the Rite of Holy Matrimony we must now solemnly inquire upon each of you as to your qualification, intentions and faithfulness in order to properly receive the Sacrament of Unification through the Rite of Holy Matrimony.

N. and N. have you come here freely and without mental reservation to give yourselves to each other in sacred marriage?

BRIDE AND GROOM

Yes.

CELEBRANT

(To bride and groom)

N. and N. do you fully understand the solemn obligations that sacred marriage entails; and to respect, honour and love one another in times of health and in times of illness; and in times of joy and midst times of difficulty; and to strive always to overcome together whatever obstacles or challenges that the journey of life may bring you?

BRIDE AND GROOM

Yes.

CELEBRANT

(To bride and groom)

N. and N. do you both fully understand that even if the challenges of life in the future may cause such loss or separation between you so that you were no longer able to be physically together, in the eyes of the Divine Creator of all Existence and all Heaven and Earth, the unity of your souls forged through this Holy Sacrament cannot be broken?

BRIDE AND GROOM

Yes.

CELEBRANT

(To bride and groom)

N. and N. are you both certain you come here without any impediment that would otherwise disqualify you from properly receiving the Sacrament of Unification and Marriage through the Rite of Holy Matrimony?

BRIDE AND GROOM

Yes.

PURIFICATION

Matrimony
Purification

CELEBRANT

(To all assembled while preparing holy water to sprinkle over the couple)

Dearly beloved, N. and N. have clearly demonstrated their deep love and affection for one another, their respect for the solemn obligations of the Sacrament of Unification and Marriage and the Rite of Holy Matrimony.

In the name of ✠ the Father, and of the Son, and of the Holy Spirit, I do bless N. and N. as a symbol of the purity of their intentions and so that all forces temporal and spiritual respect and honour their wishes.

OBLIGATION

Matrimony
Obligation

CELEBRANT

(To Bride and Groom)

I call upon N. and N. to each give their solemn vows to one another.

CELEBRANT

(To Groom)

N. will you take N. to become your best friend? Do you promise to always be truthful to her in good times and in bad, and in times of sickness and distress?

GROOM

I do.

CELEBRANT

(To Groom)

N. do you take N. to be your life partner? Do you promise to be gentle and love her, and to always be kind and forgive one other throughout this journey of life together?

GROOM

I do.

CELEBRANT

(To Groom)

N. do you take N. to be your wife? Do you promise to be loyal and support her and any children between you, every day of your life?

GROOM

I do.

CELEBRANT

(To Bride)

N. will you take N. to become your best friend? Do you promise to always be truthful to him in good times and in bad, and in times of sickness and distress?

BRIDE

I do.

CELEBRANT

(To Bride)

N. do you take N. to be your life partner? Do you promise to be gentle and love him, and to always be kind and forgive one other throughout this journey of life together?

BRIDE

I do.

CELEBRANT

(To Bride)

N. do you take N. to be your husband? Do you promise to

be loyal and support him and any children between you, every day of your life?

BRIDE

I do.

CELEBRANT

(To Bride and Groom)

N. and N. You have each declared your sacred vows and your consent and become united before the Universal Church. May all the Angels and Saints of Heaven strengthen your unity and fill you both always with their blessings. What God has now joined, let none seek to divide.

ALL

Amen.

DEDICATION (BLESSING OF THE RINGS)

Matrimony
Dedication (Blessing of the Rings)

CELEBRANT

(With the rings)

May the Angels and Saints bless ✠ these rings that you seek to give each other as an outward sign of your love and fidelity to one another.

ALL

Amen

VOCATION

Matrimony
Vocation

GROOM

(To the Bride whilst placing the ring on her finger)

N. Accept and receive this ring as a sign of my vows and my fidelity, love and loyalty to you.

BRIDE

(To the Groom whilst placing the ring on his finger)

N. Accept and receive this ring in return as a sign of my vows and my fidelity, love and trust in you.

CELEBRANT
(To the Bride and Groom)

By the ecclesial and legal powers vested in my Office; and by the conclusion of this outward sign of your Vows, your Love and Unity, I now pronounce you Husband and Wife.

You may each kiss one another.

UNIFICATION

Matrimony
Unification

CELEBRANT
(Raises his hands as the Bride and Groom now separate and kneel)

Divine Father, by your will you made everything out of nothing. In the beginning you created the universe and made man and woman in your likeness.

Grant N. and N. every possible blessing ✠ as they set out on this journey of life together. Keep them safe, guard them and strengthen them against those who would seek to weaken them and divide them.

All the Angels and Saints of Heaven, bestow your blessings ✠ upon N. and N. and keep them safe from harm and danger.

Mother Mary, Guardian of the Church and all Families, grant your blessings ✠ upon N. and N. and all those souls who may join their family. Grant them the serenity and courage to preserve with your help.

We humbly invoke these blessings in the name of Jesus Christ, our Lord.

ALL

Amen.

XII.VIII – EXTRAORDINARY RITE OF MATRIMONY

1. The *Extraordinary Rite of Matrimony* celebrated as a separate ceremony on its own shall be as follows:

Extraordinary Rite of Matrimony

GREETING

Extraordinary Rite of Matrimony

CELEBRANT

In the name of ✠ the Father, and of the Son, and of the Holy Spirit. Greeting

ALL

Amen.

CELEBRANT

(C. joins his hands, then extends outward his hands:)

May the love of our Saviour Jesus Christ, the mercy of God and the strength of the Holy Spirit be with you all.

CONGREGATION

(Congregation all sit at conclusion of reply.)

And also with you.

PETITION

Extraordinary Rite of Matrimony Petition

CELEBRANT

(To all assembled)

I call upon those who seek to make their solemn petition today in the name of Christ our Saviour to now come forward and make their presence and prayer known.

(The bride and groom come forward)

CELEBRANT

What is it you ask in the name of the Father and of the Son and of the Holy Spirit?

BRIDE AND GROOM

Matrimony.

CELEBRANT

(To bride and groom)

The Sacrament of Unification that you ask to receive through the Rite of Holy Matrimony is a supremely sacred and solemn gift and obligation.

It is the sacred foundation of our community and society that ensures children may be raised in a loving and united family; and that through the support, guidance and intercession of all the angels and saints, a husband and wife may continue to grow and experience a deeper and richer life together.

The Rite of Holy Matrimony as instituted by Christ himself is a manifest sign of unity with Heaven; and with one another through the mystery of two people becoming a greater singular spiritual presence in the eyes of all Heaven and Earth.

As a consequence, the Sacrament of Unification through the Rite of Holy Matrimony may only be imparted once to a man or woman in their lifetime as it imprints a permanent character of Divine unity.

Even if the challenges and trials of life may seek to conspire to try to break such unity, in Heaven what is promised cannot be broken; and what is made cannot be unmade.

Knowing then the significance and obligation of what you ask, and the inquiry that must be first made as to your qualification, intentions and faithfulness, is the Rite of Holy Matrimony of the Universal Ecclesia what you truly seek?

BRIDE AND GROOM

Yes.

INQUISITION

CELEBRANT

(To bride and groom)

To proceed with the Rite of Holy Matrimony we must now solemnly inquire upon each of you as to your qualification, intentions and faithfulness in order to properly receive the Sacrament of Unification through the Rite of Holy Matrimony.

N. and N. have you come here freely and without mental reservation to give yourselves to each other in sacred marriage?

BRIDE AND GROOM

Yes.

CELEBRANT

(To bride and groom)

N. and N. do you fully understand the solemn obligations that sacred marriage entails; and to respect, honour and love one another in times of health and in times of illness; and in times of joy and midst times of difficulty; and to strive always to overcome together whatever obstacles or challenges that the journey of life may bring you?

BRIDE AND GROOM

Yes.

CELEBRANT

(To bride and groom if younger)

N. and N. do you both fully understand that even if the challenges of life in the future may cause such loss or separation between you so that you were no longer able to be physically together, in the eyes of the Divine Creator of all Existence and all Heaven and Earth, the unity of your souls forged through this Holy Sacrament cannot be broken?

BRIDE AND GROOM

Yes.

CELEBRANT

(To bride and groom)

N. and N. are you both certain you come here without any impediment that would otherwise disqualify you from properly receiving the Sacrament of Unification and Marriage through the Rite of Holy Matrimony?

BRIDE AND GROOM

Yes.

PURIFICATION

Extraordinary Rite of Matrimony
Purification

CELEBRANT

(To all assembled while preparing holy water to sprinkle over the couple)

Dearly beloved, N. and N. have clearly demonstrated their deep love and affection for one another, their respect for the solemn obligations of the Sacrament of Unification and Marriage and the Rite of Holy Matrimony.

In the name of ✠ the Father, and of the Son, and of the Holy Spirit, I do bless N. and N. as a symbol of the purity of their intentions and so that all forces temporal and spiritual respect and honour their wishes.

OBLIGATION

Extraordinary Rite of Matrimony Obligation

CELEBRANT

(To Bride and Groom)

I call upon N. and N. to each give their solemn vows to one another.

CELEBRANT

(To Groom)

N. will you take N. to become your best friend? Do you promise to always be truthful to her in good times and in bad, and in times of sickness and distress?

GROOM

I do.

CELEBRANT

(To Groom)

N. do you take N. to be your life partner? Do you promise to be gentle and love her, and to always be kind and forgive one other throughout this journey of life together?

GROOM

I do.

CELEBRANT

(To Groom)

N. do you take N. to be your wife? Do you promise to be loyal and support her and any children between you, every day of your life?

GROOM

I do.

CELEBRANT

(To Bride)

N. will you take N. to become your best friend? Do you promise to always be truthful to him in good times and in bad, and in times of sickness and distress?

BRIDE

I do.

CELEBRANT

(To Bride)

N. do you take N. to be your life partner? Do you promise to be gentle and love him, and to always be kind and forgive one other throughout this journey of life together?

BRIDE

I do.

CELEBRANT

(To Bride)

N. do you take N. to be your husband? Do you promise to be loyal and support him and any children between you, every day of your life?

BRIDE

I do.

CELEBRANT

(To Bride and Groom)

N. and N. You have each declared your sacred vows and your consent and become united before the Universal Church. May all the Angels and Saints of Heaven strengthen your unity and fill you both always with their blessings. What God has now joined, let none seek to divide.

ALL

Amen.

DEDICATION (BLESSING OF THE RINGS)

Extraordinary Rite of Matrimony Dedication (Blessing of the Rings)

CELEBRANT

(With the rings)

May the Angels and Saints bless ✠ these rings that you seek to give each other as an outward sign of your love and fidelity to one another.

ALL

Amen

VOCATION

Extraordinary Rite of Matrimony Vocation

GROOM

(To the Bride whilst placing the ring on her finger)

N. Accept and receive this ring as a sign of my vows and my fidelity, love and loyalty to you.

BRIDE

(To the Groom whilst placing the ring on his finger)

N. Accept and receive this ring in return as a sign of my vows and my fidelity, love and trust in you.

CELEBRANT

(To the Bride and Groom)

By the ecclesial and legal powers vested in my Office; and by the conclusion of this outward sign of your Vows, your Love and Unity, I now pronounce you Husband and Wife.

You may each kiss one another.

UNIFICATION

Extraordinary Rite of Matrimony Unification

CELEBRANT

(Raises his hands as the Bride and Groom now separate and kneel)

Divine Father, by your will you made everything out of nothing. In the beginning you created the universe and made man and woman in your likeness.

Grant N. and N. every possible blessing ✠ as they set out on this journey of life together. Keep them safe, guard them and strengthen them against those who would seek to weaken them and divide them.

All the Angels and Saints of Heaven, bestow your blessings ✠ upon N. and N. and keep them safe from harm and danger.

Mother Mary, Guardian of the Church and all Families, grant your blessings ✠upon N. and N. and all those souls who may join their family. Grant them the serenity and courage to preserve with your help.

We humbly invoke these blessings in the name of Jesus Christ, our Lord.

ALL

Amen.

Title XIII – Sacrament of Authentication & Rite of Record

XIII.I – SACRAMENT OF AUTHENTICATION

1. Authentication (*Ritus Sacramentum Authentico*) is the fifth of the fourteen (14) Cardinal Sacraments, also known as the Ways of Heaven. Sacrament of Authentication (Ritus Sacramentum Authentico)

The Sacrament of Authentication and Rite of Record may also be granted and conferred on its own in accordance with the most sacred Covenants *Pactum De Singularis Caelum*, *Pactum De Singularis Christus*, and *Missale Christus* and associated approved liturgy.

2. Authentication is granted and administered upon the formal recording of the name and details of a particular object or concept in the Great Register and Public Record of One Heaven or associated Great Registers under Oath and evidence in accordance with the most sacred Covenants *Pactum De Singularis Caelum*, *Pactum De Singularis Christus* and associated approved liturgy. Divine Purpose of the Sacrament of Authentication

3. The highest form of valid Records and Instruments of Record are those derived from valid Ucadia Registers and those of the Universal Ecclesia of One Christ:- Highest form of Records

   (i) The highest authority and form of Ucadian Register is the Great Register and Public Record of One Heaven, with no Records higher; and

   (ii) The second highest authority and form of Ucadia Register is the Great Register and Public Record of a valid registered Ucadian Society; and

   (iii) The third and lowest authority and form of Records is any Record created and issued by a non-Ucadian society.

XIII.II – DIVINE GRACE AND ACTION OF AUTHENTICATION

1. The Divine Grace and Action of *Authentication* is the supernatural effect of validation and exemplification of records properly entered into registers and rolls within the custody of the Universal Ecclesia of One Christ. Divine Grace and Action of Authentication

2. *Authentication* is a wholly Divine and unmerited action, warranted by God and the Divine Creator. It is not an action effected within the temporal realm, nor can it be equated to physical terms or constructs. Understanding of action and Divine Grace of Authentication

3. The Divine Grace and Supernatural Action of *Authentication* is central to the proper effect of the Holy Rite of Record. Such supernatural presence and grace is made manifest *first* by the suitable qualification Divine Grace and Action of Sacrament of Authentication

of the recipient; and *second* by the proper authority of one administering the sacrament; and *third* by the constituent parts and order that must be established in order to effect the sacrament.

In accord with sacred liturgy, in the absence of one or more of these central requisites, no legitimate manifestation of such Divine Grace and Action can occur.

XIII.III – RITE OF RECORD

1. The Holy Rite of Record represents the constituent parts and their order that must be established in order to effect the Divine and Supernatural Sacrament of Authentication. In the absence of one or more of these central requisites, no legitimate manifestation or imprint of the Divine Grace and Action of Authentication can occur. Rite of Record

2. There are only three (3) valid and licit forms for the Rite of Record as defined by the most sacred *Missale Christus* and associated approved liturgy being Ecclesiastical, Vital and Public:- Form of the Sacrament of Authentication & Rite of Record

   (i) "**Ecclesiastical Record**" is when the Sacrament of Authentication is bestowed automatically as part of the proper formation of an Ecclesiastical Record in accord with the most sacred Covenants *Pactum De Singularis Caelum* and *Pactum De Singularis Christus*; and

   (ii) "**Vital Record**" is when the Sacrament of Authentication is bestowed automatically as part of the proper formation of a Vital Record relating to Members, in accord with the most sacred Covenants *Pactum De Singularis Caelum* and *Pactum De Singularis Christus*; and

   (iii) "**Public Record**" is when the Sacrament of Authentication is bestowed automatically as part of the proper formation of a Public Record in accord with the most sacred Covenants *Pactum De Singularis Caelum* and *Pactum De Singularis Christus*.

XIII.IV – ELEMENTS OF RITE OF RECORD

1. Elements of the Rite of Record are those constituent parts that must be established in order to effect the Holy Sacrament and manifest the Divine Grace and Action of Authentication. Elements of Rite of Record

2. A valid Record is comprised of three actions entered into three Books, consistent with the etymology of "record" from two Latin words *re* meaning "property" and *cordis* meaning "heart (body), mind (thought Valid Record

and reason) and spirit (soul)":

(i) The Event is the first action, entered into a Memorandum as a true written memorial to the "event" and associated proceedings and actions; and

(ii) The Witnessed Account is the second action, as attestation to an Account or Affidavit entered into a Journal as an attestation to the true Summary of Facts, with a unique Event Number then "posted back" to the Memorandum as well as "cancelling" those details within the Memorandum now "posted" in the Journal; and

(iii) The Conveyance is the third action, as proof of a valid "event" to a Ledger, or Summary Letter or Certificate as a True Summary of Account and Instrument of Record, with the unique Event Number then "posted forward" to the Ledger as the completion of the Record.

3. In terms of the general authority and nature of Records: Nature of Records

(i) All Records are wholly and exclusively Ecclesiastical Property and can never belong to a Trust, or Estate or Fund that formed or inherited it. Instead, all Records are the property of One Heaven; and

(ii) All Records are hierarchical in their inheritance of authority and validity from One Heaven, beginning with the highest being the Great Register and Public Record of One Heaven. A Record that cannot demonstrate the provenance of its authority, has none and is null and void from the beginning; and

(iii) As all Records are wholly and exclusively Ecclesiastical, absolutely no clerical or administrative act may take place in association with Records unless by a duly authorised Trustee under active and valid sacred Oath or Vow in a manner consistent and in accord with the most sacred Covenants *Pactum De Singularis Caelum*, *Pactum De Singularis Christus*, and *Missale Christus* and associated approved liturgy; and

(iv) The entry of the elements of a Record is wholly invalid unless the memorial of the act giving authority is done without duress, is done freely and with full knowledge and is consistent and in accord with the most sacred Covenants *Pactum De Singularis Caelum*, *Pactum De Singularis Christus*, and *Missale Christus* and associated approved liturgy.

4. Two types of valid Instrument of Record may be created being an Original and Certified

Original, or a *Certified Original*: Original Record

(i) An *Original Record* is an Instrument of Record where the existence of the Instrument itself and the number attached to it "completes" the Record and the instrument makes this clear; and

(ii) A *Certified Original Record* is when the Instrument of Record makes clear it is a Certificate or Extract or Abstract of an Original Record held somewhere else and the Jurat makes clear its status.

XIII.V – CONDITIONS OF RITE OF RECORD

1. Conditions of the Rite of Ecclesiastical Record are those requisite qualifications and contingencies permitted in the proper ministration of the Rite:- Conditions of Rite of Ecclesiastical Record

(i) That an event warranting the entry of a Record in an Ecclesiastical Register or Roll did occur and was entered into a Memorandum as a true memorial to the event and associated proceedings and actions; and

(ii) That a Witness Account to the event was received and entered into a Journal as an attestation to the true Summary of Facts, with a unique Event Number then "posted back" to the Memorandum as well as "cancelling" those details within the Memorandum now "posted" in the Journal; and

(iii) That the memorial of the event giving authority to the entry of an Ecclesiastical Record was done without duress, is done freely and with full knowledge and is consistent and in accord with the most sacred Covenants *Pactum De Singularis Caelum*, *Pactum De Singularis Christus*, and *Missale Christus* and associated approved liturgy; and

(iv) That a True Summary of Account and Instrument of Record from an appropriate Journal was duly entered into an Ecclesiastical Register or Roll.

2. Conditions of the Rite of Vital Record are those requisite qualifications and contingencies permitted in the proper ministration of the Rite:- Conditions of Rite of Vital Record

(i) That an event warranting the entry of a Vital Record in an Authorised Register or Roll did occur and was entered into a Memorandum as a true memorial to the event and associated proceedings and actions; and

(ii) That a Witness Account to the event was received and entered into a Journal as an attestation to the true Summary of Facts, with a unique Event Number then "posted back" to the Memorandum as well as "cancelling" those details within the Memorandum now "posted" in the Journal; and

(iii) That the memorial of the event giving authority to the entry of a Vital Record was done without duress, is done freely and with full knowledge and is consistent and in accord with the most sacred Covenants *Pactum De Singularis Caelum*, *Pactum De Singularis Christus*, and *Missale Christus* and associated approved liturgy; and

(iv) That a True Summary of Account and Instrument of Record from an appropriate Journal was duly entered into an Vital Register or Roll.

3. Conditions of the Rite of Public Record are those requisite qualifications and contingencies permitted in the proper ministration of the Rite:- Conditions of Rite of Public Record

(i) That an event warranting the entry of a Record in an Public Register or Roll did occur and was entered into a Memorandum as a true memorial to the event and associated proceedings and actions; and

(ii) That a Witness Account to the event was received and entered into a Journal as an attestation to the true Summary of Facts, with a unique Event Number then "posted back" to the Memorandum as well as "cancelling" those details within the Memorandum now "posted" in the Journal; and

(iii) That the memorial of the act giving authority to entry of a Public Record was done without duress, is done freely and with full knowledge and is consistent and in accord with the most sacred Covenants *Pactum De Singularis Caelum*, *Pactum De Singularis Christus*, and *Missale Christus* and associated approved liturgy; and

(iv) That a True Summary of Account and Instrument of Record from an appropriate Journal was duly entered into an Public Register or Roll.

XIII.VI – MINISTER OF RITE OF RECORD

1. Only authorised persons may validly and legitimately administer the Minister of Rite of Record

Rite of Record:

(i) Only persons properly ordained as a Minister or invested into office holding *Magisterium* or *Visium* possesses the powers and authority to confer and administer the Rite of Record under Extraordinary Conditions; and

(ii) Only persons properly invested into office holding *Administratum*, *Officium* or *Imperium* possesses the powers and authority to administer the Rite of Record under Ordinary Conditions.

Title XIV – Sacrament of Absolution & Rite of Confession

XIV.I – SACRAMENT OF ABSOLUTION

1. Absolution (*Ritus Sacramentum Absolutio*) and Rite of Confession is the sixth of the fourteen (14) Cardinal Sacraments, also known as the Ways of Heaven. Sacrament of Absolution (Ritus Sacramentum Absolutio)

The Sacrament of Absolution and Rite of Confession is granted and conferred in accordance with the most sacred Covenants *Pactum De Singularis Caelum*, *Pactum De Singularis Christus*, and *Missale Christus* and associated approved liturgy.

2. Whilst Divine Forgiveness is absolute, immediate and irrevocable to all who have transgressed, the full effect of the Divine Sacrament of Absolution can only be received upon the genuine act of Contrition through the proper conferral of the Rite of Confession, also known as the Act of Reconciliation. Divine Purpose of the Sacrament of Absolution

In the Rite of Confession, a Member who confesses their offences to a legitimate minister; and is authentically contrite and remorseful for such actions; and truly intends to reform themselves; and accepts without duress the necessary ecclesiastical or civil penalties, thereby removes any impediment to full reconciliation with God and the Divine Creator of all Heaven and Earth; and the full receipt of the absolute unconditional Divine Grace of Divine Mercy, Divine Forgiveness and Divine Love.

Thus, the proper and pious Cardinal Sacrament of Absolution, also known as the Act of Reconciliation itself does not presume to be the mechanism of conferring Divine Mercy, Divine Forgiveness and Divine Love, nor to presume to place conditions upon God and the Divine Creator of all Heaven and Earth and Christ and the Holy Spirit as to whether one is worthy or not worthy of Divine Salvation. Instead, the Sacrament of Absolution recognises the free will and choice of the penitent in openly reconciling with God and the Divine Creator of all Existence; and thus removing any impediment to the full receipt of Divine Grace.

Most importantly, within and through the authentic Sacrament of Absolution, the competent minister becomes the living embodiment of Christ the Witness and Messenger of the Good News of the Divine Mercy, Divine Forgiveness and Eternal Love of God and the Divine Creator of all Existence to each and every higher order life form and life itself.

3. There is only one form of the Sacrament of Absolution in accord with the most sacred Covenants *Pactum De Singularis Caelum* and *Pactum* Form of the Sacrament of

De Singularis Christus.

Absolution

4. Whilst it is a grievous error to consider that men or women or any church may interpret a holy position of trust into the presumption of adjudicating for Heaven the merits of a candidate for Divine Mercy, it is also a gross error to presume a man or woman is free to receive the full Grace of Divine Mercy and Divine Forgiveness without first being authentic, contrite, remorseful and pious in seeking reconciliation through the Rite of Confession.

Rite of Confession, Penance and the removal of any impediment to Divine Grace

The impediment is self inflicted and self sustaining, so long as the transgressor chooses to separate themselves from the truth of their actions and such consequences. Thus, the belligerent suffers the double ignominy of being estranged from the Grace and Divine Love of God and the Divine Creator as well as accepting by default the full spiritual liability of their actions in placing themselves as opposite to the laws of Heaven. Thus, it is the belligerent transgressor and not the Universal Ecclesia, that chooses to put themselves in such danger and suffering.

XIV.II – DIVINE GRACE AND ACTION OF ABSOLUTION

1. The Divine Grace and Action of *Absolution* is the supernatural effect of the forgiveness of transgressions; and removing any impediment to full reconciliation with God and the Divine Creator of all Heaven and Earth; and the full receipt of the absolute unconditional Divine Grace of Divine Mercy, Divine Forgiveness and Divine Love.

Divine Grace and Action of Absolution

2. *Absolution* is a wholly Divine and unmerited action, warranted by God and the Divine Creator. It is not an action effected within the temporal realm, nor can it be equated to physical terms or constructs.

Understanding of action and Divine Grace of Absolution

Article 7 (*Transgression and Sin*) of the most Holy Covenant *Pactum De Singularis Christus* states:-

> *Unification of the Living Body of Christ being the Universal Ecclesia of Christ represents a new Heaven and a new Earth and fulfilment of the Kingdom of Heaven upon the Earth and the vanquishing of all Sin.*
>
> *Whilst references and honour to historic and canonical texts and scripture shall permit the continued use of the word in Sacred Liturgy in historic context, all teachings, lessons, education and interpretation as to present and future events and the reference to "sin" is absolutely forbidden to be continued and an offence against the Living Body of One Christ.*

Furthermore, Article 29 (*Divine Mercy, Remedy & Redemption*) of the most sacred Covenant *Pactum De Singularis Caelum*, mandates by Divine Decree that the term and use of the word "Sin":-

> *is hereby forbidden, reprobate, suppressed and never to be revived. Instead, the word and the equivalent concept of "**Transgression**" shall now be used to define mistake, fault, concept, default, fraud, profanity, tyranny and impiety.*

3. In accord with Article 29 (*Divine Mercy, Remedy & Redemption*) of the most sacred Covenant *Pactum De Singularis Caelum*, there are seven (7) levels of Transgression. The higher the level of Transgression, the more serious the transgression:-

Seven levels of Transgression

(i) Mistake or Error; and

(ii) Fault (Delict); and

(iii) Contempt (Profanity); and

(iv) Default (Delinquency); and

(v) Fraud (Perfidy); and

(vi) Tyranny; and

(vii) Impiety.

4. The Divine Grace and Supernatural Action of *Absolution* is central to the proper effect of the Holy Rite of Confession. Such supernatural presence and grace is made manifest *first* by the suitable qualification of the recipient; and *second* by the proper authority of one administering the sacrament; and *third* by the constituent parts and order that must be established in order to effect the sacrament.

Divine Grace and Action of Sacrament of Absolution

In accord with sacred liturgy, in the absence of one or more of these central requisites, no legitimate manifestation of such Divine Grace and Action can occur.

XIV.III – RITE OF CONFESSION

1. The Holy Rite of Confession represents the constituent parts and their order that must be established in order to effect the Divine and Supernatural Sacrament of Absolution. In the absence of one or more of these central requisites, no legitimate manifestation or imprint of the Divine Grace and Action of Absolution can occur.

Rite of Confession

2. There are only three (3) valid and licit forms for the Holy Rite of

Form of the Rite

Confession as defined by the most sacred *Missale Christus* and associated approved liturgy being *General*, *Ordinary* and *Extraordinary*:- of Confession

(i) "**General Rite (of Confession)**" is conferred by a competent minister within a Sacred Space dedicated as a Competent Forum of Law; and

(ii) "**Ordinary Rite (of Confession)**" is conferred by a competent ordained minister to an individual penitent in private; and

(iii) "**Extraordinary Rite (of Confession)**" is conferred by a competent ordained minister during Holy Mass through the Penitential Rite.

XIV.IV – ELEMENTS OF RITE OF CONFESSION

1. Elements of the Rite of Confession are those constituent parts that must be established in order to effect the Holy Sacrament and manifest the Divine Grace and Action of Absolution. Elements of Rite of Confession

2. The Proper and Essential Order of Elements of the Rite of Confession are:- Order of Elements of Rite of Confession

   (i) Petition; and

   (ii) Confession; and

   (iii) Contrition; and

   (iv) Compunction.

3. The Proper Seal of Confession, once formed through the bond of an authentically contrite, remorseful and pious Penitent and the competent, compassionate and discerning Confessor is absolute, permanent and irrevocable. In accord with the most sacred Covenant *Pactum De Singularis Caelum*, no force within Heaven or upon the Earth is permitted to break such a properly formed Seal. Seal of Confession

   However, an incomplete or tainted Act of Contrition, particularly when a Penitent is found not to be genuinely contrite, or remorseful or pious by their lack of subsequent penance or actions, fully dissolves any bond or constraints upon the Confessor and instead impels him under the Laws of Heaven to remedy the injury of the false Penitent in giving notice of the facts pertaining to such Act:-

   (i) There can be no proper Seal of Confession or completed Rite of Confession where a Penitent continues to be culpable of sexual abuse or molestation against minors, unless such a person agrees to make a full and frank confession to the relevant ecclesiastical authorities and civil authorities within seven days of such admission under Confession; and

(ii) There can be no proper Seal of Confession or completed Rite of Confession where the Penitent is culpable of murder or terror without justifiable cause, unless such a person agrees to make a full and frank confession to the relevant ecclesiastical authorities and civil authorities within seven days of such admission under Confession.

XIV.V – CONDITIONS OF RITE OF CONFESSION

Conditions of Rite of Confession

1. Conditions of the Rite of Confession are those requisite qualifications and contingencies permitted in the proper ministration of the Rite. There shall exist only three (3) possible Conditions for the ministration of Rite of Confession being *Universal, Ordinary and General*:-

(i) *Universal* are the Conditions that apply to all forms and circumstances of the Rite of Confession, including as part of the Liturgy of Mass; and

(ii) *Ordinary* are the Conditions necessary for the conferral of the Ordinary Rite of Confession upon a living human being; and

(iii) *General* are the Conditions necessary for the conferral of the General Rite of Confession within an Oratory or Sacred Place dedicated as a Competent Forum of Law.

Universal Conditions

2. *Universal Conditions* for the conferral of the Rite of Confession apply to all forms and circumstances of the Rite:-

(i) Every baptised person having reached a state of reason and identity of self is capable of receiving (the Rite of) Confession; and

(ii) A person, whether accused by another or not, who is conscious of having committed a grave, wicked or perverse offence is capable of receiving (the Rite of) Confession.

Ordinary Conditions

3. *Ordinary Conditions* apply to the conferral of the Ordinary Rite of Confession:-

(i) That a baptised person has clearly expressed a genuine and heartfelt yearning to be reconciled with God and the Divine Creator; and

(ii) That a baptised person is conscious of having committed a grave, wicked or perverse offence; and has taken the first manifest steps to accepting personal responsibility; and has genuinely experienced remorse for their actions; and

(iii) That a baptised person is disposed to amendments of their own behaviour and actions in order to mitigate habitual grievances and offences warranting the urgent need for the Rite of Confession.

4. *General Conditions* apply to the conferral of the General Rite of Confession:- General Conditions

(i) That a baptised person is accused of having committed a grave, wicked or perverse offence warranting the General Rite of Confession.

XIV.VI – MINISTER OF RITE OF CONFESSION

1. Only authorised persons may validly and legitimately administer the Rite of Confession in accord with the most sacred Covenants *Pactum De Singularis Caelum* and *Pactum De Singularis Christus*: Minister of Rite of Confession

(i) Only persons properly ordained as a Minister or invested into Sacred Office holding *Magisterium* or *Visium* possesses the powers and authority to confer and administer the Ordinary Rite of Confession under Ordinary Conditions or the Universal Rite within the Liturgy of Mass; and

(ii) Only persons properly invested into Sacred Office holding *Administratum*, *Officium* or *Imperium* possesses the powers and authority to administer the General Rite of Confession under General Conditions.

XIV.VII – ORDINARY RITE OF CONFESSION

1. The *Ordinary Rite of Confession* shall be as follows: Ordinary Rite of Confession

GREETING

Customary Greeting

CONFESSOR

In the name of ✠ the Father, and of the Son, and of the Holy Spirit.

PENITENT

Amen.

CONFESSOR
May the love of our Saviour Jesus Christ, the mercy of God and the strength of the Holy Spirit be with you.

PENITENT
And also with you.

PETITION

Petition

CONFESSOR
What is it you ask in the name of the Father and of the Son and of the Holy Spirit today?

PENITENT
Absolution (Forgiveness)

CONFESSOR
The Sacrament of Absolution you ask through the Rite of Confession is a solemn and sacred rite. It is a foundation stone of Christian Life and Justice that our Divine Creator loves each and everyone of us, no matter how badly we transgress; and that all people can reform and change.

God truly loves you. This is a fundamental pillar of our Christian Faith. So much does your Heavenly Father love you that he forgives you and does not seek to judge or condemn you.

Yet Christ himself also taught us the importance of respecting such Divine Love, Mercy and Forgiveness by demonstrating sincere remorse for our transgressions; and a willingness to change and make amends. This is the heart of this most sacred Sacrament and Rite instituted by Christ.

Are you willing to be truthful under the Sacred Seal of Confession and disclose before God your transgressions, your remorse and your willingness to change and make amends.

PENITENT
Yes.

CONFESSION

Confession

CONFESSOR

What then is it you wish to confess?

PENITENT

(Penitent confesses their transgressions, with the Confessor gently asking and confirming the remorse of the Penitent for these transgressions and their willingness to change and make amends.)

CONTRITION

Contrition

CONFESSOR

Nothing is hidden from God. Yet by your honesty and courage, you have chosen to bring forth into this realm as in Heaven, the nature of your transgressions, your genuine remorse and your willingness to change and make amends.

As an outward sign of your genuine remorse and contrition, I ask you to recite in your own voice the prayer of contrition with me.

(To aid the Penitent, the Confessor may then recite each line so the Penitent can repeat the line in their own voice)

PENITENT

I confess before God and the Divine Creator of all Existence, that I have transgressed from your teachings and laws, by my thoughts and through my words and actions; and in what I have done and what I have failed to do.
I admit that I am truly sorry and remorseful for my thoughts, my words and my actions and call out to our Mother Blessed Mary in Heaven, to all the angels and saints and our ancestors, to intercede for me and help me change and make amends.

CONFESSOR

By the love of our Divine Creator and the power of Christ you are absolved ✠ from your transgressions and any spiritual blemish is wiped clean.

COMPUNCTION

Compunction

CONFESSOR

Just as the Divine has forgiven you, are you now prepared to demonstrate your remorse and contrition through reasonable steps to make genuine amends?

PENITENT

Yes.

CONFESSOR

(Confessor provides practical suggestions as outwards signs of penance.)

BLESSING

Blessing

CONFESSOR

May our God and Divine Creator bless you, ✠ the Father, and the Son and the Holy Spirit.

PENITENT

Amen

CONFESSOR

Go forth with the peace and love of Christ

PENITENT

Thanks be to God!

Title XV – Sacrament of Volition & Rite of Oath

XV.I – SACRAMENT OF VOLITION

1. Volition (*Ritus Sacramentum Volitio*) and Rite of Oath is the seventh of the fourteen (14) Cardinal Sacraments, also known as the Ways of Heaven. Sacrament of Volition (Ritus Sacramentum Volitio)

   The Sacrament of Volition and Rite of Oath is granted and conferred in accordance with the most sacred Covenants *Pactum De Singularis Caelum*, *Pactum De Singularis Christus*, and *Missale Christus* and associated approved liturgy.

2. The Sacrament of Holy Oath is a recognition of a binding of obligation and performance duly recorded in the Great Register and Divine Records of Heaven and the temporal records on Earth and the Solar System. Divine Purpose of the Sacrament of Volition

   The Sacrament of Holy Oath is granted and conveyed upon the pronouncement of a valid oath in accordance with the present sacred Covenant and associated approved liturgy.

XV.II – DIVINE GRACE AND ACTION OF VOLITION

1. The Divine Grace and Action of *Volition* is the supernatural effect of recognising a binding of obligation and performance duly recorded in the Great Register and Divine Records of Heaven and the temporal records on Earth and the Solar System. Divine Grace and Action of Volition

2. *Volition* is a wholly Divine and unmerited action, warranted by God and the Divine Creator. It is not an action effected within the temporal realm, nor can it be equated to physical terms or constructs. Understanding of action and Divine Grace of Volition

3. The Divine Grace and Supernatural Action of *Volition* is central to the proper effect of the Holy Rite of Oath. Such supernatural presence and grace is made manifest *first* by the suitable qualification of the recipient; and *second* by the proper authority of one administering the sacrament; and *third* by the constituent parts and order that must be established in order to effect the sacrament. Divine Grace and Action of Sacrament of Volition

   In accord with sacred liturgy, in the absence of one or more of these central requisites, no legitimate manifestation of such Divine Grace and Action can occur.

XV.III – RITE OF OATH

1. The Holy Rite of Oath represents the constituent parts and their order that must be established in order to effect the Divine and Supernatural Rite of Oath

Sacrament of Volition. In the absence of one or more of these central requisites, no legitimate manifestation or imprint of the Divine Grace and Action of Volition can occur.

A Person cannot be invested into an Office, nor hold any authority or power without a properly pronounced Oath or Vow.

3. There are only four (4) valid and licit forms for the Rite of Oath as defined by the most sacred *Missale Christus* and associated approved liturgy being *Personal, Public, Ordinary* and *Extraordinary*:- Form of the Rite of Oath

(i) "**Personal Oath**" is when the Sacrament of Volition is bestowed automatically as part of the proper formation of a Solemn and Binding Personal Oath performed and witnessed by at least one other person; and

(ii) "**Public Oath**" is when the Sacrament of Volition is bestowed automatically as part of the proper formation of a Solemn and Binding Public Oath; and

(iii) "**Ordinary Oath**" is when the Sacrament of Volition is bestowed automatically as part of the proper formation of a Solemn and Binding Sacred Oath by properly consecrated and ordained clergy; and

(iv) "**Extraordinary Oath**" is when the Sacrament of Volition is bestowed automatically as part of the proper formation of a Solemn and Binding Pious Oath by properly consecrated and ordained clergy choosing to live a heroic and virtuous life of austerity in the same manner of Christ.

XV.IV – ELEMENTS OF RITE OF OATH

1. Elements of the Rite of Oath are those constituent parts that must be established in order to effect the Holy Sacrament and manifest the Divine Grace and Action of Volition. Elements of Rite of Oath

2. By the custom and tradition throughout the history of law, an Oath can only be valid if the following criteria exist: Order of Elements

(i) The one making the Oath comes with good intention, good character and good conscience; and

(ii) The one making the Oath has the Right and proper authority to make such an Oath; and

(iii) At least one other person is present and prepared to witness the Oath and testify to such a fact; and

(iv) The candidate raises his right hand with a flat palm so that the face of the open palm can be clearly seen by all witnesses during the pronunciation of the Oath, whilst his left covers his heart as the symbol and source of truth of the spoken words; and

(v) That the pronunciation of the Oath never uses language of profanity such as "swear"; and

(vi) That some written Memorial (Memorandum) to the event exists, signed by the one making the Oath and a different person as witness.

3. In the absence of a valid and proper Oath, no person claiming possession, or occupation, or investiture or ownership of a Sacred Office holds any authority or power whatsoever and any and all actions made by such a person are completely without validity in law, whether or not the parties present did consent or decline. Effect of Oath

XV.V – MINISTER OF RITE OF OATH

1. Only authorised persons may validly and legitimately administer the Rite of Oath: Minister of Rite of Oath

(i) Only persons properly ordained as a Minister or invested into office holding *Magisterium* or *Visium* possesses the powers and authority to confer and administer the Rite of Oath under Extraordinary Conditions; and

(ii) Only persons properly invested into office holding *Administratum*, *Officium* or *Imperium* possesses the powers and authority to administer the Rite of Oath under Ordinary Conditions.

XV.VI – RITE OF PUBLIC OATH

1. Rite of Public Oath is when the Sacrament of Volition is bestowed automatically as part of the proper formation of a Solemn and Binding Public Oath; and Rite of Public Oath

PUBLIC OATH OF PHYSICIANS Public Oath of Physicians

SUPPLICANT

I invoke the favour of the Divine Creator of all Existence and Life, And implore the spirits of my ancestors to bear witness to my most solemn oath, Upon the names and lives of all my household and all those yet to come, That even upon peril against my life I shall not disavow this sacred Covenant:

First: I pledge that for as long as I shall live, I will be a seeker of truth and a servant to true knowledge; free from any superstition, prejudice, fear or malice; and

Second: I promise that to the best of my ability, I will protect the dignity of life and will promote wellness above all; and will tend to the needs of the sick and the dying; and

Third: I pledge to honour the sanctity of trust given to me and I will keep confidence and refrain from pursuing any financial or unfair advantage gained from my position; and

Fourth: I promise to use logic and reason in all my diagnosis and I will refrain at all cost from cutting or poisoning the body unless it is the only reasonable conclusion to saving a life; and

Fifth: I vow to keep firm and inviolable this sacred Covenant. May it grant me your favour and good fortune. If I do transgress, I shall be at your mercy; and if I have sworn falsely in bad faith and bad character this day, may you portion to me that which is deserved upon such profanity and disgrace before Heaven and Earth.
Amen.

PUBLIC OATH OF JUSTICE

Public Oath of Justice

SUPPLICANT

I N, do solemnly vow before God, that as a Justice of the Peace for (Name of Place), I will at all times and in all things do equal justice to all people; and discharge the duties of my office according to the law to the best of my knowledge and ability without fear, or favour or affection. So help me God! Amen

PUBLIC OATH OF OFFICE

Public Oath of Office

SUPPLICANT

I N, I, do solemnly and sincerely promise and pledge (or

declare) that I will truly and faithfully, and to the best of my skill and knowledge, execute the powers and trusts reposed in me as (office).
So help me God! Amen

PUBLIC OATH OF CITIZENSHIP

Public Oath of Citizenship

SUPPLICANT

I, N. do solemnly promise as a loyal citizen that I will be faithful and bear true allegiance to the Constitution of [country]; and that I shall defend its values and sovereign rights when called to do so; and that I will continue to respect and obey its laws to the best of my ability. So help me God!

PUBLIC OATH OF RENUNCIATION OF CITIZENSHIP

Public Oath of Renunciation of Citizenship

SUPPLICANT

I, N. do hereby declare and make these solemn promises: That I absolutely and entirely renounce and abjure all allegiance and fidelity to any foreign prince, potentate, state or sovereignty of whom or wherefore I previously have been a subject or citizen; and that I will be faithful and bear true allegiance to the Constitution of [country]; and that I shall defend its values and sovereign rights when called to do so; and that I will continue to respect and obey its laws to the best of my ability. So help me God!

XV.VII – RITE OF ORDINARY OATH

1. Rite of Ordinary Oath is when the Sacrament of Volition is bestowed automatically as part of the Rite of Ordination.

Rite of Ordinary Oath

ORDINATION (HOLY ORDERS) OATH

Ordination (Holy Orders) Oath

SUPPLICANT

(Standing facing the congregation, whilst having right hand upon the Holy Gospel)

In the Name of God the Father, Christ the Son and the Holy Spirit, I, N. do solemnly and humbly promise before all Heaven and Earth that all I have here before avowed, I will perform and keep in sacred trust for the benefit of all the People of God; and for the bishops and hierarchy of all the clergy of this country; and for the Holy Father and all the fraternal brothers and sisters of the Universal Ecclesia of One Christ.

(The Supplicant then kisses the sacred text and then signs their name to an original document of the previous Vows and Oath representing the Original Deed of a new sacred trust of Holy Orders.)

XV.VIII – RITE OF EXTRAORDINARY OATH (OF CORONATION)

1. Rite of Coronation Oath is when the Sacrament of Volition is bestowed as Rite of Coronation. Rite of Coronation Oath

CORONATION OATH Coronation Oath

(Coronation Oath always proceeds the Coronation Vows. See Rite of Coronation Vow)

SUPPLICANT (MONARCH)

(Standing facing the congregation, whilst having right hand upon the Holy Gospel)

In the Name of God the Father, Christ the Son and the Holy Spirit, I, N. do solemnly and humbly promise before all Heaven and Earth that all I have here before avowed, I will perform and keep in sacred trust for the benefit of all the people of this realm; and for the Body Politic and all its realms, dependencies and territories; and for the crown and all its ministers and officers.

(The Supplicant then kisses the sacred text and then signs their name to an original document of the previous Vows and Oath representing the Original Deed of a new sacred majestic trust for the realm.)

Title XVI – Sacrament of Vocation & Rite of Vow

XVI.I – SACRAMENT OF VOCATION

1. Vocation (*Ritus Sacramentum Vocatio*) and Rite of Vow is the eighth of the fourteen (14) Cardinal Sacraments, also known as the Ways of Heaven. Sacrament of Vocation (Ritus Sacramentum Vocatio)

 The Sacrament of Vocation and Rite of Vow is granted and conferred in accordance with the most sacred Covenants *Pactum De Singularis Caelum*, *Pactum De Singularis Christus*, and *Missale Christus* and associated approved liturgy.

2. The purpose of the sacrament of Vocation is the formal recognition and endorsement of a person pledging an act or themselves as assurance or security for the obligations of another in accordance with the present sacred Covenant and associated approved liturgy. Divine Purpose of the Sacrament of Vocation

XVI.II – DIVINE GRACE AND ACTION OF VOCATION

1. The Divine Grace and Action of *Vocation* is the supernatural effect of the formal recognition and endorsement of a person pledging an act or themselves as assurance or security for the obligations of another. Divine Grace and Action of Vocation
2. *Vocation* is a wholly Divine and unmerited action, warranted by God and the Divine Creator. It is not an action effected within the temporal realm, nor can it be equated to physical terms or constructs. Understanding of action and Divine Grace of Vocation
3. The Divine Grace and Supernatural Action of *Vocation* is central to the proper effect of the Holy Rite of Vow. Such supernatural presence and grace is made manifest *first* by the suitable qualification of the recipient; and *second* by the proper authority of one administering the sacrament; and *third* by the constituent parts and order that must be established in order to effect the sacrament. Divine Grace and Action of Sacrament of Vocation

 In accord with sacred liturgy, in the absence of one or more of these central requisites, no legitimate manifestation of such Divine Grace and Action can occur.

XVI.III – RITE OF VOW

1. The Holy Rite of Vow represents the constituent parts and their order that must be established in order to effect the Divine and Supernatural Sacrament of Vocation. In the absence of one or more of these central requisites, no legitimate manifestation or imprint of the Divine Grace and Action of Vocation can occur. Rite of Vow
2. There are only four (4) valid and licit forms for the Sacrament of Vocation (Sacramentum) as defined by the most sacred *Missale* Form of the Rite of Vow

Christus and associated approved liturgy being *Personal, Public, Ordinary* and *Extraordinary*:-

(i) "**Personal Vow**" is when the Sacrament of Vocation is bestowed automatically as part of the proper formation of a Solemn and Binding Personal Vow; and

(ii) "**Public Vow**" is when the Sacrament of Vocation is bestowed automatically as part of the proper formation of a Solemn and Binding Public Vow; and

(iii) "**Ordinary Vow**" is when the Sacrament of Vocation is bestowed automatically as part of the proper formation of a Solemn and Binding Sacred Vow by properly consecrated and ordained clergy; and

(iv) "**Extraordinary Vow**" is when the Sacrament of Vocation is bestowed automatically as part of the proper formation of a Solemn and Binding Pious Vow by properly consecrated and ordained clergy choosing to live a heroic and virtuous life of austerity in the same manner of Christ.

XVI.IV – ELEMENTS OF RITE OF VOW

1. Elements of the Rite of Vow are those constituent parts that must be established in order to effect the Holy Sacrament and manifest the Divine Grace and Action of Vocation. Elements of Rite of Vow

2. In relation to Vows: General Principles of Vows

(i) A Vow made by oration in the presence of others is always superior to a written Vow. A Vow made in secret or privately has no effect and is void from the beginning by virtue of not being made in public; and

(ii) A Vow made free from coercion, fear or deliberate deception must be fulfilled. A Vow made out of grave and unjust fear or malice, or ignorance is null by the law itself; and

(iii) A Vow ceases by the lapse of the time designated to fulfil the obligation, or by a substantial change of the matter promised, or by the absence of a condition that the vow depends upon, or by the absence of the purpose of the vow, or by dispensation, or by commutation.

3. In the absence of a valid and proper Vow associated with a valid and proper Oath, no person claiming possession, or occupation, or investiture or ownership of an Office holds any authority or power Absence of proper Vow whatsoever and any and all actions made by such a person are completely without validity in law, whether or not the parties present did consent or decline.

XVI.V – RITE OF PUBLIC VOW

1. Rite of Public Vow is when the Sacrament of Vocation is bestowed automatically as part of the proper formation of a Solemn and Binding Public Vow. Rite of Public Vow

PUBLIC VOW OF JUSTICE OF THE PEACE

Public Vow Justice of the Peace

AVOWER

I N, do solemnly vow before God, that as a Justice of the Peace for [Name of Place], I will at all times and in all things do equal justice to all people; and discharge the duties of my office according to the law to the best of my knowledge and ability without fear, or favour or affection. So help me God! Amen

XVI.VI – RITE OF ORDINARY VOWS

1. Rite of Ordinary Vow is when the Sacrament of Vocation is bestowed as part of the proper formation of a Solemn and Binding Ordinary Vows during the Rite of Ordination. Rite of Ordinary Vows

ORDINARY VOWS

Ordinary Vows

CELEBRANT

I call upon the Supplicants knelt before us to each give their solemn vows.

CELEBRANT

(To Supplicants)

Do you take your fraternity of brothers and sisters in Christ to be your new friends and family? Do you promise to always be truthful to them in good times and bad, and in times of sickness and distress?

SUPPLICANTS

I do.

CELEBRANT

Do you take this sacred calling to be your life journey? Do you promise to be trusting in your faith, and to always be gentle and kind to your soul throughout this journey with Christ?

SUPPLICANTS

I do.

CELEBRANT

Do you take your Ordinary as your instructor and guide? Do you promise always to be respectful and obedient and support your leaders and the order of hierarchy of clergy of the most holy Universal Ecclesia every day of your life?

SUPPLICANTS

I do.

XVI.VII – RITE OF EXTRAORDINARY VOWS

1. Rite of Extraordinary Vow is when the Sacrament of Vocation is bestowed as part of the proper formation of a Solemn and Binding Pious Vows during higher Rites associated with a heroic and virtuous life of austerity. Rite of Extraordinary Vows

EXTRAORDINARY VOWS (HOLY ORDERS)

Extraordinary Vows Holy Orders

CELEBRANT

I call upon the Supplicants knelt before us to each give their solemn vows.

CELEBRANT

(To Supplicants)

Do you solemnly vow a life of poverty, chastity and humility? And do you promise to forsake your own personal wants and desires for the sake of the sacred office and mission you shall hold?

SUPPLICANT

I do.

CELEBRANT

Do you solemnly vow to always uphold the gift of charity and alms to those in need? And do you promise to act with mercy, compassion and forgiveness of others, as you yourself are forgiven by God?

SUPPLICANT

I do.

CELEBRANT

Do you solemnly vow to respect and protect the rule of law, fairness and the equality of rights of all? And do you promise to pursue every remedy, relief and reform against injustice, or moral repugnancy or corruption of the laws and institutions of the Universal Ecclesia and all its bodies, institutions and fraternities?

SUPPLICANT

I do.

CELEBRANT

Do you solemnly vow to absolute obedience to the Mission and the Powers delegated to you by Christ through his Holy Universal Ecclesia with dignity, grace and the gift of wise discernment?

SUPPLICANT

I do.

EXTRAORDINARY VOWS (SOVEREIGN)

Extraordinary Vows Sovereign

CELEBRANT

I call upon the Supplicant knelt before God to give their solemn vows.

CELEBRANT

(To Supplicant)

Do you take your fraternity of clergy, peers, ministers and officers to be your new family? Do you promise to always be truthful to them in good times and bad, and in times of sickness and distress?

SUPPLICANT

I do.

CELEBRANT

Do you take this sacred calling to be your life journey? Do you promise to be trusting in your faith, and to always be loyal, trustworthy and dependable to the one true and Holy Universal Church?

SUPPLICANT

I do.

CELEBRANT

Do you take the Holy Gospel of Christ and the Maxims of Divine Law as your instruction and guide? Do you promise always to be respectful and support the well being of your government and the order of hierarchy of the Body Politic and all its dominions, dependencies, protectorates and territories every day of your life?

SUPPLICANT

I do.

CELEBRANT

Do you solemnly vow a life of self restraint, frugality and humility? And do you promise to forsake your own personal wants and desires for the sake of the sacred office and mission you shall hold?

SUPPLICANT

I do.

CELEBRANT

Do you solemnly vow to always uphold the gift of charity and alms to those in need? And do you promise to the act with mercy, compassion and forgiveness of others, as you yourself are forgiven by God?

SUPPLICANT

I do.

CELEBRANT

Do you solemnly vow to respect and protect the rule of law, fairness and the equality of rights of all? And do you with promise to pursue every remedy, relief and reform against injustice, or moral repugnancy or corruption of the laws and institutions of the Body Politic?

SUPPLICANT

I do.

CELEBRANT

Do you solemnly vow to uphold this sacred Mission and the Powers delegated to you by Christ with dignity, grace and the gift of wise discernment?

SUPPLICANT

I do.

Title XVII – Sacrament of Testification & Rite of Testimony

XVII.I – SACRAMENT OF TESTIFICATION

1. Testification (*Ritus Sacramentum Testificatio*) and the Rite of Testimony is the ninth of the fourteen (14) Cardinal Sacraments, also known as the Ways of Heaven. Sacrament of Testification (Ritus Sacramentum Testificatio)

   The Sacrament of Testification and Rite of Testimony may also be granted and conferred on its own in accordance with the most sacred Covenants *Pactum De Singularis Caelum*, *Pactum De Singularis Christus*, and *Missale Christus* and associated approved liturgy.

2. Testification is by definition the act of vocalising and giving testimony or evidence; being a vocalised act involving not only at least one Invocation, but at least one promise and obligation in relation to the performance of a valid office. All valid offices are based upon truth and trust and so no office can be formed without a proper Testification. Nature of Testification

   All communication to the *Officium Systemata* (Offices Systems) of Heaven by living Members of One Heaven shall be by Testification of an Oath and at least one Vow in accord with the most sacred Covenant *Pactum De Singularis Caelum*. The methods, rules and standards of proper Testification shall be defined by the most sacred Covenant *Pactum De Singularis Caelum* and associated covenants and no other. All properly conferred Testification shall be received, recorded and acknowledged by the Officium Systemata (Offices Systems) of One Heaven.

3. There is only one form of the Sacrament of Testification in recognition of the fact that all Testimony is predicated on the solemn attestation of the truth, without embellishment. Form of the Sacrament of Testification

XVII.II – DIVINE GRACE AND ACTION OF TESTIFICATION

1. The Divine Grace and Action of *Testification* is the supernatural effect of officially communicating with Heaven the truth as acknowledged upon the Earth. Divine Grace and Action of Testification

2. *Testification* is a wholly Divine and unmerited action, warranted by God and the Divine Creator. It is not an action effected within the temporal realm, nor can it be equated to physical terms or constructs. Understanding of action and Divine Grace of Testification

3. The Divine Grace and Supernatural Action of *Testification* is central to the proper effect of the Holy Rite of Testimony. Such supernatural presence and grace is made manifest *first* by the suitable qualification of the recipient; and *second* by the proper authority of one administering the sacrament; and *third* by the constituent parts and Divine Grace and Action of Sacrament of Testification

order that must be established in order to effect the sacrament.

In accord with sacred liturgy, in the absence of one or more of these central requisites, no legitimate manifestation of such Divine Grace and Action can occur.

XVII.III – RITE OF TESTIMONY

1. The Holy Rite of Testimony represents the constituent parts and their order that must be established in order to effect the Divine and Supernatural Sacrament of Testification. In the absence of one or more of these central requisites, no legitimate manifestation or imprint of the Divine Grace and Action of Testification can occur. Rite of Testimony

XVII.IV – ELEMENTS OF RITE OF TESTIMONY

1. Elements of the Rite of Testimony are those constituent parts that must be established in order to effect the Holy Sacrament and manifest the Divine Grace and Action of Testification. Elements of Rite of Testimony

2. The validity and therefore admissibility of Testimonial evidence relevant to an Argument is dependent upon four major qualities being *Competency, Integrity, Authenticity* and *Objectivity*, namely: Condition of Testimony

    (i) *Competency* is that the witness is capable of comprehending questions and capable of answering truthfully without influence; and

    (ii) *Integrity* is the context that the witness has not been offered any financial benefit or that reward has been offered to a witness for their testimony, nor has the witness been threatened or coerced; and

    (iii) *Authenticity* is that the words of the witness are their own and that they have not been coached in any way by any third party on what to say or not to say; and

    (iv) *Objectivity* that the answers are firsthand knowledge of fact and not hearsay.

Title XVIII – Sacrament of Compassion & Rite of Mercy

XVIII.I – SACRAMENT OF COMPASSION

1. Compassion (*Ritus Sacramentum Compassio*) and the Rite of Mercy is the tenth of the fourteen (14) Cardinal Sacraments, also known as the Ways of Heaven.

Sacrament of Compassion (Ritus Sacramentum Compassio)

The Sacrament of Compassion and Rite of Mercy may also be granted and conferred on its own in accordance with the most sacred Covenants *Pactum De Singularis Caelum*, *Pactum De Singularis Christus*, and *Missale Christus* and associated approved liturgy.

2. The purpose of the Sacrament of Compassion and Rite of Mercy is the formal blessing of charity and benevolence to those in need; and the formal remittance and discharge of part or all of an offence as well as any prescribed punishment, in accordance with the present sacred Covenant and associated approved liturgy.

Divine Purpose of the Sacrament of Compassion

XVIII.II – DIVINE GRACE AND ACTION OF COMPASSION

1. The Divine Grace and Action of *Compassion* is the supernatural effect of acknowledging and respecting the formal blessing of charity and benevolence to those in need; or the formal remittance and discharge of part or all of an offence as well as any prescribed punishment.

Divine Grace and Action of Compassion

2. *Compassion* is a wholly Divine and unmerited action, warranted by God and the Divine Creator. It is not an action effected within the temporal realm, nor can it be equated to physical terms or constructs.

Understanding of action and Divine Grace of Compassion

3. The Divine Grace and Supernatural Action of *Compassion* is central to the proper effect of the Holy Rite of Mercy (Clemency). Such supernatural presence and grace is made manifest *first* by the suitable qualification of the recipient; and *second* by the proper authority of one administering the sacrament; and *third* by the constituent parts and order that must be established in order to effect the sacrament.

Divine Grace and Action of Sacrament of Compassion

In accord with sacred liturgy, in the absence of one or more of these central requisits, no legitimate manifestation of such Divine Grace and Action can occur.

XVIII.III – RITE OF MERCY (CLEMENCY)

1. The Holy Rite of Mercy (Clemency) represents the constituent parts and their order that must be established in order to effect the Divine and Supernatural *Sacrament of Compassion*. In the absence of one or more of these central requisits, no legitimate manifestation or imprint of the Divine Grace and Action of Compassion can occur.

Rite of Mercy (Clemency)

2. There are only four (4) valid and licit corporeal forms for the Sacrament of Compassion as defined by the most sacred *Missale Christus* and associated approved liturgy being Personal, Public, Ordinary and Extraordinary:- Form of the Sacrament of Mercy

(i) "**Personal Mercy**" is when the Sacrament of Compassion is bestowed automatically as part of a formal forgiveness of some grievance between parties; or the benevolent assistance or selfless act of one to another; and

(ii) "**Public Mercy**" is when the Sacrament of Compassion is bestowed automatically as part of a formal public decree of clemency and mercy in light of some sentence; or as part of some organised charitable and benevolent support to the less fortunate; and

(iii) "**Ordinary Mercy**" is when the Sacrament of Compassion is bestowed automatically as an element of a formal sacramental ritual performed by properly consecrated and ordained clergy; and

(iv) "**Extraordinary Mercy**" is when the Sacrament of Compassion is bestowed automatically as an element of a formal sacramental ritual performed by the Supreme Patriarch.

3. The elements and conditions of the Rite of Mercy (Clemency) are reserved and incorporated with the appropriate rites and sacraments possessing Mercy. Elements and Conditions of Mercy (Clemency)

Title XIX – Sacrament of Conscription & Rite of Binding

XIX.I – SACRAMENT OF CONSCRIPTION

1. Conscription (*Ritus Sacramentum Conscripto*) is the eleventh of the fourteen (14) Cardinal Sacraments, also known as the Ways of Heaven. Sacrament of Conscription (Ritus Sacramentum Conscripto)

The Sacrament of Conscription and Rite of Binding may also be granted and conferred on its own in accordance with the most sacred Covenants *Pactum De Singularis Caelum*, *Pactum De Singularis Christus*, and *Missale Christus* and associated approved liturgy.

2. Binding is a fundamental concept of society as it permits people to engage in trusted relations of significant trust. The purpose of the sacrament of Binding is the formal recognition and acknowledgement of the Divine Authority given to the Universal Ecclesia of One Christ whereby *What is bound on Earth shall be bound in Heaven and what is loosed upon the Earth shall likewise be loosed in Heaven.* Divine Purpose of the Sacrament of Conscription

XIX.II – DIVINE GRACE AND ACTION OF CONSCRIPTION

1. The Divine Grace and Action of *Conscription* is the supernatural effect of formal recognition and acknowledgement of the Divine Authority given to the Universal Ecclesia of One Christ whereby *What is bound on Earth shall be bound in Heaven and what is loosed upon the Earth shall likewise be loosed in Heaven.* Divine Grace and Action of Conscription

2. *Conscription* is a wholly Divine and unmerited action, warranted by God and the Divine Creator. It is not an action effected within the temporal realm, nor can it be equated to physical terms or constructs. Understanding of action and Divine Grace of Conscription

3. The Divine Grace and Supernatural Action of *Conscription* is central to the proper effect of the Holy Rite of Binding. Such supernatural presence and grace is made manifest *first* by the suitable qualification of the recipient; and *second* by the proper authority of one administering the sacrament; and *third* by the constituent parts and order that must be established in order to effect the sacrament. In accord with sacred liturgy, in the absence of one or more of these central requisites, no legitimate manifestation of such Divine Grace and Action can occur. Divine Grace and Action of Sacrament of Conscription

XIX.III – RITE OF BINDING

1. The Holy Rite of Binding represents the constituent parts and their order that must be established in order to effect the Divine and Supernatural Sacrament of Conscription. In the absence of one or Rite of Binding

more of these central requisites, no legitimate manifestation or imprint of the Divine Grace and Action of Conscription can occur.

2. There are only four (4) valid and licit corporeal forms for the Sacrament of Conscription as defined by the most sacred *Missale Christus* and associated approved liturgy being Personal, Public, Ordinary and Extraordinary:- Form of the Rite of Binding

    (i) "**Personal Binding**" is when the Sacrament of Conscription is bestowed automatically as part the acceptance of a promise, or bond or surety of some written form between parties; and

    (ii) "**Public Binding**" is when the Sacrament of Conscription is bestowed automatically as part of the formal public acceptance and registration of securities, sureties, promises associated with one or more rights and property; and

    (iii) "**Ordinary Binding**" is when the Sacrament of Conscription is bestowed automatically as associated with a binding obligation accepted by a party, such as the penalty and duties associated with the Sacrament of Penance; and

    (iv) "**Extraordinary Binding**" is when the Sacrament of Conscription is bestowed automatically as an element of a formal sacramental ritual performed by the authority of the Supreme Patriarch or his agents, such as the ritual of Exorcism.

3. The elements and conditions of the Rite of Binding are reserved and incorporated with the appropriate rites and sacraments possessing Binding. Elements & Conditions of Binding

XIX.IV – RITE OF EXTRAORDINARY BINDING

1. The Holy Rite of Extraordinary Binding is when a spirit, soul, demon or other supernatural force who has demonstrated persistent and repeated contempt and injury to the Laws of Heaven and Earth enters into an unbreakable agreement between their spirit and other spirits to call upon all the most ancient Great Spirits, Arch Demons, Demons, Arch Angels, Angels and all departed spirits to bind them until their departure from the temporal world. Rite of Extraordinary Binding

    The Holy Rite of Extraordinary Binding is wholly administered by the authority of Heaven. The role and function of the Universal Ecclesia is to give proper notice in the rarest of circumstances, notably the issuance of a *Holy Writ*, or the Rite of Extraordinary Exorcism.

Title XX – Sacrament of Convocation & Rite of Convention

XX.I – SACRAMENT OF CONVOCATION

1. Convocation (*Ritus Sacramentum Convocatio*) is the twelfth of the fourteen (14) Cardinal Sacraments, also known as the Ways of Heaven. Sacrament of Convocation (Ritus Sacramentum Convocatio)

The Sacrament of Convocation may also be granted and conferred on its own in accordance with the most sacred Covenants *Pactum De Singularis Caelum*, *Pactum De Singularis Christus*, and *Missale Christus* and associated approved liturgy.

2. The purpose of the sacrament of Convocation is the formal summons to attendance with the members of a sacred body in accordance with the most sacred Covenants *Pactum De Singularis Caelum*, *Pactum De Singularis Christus* and associated approved liturgy. The meaning of Convocation is derived from the Latin word *convoco* meaning "to call meeting of". Divine Purpose of the Sacrament of Convocation

XX.II – DIVINE GRACE AND ACTION OF CONVOCATION

1. The Divine Grace and Action of *Convocation* is the supernatural effect of formal summons both of spiritual and temporal beings to attendance with the members of a sacred body in accordance with the most sacred Covenants *Pactum De Singularis Caelum*, *Pactum De Singularis Christus* and associated approved liturgy. Divine Grace and Action of Convocation

2. *Convocation* is a wholly Divine and unmerited action, warranted by God and the Divine Creator. It is not an action effected within the temporal realm, nor can it be equated to physical terms or constructs. Understanding of action and Divine Grace of Convocation

3. The Divine Grace and Supernatural Action of *Convocation* is central to the proper effect of the Holy Rite of Convention. Such supernatural presence and grace is made manifest *first* by the suitable qualification of the recipient; and *second* by the proper authority of one administering the sacrament; and *third* by the constituent parts and order that must be established in order to effect the sacrament. Divine Grace and Action of Sacrament of Convocation

In accord with sacred liturgy, in the absence of one or more of these central requisites, no legitimate manifestation of such Divine Grace and Action can occur.

XX.III – RITE OF CONVENTION

1. The Holy Rite of Convention represents the constituent parts and their order that must be established in order to effect the Divine and Supernatural Sacrament of Convocation. In the absence of one or Rite of Convention

more of these central requisites, no legitimate manifestation or imprint of the Divine Grace and Action of Absolution can occur.

2. There are only three (3) valid and licit forms for the Rite of Convention as defined by the most sacred *Missale Christus* and associated approved liturgy being General, Ordinary and Extraordinary:- Form of the Rite of Convention

(i) "**General Convention**" is when the Sacrament of Convocation is bestowed automatically as part of the proper formation of a meeting in trust, such as attendance to a competent forum of law; and

(ii) "**Ordinary Convention**" is when the Sacrament of Convocation is bestowed automatically as an element of a formal sacramental ritual performed by properly consecrated and ordained clergy; and

(iii) "**Extraordinary Convention**" is when the Sacrament of Convocation is bestowed automatically as part of an Ecumenical Council, or Conclave or Great Conclave.

3. The elements and conditions of the Rite of Convention are reserved and incorporated with the appropriate rites and sacraments possessing Convocation. Elements and Conditions of Convention

Title XXI – Sacrament of Authorisation & Rite of Prescription

XXI.I – SACRAMENT OF AUTHORISATION

1. Authorisation (*Ritus Sacramentum Auctoriso*) is the thirteenth of the fourteen (14) Cardinal Sacraments, also known as the Ways of Heaven. Sacrament of Authorisation (Ritus Sacramentum Auctoriso)

The Sacrament of Authorisation may also be granted and conferred on its own in accordance with the most sacred Covenants *Pactum De Singularis Caelum*, *Pactum De Singularis Christus*, and *Missale Christus* and associated approved liturgy.

2. The purpose of the sacrament of Authorisation is the formal blessing of a decree or judgement issued by a valid minister or one possessing the proper level of authority in accordance with the most sacred Covenants *Pactum De Singularis Caelum*, *Pactum De Singularis Christus*, and *Missale Christus* and associated approved liturgy. Divine Purpose of the Sacrament of Authorisation

XXI.II – DIVINE GRACE AND ACTION OF AUTHORISATION

1. The Divine Grace and Action of *Authorisation* is the supernatural effect of the formal blessing of a decree or judgement issued by a valid minister or one possessing the proper level of authority in accordance with the most sacred Covenants *Pactum De Singularis Caelum*, *Pactum De Singularis Christus*, and *Missale Christus* and associated approved liturgy. Divine Grace and Action of Authorisation

2. *Authorisation* is a wholly Divine and unmerited action, warranted by God and the Divine Creator. It is not an action effected within the temporal realm, nor can it be equated to physical terms or constructs. Understanding of action and Divine Grace of Authorisation

3. The Divine Grace and Supernatural Action of *Authorisation* is central to the proper effect of the Holy Rite of Prescription. Such supernatural presence and grace is made manifest *first* by the suitable qualification of the recipient; and *second* by the proper authority of one administering the sacrament; and *third* by the constituent parts and order that must be established in order to effect the sacrament. Divine Grace and Action of Sacrament of Authorisation

In accord with sacred liturgy, in the absence of one or more of these central requisites, no legitimate manifestation of such Divine Grace and Action can occur.

XXI.III – RITE OF PRESCRIPTION

1. The Holy Rite of Prescription represents the constituent parts and Rite of Prescription

their order that must be established in order to effect the Divine and Supernatural Sacrament of Authorisation. In the absence of one or more of these central requisites, no legitimate manifestation or imprint of the Divine Grace and Action of Authorisation can occur.

3. There are only three (3) valid and licit forms for the Rite of Prescription as defined by the most sacred *Missale Christus* and associated approved liturgy being Official, Ordinary and Extraordinary:- Form of the Rite of Prescription

(i) "**Official Prescription**" is when the Sacrament of Authorisation is bestowed automatically as part of the proper formation of an instrument of direction, command or order associated with the authority of the relevant position; and

(ii) "**Ordinary Prescription**" is when the Sacrament of Authorisation is bestowed automatically as part of the proper formation of an instrument of direction, command or order associated with the authority of properly consecrated and ordained clergy; and

(iii) "**Extraordinary Prescription**" is when the Sacrament of Authorisation is bestowed automatically as part of the proper formation of an instrument of direction, command or order associated with the authority of the Supreme Patriarch.

4. The elements and conditions of the Rite of Prescription are reserved and incorporated with the appropriate rites and sacraments possessing Prescription. Elements and Conditions of Prescription

Title XXII – Sacrament of Elucidation & Rite of Rescription

XXII.I – SACRAMENT OF ELUCIDATION

1. Elucidation (*Ritus Sacramentum Elucidato*) is the fourteenth of the fourteen (14) Cardinal Sacraments, also known as the Ways of Heaven.

   The Sacrament of Elucidation may also be granted and conferred on its own in accordance with the most sacred Covenants *Pactum De Singularis Caelum*, *Pactum De Singularis Christus*, and *Missale Christus* and associated approved liturgy.

   Sacrament of Elucidation (Ritus Sacramentum Elucidato)

2. The purpose of the Sacrament of Elucidation is the formal blessing of an opinion, answer or judgement promulgated by an Official Person, subject to the limits of their authority, in accordance with the most sacred Covenants *Pactum De Singularis Caelum*, *Pactum De Singularis Christus*, and *Missale Christus* and associated approved liturgy.

   Divine Purpose of the Sacrament of Elucidation

XXII.II – DIVINE GRACE AND ACTION OF ELUCIDATION

1. The Divine Grace and Action of *Elucidation* is the supernatural effect of the formal blessing of an opinion, answer or judgement promulgated by an Official Person, subject to the limits of their authority.

   Divine Grace and Action of Elucidation

2. *Elucidation* is a wholly Divine and unmerited action, warranted by God and the Divine Creator. It is not an action effected within the temporal realm, nor can it be equated to physical terms or constructs.

   Understanding of action and Divine Grace of Elucidation

3. The Divine Grace and Supernatural Action of *Elucidation* is central to the proper effect of the Holy Rite of Rescription. Such supernatural presence and grace is made manifest *first* by the suitable qualification of the recipient; and *second* by the proper authority of one administering the sacrament; and *third* by the constituent parts and order that must be established in order to effect the sacrament.

   In accord with sacred liturgy, in the absence of one or more of these central requisites, no legitimate manifestation of such Divine Grace and Action can occur.

   Divine Grace and Action of Sacrament of Elucidation

XXII.III – RITE OF RESCRIPTION

1. The Holy Rite of Rescription represents the constituent parts and their order that must be established in order to effect the Divine and Supernatural Sacrament of Elucidation. In the absence of one or more of these central requisites, no legitimate manifestation or imprint of

   Rite of Rescription

the Divine Grace and Action of Elucidation can occur.

3. There are only three (3) valid and licit forms for the Rite of Rescription as defined by the most sacred *Missale Christus* and associated approved liturgy being Official, Ordinary and Extraordinary:-

Form of the Rite of Rescription

(i) "**Official Rescription**" is when the Sacrament of Elucidation is bestowed automatically as part of the proper formation of an instrument of direction, command or order associated with the authority of the relevant position; and

(ii) "**Ordinary Rescription**" is when the Sacrament of Elucidation is bestowed automatically as part of the proper formation of an instrument of direction, command or order associated with the authority of properly consecrated and ordained clergy; and

(iii) "**Extraordinary Rescription**" is when the Sacrament of Elucidation is bestowed automatically as part of the proper formation of an instrument of direction, command or order associated with the authority of the Supreme Patriarch.

4. The elements and conditions of the Rite of Rescription are reserved and incorporated with the appropriate rites and sacraments possessing Rescription.

Elements and Conditions of Rescription

Title XXIII – Sacrament of Inspiration & Rite of Annunciation

XXIII.I – SACRAMENT OF INSPIRATION

1. Inspiration (*Ritus Sacramentum Inspiratio*) and Rite of Annunciation is the first of the twelve (12) Apostolic Life Sacraments, also known as "The Twelve", "The Twelve Apostles" and "The Means".

Sacrament of Inspiration (Ritus Sacramentum Inspiratio)

The Sacrament of Inspiration and Rite of Annunciation is granted and conferred exclusively to an expectant mother and her living unborne child according to most sacred Covenants *Pactum De Singularis Caelum*, *Pactum De Singularis Christus*, and *Missale Christus* and associated approved liturgy.

2. All life is sacred and human life is especially sacred. Thus, the journey of conception to gestation and finally birth is an extraordinary journey and gift. The purpose of the Sacrament of Inspiration and Rite of Annunciation is the recognition of the ancient custom and tradition of celebrating the certainty of pregnancy and the arrival of the Holy Spirit into the unborne child from the fiftieth day onward.

Divine Purpose of the Sacrament of Annunciation

It is the Holy Spirit that helps form the very beginnings of the human mind and consciousness and this Divine Contribution appears the moment that the fetus is unmistakably and unquestionably of the higher order life form of Homo Sapien from the end of the first trimester.

3. It is a gross error to presume the Spirit is fully present in Human Form from the precise moment of Conception. Laws and Canons that are enacted according to this error are profane against God and the Divine Creator of all Life. The reason the Spirit is not fully present in Human Form within the fetus until the end of the first trimester is threefold:-

Conception and Annunciation

(i) First, the new life must first experience and overcome each and every form and era of history of evolution of life upon planet Earth over more than two billion years in a matter of fifty to sixty days. Thus, to be human is to first experience what it is to be all other forms of lesser complex life; and

(ii) Second, the Holy Spirit must be invited into the new unborn life by the Spirit of the mother, even if the lower consciousness of the mother is unaware of such status of the pregnancy or may even be against the idea of pregnancy. If the Holy Spirit were not invited, but simply imposed itself upon the mother, then the arrival of the Divine Spirit would be a fundamental breach of all the Laws of Heaven; and

(iii) Third, the body of the mother must reach the state of no longer reacting to the pregnancy as if it were an infection and instead must demonstrate at this miraculous moment a metamorphosis whereby the body of the mother ceases to fight for the death of the new life form and instead normally begins to change in order to support by every means the successful nurturing of the unborn infant to full term; and

(iv) Therefore, any teachings or laws that seek to impose the denial of the rights of the mother prior to this key event, over an unborn life form, not yet enjoined with the Holy Spirit is morally repugnant, profane, sacrilegious, illogical and is forbidden and to be suppressed; and

(v) However, any teachings or laws that deny this momentous event and ignore the rights of the unborn child from this moment at the end of the first trimester, in favour of the mother having extended rights to destroy a life beyond the first trimester are also morally repugnant, profane, sacrilegious, illogical and is forbidden and to be suppressed.

4. Upon the estimated fiftieth day of pregnancy and before the one hundredth day, the expectant mother, or nominated guardian shall appoint a Herald by extraordinary condition to formally make known the news of the pregnancy to friends, family and the community: Annunciation as Conception of the Holy Spirit

(i) The promulgation of the news represents the Heraldic Prayer which represents the moment of conferral of the sacrament and the appointment of a Divine Guardian Angel to watch over the unborn child and the safety of the mother until birth; and

(ii) Should no Herald be appointed by the mother or nominated guardian and the Heraldic Prayer not be instanced, then by ordinary condition a Divine Guardian Angel shall be automatically appointed by the powers of Heaven to watch over her unborn child and her safety not later than one hundred and fifty days since the beginning of the pregnancy; and

(iii) In the instance that the unborn baby was not successfully delivered to full term, the sacrament of Baptism may be conferred upon all who have received the sacrament of Annunciation not earlier than two hundred days after the Sacrament of Annunciation.

XXIII.II – DIVINE GRACE AND ACTION OF INSPIRATION

1. The Divine Grace and Action of *Inspiration* is the supernatural effect of the recognition of the ancient custom and tradition of celebrating the certainty of pregnancy and the arrival of the Holy Spirit into the unborne child from the fiftieth day onward. Divine Grace and Action of Inspiration

2. *Inspiration* is a wholly Divine and unmerited action, warranted by God and the Divine Creator. It is not an action effected within the temporal realm, nor can it be equated to physical terms or constructs. Understanding of action and Divine Grace of Inspiration

3. The Divine Grace and Supernatural Action of *Inspiration* is central to the proper effect of the Holy Rite of Annunciation. Such supernatural presence and grace is made manifest *first* by the suitable qualification of the recipient; and *second* by the proper authority of one administering the sacrament; and *third* by the constituent parts and order that must be established in order to effect the sacrament. Divine Grace and Action of Sacrament of Inspiration

   In accord with sacred liturgy, in the absence of one or more of these central requisites, no legitimate manifestation of such Divine Grace and Action can occur.

XXIII.III – RITE OF ANNUNCIATION

1. The Holy Rite of Annunciation represents the constituent parts and their order that must be established in order to effect the Divine and Supernatural Sacrament of Inspiration. In the absence of one or more of these central requisites, no legitimate manifestation or imprint of the Divine Grace and Action of Inspiration can occur. Rite of Annunciation

2. There are only three (3) valid and licit forms for the Sacrament of Inspiration and Rite of Annunciation as defined by the most sacred *Missale Christus* and associated approved liturgy being General, Ordinary and Extraordinary:- Form of the Rite of Annunciation

   (i) "**General Annunciation**" is when the Sacrament of Inspiration is bestowed automatically as part of the proper medical announcements of a Therapist or Physician of an Order or College in conformity with the Universal Ecclesia; and

   (ii) "**Ordinary Annunciation**" is when the Sacrament of Inspiration is bestowed as part of the proper formation of pastoral announcements at the main Sunday mass by properly consecrated and ordained clergy; and

   (iii) "**Extraordinary Annunciation**" is when the Sacrament of Inspiration is bestowed automatically as part of the proper formation of special Patriarchal instrument of blessing from the Patriarchal Registry.

XXIII.IV – CONDITIONS OF RITE OF ANNUNCIATION

Conditions of Rite of Annunciation

1. Conditions of the Rite of Ordinary Annunciation and Extraordinary Annunciation are those requisite qualifications and contingencies permitted in the proper ministration of the Rite.

   The Sacrament of Annunciation may only be conferred if the status and circumstances permit in accord with these rubrics, namely:

   (i) That the expectant mother and father have first been Baptised into the Christian Faith; and

   (ii) That the expectant mother is wedded to the expectant father in Holy Matrimony; and

   (iii) That a period of at least fifty days has passed prior to the proposed date for ministration of the sacrament.

Annunciation and Holy Matrimony

2. The Conditions of the Rites of Ordinary and Extraordinary Annunciation may appear at first to some to be unfairly restrictive given the truth that every new life is sacred and every unborne and new born child is loved by God.

   No child or person is deprived of the right to the blessings and imprint of Divine Love, Mercy and Forgiveness through the Rite of Baptism and the Right of Christening. However the Rites of Ordinary and Extraordinary Annunciation are necessarily restrictive to honour and protect the sanctity of the Rite of Holy Matrimony.

XXIII.V – MINISTER OF RITE OF ANNUNCIATION

Minister of Rite of Annunciation

1. Only authorised persons may validly and legitimately administer the Rite of Annunciation:

   (i) Only persons properly ordained as a Minister or invested into office holding *Magisterium* or *Visium* possesses the powers and authority to confer and administer the Rite of Annunciation under Extraordinary Conditions; and

   (ii) Only persons properly invested into office holding *Administratum*, *Officium* or *Imperium* possesses the powers and authority to administer the Rite of Annunciation under Ordinary Conditions.

XXIII.VI – ORDINARY RITE OF ANNUNCIATION

1. The Rite of Ordinary Annunciation shall be as follows: Rite of Ordinary Annunciation

LITURGY OF CHRISTIAN LIFE

Liturgy of Christian Life

SALUTATION

Ordinary Annunciation Salutation

CELEBRANT

In the name of ✠ the Father, and of the Son, and of the Holy Spirit.

ALL

Amen.

CELEBRANT

(C. joins his hands, then extends outward his hands:)

May the love of our Saviour Jesus Christ, the mercy of God and the strength of the Holy Spirit be with you all.

ALL

And also with you.

PETITION

Ordinary Annunciation Petition

CELEBRANT

(C. to the mother to be)

Dear Sister, what news do you bring us today?

MOTHER TO BE

I am pregnant with child.

CELEBRANT

Praise be to God our Father, and to his son, and to our Mother Mary, Queen of Heaven for this wondrous news! Is it at least seven weeks or more, to the best of your knowledge, since the first moment of conception?

MOTHER TO BE

Yes.

CELEBRANT

Then we are truly blessed as witnesses to the development of a unique and complete human being and life - one recognised by all Heaven and the Angels and Saints and the Universal Ecclesia as having a unique soul with ecclesiastical, moral and legal rights.

How then may all of Heaven and all the angels and saints of the one true apostolic Universal Ecclesia of Christ help serve you and help your precious unborn child?

MOTHER TO BE

Bless my Child.

CELEBRANT

Do you ask this in the name of the Father and of the Son and of the Holy Spirit?

MOTHER TO BE

I do.

CELEBRANT

The Sacrament of Annunciation you ask for is a foundational blessing. It is the recognition of the appearance of the Holy Spirit and the presence of a true and unique new soul. As Parent(s), relatives and friends here assembled, you have been called by God our Father to accept a sacred responsibility for the protection, nurturing and well being of this expectant mother. Do you all understand and accept this sacred responsibility?

ALL

Yes.

RECITALS

Ordinary
Annunciation
Petition

CELEBRANT

Very well. Let us begin.

CELEBRANT

(C. joins his hands, then extends outward his hands:)

Dear brothers and sisters, it is our faith as true Christians that is founded upon the celebration of life, the sanctity and beauty of all life, especially new human life. The very words and actions of the Risen Christ revealed to every generation the authentic nature of our Divine Creator as one of Divine Love, Mercy and Forgiveness, who cherishes life; and who gives us the power of free will to make decisions and take responsibility for our lives and for the benefit of others in our care.

The incarnation of Our Saviour Jesus Christ within the womb of our holy mother Mary is a testament to the the sacredness and sacrament of Annunciation and the blessing of a new life to be. Mary reminds us all of the sanctity of motherhood and the importance of protecting and supporting mothers during pregnancy.

Most importantly, our Holy Mother reaches out to all women and all expectant mothers and calls them to herself and her son - that like her, they may call upon the angels and saints of Heaven as assistance. So it is, in the name of our heavenly Mother and her Son, I invite N. to recite the sacramental prayer of Annunciation before all here present as witnesses.

MOTHER TO BE

My soul does magnify the Lord,
And my Spirit does rejoice in God my Saviour.
For he has chosen me, and that I be the bringer of new life and a new soul,
So that generations of our species continue now and until the end of days.
For He that is mighty has magnified me,
And holy are all His Names.
And mercy is upon all that obey and follow Him,
Throughout all generations.
He that is the Divine Creator of all has shown his wisdom,
For he scatters the proud and the hardened of hearts.
He fills the hungry for truth with great treasures,
Yet leaves the rich in ignorance empty handed.
He remembers always his covenants and promises,
To all the people of God he brings redemption forever.

Amen

WILL OF THE PEOPLE

CELEBRANT

Let us pray.

Jesus, through your teachings and sacrifice we have come to no longer fear death, for you have given us eternal life so we can never die.

Heavenly Father, it is our Will and true intention in gratitude for your gifts of healing and our reconciliation into your presence, that we seek to dedicate our lives more fully to enacting your teachings.

We pray you will accept our humble petition and promises as a sign of the truth of our intentions, for the well being of N. and her expectant child through Jesus Christ your son.

ALL

Amen.

SUPPLICANT(S)

By the mystery of your life, death and resurrection, bathe this new life and soul in light, and give N. all your protection and love.

ALL

Christ hear our prayer.

SUPPLICANT(S)

Through this blessing, make this pregnancy fruitful so that this new life and soul may come to full term and witness the joy and wonderment of birth and life as a living witness to your Good News.

ALL

Christ hear our prayer.

SUPPLICANT(S)

Keep this new life and soul safe from all physical and spiritual harm.

ALL

Christ hear our prayer.

SUPPLICANT(S)
Keep this family always in your love.

ALL
Christ hear our prayer.

CELEBRANT
Almighty and ever-living God, you sent your only Son into the world to cast out the power of Satan, spirit of evil, to rescue man from the kingdom of darkness, and bring him into the splendour of your kingdom of light. We pray for every blessing for this new life and new soul: We ask these prayers through Christ our Lord.

ALL
Amen.

HOLY OIL ANOINTING

Ordinary Annunciation
Holy Oil Anointing

CELEBRANT
We anoint N. and this new life with the oil of salvation in the name of Christ our Saviour; may he strengthen them both with his power, who lives and reigns for ever and ever.

CELEBRANT
(He anoints the child on the breast with the oil of catechumens)

May you have strength in the power of Christ our Saviour, who lives and reigns for ever and ever.

ALL
Amen.

Title XXIV – Sacrament & Resurrection & Rite of Baptism

XXIV.I – SACRAMENT OF RESURRECTION

1. Resurrection (*Ritus Sacramentum Resurrectio*) and Rite of Baptism is the second of the twelve (12) Apostolic Life Sacraments, also known as "The Twelve", "The Twelve Apostles" and "The Means".

Sacrament of Resurrection (Ritus Sacramentum Resurrectio)

The Sacrament of Resurrection and Rite of Baptism is normally granted and conferred to a new born Homo Sapien child at the final stage of birth or within 90 days of being born in accordance with the most sacred Covenants *Pactum De Singularis Caelum*, *Pactum De Singularis Christus*, and *Missale Christus* and associated approved liturgy.

2. The purpose of the Sacrament of Resurrection and Rite of Baptism is the formal bestowal or presentation of a possessory or prescriptive right of Office to an incumbent including taking possession of the insignia of Office, namely the formation of the True Person.

Divine Purpose of the Sacrament of Resurrection

The birth of a child into flesh represents the birth through the Rite of Baptism of a True Trust through the conveyance of divinity, also known as Divine right of use from the Divine Personality of the spirit of the child with the flesh of the child the eventual rightful trustee of the True Trust upon age of majority. Until such time, the Divine Person of the child grants temporary guardian powers to the parent or parents, or those properly designated as immediate carer.

3. Baptism, from the ancient Greek words *bapto*, or *baptizo* (meaning to wash or immerse), is rightly considered a singular unifying sacrament of all Christians. That Christ instituted the Sacrament of Baptism is unquestionable. Holy Scripture reveals that not only did Christ command his disciples as to the mission and proper form of the sacrament, but that He declared explicitly the absolute necessity of every being to undergo the proper rite of Baptism by water, in order to be born again to a new life; and to receive the gifts of the Holy Spirit; and the promise of entry into the Kingdom of One Heaven.

The nature of Baptism

It is why every valid rite of Christianity places the Rite of Baptism as a central and fundamental ritual for salvation; and as an indelible *mark* distinguishing those who are true followers of the Risen Christ and those who are not.

Baptism therefore, is rightly described throughout tradition and writings as a "gateway" and "door" to the other valid life sacraments of the Universal Ecclesia of One Christ.

4. Through the Sacrament of Baptism, as unequivocally instructed by the Crucified and Living Christ Himself, a being experiences being born to a second life, beyond the physical first life as a human being.

Second Birth and Life of Baptism

Christ made this clear throughout his authentic teachings as expressed in Holy Scripture, that this second birth and this second life represent a positive growth and expansion, not a regression or regeneration.

This second birth and second life, celebrated through the permanent imprint of the valid Sacrament of Baptism, is a spiritual birth and an immortal spiritual life beyond our first physical birth and physical life as mortal beings. Not only is the second birth through Baptism a wholly different form of birth to our physical birth, it logically depends upon the first physical formation in human form.

5. By the longest and most firmly held traditions, the Sacrament of valid Baptism is seen as essential to being able to receive the Gifts of the Holy Spirit. This logically follows why Baptism is recognised therefore as the "gateway" or "door" to the other valid life sacraments of the Universal Ecclesia of One Christ, as the true doctrines of Christianity have always recognised the valid sacraments as gifts of the Holy Spirit.

Baptism and the Gifts of the Holy Spirit

Thus, without receiving the indelible mark of Baptism, the Universal Ecclesia of One Christ properly view that a being is prevented from authentically receiving the other valid sacraments, even if such sacraments are bestowed in the same form and rites as prescribed. Baptism therefore unlocks the capacity of other dimensions to our existence, beyond the physical realm and makes all such gifts of the Holy Spirit possible.

Importantly, the teachings of Christ do not in anyway preclude the fact of the presence of the Holy Spirit prior to the Sacrament of Baptism, nor of the absence of the gift of the soul. The true teachings and doctrines of those who follow and obey the Risen Christ as authentic Christians recognise that the form of human life from forty to sixty days from conception is the sacred moment of recognition not only of the power of the Holy Spirit, but the presence of the divine spark, as celebrated by the sacrament of Annunciation.

Therefore, to imply that an absence of the mark of Baptism is an absence of the presence of the Holy Spirit or of the soul, is absurd and heretical to the very words of Christ. Indeed, Christ made clear that Baptism is vital and essential to salvation, not to being human.

To deny the presence of humanity or the presence of the soul in the absence of Baptism is an anathema to the true teachings of Christ; and no man or woman may hold a teaching or clerical position of authority if they hold to such contrary views to the authentic teachings of the Risen Christ.

6. The true purpose and enabling powers of Baptism are ultimately revealed through the promise of the entry into the Kingdom of God as the Kingdom of One Heaven. Baptism and the Promise of Entry into the Kingdom of One Heaven

It is a promise beyond merely an existence beyond life. Many religions and faiths for millennia have espoused some forms of immortal existence beyond the physical death of the body. Yet it is the authentic Christian body and teachings that uniquely offers a moral, just, useful and fulfilled existence beyond the physical realm.

The Kingdom of One Heaven is not some replica of earthly imperfections of social order, nor some misguided utopia of uniformity. In fact, Christ was at pains to express our limitations in understanding and even beginning to comprehend the vastness, complexity, beauty and divinity of the model of One Heaven of the Divine Creator.

Instead, what Christ made abundantly clear to his disciples and to all men and women throughout history is that unless a man or woman is prepared to learn, to apply and to willingly accept the blessings and obligations of the gifts of the Holy Spirit, beginning with the Sacrament of Baptism, then this is a path denied, not by God, but by our own limitations and free will.

XXIV.II – DIVINE GRACE AND ACTION OF RESURRECTION

1. The Divine Grace and Action of *Resurrection* is the supernatural effect of the formation of Sacred Circumscribed Space as a True Person, possessing certain sacred rights and character. Divine Grace and Action of Resurrection

2. *Resurrection* is a wholly Divine and unmerited action, warranted by God and the Divine Creator. It is not an action effected within the temporal realm, nor can it be equated to physical terms or constructs. Understanding of action and Divine Grace of Resurrection

3. The Divine Grace and Supernatural Action of *Resurrection* is central to the proper effect of the Holy Rite of Baptism. Such supernatural presence and grace is made manifest *first* by the suitable qualification of the recipient; and *second* by the proper authority of one administering the sacrament; and *third* by the constituent parts and order that must be established in order to effect the sacrament. Divine Grace and Action of Sacrament of Resurrection

In accord with sacred liturgy, in the absence of one or more of these central requisites, no legitimate manifestation of such Divine Grace and Action can occur.

XXIV.III – RITE OF BAPTISM

1. The Holy Rite of Baptism represents the constituent parts and their order that must be established in order to effect the Divine and Supernatural Sacrament of Resurrection. In the absence of one or more of these central requisites, no legitimate manifestation or imprint of the Divine Grace and Action of Resurrection can occur. Rite of Baptism

2. There are only three (3) valid and licit forms for the Sacrament of Resurrection and Rite of Baptism as defined by the most sacred *Missale Christus* and associated approved liturgy being General, Ordinary and Extraordinary:- Form of the Rite of Baptism

    (i) "**General Baptism**" is conferred by the delivery, by a Therapist or Physician of an Order or College in conformity with the Universal Ecclesia, of a child without the presence of an ordained minister and through the witness of the birth by two (2) or more qualified and credible witnesses; and

    (ii) "**Ordinary Baptism**" is conferred by the delivery of a child in the presence of an ordained minister; and

    (iii) "**Extraordinary Baptism**" is conferred by an ordained minister in the presence of the body of a still born infant, or in formal dedication of the spirit of the still born infant at the next celebration of the Eucharist and then such record entered into the Rolls to the fact of such sacred act.

3. In accordance with Divine Law and the most sacred covenant *Pactum De Singularis Caelum*, if a fetus having received the sacrament of Annunciation dies before being born, then this unique Divine Immortal Spirit shall be fully entitled to receive the sacrament of Baptism after what otherwise would have been its born day and all Life Sacraments thereafter at their appointed time. Extraordinary Baptism

4. The Sacrament of Resurrection and Rite of Baptism negates the presumptions, validity and existence of any claimed Cestui Que Vie Trusts, or Secret Trusts or any other curses, spells and unlawful conveyances. Unlawful and invalid presumptions

XXIV.IV – CONDITIONS OF RITE OF BAPTISM

1. Conditions of the Rite of Baptism are those requisite qualifications and contingencies permitted in the proper ministration of the Rite. There shall exist only four possible Conditions for the ministration of Rite of Baptism being *Universal, General, Ordinary* and *Extraordinary*:- Conditions of Rite of Baptism

(i) *Universal* are the Conditions that apply to all forms and circumstances of the Rite of Baptism; and

(ii) *General* are the Conditions necessary for the conferral of the General Rite of Baptism upon a living person under the age of one year; and

(iii) *Ordinary* are the Conditions necessary for the conferral of the Ordinary Rite of Baptism upon a living person under the age of one year within a Sacred Place by an ordained minister; and

(iv) *Extraordinary* are the Conditions necessary for the conferral of the Rite of Baptism upon a deceased child or adult.

Universal Conditions

2. *Universal Conditions* for the conferral of the Rite of Baptism apply to all forms and circumstances of the Rite:-

(i) Every person not yet baptised and only such a person is capable of receiving (the Rite of) Baptism; and

(ii) An authorised person holding a Sacred Office with sufficient clerical powers who administers baptism is to take care that, unless a sponsor is present, there is at least a witness who can attest to the conferral of the baptism; and

(iii) To prove the conferral of (the Rite of) Baptism, if prejudicial to no one, the declaration of one witness beyond all exception is sufficient or the oath of the one baptised if the person receiving baptism as an adult; and

(iv) The pastor of the place where the baptism is celebrated must carefully and without any delay record in the baptismal register the names of the baptised, with mention made of the minister, parents, sponsors, witnesses, if any, the place and date of the conferral of the baptism, and the date and place of birth; and

(v) If it concerns a child born to an unmarried mother, the name of the mother must be inserted, if her maternity is established publicly or if she seeks it willingly in writing or before two witnesses. Moreover, the name of the father must be inscribed if a public document or his own declaration before the pastor and two witnesses proves his paternity; in other cases, the name of the baptised is inscribed with no mention of the name of the father or the parents; and

(vi) If it concerns an adopted child, the names of those adopting are to be inscribed and, at least if it is done in the civil records of the region, also the names of the natural parents; and

(vii) If the baptism was not administered by the pastor or in his presence, the minister of baptism, whoever it is, must inform the pastor of the parish in which it was administered of the conferral of the baptism, so that he records the baptism according to the norms of flaw.

3. *General Conditions* apply for the conferral of the (General) Rite of Baptism:- General Conditions

(i) Ordinary Members are baptised and incorporated with the Living Body of One Christ by two means: The Nature and Circumstance of Birth and secondly by the imprint and character of the most sacred Rite of Baptism bestowed upon those not naturally born into the Living Body of Christ; and

(ii) When a child is born within the bounds of a professed and Sacred Christian or Jewish community, such a community is properly declared Sacred Circumscribed Space and those that service in medical and health and legal capacity as being capable to dispense certain key Sacraments as a function of community significance, such as the delivery of a new born baby; and

(iii) The recorded fact of a birth within the Sacred Circumscribed Space of One Christ is absolute proof recording of an Ordinary Member within the Great Register and Public Record of Heaven, held in temporal custody by the Universal Ecclesia of One Christ; and

(iv) When a person not born within the bounds of a professed and Sacred Christian or Jewish community and not yet Baptised, chooses of their own volition to confirm their intention and will to be incorporated into the Living Body of One Christ.

XXIV.V – CELEBRATION OF RITE OF BAPTISM

1. The proper place for the celebration of the Rite of Baptism is a church or oratory. As a rule an adult is to be baptised in his or her parish church and an infant in the parish church of the parents unless a just cause suggests otherwise. Celebration of Rite of Baptism

If because of distance or other circumstances the one to be baptised cannot go or be brought to his or her parish church or the parish church of the parents without grave inconvenience, baptism can and must be conferred in another nearer church or oratory, or even in another fitting place.

Apart from a case of necessity, the Rite of Baptism is not to be conferred in private houses, unless the local clerical authority has permitted it for a grave cause.

Except in a case of necessity or for some other compelling pastoral reason, the Rite of Baptism is not to be celebrated in hospitals unless the Diocesan Bishop has established otherwise.

2. Every parish church is to have a baptismal font, without prejudice to the cumulative right already acquired by other churches. Baptismal Font and Water

The local clerical authority can permit or order for the convenience of the faithful that there also be a baptismal font in another church or oratory within the boundaries of the parish.

Apart from a case of necessity, the water to be used in conferring baptism must be blessed according to the prescripts of the present sacred Liturgical books. Baptism is to be conferred either by immersion or by pouring whilst observing and respecting the prescripts of the appropriate denomination of the Universal Ecclesia.

3. The Rite of Baptism may be celebrated on any day, except Good Friday, Easter Sunday and Christmas Day. Day of Celebrating Baptism

XXIV.VI – MINISTER OF RITE OF BAPTISM

1. Baptism is administered according to the order prescribed herein, except in the case of urgent necessity when only those things required for the validity of the sacrament must be observed: Minister of Rite of Baptism

(i) The ordinary minister of baptism is a bishop, a presbyter, or a deacon; and

(ii) When an ordinary minister is absent or impeded, a catechist or another person designated for this function by the local ordinary, or in a case of necessity any person with the right intention, confers baptism licitly. Pastors of souls, especially the pastor of a parish, are to be concerned that the Christian faithful are taught the correct way to baptise; and

(iii) Except in a case of necessity, no one is permitted to confer baptism in the territory of another without the required permission, not even upon his own subjects; and

(iv) The baptism of adults, at least of those who have completed their fourteenth year, is to be deferred to the diocesan bishop so that he himself administers it if he has judged it Expedient.

2. Only authorised persons may validly and legitimately administer the Minister of Rite

Rite of Baptism: of Baptism

(i) Only persons properly ordained as a Minister or invested into office holding *Magisterium* or *Visium* possesses the powers and authority to confer and administer the Rite of Baptism under Extraordinary Conditions; and

(ii) Only persons properly invested into office holding *Administratum*, *Officium* or *Imperium* possesses the powers and authority to administer the Rite of Baptism under Ordinary Conditions.

XXIV.VII – RITE OF GENERAL BAPTISM

xx. Rite of General Baptism is conferred by the delivery, by a Therapist or Physician of an Order or College in conformity with the most sacred Covenant *Pactum De Singularis Caelum*, of a child without the presence of an ordained minister and through the witness of the birth by two or more people apart from the mother; and Rite of General Baptism

XXIV.VIII – RITE OF ORDINARY BAPTISM

1. The Rite of *Ordinary Baptism*, as conferred in accord with the prescribed rubrics and conditions, shall be as follows: Rite of Ordinary Baptism

IMMERSION Holy Water Blessing

CELEBRANT

Is it your will that N. should be baptised in the faith of the Church, which we have all professed with you?

PARENT(S) AND SPONSOR(S)

It is.

CELEBRANT

(Pronounced simultaneously with the pouring of the water.)

I baptise you in the name of the Father, and of the Son and of the Holy Spirit.
Let no wicked force or malevolent spirit impede you;
May the angels and saints protect you;
And may you live a fruitful and obedient life in the name of the Risen Christ.

CELEBRANT

God the Father of our Lord Jesus Christ has freed you from any and all spiritual impediments, given you a new birth by water and the Holy Spirit, and welcomed you into his holy people. He now anoints you with the chrism of salvation. As Christ was anointed Priest, Prophet, and King, so may you live always as a member of his body, sharing everlasting life.

ALL

Amen.

XXIV.IX – RITE OF EXTRAORDINARY BAPTISM

1. The *Rite of Extraordinary Baptism* shall be as follows: Rite of Extraordinary Baptism

INTROIT Introit

CELEBRANT

(Whisper quietly.)

In the name of ✠ the Father, and of the Son, and of the Holy Spirit. Amen.

(C. joins his hands, then extends outward his hands:)

May the love of our Saviour Jesus Christ, the mercy of God and the strength of the Holy Spirit be present.

(C. joins his hands:)

Our Father in Heaven, you called me to witness and testify to the extraordinary power and mysteries of our faith, by following in the footsteps and true teachings of your son the Risen Christ.

To cast off any doubt or uncertainties; and to guard against the false securities and material desires of this world; and to reject the temptations of comfortable indifference to the real suffering of others in this world.

Look kindly therefore upon us; May you forgive your humble servant for all our transgressions and our weaknesses and inadequacies in failing to more completely devote ourselves to fulfilling your Divine Mission.

Verily, may you hear and accept our calls to you; not only

for our sake, but for the benefit of all in whose name we make these petitions, invocations and blessings.

Today we acknowledge the extremely sad event in the lives of the (name of family) of a beloved Infant. We recognise the tremendous grief of the (Parent/Family) and we seek to give our comfort and heart felt compassion to them, to help them through this time.

Yet, we also come here today to witness the true power of our faith in the fulfilment of a promise made by our Saviour the Risen Christ, that none be abandoned, none be forgotten, and none be condemned by our Eternal Father.

Today then we celebrate the extraordinary gift and sacrament of Baptism; and the fact that through the continued and steadfast faith and trust of the living members of the one true Apostolic Universal Ecclesia of One Christ, all of One Heaven hears our call and recognises the valid Baptism of those who are no longer with us in the same legitimacy and validity as if they were present with us today in one mind body and spirit.

WILL OF THE PEOPLE

Ordinary Infant
Will of the People

CELEBRANT

Jesus, through your teachings and sacrifice we have come to no longer fear death, for you have given us eternal life so we can never die.

Heavenly Father, it is our Will and true intention in gratitude for your gifts of healing and our reconciliation into your presence, that we seek to dedicate our lives more fully to enacting your teachings.

We pray you will accept our humble petition and promises as a sign of the truth of our intentions, through Jesus Christ your son.

By the mystery of your death and resurrection, bathe this child in light, give him (her) the new life of baptism and welcome him (her) into your holy Church.

Through baptism, make him (her) your faithful follower and a witness to your gospel.

Lead him (her) by a holy life to the joys of God's kingdom.

Keep his (her) family always in your love.

Renew the grace of our baptism in each one of us.

Almighty and ever-living God, you sent your only Son into the world to cast out the power of Satan, spirit of evil, to rescue man from the kingdom of darkness, and bring him into the splendour of your kingdom of light. We pray for this child: set him (her) free from any spiritual impediment, make him (her) a temple of your glory, and send your Holy Spirit to dwell with him (her). We ask this through Christ our Lord.

Amen.

Title XXV – Sacrament of Incarnation & Rite of Christening

XXV.I – SACRAMENT OF INCARNATION

1. Incarnation (*Ritus Sacramentum Incarnatio*) and Rite of Christening is the third of the twelve (12) Apostolic Life Sacraments, also known as "The Twelve", "The Twelve Apostles" and "The Means".

   Sacrament of Incarnation (Ritus Sacramentum Incarnatio)

   The Sacrament of Incarnation and Rite of Christening shall be granted and administered by the second (2nd) birthday of a child that has received the Sacrament of Resurrection and Rite of Baptism in accordance with the most sacred Covenants *Pactum De Singularis Caelum*, *Pactum De Singularis Christus*, and *Missale Christus* and associated approved liturgy.

2. The purpose of the Sacrament of Incarnation and Rite of Christening is to officially recognise the transition of a baby to a child and their commencement of valid organised learning systems of the community. The child is now welcomed into the tribe and protection is given in exchange for the child understanding that it is time to learn.

   Divine Purpose of the Sacrament of Incarnation and Rite of Christening

XXV.II – DIVINE GRACE AND ACTION OF INCARNATION

1. The Divine Grace and Action of *Incarnation* is the supernatural effect of the proper ministration of the Rite of Christening to officially recognise the transition of a baby to a child and their commencement of valid organised learning systems of the community.

   Divine Grace and Action of Incarnation

2. *Incarnation* is a wholly Divine and unmerited action, warranted by God and the Divine Creator. It is not an action effected within the temporal realm, nor can it be equated to physical terms or constructs.

   Understanding of action and Divine Grace of Incarnation

3. The Divine Grace and Supernatural Action of *Incarnation* is central to the proper effect of the Holy Rite of Christening. Such supernatural presence and grace is made manifest *first* by the suitable qualification of the recipient; and *second* by the proper authority of one administering the sacrament; and *third* by the constituent parts and order that must be established in order to effect the sacrament.

   Divine Grace and Action of Sacrament of Incarnation

   In accord with sacred liturgy, in the absence of one or more of these central requisites, no legitimate manifestation of such Divine Grace and Action can occur.

XXV.III – RITE OF CHRISTENING

1. The Holy Rite of Christening represents the constituent parts and their order that must be established in order to effect the Divine and

   Rite of Christening

Supernatural Sacrament of Incarnation. In the absence of one or more of these central requisites, no legitimate manifestation or imprint of the Divine Grace and Action of Incarnation can occur.

2. There are only two (2) valid and licit forms for the Sacrament of Incarnation and Rite of Christening as defined by the most sacred *Missale Christus* and associated approved liturgy being Ordinary and Extraordinary:- Form of the Sacrament of Incarnation

   (i) "**Ordinary Christening**" is conferred by a competent minister upon a child having reached the age of two (2) years; and

   (ii) "**Extraordinary Christening**" is conferred by a competent minister in formal dedication to the spirit of a still-borne infant, or deceased child upon the calculation of what would have been their second birthday. Such a ceremony may be conducted as a Special Mass, with such records then entered into the rolls to the fact of such sacred act.

3. In accordance with Divine Law and the most sacred covenant *Pactum De Singularis Caelum*, if a child having received the sacrament of Baptism dies at or prior to the age of two, then this unique Divine Immortal Spirit shall be fully entitled to receive the sacrament of Christening two years since being borne and all Life Sacraments thereafter at their appointed time. Extraordinary Christening of Deceased Child

4. In accordance with Divine Law and the most sacred covenant Pactum De Singularis Caelum, the mother or father or next of living kin of any child that died at or prior to the age of two yet was not previously granted the sacrament of Baptism may apply for the special ceremony of Life Sacraments where all sacraments are granted beginning with Annunciation to the sacrament representing the same age as if the child had lived and grown up to the present day. Extraordinary Christening of Deceased Person

XXV.IV – CONDITIONS OF RITE OF CHRISTENING

1. Conditions of the Rite of Christening are those requisite qualifications and contingencies permitted in the proper ministration of the Rite. There shall exist only two (2) possible Conditions for the ministration of Rite of Christening being *Ordinary and Extraordinary*:- Conditions of Rite of Christening

   (i) *Ordinary* are the Conditions necessary for the conferral of the Ordinary Rite of Christening upon a living human being under the age of two years; and

   (ii) *Extraordinary* are the Conditions necessary for the conferral of the Rite of Christening upon a deceased child or adult.

2. The conditions for the Ordinary Rite of Christening are:- *Ordinary Conditions*

(i) The Sponsors, whether parents or immediate family members, have at least all received the Rite of Baptism, the Rite of Christening and the Rite of First Communion; and

(ii) Sufficient confidence exists that the Sponsors have attended Holy Mass for at least one Universal Feast from each of the seven Liturgical Cycles of the Mysteries of Christ of the previous year, being *Immanent, Filial, Eucharistic, Transcendent, Sacred Heart, Redemption* and *Apostolic*, unless a special exemption is granted by the local Ordinary.

3. The conditions for the Extraordinary Rite of Christening are:- *Extraordinary Conditions*

(i) The Sponsors, whether parents or immediate family members, have at least all received the Rite of Baptism, the Rite of Christening and the Rite of First Communion; and

(ii) Sufficient confidence exists that the Sponsors have attended Holy Mass for at least one Universal Feast from each of the seven Liturgical Cycles of the Mysteries of Christ of the previous year, being *Immanent, Filial, Eucharistic, Transcendent, Sacred Heart, Redemption* and *Apostolic*, unless a special exemption is granted by the local Ordinary.

XXV.V – CELEBRATION OF RITE OF CHRISTENING

1. Only legitimately and validly ordained ministers may minister the Rite of Christening. *Minister of Rite of Christening*

2. The Rite of Christening may be celebrated on any Day, except those reserved for Holy Feast Days during the liturgical season of the Eucharistic Mystery of Christ. *Valid days of celebration*

XXV.VI – ORDINARY RITE OF CHRISTENING

1. The *Rite of Ordinary Christening* conferred by a competent minister upon a child having reached the age of two years, shall be as follows: *Ordinary Rite of Christening*

SALUTATION *Ordinary Christening Salutation*

CELEBRANT

In the name of ✠ the Father, and of the Son, and of the Holy Spirit.

ALL

Amen.

CELEBRANT

(C. joins his hands, then extends outward his hands:)

May the love of our Saviour Jesus Christ, the mercy of God and the strength of the Holy Spirit be with you all.

ALL

And also with you.

PETITION

CELEBRANT

(To all assembled)

I call upon those who seek to make their solemn petition today in the name of Christ our Saviour to now come forward and make their presence and prayer known.

(The parents with their child come forward)

CELEBRANT

What then is it you ask in the name of the Father and of the Son and of the Holy Spirit today?

PARENT(S)

Christening.

CELEBRANT

(To the Parent(s))

Are you the Parent(s) (or Lawful Guardian) of this Child?

PARENT(S)

Yes

CELEBRANT

What is the name you give to your Child?

PARENT(S)

N.

CELEBRANT

(Turning to Sponsor(s).)

In what capacity have you come here today with N.?

SPONSOR(S)

Godparents.

CELEBRANT

(Turning to Parents(s).)

The Sacrament of Christening you ask is a significant blessing. It is a foundation stone of our community of faith to bless and recognise all new members of our community; and that our future depends in part upon each new generation. The Sacrament of Christening as instituted by Christ himself is a manifest sign of this vital bond and the necessity that each and every child be properly educated and nurtured to their full potential, safe from the dangers of this temporal world. As Parent(s) and Godparent(s) here assembled, in the name of N., you have been called by God our Father to accept a sacred responsibility for the spiritual well being as well as the physical and mental well being of N. Do each of you understand this sacred responsibility?

ALL

Yes.

RECITALS

Ordinary Christening Recitals

CELEBRANT

Very well, before we proceed, I ask all of you three simple questions of faith and trust in the name of Christ:

CELEBRANT

(Opens his palms before all present before briefly looking to Heaven and then back to all present)

Do you solemnly promise to care for the needs of N.? To protect N. from any danger or harm, to the best of your abilities?

ALL

We do (promise).

CELEBRANT

And do you solemnly promise to educate N. into the faith of Christ and the one true Apostolic Universal Ecclesia? To teach by example by nurturing your own faith and actively participating in and attending the celebrations of your own Christian community with N.?

ALL

We do (promise).

CELEBRANT

And do you solemnly promise to uphold the Christian values of care for one another, so that you promise to help one another for the sake of N.?

ALL

We do (promise).

OBSIGNATION

CELEBRANT

Then truly this is a joyous day, for we welcome into our Christian community a new member. Upon the strength of faith of all here present.

CELEBRANT

(Gently makes the sign of the cross on the forehead of the infant with Holy Water)

I now gently trace the sign ✠ of the cross upon the forehead of N. as a sign and seal of the promise made in the name of our Divine Father.

CELEBRANT

I invite the Parents and Godparents if you so choose, as a mark of your solemn commitment to the promises made here today to gently do the same.

PARENT(S) AND SPONSOR(S)

(Each gently make the sign of the cross on the forehead of the infant)

CELEBRANT

Dear Brothers and Sisters, let us ask that all of Heaven

look lovingly upon this child who is about to be anointed and upon the Parent(s) and Godparent(s) and all here present as an embodiment of his holy Church. We ask this in the name of Christ.

ALL

Amen.

WILL OF THE PEOPLE

Ordinary Christening Will of the People

CELEBRANT

Let us pray.

Jesus, through your teachings and sacrifice we have come to no longer fear death, for you have given us eternal life so we can never die.

Heavenly Father, it is our Will and true intention in gratitude for your gifts of healing and our reconciliation into your presence, that we seek to dedicate our lives more fully to enacting your teachings.

We pray you will accept our humble petition and promises as a sign of the truth of our intentions, through Jesus Christ your son.

ALL

Amen.

SPONSOR(S)

By the mystery of your death and resurrection, bathe this child in light, give him (her) new life and welcome him (her) into your Church that is your Living Body.

ALL

Christ hear our prayer.

SPONSOR(S)

Through anointing, make him (her) your faithful follower and a witness to your gospel.

ALL

Christ hear our prayer.

SPONSOR(S)

Lead him (her) by a holy life to the joys of God's kingdom.

ALL
Christ hear our prayer.

SPONSOR(S)
Make the lives of his (her) parents and godparents examples of faith to inspire this child.

ALL
Christ hear our prayer.

SPONSOR(S)
Keep his (her) family always in your love.

ALL
Christ hear our prayer.

SPONSOR(S)
Renew the grace of our baptism in each one of us.

ALL
Christ hear our prayer.

EXORCISM PRAYER

CELEBRANT
Almighty and ever-living God, you sent your only Son into the world to cast out the power of Satan, the personification of evil, to rescue man from the kingdom of darkness, and bring him into the splendour of your kingdom of light. We pray for this child: set him (her) free from any spiritual impediment, make him (her) a temple of your glory, and send your Holy Spirit to dwell with him (her). We ask this through Christ our Lord.

ALL
Amen.

HOLY OIL ANOINTING

CELEBRANT
We anoint you with the oil of salvation in the name of

Christ our Saviour; may he strengthen you with his power, who lives and reigns for ever and ever.

CELEBRANT

(He anoints the child on the breast with the oil of catechumens)

May you have strength in the power of Christ our Saviour, who lives and reigns for ever and ever.

ALL

Amen.

UNIVERSAL PROFESSION OF FAITH

Ordinary Christening
Universal Profession of Faith

CELEBRANT

My dear brothers and sisters, Our faith is borne of trust in the truth of the Good News of the Risen Christ; and nurtured through our concrete actions as Christians. It is not a message of fear or superstition, but one of genuine certainty in the divine love, mercy and forgiveness of our Eternal Father and Creator. So it is as Christians, we freely and joyfully proclaim by our own will the Good News of Christ. In the spirit of this occasion then, I invite each of you once more to consent and make the seven solemn professions of Christian Faith with a loud and clear voice:

CELEBRANT

First, Do you accept that God the one true Divine Creator exists?; and that everything is part of the divine laws of creation, even if we do not always understand?

ALL

I do.

CELEBRANT

Second, Do you agree that our Eternal Father made humanity in his image?; and that everything in life has a purpose?; and that he has a divine plan for us, even if sometimes we reject his laws?

ALL

I do.

CELEBRANT

Third, Do you reject all forms of evil in this world? and all that seeks to confuse us?; and all forms of wickedness that seeks to entrap our minds and harden our hearts, especially all forms of addiction, exploitation, nihilism and cruelty?

ALL

I do.

CELEBRANT

Fourth, Do you recognise Christ as your Saviour?; and as the embodiment of every person who has lived or will ever live?; and that as a Divine singularity, He truly was borne of flesh; and lived and suffered in life as we do?; and that He willingly sacrificed himself to free all of us, without condition, from the bondage of our transgressions?; and that through such an act of Divine Redemption of Divine Mercy and love, He did make it possible so that all may rise from the death of transgression and have eternal life?

ALL

I do.

CELEBRANT

Fifth, Do you trust in the true teachings and Good News of the Risen Christ? That our Divine Creator is a loving god, who is merciful and loves us, despite our weaknesses? And that because of the gift of the universal law of free will, God does not seek to condemn us, or punish us, or directly cause us pain? And that no person has the right to curse or abuse or kill in the name of God?

ALL

I do.

CELEBRANT

Sixth, Do you welcome the Holy Spirit, the bringer of light and hope? Who illuminated the hearts and minds of the apostles at Pentecost and today is present with us through the celebration of this holy sacrament?

ALL

I do.

CELEBRANT

Seventh, Do you have faith in the one, holy apostolic Universal Ecclesia of Christ? As the one true living apostolic body of Christ and of all Christians?

ALL

I do.

CELEBRANT

This is our faith. This is the same faith of the disciples and Christian Founders. We joyfully profess it in the name of Christ our Saviour.

ALL

Amen.

BLESSING

CELEBRANT

Father, you give us grace through sacramental signs, which tell us of the wonders of your unseen power. In baptism we used your gift of water, which you have made a rich symbol of the grace you give us in this sacrament. At the very dawn of creation your Spirit breathed on the waters, making them the wellspring of all holiness. The waters of the great flood you made a sign of the waters of baptism, that make an end of spiritual impediments and a new beginning of goodness.

Through the waters of the Red Sea you led Israel out of slavery, to be an image of God's holy people, set free from all transgressions by baptism. In the waters of the Jordan your Son was baptised by John and anointed with the Spirit.

God the Father of our Lord Jesus Christ has freed you from spiritual transgression, given you a new birth by water and oil, and welcomed you into his holy people. He now anoints you with the chrism of salvation. As Christ was anointed Priest, Prophet, and King, so may you live always as a member of his body, sharing everlasting life.

ALL

Amen.

XXV.VII – EXTRAORDINARY RITE OF CHRISTENING

1. The *Rite of Extraordinary Christening* conferred by a competent minister in formal dedication as the second Liturgy of Mass to the spirit of one or more still-born infants, or deceased children upon the calculation of what would have been the year of their second birthday, shall be as follows:- Extraordinary Rite of Christening

LITURGY OF CHRISTIAN LIFE

Liturgy of Christian Life

(Appropriate memorial pictures of the deceased infants and children are positioned on display around the altar so that the whole congregation may observe.)

PETITION

Extraordinary Petition

CELEBRANT
(To the Parent(s) or Relative(s))

Are you the Parent(s) or Relative of a beautiful and pure soul that has reunited with God to continue their unique life in the hereafter?

PARENT(S)
Yes

CELEBRANT
(To each Parent or Relative)

What is the name of your Child?

PARENT(S)
N.

CELEBRANT
(To the Parent(s) or Relative(s))

What then is it you ask in the name of the Father and of the Son and of the Holy Spirit for N. today?

PARENT(S)
Christening.

CELEBRANT

The Rite of Holy Christening you ask for is a significant blessing. It is a foundation stone of our community of faith to bless and recognise all new members of our community; and that our future depends in part upon each new generation. The Sacrament of Christening as instituted by Christ himself is a manifest sign of this vital bond and the necessity that each and every child be properly educated and nurtured to their full potential, safe from the dangers of this temporal world.

As Parent(s) and Relative(s) here assembled, you have been called by God our Father to demonstrate your commitment to a fundamental article of Christian faith that our saviour Jesus Christ did open the door to eternal life for all of us; and that our lives do not end with physical death; and that we may continue to grow and learn and evolve as unique spiritual beings in the hereafter. Do each of you understand this sacred responsibility?

ALL

Yes.

RECITALS

Extraordinary Christening Recitals

CELEBRANT

Very well, before we proceed, I ask all of you three simple questions of faith and trust in the name of Christ:

CELEBRANT

(Opens his palms before all present before briefly looking to Heaven and then back to all present)

Do you solemnly promise to always keep the memory of your beloved in your hearts and to care for the needs of those still with us in flesh? And to continue to live, experience and give thanks for life to the best of your abilities?

ALL

We do (promise).

CELEBRANT

And do you solemnly promise to trust Christ and your faith

in the one true Apostolic Universal Ecclesia that your beloved can never truly die and are always with you? And to honour their memory by accepting the mystery of faith that they may continue to grow and experience a new life in Heaven as we continue to grow and learn and experience life on Earth?

ALL

We do (promise).

CELEBRANT

And do you solemnly promise to uphold the Christian values of care for one another, and not to shut yourself off from life or others? And that you look to express your love and care and respect of all whom we love, by helping those in our community who still need our love and support?

ALL

We do (promise).

OBSIGNATION

Extraordinary Christening Obsignation

CELEBRANT

Then truly this is a joyous day, for we recognise and welcome into our spiritual Christian community a new member. Upon the strength of faith of all here present.

CELEBRANT

(Gently makes the sign of the cross on each picture of the departed at the front of the church)

I now gently trace the sign ✠ of the cross upon the memorial of each of our beloved as a sign and seal of the promise made in the name of our Divine Father.

CELEBRANT

I invite the Parents and Godparents if you so choose, as a mark of your solemn commitment to the promises made here today to gently do the same.

PARENT(S) AND SPONSOR(S)

(Each gently make the sign of the cross on the memory of their beloved)

CELEBRANT

Dear Brothers and Sisters, let us ask that all of Heaven look lovingly upon this child who is about to be anointed and upon the Parent(s) and Godparent(s) and all here present as an embodiment of his holy Church. We ask this in the name of Christ.

ALL

Amen.

WILL OF THE PEOPLE

CELEBRANT

Let us pray.

Jesus, through your teachings and sacrifice we have come to no longer fear death, for you have given us eternal life so we can never die.

Heavenly Father, it is our Will and true intention in gratitude for your gifts of healing and our reconciliation into your presence, that we seek to dedicate our lives more fully to enacting your teachings.

We pray you will accept our humble petition and promises as a sign of the truth of our intentions, through Jesus Christ your son.

ALL

Amen.

SPONSOR(S)

By the mystery of your death and resurrection, bathe this child in light, give him (her) new life and welcome him (her) into your spiritual home in Heaven.

ALL

Christ hear our prayer.

SPONSOR(S)

Through the ceremony of anointing here on Earth, make him (her) your faithful follower and a witness to your gospel.

ALL

Christ hear our prayer.

SPONSOR(S)
Lead him (her) to a full life and the joys of your Kingdom in Heaven.

ALL
Christ hear our prayer.

SPONSOR(S)
Make the lives of his (her) parents and godparents examples of faith to inspire all people of the community.

ALL
Christ hear our prayer.

SPONSOR(S)
Keep his (her) family always in your love.

ALL
Christ hear our prayer.

SPONSOR(S)
Renew the grace of our baptism in each one of us.

ALL
Christ hear our prayer.

HOLY OIL ANOINTING

Extraordinary Christening
Holy Oil Anointing

CELEBRANT
We anoint the memory of each of our beloved with the oil of salvation in the name of Christ our Saviour; may he strengthen you with his power, who lives and reigns for ever and ever.

CELEBRANT
(Gently makes the sign of the cross on each picture of the departed with anointing oil at the front of the church)

May you have strength in the power of Christ our Saviour, who lives and reigns for ever and ever.

ALL

Amen.

UNIVERSAL PROFESSION OF FAITH

CELEBRANT

My dear brothers and sisters, Our faith is borne of trust in the truth of the Good News of the Risen Christ; and nurtured through our concrete actions as Christians. It is not a message of fear or superstition, but one of genuine certainty in the divine love, mercy and forgiveness of our Eternal Father and Creator. So it is as Christians, we freely and joyfully proclaim by our own will the Good News of Christ. In the spirit of this occasion then, I invite each of you once more to consent and make the seven solemn professions of Christian Faith with a loud and clear voice:

CELEBRANT

First, Do you accept that God the one true Divine Creator exists?; and that everything is part of the divine laws of creation, even if we do not always understand?

ALL

I do.

CELEBRANT

Second, Do you agree that our Eternal Father made humanity in his image?; and that everything in life has a purpose?; and that he has a divine plan for us, even if sometimes we reject his laws?

ALL

I do.

CELEBRANT

Third, Do you reject all forms of evil in this world? and all that seeks to confuse us?; and all forms of wickedness that seeks to entrap our minds and harden our hearts, especially all forms of addiction, exploitation, nihilism and cruelty?

ALL

I do.

CELEBRANT

Fourth, Do you recognise Christ as your Saviour?; and as the embodiment of every person who has lived or will ever live?; and that as a Divine singularity, He truly was borne of flesh; and lived and suffered in life as we do?; and that He willingly sacrificed himself to free all of us, without condition, from the bondage of our transgressions?; and that through such an act of Divine Redemption of Divine Mercy and love, He did make it possible so that all may rise from the death of transgressions and have eternal life?

ALL

I do.

CELEBRANT

Fifth, Do you trust in the true teachings and Good News of the Risen Christ? That our Divine Creator is a loving god, who is merciful and loves us, despite our weaknesses? And that because of the gift of the universal law of free will, God does not seek to condemn us, or punish us, or directly cause us pain? And that no person has the right to curse or abuse or kill in the name of God?

ALL

I do.

CELEBRANT

Sixth, Do you welcome the Holy Spirit, the bringer of light and hope? Who illuminated the hearts and minds of the apostles at Pentecost and today is present with us through the celebration of this holy sacrament?

ALL

I do.

CELEBRANT

Seventh, Do you have faith in the one, holy apostolic Universal Ecclesia of Christ? As the one true living apostolic body of Christ and of all Christians?

ALL

I do.

CELEBRANT

This is our faith. This is the same faith of the disciples and Christian Founders. We joyfully profess it in the name of Christ our Saviour.

ALL

Amen.

BLESSING

CELEBRANT

Father, you give us grace through sacramental signs, which tell us of the wonders of your unseen power. In baptism we used your gift of water, which you have made a rich symbol of the grace you give us in this sacrament. At the very dawn of creation your Spirit breathed on the waters, making them the wellspring of all holiness. The waters of the great flood you made a sign of the waters of baptism, that make an end of spiritual impediments and a new beginning of goodness.

Through the waters of the Red Sea you led Israel out of slavery, to be an image of God's holy people, set free from all transgressions by baptism. In the waters of the Jordan your Son was baptised by John and anointed with the Spirit.

God the Father of our Lord Jesus Christ has freed you from spiritual transgression, given you a new birth by water and oil, and welcomed you into his holy people. He now anoints you with the chrism of salvation. As Christ was anointed Priest, Prophet, and King, so may you live always as a member of his body, sharing everlasting life.

ALL

Amen.

Title XXVI – Sacrament of Confirmation & Rite of First Communion

XXVI.I – SACRAMENT OF OF CONFIRMATION

1. Confirmation (*Ritus Sacramentum Confirmatio*) and Rite of First Communion is the fourth of the twelve (12) Apostolic Life Sacraments, also known as "The Twelve", "The Twelve Apostles" and "The Means". Sacrament of Confirmation (Ritus Sacramentum Confirmatio)

   The Sacrament of Confirmation and Rite of First Communion shall be granted and administered by the twelfth (12th) birthday of a child that has received the Sacrament of Incarnation and Rite of Christening in accordance with the most sacred Covenants *Pactum De Singularis Caelum*, *Pactum De Singularis Christus*, and *Missale Christus* and associated approved liturgy.

2. The Divine purpose of the Sacrament of Confirmation and Rite of First Communion is to celebrate the admittance of a child into the rights of possessions and responsibility of their respective community through the formal celebration and bestowal of certain Ecclesiastical and Public rights to the child as a member of the community. Upon a child demonstrating their ability to distinguish right from wrong; and the basic competence of logic, reason and discernment; and an essential understanding of morals and consequences, a child is permitted to own property in their own name and to participate in the Holy Eucharist. A child having received Holy Communion is also expected to acknowledge their responsibilities and duties to their family and community. Apostolic Life Sacrament of Confirmation

XXVI.II – DIVINE GRACE AND ACTION OF CONFIRMATION

1. The Divine Grace and Action of *Confirmation* is the supernatural effect of the proper ministration of the Rite of First Communion to celebrate the admittance of a child into the rights of possessions and responsibility of their respective community through the formal celebration and bestowal of certain Ecclesiastical and Public rights to the child as a member of the community. Divine Grace and Action of Confirmation

2. *Confirmation* is a wholly Divine and unmerited action, warranted by God and the Divine Creator. It is not an action effected within the temporal realm, nor can it be equated to physical terms or constructs. Understanding of action and Divine Grace of Confirmation

3. The Divine Grace and Supernatural Action of *Confirmation* is central to the proper effect of the Holy Rite of First Communion. Such supernatural presence and grace is made manifest *first* by the suitable qualification of the recipient; and *second* by the proper authority of Divine Grace and Action of Sacrament of Confirmation

one administering the sacrament; and *third* by the constituent parts and order that must be established in order to effect the sacrament.

In accord with sacred liturgy, in the absence of one or more of these central requisites, no legitimate manifestation of such Divine Grace and Action can occur.

XXVI.III – RITE OF FIRST COMMUNION

Rite of First Communion

1. The Holy Rite of First Communion represents the constituent parts and their order that must be established in order to effect the Divine and Supernatural Sacrament of Confirmation. In the absence of one or more of these central requisites, no legitimate manifestation or imprint of the Divine Grace and Action of Confirmation can occur.

Form of the Sacrament of Confirmation

2. There are only two (2) valid and licit forms for the Sacrament of Confirmation and Rite of First Communion as defined by the most sacred *Missale Christus* and associated approved liturgy being Ordinary and Extraordinary:

   (i) "**Ordinary Communion**" is conferred by a competent minister upon a child having reached the age of twelve (12) years; and

   (ii) "**Extraordinary Communion**" is conferred by a competent minister in formal dedication to the spirit of a still-borne infant, or deceased child upon the calculation of what would have been their twelfth birthday. Such a ceremony may be conducted as a Special Mass, with such records then entered into the rolls to the fact of such sacred act.

3. In accordance with Divine Law and the most sacred covenant *Pactum De Singularis Caelum*, if a child having received the Rite of Christening dies before being the age of twelve (12), then this unique Divine Immortal Spirit shall be fully entitled to receive the sacrament of Communion within 60 days of 12 years since being borne.

4. In accordance with Divine Law and the most sacred covenant *Pactum De Singularis Caelum*, the mother or father or next of living kin of any child that died prior to the age of twelve (12) yet was not previously granted the Rite of Christening may apply for the special ceremony of Life Sacraments where all sacraments are granted beginning with Annunciation to the sacrament representing the same age as if the child had lived and grown up to the present day.

XXVI.IV – CONDITIONS OF RITE OF FIRST COMMUNION

1. Conditions of the Rite of First Communion are those requisite qualifications and contingencies permitted in the proper ministration of the Rite. There shall exist only two (2) possible Conditions for the ministration of Rite of First Communion being *Ordinary* and *Extraordinary*:-

Conditions of Rite of First Communion

(i) *Ordinary* are the Conditions necessary for the conferral of the Ordinary Rite of First Communion upon a child having reached the age of twelve (12) years; and

(ii) *Extraordinary* are the Conditions necessary for the conferral of the Rite of First Communion upon a deceased child or adult.

2. The Ordinary Form of the Rite of Holy Communion cannot be conferred unless the child is clearly prepared and able to become a productive and exemplary member of their community. Thus, the priority of education and preparation must pertain to skills of reason, logic, discernment, morality, ethics and the consequences of actions before any general knowledge of the Maxims of Divine Law are then necessary:

Expectation of Knowledge and Education of Child

(i) A child that is able to recite scripture, yet is unable to apply reason, logic and virtue to their decisions is not competent for First Communion and those that failed to adequately prepare such a child are not competent to teach, until they acknowledge such failings; and

(ii) This is because, to be a member of a community under Heaven is to be an ambassador of the Divine Creator; and an exemplary to the world. First Communion is a sacred ceremony that heralds such a moment. Therefore an absence of proper preparation is a grave offence against the child and the most sacred Covenant Pactum De Singularis Caelum itself.

3. The conditions for the Ordinary Rite of First Communion are:-

Ordinary Conditions

(i) The Sponsors, whether parents or immediate family members, have at least all received the Rite of Baptism, the Rite of Christening and the Rite of First Communion; and

(ii) Sufficient confidence exists that the Sponsors have attended Holy Mass for at least one Universal Feast from each of the seven Liturgical Cycles of the Mysteries of Christ of the previous year, being *Immanent, Filial, Eucharistic, Transcendent, Sacred Heart, Redemption* and *Apostolic*, unless a special exemption is granted by the local Ordinary; and

(iii) That the child is sufficiently prepared and competent with their faith to make an informed decision of their own accord during the sacred Rite.

Extraordinary Form of the Sacrament of Confirmation

4. In accordance with Divine Law and the most sacred Covenant *Pactum De Singularis Caelum*, if a child having received the Sacrament of Confirmation and Rite of First Communion dies before being the age of twelve (12), then this unique Divine Immortal Spirit shall be fully entitled to receive the Sacrament of Confirmation and Rite of First Communion within sixty (60) days of twelve (12) years since being borne.

In accordance with Divine Law and the most sacred Covenant *Pactum De Singularis Caelum*, the mother or father or next of living kin of any child that died prior to the age of twelve (12) yet was not previously granted the Sacrament of Confirmation and Rite of First Communion may apply for the special ceremony of Life Sacraments where all sacraments are granted beginning with Sacrament of Inspiration and Rite of Annunciation to the sacrament representing the same age as if the child had lived and grown up to the present day.

Extraordinary Conditions

5. The conditions for the Extraordinary Rite of First Communion are:-

(i) The Sponsors, whether parents or immediate family members, have at least all received the Rite of Baptism, the Rite of Christening and the Rite of First Communion; and

(ii) Sufficient confidence exists that the Sponsors have attended Holy Mass for at least one Universal Feast from each of the seven Liturgical Cycles of the Mysteries of Christ of the previous year, being *Immanent, Filial, Eucharistic, Transcendent, Sacred Heart, Redemption* and *Apostolic*, unless a special exemption is granted by the local Ordinary.

XXVI.V – CELEBRATION OF RITE OF FIRST COMMUNION

Celebration of Rite of First Communion

1. Only the local Ordinary, or visiting Bishop may minister the Ordinary Rite of First Communion. Only a legitimately and validly ordained minister may minister the Extraordinary Rite of First Communion.

Valid days of celebration

2. The Ordinary Rite of First Communion may be celebrated on any Day, except those reserved for Holy Feast Days of Good Friday, Easter Sunday and Christmas Day. The Extraordinary Rite of First Communion may not be celebrated on any day reserved for any of the sixty-six (66) Holy Feast Days of the Liturgical Season of the Seven

Mysteries of Christ.

The Sacred Colour for the Liturgy of Mass shall be **White** if three (3) or more Supplicants or Sponsors are present for the Rite. Otherwise, the Sacred Colour for the Liturgy of Mass shall remain the same for the liturgical season that the particular Mass is celebrated.

XXVI.VI – ORDINARY RITE OF FIRST COMMUNION

1. *The Ordinary Rite of First Communion* conferred by a competent minister upon a child having reached the age of twelve years shall be as follows:

Ordinary Rite of First Communion

LITURGY OF CHRISTIAN LIFE

Liturgy of Christian Life

PETITION

Ordinary First Communion
Petition

CELEBRANT

(To all assembled)

I call upon those who seek to make their solemn petition today in the name of Christ our Saviour to now stand and make their presence and prayer known.

(The young boys and girls in the front rows stand)

CELEBRANT

What Holy Rite then is it you ask in the name of the Father and of the Son and of the Holy Spirit today?

COMMUNICANT(S)

Holy Communion.

CELEBRANT

(Turning to Communicants.)

The Sacrament of Holy Communion that each of you ask is a moment of great importance, not only for you and your family and this community, but our wider community of the people of God. It signifies the arrival of each of you unto the age of Reason - a time where you have demonstrated to those who prepared you for this occasion, that you comprehend the differences between right from wrong, between truth and falsity, between kindness and cruelty, between logic and irrationality, between discernment and stupidity, between self discipline and reckless abandon, between love and hate and between virtue and evil.

What is more, each of you have willingly and freely accepted that with such gifts of knowledge and competence comes the acceptance of moral and personal responsibility.

As your teachers have explained, accepting and living life according to moral and personal responsibility does not mean being deprived of the joy and fun and happiness of being young. In fact, your acceptance that what you think, or say or do has consequences; and that you are accountable for your own actions means you have the chance to avoid many of the mistakes that can lead to regret, sadness and misery.

The idea that anyone can do or say whatever they please without consideration or consequences is a wicked lie. You share a common home and planet we call Earth. You live in a community and have friends and neighbours. Everything you do has consequences.

Without such knowledge in action, without such competency among the members of a community, such a society cannot survive. Whilst it may appear for a time that corruption and injustice prevail, no civilisation can stand, when these self-evident foundations of reason are abandoned.

You are loved by your parents and this family and community. You are our future and the future of our wider community because you are welcomed today as true Christians as followers in the teachings and actions of Christ.

Many faiths and cultures celebrate a similar moment by different names. As Christians, we call this moment in time First Communion, because we celebrate your maturity in welcoming you to partake for the first time in the Holy Eucharist as centre of our spiritual and communal rite through Mass. Furthermore, because each of you have demonstrated your capacity for reason, we invite you by your own free will and choice to renew the vows of Baptism that your parents, godparents and witnesses took in your name when you were new born infants; and to be sealed with holy oil as a permanent sign that you are loved by God and his son Jesus Christ; and that you are protected by the Holy Spirit and that you are truly blessed, even if in the difficult times of life such blessings and love may feel distant.

May you never forget the abundant blessings bestowed upon each of you today. May you never lose hope or surrender your faith, no matter how challenging the events of life to come.

God so loves this world and our species, that he sent his only son Jesus Christ into our midst to teach us by example, to show us the extraordinary capacity each and everyone of us have to overcome even the most horrible of injustices and cruelties and to help heal even the deepest wounds through virtue and moral responsibility to others.

Let us always remember that to be Christians is to follow and live the example of Christ. Do each of you understand these sacred responsibilities?

ALL

Yes.

OBLIGATION

Ordinary First Confirmation Obligation

CELEBRANT

I call upon the Supplicants to kneel and give their solemn vows to their family, their community and the Divine Creator.

CELEBRANT

(Opens his palms before all present before briefly looking to Heaven and then back to all present)

Will you take and accept your immediate family as they are? Do you promise to always be truthful to them in good times and in bad, and in times of sickness and distress?

SUPPLICANT(S)

I do.

CELEBRANT

Will you take and accept education and learning to be a key part of your life? Do you promise to be gentle and persistent in acquiring deeper knowledge and skills, and to always be kind and forgive others throughout this journey of life experience?

ALL

I do.

CELEBRANT

Will you take and accept your church to be part of your wider family? Do you promise to be loyal and support your community and your faith, every day of your life?

ALL

I do.

OBSIGNATION

CELEBRANT

Then truly this is a joyous day, for we welcome into our Christian community new member(s) of equal standing with the power of discernment and reasoning.

CELEBRANT

(Gently makes the sign of the cross on the forehead of each supplicant with Holy Water and then lays their hands on their head.)

Upon the strength of faith of all here present. I now gently trace the sign ✠ of the cross upon the forehead of N. as a sign and seal of the promise made in the name of our Divine Father at the time of the Rite of Holy Baptism.

CELEBRANT

(Celebrant returns and faces the kneeling Supplicants and extends his hands over them)

Heavenly Father, by the teachings of your son Jesus Christ and with the power for the Holy Spirit you transformed these sons and daughters into Persons unblemished by inherited spiritual impediments and with the full rights you promised. Send your Holy Spirit upon them once more to be their helper and guide.

Give them the spirit of wisdom of understanding, the spirit of right judgement and courage and the spirit of knowledge and reverence. Fill them with the spirit of wise discernment and compassion. We ask this in the name of Christ.

ALL

Amen.

WILL OF THE PEOPLE

CELEBRANT

Let us pray.

Jesus, through your teachings and sacrifice we have come to no longer fear death, for you have given us eternal life so we can never die.

Heavenly Father, it is our Will and true intention in gratitude for your gifts of healing and our reconciliation into your presence, that we seek to dedicate our lives more fully to enacting your teachings.

We pray you will accept our humble petition and promises as a sign of the truth of our intentions, through Jesus Christ your son.

ALL

Amen.

SPONSOR(S)

By the mystery of your death and resurrection, bathe these sons and daughters in light, give them new life and welcome them as equals into your Church that is the fulfilment of your Living Body.

ALL

Christ hear our prayer.

SPONSOR(S)

Through anointing, make these sons and daughters your faithful followers and witnesses to your gospel.

ALL

Christ hear our prayer.

SPONSOR(S)
Lead them by a holy life to the joys of God's kingdom.

ALL
Christ hear our prayer.

SPONSOR(S)
Make the lives of their parents and godparents examples of faith to inspire them.

ALL
Christ hear our prayer.

SPONSOR(S)
Keep all the families here always in your love.

ALL
Christ hear our prayer.

SPONSOR(S)
Renew the grace of our baptism in each one of us.

ALL
Christ hear our prayer.

HOLY OIL ANOINTING

CELEBRANT
We anoint you with the most sacred Oil of Christ in the name of our Lord and our Saviour; may he strengthen you with his power, who lives and reigns for ever and ever.

CELEBRANT
(He anoints each child on the forehead with Chrism Oil)

Be sealed with the gift of the Holy Spirit. May you have strength in the power of Christ our Saviour, who lives and reigns for ever and ever.

ALL
Amen.

UNIVERSAL PROFESSION OF FAITH

CELEBRANT
My dear brothers and sisters, Our faith is borne of trust in the truth of the Good News of the Risen Christ; and nurtured through our concrete actions as Christians. It is not a message of fear or superstition, but one of genuine certainty in the divine love, mercy and forgiveness of our Eternal Father and Creator. So it is as Christians, we freely and joyfully proclaim by our own will the Good News of Christ. In the spirit of this occasion then, I invite each of you once more to consent and make the seven solemn professions of Christian Faith with a loud and clear voice:

CELEBRANT
First, Do you accept that God the one true Divine Creator exists?; and that everything is part of the divine laws of creation, even if we do not always understand?

ALL
I do.

CELEBRANT
Second, Do you agree that our Eternal Father made humanity in his image?; and that everything in life has a purpose?; and that he has a divine plan for us, even if sometimes we reject his laws?

ALL
I do.

CELEBRANT
Third, Do you reject all forms of evil in this world? and all that seeks to confuse us?; and all forms of wickedness that seeks to entrap our minds and harden our hearts, especially all forms of addiction, exploitation, nihilism and cruelty?

ALL
I do.

CELEBRANT
Fourth, Do you recognise Christ as your Saviour?; and as

the embodiment of every person who has lived or will ever live?; and that as a Divine singularity, He truly was borne of flesh; and lived and suffered in life as we do?; and that He willingly sacrificed himself to free all of us, without condition, from the bondage of our transgressions?; and that through such an act of Divine Redemption of Divine Mercy and love, He did make it possible so that all may rise from the death of transgressions and have eternal life?

ALL

I do.

CELEBRANT

Fifth, Do you trust in the true teachings and Good News of the Risen Christ? That our Divine Creator is a loving god, who is merciful and loves us, despite our weaknesses? And that because of the gift of the universal law of free will, God does not seek to condemn us, or punish us, or directly cause us pain? And that no person has the right to curse or abuse or kill in the name of God?

ALL

I do.

CELEBRANT

Sixth, Do you welcome the Holy Spirit, the bringer of light and hope? Who illuminated the hearts and minds of the apostles at Pentecost and today is present with us through the celebration of this holy sacrament?

ALL

I do.

CELEBRANT

Seventh, Do you have faith in the one, holy apostolic Universal Ecclesia of Christ? As the one true living apostolic body of Christ and of all Christians?

ALL

I do.

CELEBRANT

This is our faith. This is the same faith of the disciples and Christian Founders. We joyfully profess it in the name of

Christ our Saviour.

ALL

Amen.

BLESSING

Ordinary First Confirmation
Blessing

CELEBRANT

Father, you give us grace through sacramental signs, which tell us of the wonders of your unseen power. In baptism we used your gift of water, which you have made a rich symbol of the grace you give us in this sacrament. At the very dawn of creation your Spirit breathed on the waters, making them the wellspring of all holiness.

Now with your most Holy Oil, we recognise the newest equal members of our family, who have demonstrated their capacity to discern and choose their faith unto you.

God the Father of our Lord Jesus Christ has freed you from spiritual transgression, given you a new birth by water and oil, and welcomed you into his holy people. As Christ was anointed Priest, Prophet, and King, so may you live always as a member of his body, sharing everlasting life.

ALL

Amen.

XXVI.VII – RITE OF EXTRAORDINARY COMMUNION

1. The *Rite of Extraordinary Communion* conferred by a competent minister in formal dedication as the second Liturgy of Mass to the spirit of one or more deceased children upon the calculation of what would have been the year of their twelfth birthday shall be as follows:

Rite of Extraordinary First Communion

LITURGY OF CHRISTIAN LIFE

Liturgy of Christian Life

(Appropriate memorial pictures of the deceased as children around the age of twelve are positioned on display around the altar so that the whole congregation may observe. A White Ribbon is tied to the side of each picture as a sign of the Rite of First Communion.)

PETITION

CELEBRANT
(To the Parent(s) or Relative(s))

Are you the Parent(s) or Relative of a beautiful child that has returned to our Divine Creator to continue their unique life in the hereafter?

PARENT(S)
Yes

CELEBRANT
(To each Parent or Relative)

What is the name of your Child?

PARENT(S)
N.

CELEBRANT
(To the Parent(s) or Relative(s))

What Holy Rite then is it you ask in the name of the Father and of the Son and of the Holy Spirit for N. today?

PARENT(S)
First Communion

CELEBRANT
The Rite of First Communion you ask for is a significant blessing. It is a foundation of our faith in our Divine Creator as the doorway to eternal life. As Parent(s) and Relative(s) here assembled, you have been called by God our Father to demonstrate to all here present your commitment to a fundamental article of Christian faith that our saviour Jesus Christ has opened the door to eternal life for all of us; and our life does not end with physical death; and that we continue to grow and learn and evolve as unique spiritual beings in the hereafter. Do each of you understand this sacred responsibility?

PARENT(S)
Yes.

RECITALS

Extraordinary First Communion Recitals

CELEBRANT
Very well, before we proceed, I ask all of you three simple questions of faith and trust in the name of Christ:

CELEBRANT
(Opens his palms before all present before briefly looking to Heaven and then back to all present)

Do you solemnly promise to always keep the memory of your beloved in your hearts and to care for the needs of those still with us in flesh? And to continue to live, experience and give thanks for life to the best of your abilities?

ALL
We do (promise).

CELEBRANT
And do you solemnly promise to trust Christ and your faith in the one true Apostolic Universal Ecclesia that your beloved can never truly die and are always with you? And to honour their memory by accepting the mystery of faith that they may continue to grow and experience a new life in Heaven as we continue to grow and learn and experience life on Earth?

ALL
We do (promise).

CELEBRANT
And do you solemnly promise to uphold the Christian values of care for one another, and not to shut yourself off from life or others? And that you look to express your love and care and respect of all whom we love, by helping those in our community who still need our love and support?

ALL
We do (promise).

OBSIGNATION

Extraordinary First Communion

Obsignation

CELEBRANT

Then truly this is a joyous day, for we recognise and welcome into our spiritual Christian community a new equal member. Upon the strength of faith of all here present.

CELEBRANT

(Gently makes the sign of the cross on each picture of the departed at the front of the church)

I now gently trace the sign ✠ of the cross upon the memorial of each of our beloved as a sign and seal of the promise made in the name of our Divine Father that all Baptised in the faith are saved and none be condemned.

CELEBRANT

I invite the Parents and Godparents if you so choose, as a mark of your solemn commitment to the promises made here today to gently do the same.

PARENT(S) AND SPONSOR(S)

(Each gently make the sign of the cross on the memory of their beloved)

CELEBRANT

Dear Brothers and Sisters, let us ask that all of Heaven look lovingly upon this child who is about to be anointed as an equal member of our spiritual and temporal family; and upon the Parent(s) and Godparent(s) and all here present as an embodiment of his holy Church. We ask this in the name of Christ.

ALL

Amen.

WILL OF THE PEOPLE

Extraordinary First Communion
Will of the People

CELEBRANT

Let us pray.

Jesus, through your teachings and sacrifice we have come to no longer fear death, for you have given us eternal life so we can never die.

Heavenly Father, it is our Will and true intention in

gratitude for your gifts of healing and our reconciliation into your presence, that we seek to dedicate our lives more fully to enacting your teachings.

We pray you will accept our humble petition and promises as a sign of the truth of our intentions, through Jesus Christ your son.

ALL

Amen.

SPONSOR(S)

By the mystery of your death and resurrection, bathe these sons and daughters in light, give them new life and welcome them as equals into your Church that is the fulfilment of your Living Body.

ALL

Christ hear our prayer.

SPONSOR(S)

Through anointing, make these sons and daughters your faithful followers and witnesses to your gospel.

ALL

Christ hear our prayer.

SPONSOR(S)

Lead them by a holy life to the joys of God's kingdom.

ALL

Christ hear our prayer.

SPONSOR(S)

Make the lives of their parents and godparents examples of faith to inspire all people.

ALL

Christ hear our prayer.

SPONSOR(S)

Keep all the families here always in your love.

ALL

Christ hear our prayer.

SPONSOR(S)
Renew the grace of our baptism in each one of us.

ALL
Christ hear our prayer.

HOLY OIL ANOINTING

Extraordinary First Communion Holy Oil Anointing

CELEBRANT
We anoint the memory of each of our beloved with the oil of salvation in the name of Christ our Saviour; may he strengthen you with his power, who lives and reigns for ever and ever.

CELEBRANT
(Gently makes the sign of the cross on each picture of the departed with anointing oil at the front of the church)

May you have strength in the power of Christ our Saviour, who lives and reigns for ever and ever.

ALL
Amen.

UNIVERSAL PROFESSION OF FAITH

Extraordinary First Communion Universal Profession of Faith

CELEBRANT
My dear brothers and sisters, Our faith is borne of trust in the truth of the Good News of the Risen Christ; and nurtured through our concrete actions as Christians. It is not a message of fear or superstition, but one of genuine certainty in the divine love, mercy and forgiveness of our Eternal Father and Creator. So it is as Christians, we freely and joyfully proclaim by our own will the Good News of Christ. In the spirit of this occasion then, I invite each of you once more to consent and make the seven solemn professions of Christian Faith with a loud and clear voice:

CELEBRANT
First, Do you accept that God the one true Divine Creator exists?; and that everything is part of the divine laws of creation, even if we do not always understand?

ALL
I do.

CELEBRANT

Second, Do you agree that our Eternal Father made humanity in his image?; and that everything in life has a purpose?; and that he has a divine plan for us, even if sometimes we reject his laws?

ALL

I do.

CELEBRANT

Third, Do you reject all forms of evil in this world? and all that seeks to confuse us?; and all forms of wickedness that seeks to entrap our minds and harden our hearts, especially all forms of addiction, exploitation, nihilism and cruelty?

ALL

I do.

CELEBRANT

Fourth, Do you recognise Christ as your Saviour?; and as the embodiment of every person who has lived or will ever live?; and that as a Divine singularity, He truly was borne of flesh; and lived and suffered in life as we do?; and that He willingly sacrificed himself to free all of us, without condition, from the bondage of our transgressions?; and that through such an act of Divine Redemption of Divine Mercy and love, He did make it possible so that all may rise from the death of transgressions and have eternal life?

ALL

I do.

CELEBRANT

Fifth, Do you trust in the true teachings and Good News of the Risen Christ? That our Divine Creator is a loving god, who is merciful and loves us, despite our weaknesses? And that because of the gift of the universal law of free will, God does not seek to condemn us, or punish us, or directly cause us pain? And that no person has the right to curse or abuse or kill in the name of God?

ALL

I do.

CELEBRANT

Sixth, Do you welcome the Holy Spirit, the bringer of light and hope? Who illuminated the hearts and minds of the apostles at Pentecost and today is present with us through the celebration of this holy sacrament?

ALL

I do.

CELEBRANT

Seventh, Do you have faith in the one, holy apostolic Universal Ecclesia of Christ? As the one true living apostolic body of Christ and of all Christians?

ALL

I do.

CELEBRANT

This is our faith. This is the same faith of the disciples and Christian Founders. We joyfully profess it in the name of Christ our Saviour.

ALL

Amen.

BLESSING

CELEBRANT

Father, you give us grace through sacramental signs, which tell us of the wonders of your unseen power. In baptism we used your gift of water, which you have made a rich symbol of the grace you give us in this sacrament. At the very dawn of creation your Spirit breathed on the waters, making them the wellspring of all holiness.

Now with your most Holy Oil, we recognise the newest equal members of our family, who have demonstrated their capacity to discern and choose their faith unto you.

God the Father of our Lord Jesus Christ has freed you from spiritual transgression, given you a new birth by water and oil, and welcomed you into his holy people. As Christ was anointed Priest, Prophet, and King, so may you live always as a member of his body, sharing everlasting life.

ALL

Amen.

Title XXVII – Sacrament of Illumination & Rite of Majority

XXVII.I – SACRAMENT OF ILLUMINATION

1. Illumination (*Ritus Sacramentum Illuminatio*) is the fifth of the twelve (12) Apostolic Life Sacraments, also known as "The Twelve", "The Twelve Apostles" and "The Means". Sacrament of Illumination (Ritus Sacramentum Illuminatio)

The Sacrament of Illumination and Rite of Majority shall be granted and administered by the twenty-first (21st) birthday of a young adult in accordance with the most sacred Covenants *Pactum De Singularis Caelum*, *Pactum De Singularis Christus*, and *Missale Christus* and associated approved liturgy.

2. Every enlightened and civilised culture of history has recognised the significance of the moment of welcoming a new member of the community as an adult, whatever age was prescribed for such tradition. Since then, the age of adulthood has progressively increased to eighteen in some societies and to the age of twenty one in others. Divine Purpose of the Sacrament of Illumination

The purpose of the Sacrament of Illumination and Rite of Majority is to formalise the welcoming of new adults into the community at an age whereby most should have successfully finished some learning and qualification of useful skills.

Most importantly, the Sacrament of Illumination and Rite of Majority is essential to the Christian and Jewish community of the Living Body of Christ to ensure all new Adult Members are fully competent in their moral, spiritual and behavioural obligations, particularly in the forming and supporting of their own families. Thus the Sacrament of Illumination and Rite of Majority is a necessary element to stable and fruitful Matrimonial relations throughout a healthy, productive and joyous society.

XXVII.II – DIVINE GRACE AND ACTION OF ILLUMINATION

1. The Divine Grace and Action of *Illumination* is the supernatural effect of the proper ministration of the Rite of Majority with the the welcoming of new adults into the community at an age whereby most should have successfully finished some learning and qualification of useful skills. Divine Grace and Action of Illumination

2. *Illumination* is a wholly Divine and unmerited action, warranted by God and the Divine Creator. It is not an action effected within the temporal realm, nor can it be equated to physical terms or constructs. Understanding of action and Divine Grace of Illumination

3. The Divine Grace and Supernatural Action of *Illumination* is central to the proper effect of the Holy Rite of Majority. Such supernatural Divine Grace and Action of

presence and grace is made manifest *first* by the suitable qualification of the recipient; and *second* by the proper authority of one administering the sacrament; and *third* by the constituent parts and order that must be established in order to effect the sacrament. Sacrament

In accord with sacred liturgy, in the absence of one or more of these central requisites, no legitimate manifestation of such Divine Grace and Action can occur.

XXVII.III – RITE OF MAJORITY

1. The Holy Rite of Majority represents the constituent parts and their order that must be established in order to effect the Divine and Supernatural Sacrament of Illumination. In the absence of one or more of these central requisites, no legitimate manifestation or imprint of the Divine Grace and Action of Illumination can occur. Rite of Majority

2. There are only two (2) valid and licit forms for the Sacrament of Illumination and Rite of Majority as defined by the most sacred *Missale Christus* and associated approved liturgy being Ordinary and Extraordinary:- Form of the Sacrament of Illumination & Rite of Majority

   (i) "**Ordinary Majority Rite**" is conferred by a competent minister upon a youth having reached the age of twenty one years; and

   (ii) "**Extraordinary Majority Rite**" is conferred by a competent minister in formal dedication to the spirit of a still-borne infant, or deceased child or youth upon the calculation of what would have been their twenty first birthday. Such a ceremony may be conducted as a Special Mass, with such records then entered into the rolls to the fact of such sacred act.

3. In accordance with Divine Law and the most sacred covenant *Pactum De Singularis Caelum*, if a teenager having received the Rite of First Communion dies before being the age of twenty one (21), then this unique Divine Immortal Spirit shall be fully entitled to receive the sacrament of Rite of Majority within 30 days of 21 years since being borne and all Life Sacraments thereafter at their appointed time. Extraordinary Rite of Majority for Deceased Person

4. In accordance with Divine Law and the most sacred covenant *Pactum De Singularis Caelum*, the mother or father or next of living kin of any child that died prior to the age of twenty-one (21) yet was not previously granted the Rite of First Communion may apply for the special ceremony of Life Sacraments where all sacraments including Rite of Majority are granted beginning with Annunciation to the sacrament representing the same age as if the child had lived and Extraordinary Rite of Majority for Deceased Child

grown up to the present day.

XXVII.IV – CONDITIONS OF RITE OF MAJORITY

1. Conditions of the Rite of Majority are those requisite qualifications and contingencies permitted in the proper ministration of the Rite. There shall exist only two possible Conditions for the ministration of Rite of Majority being *Ordinary* and *Extraordinary*:- Conditions of Rite of Majority

   (i) *Ordinary* are the Conditions necessary for the conferral of the Ordinary Rite of Majority upon a living human being at the age of twenty-one (21) years; and

   (ii) *Extraordinary* are the Conditions necessary for the conferral of the Rite of Majority upon a deceased child or adult at what would have been their twenty first year.

2. A condition of the Rite of Majority is that the youth knowingly and willingly consents to dedicating their life to continuous self improvement and virtue and to contributing to the benefit and improvement of their community and society. Expectation of Knowledge and Education of Young Adult

3. The conditions for the Ordinary Rite of Majority are:- Ordinary Conditions

   (i) The Supplicant has received the Rite of Baptism, the Rite of Christening and the Rite of First Communion; and

   (ii) Sufficient confidence exists that the Supplicant has attended Holy Mass for at least one Universal Feast from each of the seven Liturgical Cycles of the Mysteries of Christ of the previous year, being *Immanent, Filial, Eucharistic, Transcendent, Sacred Heart, Redemption* and *Apostolic*, unless a special exemption is granted by the local Ordinary; and

4. The conditions for the Extraordinary Rite of Majority are:- Extraordinary Conditions

   (i) The Sponsors, whether parents or immediate family members, have at least all received the Rite of Baptism, the Rite of Christening and the Rite of First Communion; and

   (ii) Sufficient confidence exists that the Sponsors have attended Holy Mass for at least one Universal Feast from each of the seven Liturgical Cycles of the Mysteries of Christ of the previous year, being *Immanent, Filial, Eucharistic, Transcendent, Sacred Heart, Redemption* and *Apostolic*, unless a special exemption is granted by the local Ordinary.

XXVII.V – CELEBRATION OF RITE OF MAJORITY

1. Only a legitimately and validly ordained minister may minister the Rite of Majority. Celebration of Rite of Majority

2. The Ordinary Rite of Majority may be celebrated on any Day, except those reserved for Holy Feast Days of Good Friday, Easter Sunday and Christmas Day. The Extraordinary Rite of Majority may not be celebrated on any day reserved for any of the sixty-six (66) Holy Feast Days of the Liturgical Season of the Seven Mysteries of Christ. Valid days of celebration

The Sacred Colour for the Liturgy of Mass shall be **Red** if three (3) or more Supplicants or Sponsors are present for the Rite. Otherwise, the Sacred Colour for the Liturgy of Mass shall remain the same for the liturgical season that the particular Mass is celebrated.

XXVII.VI – ORDINARY RITE OF MAJORITY

1. The *Ordinary Rite of Majority* conferred by a competent minister upon a youth having reached the age of twenty one years, shall be as follows:- Ordinary Rite of Majority

LITURGY OF CHRISTIAN LIFE

Liturgy of Christian Life

(Red sashes are prepared for each Supplicant to be placed over their head and shoulder upon the anointing ceremony.)

PETITION

Ordinary Majority Petition

CELEBRANT

(To all assembled)

I call upon those who seek to make their humble and solemn petition today in the name of Christ our Saviour to now come forward and make their presence and prayer known.

CELEBRANT

What Holy Rite then is it you ask in the name of the Father and of the Son and of the Holy Spirit today?

INITIATE(S)

Majority

CELEBRANT

The Rite of Majority you ask is a most solemn and profound blessing in recognising each of you not only as fully fledged members of our entire society but as fully capable and responsible adults and the future of our church and our people.

Throughout the centuries, enlightened cultures have recognised the example of Christ, that despite all his power and capacity, chose to come to the people in the simplest of garments and means - not upon a throne, or wearing the finest clothes or scents, but as a person stripped of material possessions.

So it was for a time, that Christian kings and even queens would present themselves to the people in remembrance of this example, stripped of all their regal glory, power and wealth at the beginning of the ceremony of coronation and only through the will of the people and their true faith did they transform into the monarch.

In a world that has so immersed itself in material possessions, even a person from a modest upbringing today possesses such material riches that even a wealthy person a few hundred years ago could only imagine. Yet with such material wealth and focus, it is tempting to forget the truth of life and your life as a human being.

The humble garments you wear today and the sense of unease and even possible embarrassment in prostrating yourself before your family and friends today is not a deliberate act of public humiliation, but a profound gift - a gift that I pray you will all never forget throughout your adult lives.

As Christ himself taught us, the last shall be first and the first last. As Scripture teaches us many times, there are some in every generation who find it impossible to humble themselves before their Divine Creator, like the wealthy young man who could not give up his riches to follow Christ.

By your presence and humility today, you allow God to raise you up and embrace you and help you and show his unquenchable love for you in fulfilment of his promises to you.

Today, we thank you in reminding us of the impermanence of material things, and the unyielding strength of a faith founded on love, respect, humility, discipline, enthusiasm, compassion and discernment. Do each of you understand these sacred responsibilities?

ALL

Yes.

OBLIGATION

CELEBRANT

I call upon the Supplicants to kneel and give their solemn vows to their family, their community and the Divine Creator.

CELEBRANT

(Opens his palms before all present before briefly looking to Heaven and then back to all present)

Will you take and accept responsibility for your own actions and consequences? Do you promise to always be truthful to those who depend on you in good times and in bad, and in times of sickness and distress?

SUPPLICANT(S)

I do.

CELEBRANT

Will you take and accept the obligations that come with being a young adult in our community? Do you promise to be humble and persistent in your work and your career, and to always be respectful and mindful of others throughout this journey of life experience?

ALL

I do.

CELEBRANT

Will you take and accept a more active role in the life of

your church? Do you promise to continue to be loyal and support your community and your faith, every day of your life?

ALL

I do.

OBSIGNATION

Ordinary
Majority
Obsignation

CELEBRANT

Then truly this is a joyous day, for we recognise in our spiritual Christian community the continued experiences, growth and life of our beloved in Heaven. Upon the strength of faith of all here present.

CELEBRANT

(Gently makes the sign of the cross on the forehead of each supplicant with Holy Water)

I now gently trace the sign ✠ of the cross upon the forehead of each of you as a sign and seal of the promise made in the name of our Divine Father.

CELEBRANT

Dear Brothers and Sisters, let us ask that all of Heaven look lovingly upon this person who is about to be anointed and upon all here present as an embodiment of his holy Church. We ask this in the name of Christ.

ALL

Amen.

WILL OF THE PEOPLE

Ordinary
Majority
Will of the People

CELEBRANT

Let us pray.

Jesus, through your teachings and sacrifice we have come to no longer fear death, for you have given us eternal life so we can never die.

Heavenly Father, it is our Will and true intention in gratitude for your gifts of healing and our reconciliation into your presence, that we seek to dedicate our lives more fully to enacting your teachings.

We pray you will accept our humble petition and promises as a sign of the truth of our intentions, through Jesus Christ your son.

ALL

Amen.

SPONSOR(S)

By the mystery of your death and resurrection, bathe these sons and daughters in light, give them new life and welcome them as equals into your Church that is the fulfilment of your Living Body.

ALL

Christ hear our prayer.

SPONSOR(S)

Through anointing, make these sons and daughters your faithful followers and witnesses to your gospel.

ALL

Christ hear our prayer.

SPONSOR(S)

Lead them by a holy life to the joys of God's kingdom.

ALL

Christ hear our prayer.

SPONSOR(S)

Make the lives of their parents and godparents examples of faith to inspire them.

ALL

Christ hear our prayer.

SPONSOR(S)

Keep all the families here always in your love.

ALL

Christ hear our prayer.

SPONSOR(S)

Renew the grace of our baptism in each one of us.

ALL

Christ hear our prayer.

HOLY OIL ANOINTING

Ordinary Majority Holy Oil Anointing

(Red sash placed over the head and shoulder of each Supplicant.)

CELEBRANT

We anoint you with the most sacred Oil of Christ in the name of our Lord and our Saviour; may he strengthen you with his power, who lives and reigns for ever and ever.

CELEBRANT

(He anoints each supplicant on the forehead with Chrism Oil)

Be sealed with the gift of the Illumination of the Holy Spirit. May you have strength in the power of Christ our Saviour, who lives and reigns for ever and ever.

ALL

Amen.

UNIVERSAL PROFESSION OF FAITH

Ordinary Majority Universal Profession of Faith

CELEBRANT

My dear brothers and sisters, Our faith is borne of trust in the truth of the Good News of the Risen Christ; and nurtured through our concrete actions as Christians. It is not a message of fear or superstition, but one of genuine certainty in the divine love, mercy and forgiveness of our Eternal Father and Creator. So it is as Christians, we freely and joyfully proclaim by our own will the Good News of Christ. In the spirit of this occasion then, I invite each of you once more to consent and make the seven solemn professions of Christian Faith with a loud and clear voice:

CELEBRANT

First, Do you accept that God the one true Divine Creator exists?; and that everything is part of the divine laws of creation, even if we do not always understand?

ALL

I do.

CELEBRANT

Second, Do you agree that our Eternal Father made humanity in his image?; and that everything in life has a purpose?; and that he has a divine plan for us, even if sometimes we reject his laws?

ALL

I do.

CELEBRANT

Third, Do you reject all forms of evil in this world? and all that seeks to confuse us?; and all forms of wickedness that seeks to entrap our minds and harden our hearts, especially all forms of addiction, exploitation, nihilism and cruelty?

ALL

I do.

CELEBRANT

Fourth, Do you recognise Christ as your Saviour?; and as the embodiment of every person who has lived or will ever live?; and that as a Divine singularity, He truly was borne of flesh; and lived and suffered in life as we do?; and that He willingly sacrificed himself to free all of us, without condition, from the bondage of our transgressions?; and that through such an act of Divine Redemption of Divine Mercy and love, He did make it possible so that all may rise from the death of transgressions and have eternal life?

ALL

I do.

CELEBRANT

Fifth, Do you trust in the true teachings and Good News of the Risen Christ? That our Divine Creator is a loving god, who is merciful and loves us, despite our weaknesses? And that because of the gift of the universal law of free will, God does not seek to condemn us, or punish us, or directly cause us pain? And that no person has the right to curse or abuse or kill in the name of God?

ALL

I do.

CELEBRANT

Sixth, Do you welcome the Holy Spirit, the bringer of light and hope? Who illuminated the hearts and minds of the apostles at Pentecost and today is present with us through the celebration of this holy sacrament?

ALL

I do.

CELEBRANT

Seventh, Do you have faith in the one, holy apostolic Universal Ecclesia of Christ? As the one true living apostolic body of Christ and of all Christians?

ALL

I do.

CELEBRANT

This is our faith. This is the same faith of the disciples and Christian Founders. We joyfully profess it in the name of Christ our Saviour.

ALL

Amen.

BLESSING

CELEBRANT

Father, you give us grace through sacramental signs, which tell us of the wonders of your unseen power. In baptism we used your gift of water, which you have made a rich symbol of the grace you give us in this sacrament. At the very dawn of creation your Spirit breathed on the waters, making them the wellspring of all holiness.

Now with your most Holy Oil, we recognise the newest equal members of our family, who have demonstrated their capacity to discern and choose their faith unto you.

God the Father of our Lord Jesus Christ has freed you from spiritual transgression, given you a new birth by water and oil, and welcomed you into his holy people. As Christ was anointed Priest, Prophet, and King, so may you live always as a member of his body, sharing everlasting life.

ALL

Amen.

XXVII.VII – EXTRAORDINARY RITE OF MAJORITY

1. The *Extraordinary Rite of Majority* conferred by a competent minister in formal dedication as the second Liturgy of Mass to the spirit of one or more deceased children or youth upon the calculation of what would have been the year of their twenty first birthday, shall be as follows: Extraordinary Rite of Majority

LITURGY OF CHRISTIAN LIFE

Liturgy of Christian Life

(Appropriate memorial pictures of the deceased as young adults around the age of twenty one are positioned on display around the altar so that the whole congregation may observe. A Red Ribbon is tied to the side of each picture as a sign of the Rite of Majority.)

PETITION

Extraordinary Majority Petition

CELEBRANT

(To the Sponsors)

Are you the Parent(s) or Relative of a beautiful young life that has reunited with God to continue their unique life in the afterlife?

SPONSOR(S)

Yes

CELEBRANT

(To each Sponsor)

What is the name of your Beloved?

SPONSOR(S)

N.

CELEBRANT

(To the Sponsors)

What Holy Rite then is it you ask in the name of the Father and of the Son and of the Holy Spirit for N. today?

SPONSOR(S)

Majority.

CELEBRANT

The Rite of Majority you ask for is a significant blessing. It is a foundation of our faith in our Divine Creator as the doorway to eternal life. As Parent(s) and Relative(s) here assembled, you have been called by God our Father to demonstrate to all here present your commitment to a fundamental article of Christian faith that our saviour Jesus Christ has opened the door to eternal life for all of us; and our life does not end with physical death; and that we continue to grow and learn and evolve as unique spiritual beings in the hereafter. Do each of you understand these sacred responsibilities?

SPONSOR(S)

Yes.

RECITALS

Extraordinary Majority Recitals

CELEBRANT

Very well, before we proceed, I ask all of you three simple questions of faith and trust in the name of Christ:

CELEBRANT

(Opens his palms before all present before briefly looking to Heaven and then back to all present)

Do you solemnly promise to always keep the memory of your beloved in your hearts and to care for the needs of those still with us in flesh? And to continue to live, experience and give thanks for life to the best of your abilities?

SPONSOR(S)

We do (promise).

CELEBRANT
And do you solemnly promise to trust Christ and your faith in the one true Apostolic Universal Ecclesia that your beloved can never truly die and are always with you? And to honour their memory by accepting the mystery of faith that they may continue to grow and experience a new life in Heaven as we continue to grow and learn and experience life on Earth?

SPONSOR(S)
We do (promise).

CELEBRANT
And do you solemnly promise to uphold the Christian values of care for one another, and not to shut yourself off from life or others? And that you look to express your love and care and respect of all whom we love, by helping those in our community who still need our love and support?

SPONSOR(S)
We do (promise).

OBSIGNATION

CELEBRANT
Then truly this is a joyous day, for we recognise and welcome into our spiritual Christian community a new equal member. Upon the strength of faith of all here present.

CELEBRANT
(Gently makes the sign of the cross on each picture of the departed at the front of the church)

I now gently trace the sign ✠ of the cross upon the memorial of each of our beloved as a sign and seal of the promise made in the name of our Divine Father that all Baptised in the faith are saved and none be condemned.

CELEBRANT
I invite the Parents and Godparents if you so choose, as a mark of your solemn commitment to the promises made here today to gently do the same.

PARENT(S) AND SPONSOR(S)

(Each gently make the sign of the cross on the memory of their beloved)

CELEBRANT

Dear Brothers and Sisters, let us ask that all of Heaven look lovingly upon this person who is about to be anointed as an equal member of our spiritual and temporal family; and upon the Parent(s) and Relatives(s) and all here present as an embodiment of his holy Church. We ask this in the name of Christ.

ALL

Amen.

WILL OF THE PEOPLE

Extraordinary Majority
Will of the People

CELEBRANT

Let us pray.

Jesus, through your teachings and sacrifice we have come to no longer fear death, for you have given us eternal life so we can never die.

Heavenly Father, it is our Will and true intention in gratitude for your gifts of healing and our reconciliation into your presence, that we seek to dedicate our lives more fully to enacting your teachings.

We pray you will accept our humble petition and promises as a sign of the truth of our intentions, through Jesus Christ your son.

ALL

Amen.

SPONSOR(S)

By the mystery of your death and resurrection, bathe these sons and daughters in light, give them new life and welcome them as equals into your Church that is the fulfilment of your Living Body.

ALL

Christ hear our prayer.

SPONSOR(S)
Through anointing, make these sons and daughters your faithful followers and witnesses to your gospel.

ALL
Christ hear our prayer.

SPONSOR(S)
Lead them by a holy life to the joys of God's kingdom.

ALL
Christ hear our prayer.

SPONSOR(S)
Make the lives of their parents and godparents examples of faith to inspire all people.

ALL
Christ hear our prayer.

SPONSOR(S)
Keep all the families here always in your love.

ALL
Christ hear our prayer.

SPONSOR(S)
Renew the grace of our baptism in each one of us.

ALL
Christ hear our prayer.

HOLY OIL ANOINTING

CELEBRANT
We anoint the memory of each of our beloved with the oil of salvation in the name of Christ our Saviour; may he strengthen you with his power, who lives and reigns for ever and ever.

CELEBRANT

(Gently makes the sign of the cross on each picture of the departed with anointing oil at the front of the church)

May you have strength in the power of Christ our Saviour, who lives and reigns for ever and ever.

ALL

Amen.

UNIVERSAL PROFESSION OF FAITH

Extraordinary Majority
Universal Profession of Faith

CELEBRANT

My dear brothers and sisters, Our faith is borne of trust in the truth of the Good News of the Risen Christ; and nurtured through our concrete actions as Christians. It is not a message of fear or superstition, but one of genuine certainty in the divine love, mercy and forgiveness of our Eternal Father and Creator. So it is as Christians, we freely and joyfully proclaim by our own will the Good News of Christ. In the spirit of this occasion then, I invite each of you once more to consent and make the seven solemn professions of Christian Faith with a loud and clear voice:

CELEBRANT

First, Do you accept that God the one true Divine Creator exists?; and that everything is part of the divine laws of creation, even if we do not always understand?

ALL

I do.

CELEBRANT

Second, Do you agree that our Eternal Father made humanity in his image?; and that everything in life has a purpose?; and that he has a divine plan for us, even if sometimes we reject his laws?

ALL

I do.

CELEBRANT

Third, Do you reject all forms of evil in this world? and all that seeks to confuse us?; and all forms of wickedness that seeks to entrap our minds and harden our hearts, especially all forms of addiction, exploitation, nihilism and cruelty?

ALL

I do.

CELEBRANT

Fourth, Do you recognise Christ as your Saviour?; and as the embodiment of every person who has lived or will ever live?; and that as a Divine singularity, He truly was borne of flesh; and lived and suffered in life as we do?; and that He willingly sacrificed himself to free all of us, without condition, from the bondage of our transgressions?; and that through such an act of Divine Redemption of Divine Mercy and love, He did make it possible so that all may rise from the death of transgressions and have eternal life?

ALL

I do.

CELEBRANT

Fifth, Do you trust in the true teachings and Good News of the Risen Christ? That our Divine Creator is a loving god, who is merciful and loves us, despite our weaknesses? And that because of the gift of the universal law of free will, God does not seek to condemn us, or punish us, or directly cause us pain? And that no person has the right to curse or abuse or kill in the name of God?

ALL

I do.

CELEBRANT

Sixth, Do you welcome the Holy Spirit, the bringer of light and hope? Who illuminated the hearts and minds of the apostles at Pentecost and today is present with us through the celebration of this holy sacrament?

ALL

I do.

CELEBRANT

Seventh, Do you have faith in the one, holy apostolic

Universal Ecclesia of Christ? As the one true living apostolic body of Christ and of all Christians?

ALL

I do.

CELEBRANT

This is our faith. This is the same faith of the disciples and Christian Founders. We joyfully profess it in the name of Christ our Saviour.

ALL

Amen.

BLESSING

CELEBRANT

Father, you give us grace through sacramental signs, which tell us of the wonders of your unseen power. In baptism we used your gift of water, which you have made a rich symbol of the grace you give us in this sacrament. At the very dawn of creation your Spirit breathed on the waters, making them the wellspring of all holiness.

Now with your most Holy Oil, we recognise the newest equal members of our family, who have demonstrated their capacity to discern and choose their faith unto you.

God the Father of our Lord Jesus Christ has freed you from spiritual transgression, given you a new birth by water and oil, and welcomed you into his holy people. As Christ was anointed Priest, Prophet, and King, so may you live always as a member of his body, sharing everlasting life.

ALL

Amen.

Title XXVIII – Sacrament of Exultation & Rite of Maturity

XXVIII.I – SACRAMENT OF EXULTATION

1. Exultation (*Ritus Sacramentum Exultatio*) is the sixth of the twelve (12) Apostolic Life Sacraments, also known as "The Twelve", "The Twelve Apostles" and "The Means". Sacrament of Exultation (Ritus Sacramentum Exultatio)

The Sacrament of Exultation and Rite of Maturity shall be granted and administered by the thirty-third (33rd) birthday of an adult in accordance with the most sacred Covenants *Pactum De Singularis Caelum*, *Pactum De Singularis Christus*, and *Missale Christus* and associated approved liturgy.

2. The Sacrament of Exultation and Rite of Maturity is the celebration of the point of transition from being a Young Adult to a fully mature Adult. Divine Purpose of the Sacrament of Exultation Rite of Maturity

XXVIII.II – DIVINE GRACE AND ACTION OF EXULTATION

1. The Divine Grace and Action of *Exultation* is the supernatural effect of the proper ministration of the Rite of Maturity as celebration of the point of transition from being a Young Adult to a fully mature Adult. Divine Grace and Action of Exultation

2. *Exultation* is a wholly Divine and unmerited action, warranted by God and the Divine Creator. It is not an action effected within the temporal realm, nor can it be equated to physical terms or constructs. Understanding of action and Divine Grace of Exultation

3. The Divine Grace and Supernatural Action of *Exultation* is central to the proper effect of the Holy Rite of Maturity. Such supernatural presence and grace is made manifest *first* by the suitable qualification of the recipient; and *second* by the proper authority of one administering the sacrament; and *third* by the constituent parts and order that must be established in order to effect the sacrament. Divine Grace and Action of Sacrament of Exultation

In accord with sacred liturgy, in the absence of one or more of these central requisites, no legitimate manifestation of such Divine Grace and Action can occur.

XXVIII.III – RITE OF MATURITY

1. The Holy Rite of Maturity represents the constituent parts and their order that must be established in order to effect the Divine and Supernatural Sacrament of Exultation. In the absence of one or more of these central requisites, no legitimate manifestation or imprint of the Divine Grace and Action of Exultation can occur. Rite of Maturity

2. There are only two (2) valid and licit forms for the Sacrament of Form of the

Exultation and Rite of Maturity as defined by the most sacred *Missale Christus* and associated approved liturgy being Ordinary and Extraordinary: Sacrament of Exultation Rite of Maturity

(i) "**Ordinary Maturity**" is conferred by a competent minister upon an adult having reached the age of thirty-three (33) years; and

(ii) "**Extraordinary Maturity**" is conferred by a competent minister in formal dedication to the spirit of a still-borne infant, or deceased child or youth or adult upon the calculation of what would have been their thirty-third birthday. Such a ceremony may be conducted as a Special Mass, with such records then entered into the rolls to the fact of such sacred act.

XXVIII.IV – CONDITIONS OF RITE OF MATURITY

1. Conditions of the Rite of Maturity are those requisite qualifications and contingencies permitted in the proper ministration of the Rite. There shall exist only two possible Conditions for the ministration of Rite of Maturity being *Ordinary* and *Extraordinary*:- Conditions of Rite of Maturity

   (i) *Ordinary* are the Conditions necessary for the conferral of the Ordinary Rite of Maturity upon a living human being of the age of thirty-three (33) years; and

   (ii) *Extraordinary* are the Conditions necessary for the conferral of the Rite of Maturity upon a deceased child or adult at the time they would be aged thirty-three on Earth.

2. The conditions for the Ordinary Rite of Maturity are:- Ordinary Conditions

   (i) The Supplicant has received the Rite of Baptism, the Rite of Christening and the Rite of First Communion and the Rite of Majority; and

   (ii) Sufficient confidence exists that the Supplicant has attended Holy Mass for at least one Universal Feast from each of the seven Liturgical Cycles of the Mysteries of Christ of the previous three (3) years, being *Immanent, Filial, Eucharistic, Transcendent, Sacred Heart, Redemption* and *Apostolic*, unless a special exemption is granted by the local Ordinary.

3. The conditions for the Extraordinary Rite of Maturity are:- Extraordinary Conditions

   (i) The Sponsors, whether parents or immediate family members, have received the Rite of Baptism, the Rite of Christening, the Rite of First Communion and the Rite of Majority; and

(ii) Sufficient confidence exists that the Sponsors have attended Holy Mass for at least one Universal Feast from each of the seven Liturgical Cycles of the Mysteries of Christ of the previous three (3) years, being *Immanent, Filial, Eucharistic, Transcendent, Sacred Heart, Redemption* and *Apostolic,* unless a special exemption is granted by the local Ordinary.

XXVIII.V – CELEBRATION OF RITE OF MATURITY

1. Only a legitimately and validly ordained minister may minister the Rite of Maturity. Celebration of Rite of Maturity

2. The Ordinary Rite of Maturity may be celebrated on any Day, except those reserved for Holy Feast Days of Good Friday, Easter Sunday and Christmas Day. The Extraordinary Rite of Maturity may not be celebrated on any day reserved for any of the sixty-six (66) Holy Feast Days of the Liturgical Season of the Seven Mysteries of Christ. Valid days of celebration

The Sacred Colour for the Liturgy of Mass shall be **Blue** if three (3) or more Supplicants or Sponsors are present for the Rite. Otherwise, the Sacred Colour for the Liturgy of Mass shall remain the same for the liturgical season that the particular Mass is celebrated.

XXVIII.VI – ORDINARY RITE OF MATURITY

1. The *Ordinary Rite of Maturity* conferred by a competent minister upon an adult having reached the age of thirty three years, shall be as follows: Ordinary Rite of Maturity

LITURGY OF CHRISTIAN LIFE

Liturgy of Christian Life

(Blue sashes are prepared for each Supplicant to be placed over their head and shoulder upon the anointing ceremony.)

PETITION

Ordinary Maturity Petition

CELEBRANT

(To all assembled)

I call upon those who seek to make their humble and solemn petition today in the name of Christ our Saviour to now come forward and make their presence and prayer known.

(The young adults in simple plain garments

come forward and kneel before the celebrant)

CELEBRANT

What Holy Rite then is it you ask in the name of the Father and of the Son and of the Holy Spirit today?

INITIATE(S)

Maturity

CELEBRANT

The Rite of Maturity you ask is a most solemn and key blessing in recognising each of you as adult members of our entire society and the future of our church and our people. It is an important and necessary time of discernment. How many risks are we prepared to take? How may we further our careers and financial and social condition? How much we are prepared to assume obligations that must be repaid in the future?

The Age of Maturity is an age when we must make more and more prudent decisions against limited resources and time and the many that may call upon our support and time. Yet fine garments do not make you more special or who you are. Acquiring more and more material possessions for the sake of it does not make a person extraordinary or truly memorable. Today you are witnesses to the living words of Christ. At this moment, you follow in the footsteps of some of the greatest people of history by humbling yourself before your Loving Eternal Father and reminding yourself that though your body will ultimately decay and die, your mind and spirit is immortal and can never die.

The Rite of Maturity is a key remembrance that you are not alone. Christ and the Holy Spirit are with you to help guide you and support you. Today, we are once again reminded of the impermanence of material things, and the unyielding strength of a faith founded on love, respect, humility, discipline, enthusiasm, compassion and discernment. Do each of you understand these sacred responsibilities?

ALL

Yes.

OBLIGATION

Ordinary
Maturity
Obligation

CELEBRANT

I call upon the Supplicants to kneel and give their solemn vows to their family, their community and the Divine Creator.

CELEBRANT

(Opens his palms before all present before briefly looking to Heaven and then back to all present)

Will you provide and pledge fair and reasonable support to those of your own blood and family that depend on you? Do you promise to be prudent and wise in your financial and personal affairs?

SUPPLICANT(S)

I do.

CELEBRANT

Will you provide and pledge a deeper commitment and interest in the health and well being of your colleagues, friends and community? Do you promise to be compassionate and kind without having to accept other peoples burdens and life lessons that are not your own?

ALL

I do.

CELEBRANT

Will you provide and pledge regular contributions to the life of your local church? Do you promise to continue to be a loyal and active member of your community and your faith?

ALL

I do.

OBSIGNATION

Ordinary
Maturity
Obsignation

CELEBRANT

Then truly this is a joyous day, for we welcome into our Christian community a new adult member. Upon the strength of faith of all here present.

CELEBRANT

(Gently makes the sign of the cross on the forehead of each supplicant with Holy Water)

I now gently trace the sign ✠ of the cross upon the forehead of each of you as a sign and seal of the promise made in the name of our Divine Father.

CELEBRANT

Dear Brothers and Sisters, let us ask that all of Heaven look lovingly upon this person who is about to be anointed and upon all here present as an embodiment of his holy Church. We ask this in the name of Christ.

ALL

Amen.

WILL OF THE PEOPLE

Ordinary Maturity Will of the People

CELEBRANT

Let us pray.

Jesus, through your teachings and sacrifice we have come to no longer fear death, for you have given us eternal life so we can never die.

Heavenly Father, it is our Will and true intention in gratitude for your gifts of healing and our reconciliation into your presence, that we seek to dedicate our lives more fully to enacting your teachings.

We pray you will accept our humble petition and promises as a sign of the truth of our intentions, through Jesus Christ your son.

ALL

Amen.

CELEBRANT

By the mystery of your death and resurrection, bathe these sons and daughters in light, give them renewed strength, courage and mission of life as members of your Church that is your Living Body.

ALL

Christ hear our prayer.

CELEBRANT
Through anointing, make these sons and daughters your faithful followers and witnesses to your gospel.

ALL
Christ hear our prayer.

CELEBRANT
Lead them by a holy life to the joys of God's kingdom.

ALL
Christ hear our prayer.

CELEBRANT
Make their lives an inspiration to all as that of perseverance, forgiveness and compassion.

ALL
Christ hear our prayer.

CELEBRANT
Keep all the families here always in your love.

ALL
Christ hear our prayer.

CELEBRANT
Renew the grace of our baptism in each one of us.

ALL
Christ hear our prayer.

HOLY OIL ANOINTING

CELEBRANT
We anoint you with the most sacred Oil of Christ in the name of our Lord and our Saviour; may he strengthen you with his power, who lives and reigns for ever and ever.

CELEBRANT

(He anoints each person on the forehead with Chrism Oil)

Be sealed with the gift of Exultation of the Holy Spirit. May you have strength in the power of Christ our Saviour, who lives and reigns for ever and ever.

ALL

Amen.

UNIVERSAL PROFESSION OF FAITH

CELEBRANT

My dear brothers and sisters, Our faith is borne of trust in the truth of the Good News of the Risen Christ; and nurtured through our concrete actions as Christians. It is not a message of fear or superstition, but one of genuine certainty in the divine love, mercy and forgiveness of our Eternal Father and Creator. So it is as Christians, we freely and joyfully proclaim by our own will the Good News of Christ. In the spirit of this occasion then, I invite each of you once more to consent and make the seven solemn professions of Christian Faith with a loud and clear voice:

CELEBRANT

First, Do you accept that God the one true Divine Creator exists?; and that everything is part of the divine laws of creation, even if we do not always understand?

ALL

I do.

CELEBRANT

Second, Do you agree that our Eternal Father made humanity in his image?; and that everything in life has a purpose?; and that he has a divine plan for us, even if sometimes we reject his laws?

ALL

I do.

CELEBRANT

Third, Do you reject all forms of evil in this world? and all that seeks to confuse us?; and all forms of wickedness that seeks to entrap our minds and harden our hearts, especially all forms of addiction, exploitation, nihilism and cruelty?

ALL

I do.

CELEBRANT

Fourth, Do you recognise Christ as your Saviour?; and as the embodiment of every person who has lived or will ever live?; and that as a Divine singularity, He truly was borne of flesh; and lived and suffered in life as we do?; and that He willingly sacrificed himself to free all of us, without condition, from the bondage of our transgressions?; and that through such an act of Divine Redemption of Divine Mercy and love, He did make it possible so that all may rise from the death of transgressions and have eternal life?

ALL

I do.

CELEBRANT

Fifth, Do you trust in the true teachings and Good News of the Risen Christ? That our Divine Creator is a loving god, who is merciful and loves us, despite our weaknesses? And that because of the gift of the universal law of free will, God does not seek to condemn us, or punish us, or directly cause us pain? And that no person has the right to curse or abuse or kill in the name of God?

ALL

I do.

CELEBRANT

Sixth, Do you welcome the Holy Spirit, the bringer of light and hope? Who illuminated the hearts and minds of the apostles at Pentecost and today is present with us through the celebration of this holy sacrament?

ALL

I do.

CELEBRANT

Seventh, Do you have faith in the one, holy apostolic Universal Ecclesia of Christ? As the one true living apostolic body of Christ and of all Christians?

ALL

I do.

CELEBRANT

This is our faith. This is the same faith of the disciples and Christian Founders. We joyfully profess it in the name of Christ our Saviour.

ALL

Amen.

BLESSING

Ordinary Maturity Blessing

CELEBRANT

Father, you give us grace through sacramental signs, which tell us of the wonders of your unseen power. In baptism we used your gift of water, which you have made a rich symbol of the grace you give us in this sacrament. At the very dawn of creation your Spirit breathed on the waters, making them the wellspring of all holiness.

Now with you most Holy Oil, we recognise the newest equal members of our family, who have demonstrated their capacity to discern and choose their faith unto you.

God the Father of our Lord Jesus Christ has freed you from spiritual transgression, given you a new birth by water and oil, and welcomed you into his holy people. As Christ was anointed Priest, Prophet, and King, so may you live always as a member of his body, sharing everlasting life.

ALL

Amen.

XXVIII.VII – EXTRAORDINARY RITE OF MATURITY

Extraordinary Rite of Maturity

1. The *Extraordinary Rite of Maturity* conferred by a competent minister in formal dedication to the spirit of a still-born infant, or deceased child or youth or adult upon the calculation of what would have been their thirty-third birthday, shall be as follows:

LITURGY OF CHRISTIAN LIFE

Liturgy of Christian Life

(Appropriate memorial pictures of the deceased as adults around the age of thirty three are positioned on display around the altar so that the whole congregation may observe. A Blue Ribbon is tied to the side of each picture as a sign of the Rite of Maturity.)

PETITION

Extraordinary Maturity
Petition

CELEBRANT

(To the Sponsors)

Are you the Parent(s) or Relative(s) of a unique life and soul that has reunited with God and continues their journey in the hereafter?

SPONSOR(S)

Yes

CELEBRANT

(To each Sponsor)

What is the name of your Beloved?

SPONSOR(S)

N.

CELEBRANT

(To the Sponsors)

What Holy Rite then is it you ask in the name of the Father and of the Son and of the Holy Spirit for N. today?

SPONSOR(S)

Maturity.

CELEBRANT

The Rite of Maturity you ask for is a significant blessing. It is a foundation of our faith in our Divine Creator as the doorway to eternal life. As Parent(s) and Relative(s) here assembled, you have been called by God our Father to demonstrate to all here present your commitment to a fundamental article of Christian faith that our saviour Jesus Christ has opened the door to eternal life for all of us; and our life does not end with physical death; and that we continue to grow and learn and evolve as unique spiritual beings in the hereafter. Do each of you understand this sacred responsibility?

SPONSOR(S)

Yes.

RECITALS

CELEBRANT

Very well, before we proceed, I ask all of you three simple questions of faith and trust in the name of Christ:

CELEBRANT

(Opens his palms before all present before briefly looking to Heaven and then back to all present)

Do you solemnly promise to always keep the memory of your beloved in your hearts and to care for the needs of those still with us in flesh? And to continue to live, experience and give thanks for life to the best of your abilities?

SPONSOR(S)

We do (promise).

CELEBRANT

And do you solemnly promise to trust Christ and your faith in the one true Apostolic Universal Ecclesia that your beloved can never truly die and are always with you? And to honour their memory by accepting the mystery of faith that they may continue to grow and experience a new life in Heaven as we continue to grow and learn and experience life on Earth?

SPONSOR(S)

We do (promise).

CELEBRANT

And do you solemnly promise to uphold the Christian values of care for one another, and not to shut yourself off from life or others? And that you look to express your love and care and respect of all whom we love, by helping those in our community who still need our love and support?

SPONSOR(S)

We do (promise).

OBSIGNATION

Extraordinary
Maturity
Obsignation

CELEBRANT

Then truly this is a joyous day, for we recognise in our spiritual Christian community the continued experiences, growth and life of our beloved in Heaven. Upon the strength of faith of all here present.

CELEBRANT

(Gently makes the sign of the cross on each picture of the departed at the front of the church)

I now gently trace the sign ✠ of the cross upon the memorial of each of our beloved as a sign and seal of the promise made in the name of our Divine Father that all Baptised in the faith are saved and none be condemned.

CELEBRANT

I invite the Parents and Godparents if you so choose, as a mark of your solemn commitment to the promises made here today to gently do the same.

PARENT(S) AND SPONSOR(S)

(Each gently make the sign of the cross on the memory of their beloved)

CELEBRANT

Dear Brothers and Sisters, let us ask that all of Heaven look lovingly upon this person who is about to be anointed as an equal member of our spiritual and temporal family; and upon the Parent(s) and Godparent(s) and all here present as an embodiment of his holy Church. We ask this in the name of Christ.

ALL

Amen.

WILL OF THE PEOPLE

CELEBRANT

Let us pray.

Jesus, through your teachings and sacrifice we have come to no longer fear death, for you have given us eternal life so we can never die.

Heavenly Father, it is our Will and true intention in gratitude for your gifts of healing and our reconciliation into your presence, that we seek to dedicate our lives more fully to enacting your teachings.

We pray you will accept our humble petition and promises as a sign of the truth of our intentions, through Jesus Christ your son.

ALL

Amen.

SPONSOR(S)

By the mystery of your death and resurrection, bathe these sons and daughters in light, give them new life and welcome them as equals into your Church that is the fulfilment of your Living Body.

ALL

Christ hear our prayer.

SPONSOR(S)

Through anointing, make these sons and daughters your faithful followers and witnesses to your gospel.

ALL

Christ hear our prayer.

SPONSOR(S)

Lead them by a holy life to the joys of God's kingdom.

ALL

Christ hear our prayer.

SPONSOR(S)

Make the lives of their parents and godparents examples of

faith to inspire all people.

ALL

Christ hear our prayer.

SPONSOR(S)

Keep all the families here always in your love.

ALL

Christ hear our prayer.

SPONSOR(S)

Renew the grace of our baptism in each one of us.

ALL

Christ hear our prayer.

HOLY OIL ANOINTING

Extraordinary Maturity
Holy Oil Anointing

CELEBRANT

We anoint the memory of each of our beloved with the oil of salvation in the name of Christ our Saviour; may he strengthen you with his power, who lives and reigns for ever and ever.

CELEBRANT

(Gently makes the sign of the cross on each picture of the departed with anointing oil at the front of the church)

May you have strength in the power of Christ our Saviour, who lives and reigns for ever and ever.

ALL

Amen.

UNIVERSAL PROFESSION OF FAITH

Extraordinary Maturity
Universal Profession of Faith

CELEBRANT

My dear brothers and sisters, Our faith is borne of trust in the truth of the Good News of the Risen Christ; and nurtured through our concrete actions as Christians. It is not a message of fear or superstition, but one of genuine certainty in the divine love, mercy and forgiveness of our Eternal Father and Creator. So it is as Christians, we freely and joyfully proclaim by our own will the Good News of Christ. In the spirit of this occasion then, I invite each of you once more to consent and make the seven solemn professions of Christian Faith with a loud and clear voice:

CELEBRANT

First, Do you accept that God the one true Divine Creator exists?; and that everything is part of the divine laws of creation, even if we do not always understand?

ALL

I do.

CELEBRANT

Second, Do you agree that our Eternal Father made humanity in his image?; and that everything in life has a purpose?; and that he has a divine plan for us, even if sometimes we reject his laws?

ALL

I do.

CELEBRANT

Third, Do you reject all forms of evil in this world? and all that seeks to confuse us?; and all forms of wickedness that seeks to entrap our minds and harden our hearts, especially all forms of addiction, exploitation, nihilism and cruelty?

ALL

I do.

CELEBRANT

Fourth, Do you recognise Christ as your Saviour?; and as the embodiment of every person who has lived or will ever live?; and that as a Divine singularity, He truly was borne of flesh; and lived and suffered in life as we do?; and that He willingly sacrificed himself to free all of us, without condition, from the bondage of our transgressions?; and that through such an act of Divine Redemption of Divine Mercy and love, He did make it possible so that all may rise from the death of transgressions and have eternal life?

ALL

I do.

CELEBRANT

Fifth, Do you trust in the true teachings and Good News of the Risen Christ? That our Divine Creator is a loving god, who is merciful and loves us, despite our weaknesses? And that because of the gift of the universal law of free will, God does not seek to condemn us, or punish us, or directly cause us pain? And that no person has the right to curse or abuse or kill in the name of God?

ALL

I do.

CELEBRANT

Sixth, Do you welcome the Holy Spirit, the bringer of light and hope? Who illuminated the hearts and minds of the apostles at Pentecost and today is present with us through the celebration of this holy sacrament?

ALL

I do.

CELEBRANT

Seventh, Do you have faith in the one, holy apostolic Universal Ecclesia of Christ? As the one true living apostolic body of Christ and of all Christians?

ALL

I do.

CELEBRANT

This is our faith. This is the same faith of the disciples and Christian Founders. We joyfully profess it in the name of Christ our Saviour.

ALL

Amen.

BLESSING

CELEBRANT

Father, you give us grace through sacramental signs, which tell us of the wonders of your unseen power. In baptism we used your gift of water, which you have made a rich symbol of the grace you give us in this sacrament. At the very dawn of creation your Spirit breathed on the waters, making them the wellspring of all holiness.

Now with you most Holy Oil, we recognise the newest equal members of our family, who have demonstrated their capacity to discern and choose their faith unto you.

God the Father of our Lord Jesus Christ has freed you from spiritual transgression, given you a new birth by water and oil, and welcomed you into his holy people. As Christ was anointed Priest, Prophet, and King, so may you live always as a member of his body, sharing everlasting life.

ALL

Amen.

Title XXIX – Sacrament of Glorification & Rite of Seniority

XXIX.I – SACRAMENT OF GLORIFICATION

1. Glorification (*Ritus Sacramentum Glorificatio*) is the seventh of the twelve (12) Apostolic Life Sacraments, also known as "The Twelve", "The Twelve Apostles" and "The Means". Sacrament of Glorification (Ritus Sacramentum Glorificatio)

The Sacrament of Glorification and Rite of Seniority shall be granted and administered by the fifty-fifth (55th) birthday of an adult in accordance with the most sacred Covenants *Pactum De Singularis Caelum*, *Pactum De Singularis Christus*, and *Missale Christus* and associated approved liturgy.

2. The Sacrament of Glorification and Rite of Seniority is the celebration of the point of transition from Maturity to Seniority. It recognises the experience and contribution of older adults while they are still active members of their society. Divine Purpose of the Sacrament of Glorification

XXIX.II – DIVINE GRACE AND ACTION OF GLORIFICATION

1. The Divine Grace and Action of *Glorification* is the supernatural effect of the proper ministration of the Rite of Seniority as celebration of the point of transition from Maturity to Seniority. Divine Grace and Action of Glorification

2. *Glorification* is a wholly Divine and unmerited action, warranted by God and the Divine Creator. It is not an action effected within the temporal realm, nor can it be equated to physical terms or constructs. Understanding of action and Divine Grace of Glorification

3. The Divine Grace and Supernatural Action of *Glorification* is central to the proper effect of the Holy Rite of Seniority. Such supernatural presence and grace is made manifest *first* by the suitable qualification of the recipient; and *second* by the proper authority of one administering the sacrament; and *third* by the constituent parts and order that must be established in order to effect the sacrament. Divine Grace and Action of Sacrament of Glorification

In accord with sacred liturgy, in the absence of one or more of these central requisites, no legitimate manifestation of such Divine Grace and Action can occur.

XXIX.III – RITE OF SENIORITY

1. The Holy Rite of Seniority represents the constituent parts and their order that must be established in order to effect the Divine and Supernatural Sacrament of Glorification. In the absence of one or more of these central requisites, no legitimate manifestation or imprint of the Divine Grace and Action of Glorification can occur. Rite of Seniority

2. There are only two (2) valid and licit forms for the the Sacrament of Glorification and Rite of Seniority as defined by the most sacred *Missale Christus* and associated approved liturgy being Ordinary and Extraordinary:- Form of the Sacrament of Glorification

   (i) "**Ordinary Seniority**" is conferred by a competent minister upon an adult having reached the age of fifty-five (55) years; and

   (i) "**Extraordinary Seniority**" is conferred by a competent minister in formal dedication to the spirit of a still-borne infant, or deceased child or youth or adult upon the calculation of what would have been their fifty-fifth birthday with such records then entered into the rolls to the fact of such sacred act.

XXIX.IV – CONDITIONS OF RITE OF SENIORITY

1. Conditions of the Rite of Seniority are those requisite qualifications and contingencies permitted in the proper ministration of the Rite. There shall exist only two (2) possible Conditions for the ministration of Rite of Seniority being *Ordinary* and *Extraordinary*:- Conditions of Rite of Seniority

   (i) *Ordinary* are the Conditions necessary for the conferral of the Ordinary Rite of Seniority upon a living human being of the age of fifty-five (55) years; and

   (ii) *Extraordinary* are the Conditions necessary for the conferral of the Rite of Seniority upon a deceased child or adult at the time they would be fifty-five (55) years on Earth.

2. The conditions for the Ordinary Rite of Seniority are:- Ordinary Conditions

   (i) The Supplicant has received the Rite of Baptism, the Rite of Christening, the Rite of First Communion, the Rite of Majority and the Rite of Maturity; and

   (ii) Sufficient confidence exists that the Supplicant has attended Holy Mass for at least one Universal Feast from each of the seven Liturgical Cycles of the Mysteries of Christ of the previous three (3) years, being *Immanent, Filial, Eucharistic, Transcendent, Sacred Heart, Redemption* and *Apostolic*, unless a special exemption is granted by the local Ordinary.

3. The conditions for the Extraordinary Rite of Seniority are:- Extraordinary Conditions

   (i) The Sponsors, whether parents or immediate family members, have received the Rite of Baptism, the Rite of Christening, the Rite of First Communion and the Rite of Majority; and

(ii) Sufficient confidence exists that the Sponsors have attended Holy Mass for at least one Universal Feast from each of the seven Liturgical Cycles of the Mysteries of Christ of the previous three (3) years, being *Immanent, Filial, Eucharistic, Transcendent, Sacred Heart, Redemption* and *Apostolic*, unless a special exemption is granted by the local Ordinary.

XXIX.V – CELEBRATION OF RITE OF SENIORITY

1. Only a legitimately and validly ordained minister may minister the Rite of Seniority. Celebration of Rite of Seniority

2. The Ordinary Rite of Seniority may be celebrated on any Day, except those reserved for Holy Feast Days of Good Friday, Easter Sunday and Christmas Day. The Extraordinary Rite of Seniority may not be celebrated on any day reserved for any of the sixty-six (66) Holy Feast Days of the Liturgical Season of the Seven Mysteries of Christ. Valid days of celebration

The Sacred Colour for the Liturgy of Mass shall be **Gold** if three (3) or more Supplicants or Sponsors are present for the Rite. Otherwise, the Sacred Colour for the Liturgy of Mass shall remain the same for the liturgical season that the particular Mass is celebrated.

XXIX.VI – ORDINARY RITE OF SENIORITY

1. The *Ordinary Rite of Seniority* conferred by a competent minister upon an adult having reached the age of fifty-five (55) years, shall be as follows:- Ordinary Rite of Seniority

LITURGY OF CHRISTIAN LIFE

Liturgy of Christian Life

(Gold sashes are prepared for each Supplicant to be placed over their head and shoulder upon the anointing ceremony.)

PETITION

Ordinary Seniority Petition

CELEBRANT

(To all assembled)

I call upon those who seek to make their humble and solemn petition today in the name of Christ our Saviour to now come forward and make their presence and prayer known.

(The supplicants come forward and kneel before the celebrant)

CELEBRANT

What Holy Rite then is it you ask in the name of the Father and of the Son and of the Holy Spirit today?

INITIATE(S)

Seniority

CELEBRANT

The Rite of Seniority you ask is a most solemn and significant blessing in recognising a milestone age of life and of trials; and of accomplishments and failures; at a time where we may still be physically strong or facing real struggles of health. A pivotal time of recognition of the experience and contribution of older adults whilst hopefully still active members of society.

Our Saviour Jesus Christ taught us through his own words and actions how to discern and avoid the traps of a material and sometimes misguided world: To reject the egoistic temptations of nihilism in all its forms; and To reject all false notions that would simply reduce life to its mere relative parts; and above all To reject all forms of fear and superstition that would seek to worship death or bigotry or false notions of pious judgement.

God gave us the gift of intellect, so that we might think for our selves and have the capacity to discern truth from falsity; and positive action from negative action. It is why God gave us the gift of free will so that we might use such a gift with discernment and choose wisely.

Christ calls everyone of us to use the talents given to us. Not to squander this precious gift of life or to suffocate under a mountain of regrets and anguish. The Age of Seniority is a time to be cherished as much as any age of our life journey. To continue to learn, to discover and to contribute positively to our community and world.

Through the Rite of Seniority we are reminded through the Holy Spirit that with greater knowledge and resources we must make even greater contributions to the well being of our community. Acquiring more and more material possessions for the sake of it does not make a person extraordinary or truly memorable. The legacy of a person is not granite or marble but consists of goodness, their deeds, love and compassion.

Today you are witnesses again to the living words of Christ. By humbling yourself before your Loving Eternal Father and reminding yourself that though your body will ultimately decay and die, your mind and spirit is immortal and can never die. Today, we thank you in reminding us of the impermanence of material things, but the unyielding strength of a faith founded on love, respect, humility, discipline enthusiasm, compassion and discernment. Do each of you understand these sacred responsibilities?

ALL

Yes.

OBLIGATION

Ordinary
Seniority
Obligation

CELEBRANT

I call upon the Supplicants to kneel and give their solemn vows to their family, their community and the Divine Creator.

CELEBRANT

(Opens his palms before all present before briefly looking to Heaven and then back to all present)

Will you provide and pledge prudent and wise support to those of your own family and friends that depend on you? Do you promise to forgive those that have hurt you and make amends with those you yourself have hurt?

SUPPLICANT(S)

I do.

CELEBRANT

Will you provide and pledge a real commitment and interest in the health and well being of your colleagues, friends and community? Do you promise to be compassionate and kind without having to accept other peoples burdens and life lessons that are not your own?

ALL

I do.

CELEBRANT

Will you provide and pledge regular contributions to the life of your local church? Do you promise to continue to be a loyal and active member of your community and your faith?

ALL

I do.

OBSIGNATION

Ordinary Seniority Obsignation

CELEBRANT

Then truly this is a joyous day, for we welcome into our Christian community a new senior member. Upon the strength of faith of all here present.

CELEBRANT

(Gently makes the sign of the cross on the forehead of each supplicant with Holy Water)

I now gently trace the sign ✠ of the cross upon the forehead of each of you as a sign and seal of the promise made in the name of our Divine Father.

CELEBRANT

Dear Brothers and Sisters, let us ask that all of Heaven look lovingly upon this person who is about to be anointed and upon all here present as an embodiment of his holy Church. We ask this in the name of Christ.

ALL

Amen.

WILL OF THE PEOPLE

Ordinary Seniority Will of the People

CELEBRANT

Let us pray.

Jesus, through your teachings and sacrifice we have come to no longer fear death, for you have given us eternal life so we can never die.

Heavenly Father, it is our Will and true intention in gratitude for your gifts of healing and our reconciliation into your presence, that we seek to dedicate our lives more fully to enacting your teachings.

We pray you will accept our humble petition and promises

as a sign of the truth of our intentions, through Jesus Christ your son.

ALL

Amen.

SPONSOR(S)

By the mystery of your death and resurrection, bathe these sons and daughters in light, give them renewed strength, courage and mission of life as members of your Church that is your Living Body.

ALL

Christ hear our prayer.

SPONSOR(S)

Through anointing, make these sons and daughters your faithful followers and witnesses to your gospel.

ALL

Christ hear our prayer.

SPONSOR(S)

Lead them by a holy life to the joys of God's kingdom.

ALL

Christ hear our prayer.

SPONSOR(S)

Make the lives of their parents and godparents examples of faith to inspire them.

ALL

Christ hear our prayer.

SPONSOR(S)

Keep all the families here always in your love.

ALL

Christ hear our prayer.

SPONSOR(S)

Renew the grace of our baptism in each one of us.

ALL
Christ hear our prayer.

HOLY OIL ANOINTING

Ordinary Seniority Holy Oil Anointing

CELEBRANT
We anoint you with the most sacred Oil of Christ in the name of our Lord and our Saviour; may he strengthen you with his power, who lives and reigns for ever and ever.

CELEBRANT
(He anoints each person on the forehead with Chrism Oil)

Be sealed with the gift of Glorification of the Holy Spirit. May you have strength in the power of Christ our Saviour, who lives and reigns for ever and ever.

ALL
Amen.

UNIVERSAL PROFESSION OF FAITH

Ordinary Seniority Universal Profession of Faith

CELEBRANT
My dear brothers and sisters, Our faith is borne of trust in the truth of the Good News of the Risen Christ; and nurtured through our concrete actions as Christians. It is not a message of fear or superstition, but one of genuine certainty in the divine love, mercy and forgiveness of our Eternal Father and Creator. So it is as Christians, we freely and joyfully proclaim by our own will the Good News of Christ. In the spirit of this occasion then, I invite each of you once more to consent and make the seven solemn professions of Christian Faith with a loud and clear voice:

CELEBRANT
First, Do you accept that God the one true Divine Creator exists?; and that everything is part of the divine laws of creation, even if we do not always understand?

ALL
I do.

CELEBRANT

Second, Do you agree that our Eternal Father made humanity in his image?; and that everything in life has a purpose?; and that he has a divine plan for us, even if sometimes we reject his laws?

ALL

I do.

CELEBRANT

Third, Do you reject all forms of evil in this world? and all that seeks to confuse us?; and all forms of wickedness that seeks to entrap our minds and harden our hearts, especially all forms of addiction, exploitation, nihilism and cruelty?

ALL

I do.

CELEBRANT

Fourth, Do you recognise Christ as your Saviour?; and as the embodiment of every person who has lived or will ever live?; and that as a Divine singularity, He truly was borne of flesh; and lived and suffered in life as we do?; and that He willingly sacrificed himself to free all of us, without condition, from the bondage of our transgressions?; and that through such an act of Divine Redemption of Divine Mercy and love, He did make it possible so that all may rise from the death of transgressions and have eternal life?

ALL

I do.

CELEBRANT

Fifth, Do you trust in the true teachings and Good News of the Risen Christ? That our Divine Creator is a loving god, who is merciful and loves us, despite our weaknesses? And that because of the gift of the universal law of free will, God does not seek to condemn us, or punish us, or directly cause us pain? And that no person has the right to curse or abuse or kill in the name of God?

ALL

I do.

CELEBRANT

Sixth, Do you welcome the Holy Spirit, the bringer of light and hope? Who illuminated the hearts and minds of the apostles at Pentecost and today is present with us through the celebration of this holy sacrament?

ALL

I do.

CELEBRANT

Seventh, Do you have faith in the one, holy apostolic Universal Ecclesia of Christ? As the one true living apostolic body of Christ and of all Christians?

ALL

I do.

CELEBRANT

This is our faith. This is the same faith of the disciples and Christian Founders. We joyfully profess it in the name of Christ our Saviour.

ALL

Amen.

BLESSING

CELEBRANT

Father, you give us grace through sacramental signs, which tell us of the wonders of your unseen power. In baptism we used your gift of water, which you have made a rich symbol of the grace you give us in this sacrament. At the very dawn of creation your Spirit breathed on the waters, making them the wellspring of all holiness.

Now with you most Holy Oil, we recognise the newest equal members of our family, who have demonstrated their capacity to discern and choose their faith unto you.

God the Father of our Lord Jesus Christ has freed you from spiritual transgression, given you a new birth by water and oil, and welcomed you into his holy people. As Christ was anointed Priest, Prophet, and King, so may you live always as a member of his body, sharing everlasting life.

ALL

Amen.

XXIX.VII – EXTRAORDINARY RITE OF SENIORITY

1. The *Extraordinary Rite of Seniority* conferred by a competent minister in formal dedication to the spirit of a still-born infant, or deceased child or youth or adult upon the calculation of what would have been their fifty-fifth birthday, shall be as follows:

Extraordinary Rite of Seniority

LITURGY OF CHRISTIAN LIFE

Liturgy of Christian Life

(Appropriate memorial pictures of the deceased as adults around the age of thirty three (33) years if they passed before the age of 33 or a picture of their age when they died if before the age of 55 years are positioned on display around the altar so that the whole congregation may observe. A Gold Ribbon is tied to the side of each picture as a sign of the Rite of Seniority.)

PETITION

Extraordinary Seniority Petition

CELEBRANT

(To the Sponsors)

Are you Parent(s) or Relative(s) of a unique life and spirit that has reunited with God and continues their journey in the hereafter?

SPONSOR(S)

Yes

CELEBRANT

(To each Sponsor)

What is the name of your Beloved?

SPONSOR(S)

N.

CELEBRANT

(To the Sponsors)

What Holy Rite then is it you ask in the name of the Father and of the Son and of the Holy Spirit for N. today?

SPONSOR(S)

Seniority.

CELEBRANT

The Rite of Seniority you ask for is a significant blessing. It is a foundation of our faith in our Divine Creator as the doorway to eternal life. As Parent(s) and Relative(s) here assembled, you have been called by God our Father to demonstrate to all here present your commitment to a fundamental article of Christian faith that our saviour Jesus Christ has opened the door to eternal life for all of us; and our life does not end with physical death; and that we continue to grow and learn and evolve as unique spiritual beings in the hereafter. Do each of you understand this sacred responsibility?

SPONSOR(S)

Yes.

RECITALS

CELEBRANT

Very well, before we proceed, I ask all of you three simple questions of faith and trust in the name of Christ:

CELEBRANT

(Opens his palms before all present before briefly looking to Heaven and then back to all present)

Do you solemnly promise to always keep the memory of your beloved in your hearts and to care for the needs of those still with us in flesh? And to continue to live, experience and give thanks for life to the best of your abilities?

ALL

We do (promise).

CELEBRANT

And do you solemnly promise to trust Christ and your faith in the one true Apostolic Universal Ecclesia that your beloved can never truly die and are always with you? And to honour their memory by accepting the mystery of faith that they may continue to grow and experience a new life in Heaven as we continue to grow and learn and experience life on Earth?

ALL

We do (promise).

CELEBRANT

And do you solemnly promise to uphold the Christian values of care for one another, and not to shut yourself off from life or others? And that you look to express your love and care and respect of all whom we love, by helping those in our community who still need our love and support?

ALL

We do (promise).

OBSIGNATION

Extraordinary
Seniority
Obsignation

CELEBRANT

Then truly this is a joyous day, for we recognise in our spiritual Christian community the continued experiences, growth and life of our beloved in Heaven. Upon the strength of faith of all here present.

CELEBRANT

(Gently makes the sign of the cross on each picture of the departed at the front of the church)

I now gently trace the sign ✠ of the cross upon the memorial of each of our beloved as a sign and seal of the promise made in the name of our Divine Father that all Baptised in the faith are saved and none be condemned.

CELEBRANT

I invite the Family and Sponsors if you so choose, as a mark of your solemn commitment to the promises made here today to gently do the same.

PARENT(S) AND SPONSOR(S)

(Each gently make the sign of the cross on the

memory of their beloved)

CELEBRANT
Dear Brothers and Sisters, let us ask that all of Heaven look lovingly upon this person who is about to be anointed and all here present as an embodiment of his holy Church. We ask this in the name of Christ.

ALL
Amen.

WILL OF THE PEOPLE

CELEBRANT
Let us pray.

Jesus, through your teachings and sacrifice we have come to no longer fear death, for you have given us eternal life so we can never die.

Heavenly Father, it is our Will and true intention in gratitude for your gifts of healing and our reconciliation into your presence, that we seek to dedicate our lives more fully to enacting your teachings.

We pray you will accept our humble petition and promises as a sign of the truth of our intentions, through Jesus Christ your son.

ALL
Amen.

SPONSOR(S)
By the mystery of your death and resurrection, bathe these sons and daughters in light, give them new life and welcome them as equals into your Church that is the fulfilment of your Living Body.

ALL
Christ hear our prayer.

SPONSOR(S)
Through anointing, make these sons and daughters your faithful followers and witnesses to your gospel.

ALL
Christ hear our prayer.

SPONSOR(S)
Lead them by a holy life to the joys of God's kingdom.

ALL
Christ hear our prayer.

SPONSOR(S)
Make the lives of their parents and godparents examples of faith to inspire all people.

ALL
Christ hear our prayer.

SPONSOR(S)
Keep all the families here always in your love.

ALL
Christ hear our prayer.

SPONSOR(S)
Renew the grace of our baptism in each one of us.

ALL
Christ hear our prayer.

HOLY OIL ANOINTING

Extraordinary Seniority
Holy Oil Anointing

CELEBRANT
We anoint the memory of each of our beloved with the oil of salvation in the name of Christ our Saviour; may he strengthen you with his power, who lives and reigns for ever and ever.

CELEBRANT
(Gently makes the sign of the cross on each picture of the departed with anointing oil at the front of the church)

May you have strength in the power of Christ our Saviour,

who lives and reigns for ever and ever.

ALL

Amen.

UNIVERSAL PROFESSION OF FAITH

CELEBRANT

My dear brothers and sisters, Our faith is borne of trust in the truth of the Good News of the Risen Christ; and nurtured through our concrete actions as Christians. It is not a message of fear or superstition, but one of genuine certainty in the divine love, mercy and forgiveness of our Eternal Father and Creator. So it is as Christians, we freely and joyfully proclaim by our own will the Good News of Christ. In the spirit of this occasion then, I invite each of you once more to consent and make the seven solemn professions of Christian Faith with a loud and clear voice:

CELEBRANT

First, Do you accept that God the one true Divine Creator exists?; and that everything is part of the divine laws of creation, even if we do not always understand?

ALL

I do.

CELEBRANT

Second, Do you agree that our Eternal Father made humanity in his image?; and that everything in life has a purpose?; and that he has a divine plan for us, even if sometimes we reject his laws?

ALL

I do.

CELEBRANT

Third, Do you reject all forms of evil in this world? and all that seeks to confuse us?; and all forms of wickedness that seeks to entrap our minds and harden our hearts, especially all forms of addiction, exploitation, nihilism and cruelty?

ALL

I do.

CELEBRANT

Fourth, Do you recognise Christ as your Saviour?; and as the embodiment of every person who has lived or will ever live?; and that as a Divine singularity, He truly was borne of flesh; and lived and suffered in life as we do?; and that He willingly sacrificed himself to free all of us, without condition, from the bondage of our transgressions?; and that through such an act of Divine Redemption of Divine Mercy and love, He did make it possible so that all may rise from the death of transgressions and have eternal life?

ALL

I do.

CELEBRANT

Fifth, Do you trust in the true teachings and Good News of the Risen Christ? That our Divine Creator is a loving god, who is merciful and loves us, despite our weaknesses? And that because of the gift of the universal law of free will, God does not seek to condemn us, or punish us, or directly cause us pain? And that no person has the right to curse or abuse or kill in the name of God?

ALL

I do.

CELEBRANT

Sixth, Do you welcome the Holy Spirit, the bringer of light and hope? Who illuminated the hearts and minds of the apostles at Pentecost and today is present with us through the celebration of this holy sacrament?

ALL

I do.

CELEBRANT

Seventh, Do you have faith in the one, holy apostolic Universal Ecclesia of Christ? As the one true living apostolic body of Christ and of all Christians?

ALL

I do.

CELEBRANT

This is our faith. This is the same faith of the disciples and Christian Founders. We joyfully profess it in the name of Christ our Saviour.

ALL

Amen.

BLESSING

CELEBRANT

Father, you give us grace through sacramental signs, which tell us of the wonders of your unseen power. In baptism we used your gift of water, which you have made a rich symbol of the grace you give us in this sacrament. At the very dawn of creation your Spirit breathed on the waters, making them the wellspring of all holiness.

Now with you most Holy Oil, we recognise the newest equal members of our family, who have demonstrated their capacity to discern and choose their faith unto you.

God the Father of our Lord Jesus Christ has freed you from spiritual transgression, given you a new birth by water and oil, and welcomed you into his holy people. As Christ was anointed Priest, Prophet, and King, so may you live always as a member of his body, sharing everlasting life.

ALL

Amen.

Title XXX – Sacrament of Divination & Rite of Elderity

XXX.I – SACRAMENT OF DIVINATION

1. Divination (*Ritus Sacramentum Divinatio*) is the eighth of the twelve (12) Apostolic Life Sacraments, also known as "The Twelve", "The Twelve Apostles" and "The Means".

Sacrament of Divination (Ritus Sacramentum Divinatio)

The Sacrament of Divination and Rite of Elders shall be granted and administered by the seventy-seventh (77th) birthday of a senior in accordance with the most sacred Covenants *Pactum De Singularis Caelum*, *Pactum De Singularis Christus*, and *Missale Christus* and associated approved liturgy.

2. An enlightened society venerates its elders, protects them and seeks their counsel and wisdom. The Sacrament of Divination and Rite of Elderity is the celebration of the point of transition from Seniority to Elderity. It is the celebration of becoming an elder.

Divine Purpose of the Sacrament of Divination

XXX.II – DIVINE GRACE AND ACTION OF DIVINATION

1. The Divine Grace and Action of *Divination* is the supernatural effect of the proper ministration of the Rite of Elderity as celebration of the point of transition from Seniority to Elderity. It is the celebration of becoming an elder.

Divine Grace and Action of Divination

2. *Divination* is a wholly Divine and unmerited action, warranted by God and the Divine Creator. It is not an action effected within the temporal realm, nor can it be equated to physical terms or constructs.

Understanding of action and Divine Grace of Divination

3. The Divine Grace and Supernatural Action of *Divination* is central to the proper effect of the Holy Rite of Elderity. Such supernatural presence and grace is made manifest *first* by the suitable qualification of the recipient; and *second* by the proper authority of one administering the sacrament; and *third* by the constituent parts and order that must be established in order to effect the sacrament.

Divine Grace and Action of Sacrament of Divination

In accord with sacred liturgy, in the absence of one or more of these central requisites, no legitimate manifestation of such Divine Grace and Action can occur.

XXX.III – RITE OF ELDERITY

1. The Holy Rite of Elderity represents the constituent parts and their order that must be established in order to effect the Divine and Supernatural Sacrament of Divination. In the absence of one or more of these central requisites, no legitimate manifestation or imprint of

Rite of Elderity

the Divine Grace and Action of Divination can occur.

2. There are only two (2) valid and licit forms for the Sacrament of Divination and Rite of Elders as defined by the most sacred *Missale Christus* and associated approved liturgy being Ordinary and Extraordinary:- Form of the Sacrament of Divination

(i) "**Ordinary Elder**" is conferred by a competent minister upon an adult having reached the age of seventy-seven (77) years; and

(ii) "**Extraordinary Elder**" is conferred by a competent minister in formal dedication to the spirit of a still-borne infant, or deceased child or youth or adult upon the calculation of what would have been their seventy-seventh (77th) birthday. Such a ceremony may be conducted as a Special Mass, with such records then entered into the rolls to the fact of such sacred act.

XXX.IV – CONDITIONS OF RITE OF ELDERITY

1. Conditions of the Rite of Elderity are those requisite qualifications and contingencies permitted in the proper ministration of the Rite. There shall exist only two (2) possible Conditions for the ministration of Rite of Elderity being *Ordinary* and *Extraordinary*:- Conditions of Rite of Elderity

(i) *Ordinary* are the Conditions necessary for the conferral of the Ordinary Rite of Elderity upon a living person aged seventy-seven (77) years; and

(ii) *Extraordinary* are the Conditions necessary for the conferral of the Rite of Elderity upon a deceased child or adult at what would have been their 77th year.

2. The Ordinary Form of the Rite of Elderity cannot be conferred unless the person is clearly a productive and exemplary member of their community:- Expectation of Knowledge and Actions of Supplicant for Ordinary Rite of Elderity

(i) The piety, actions and tangible help of others should be the first measure of qualification, not the personal wealth of the supplicant; and

(ii) The supplicant, if still blessed and capable with reason and faculty of discernment, should also demonstrate a commitment to learning and knowledge; as well as the imparting of such knowledge as a virtuous mentor to others.

3. The conditions for the Ordinary Rite of Elderity are:- Ordinary Conditions

(i) The Supplicant has received the Rite of Baptism, the Rite of

Christening, the Rite of First Communion, the Rite of Majority, the Rite of Maturity and the Rite of Seniority; and

(ii) Sufficient confidence exists that the Supplicant has attended Holy Mass for at least one Universal Feast from each of the seven Liturgical Cycles of the Mysteries of Christ of the previous three (3) years, being *Immanent, Filial, Eucharistic, Transcendent, Sacred Heart, Redemption* and *Apostolic*, unless a special exemption is granted by the local Ordinary.

4. The conditions for the Extraordinary Rite of Elderity are:-

Extraordinary Conditions

(i) The Sponsors, whether parents or immediate family members, have received the Rite of Baptism, the Rite of Christening, the Rite of First Communion and the Rite of Majority; and

(ii) Sufficient confidence exists that the Sponsors have attended Holy Mass for at least one Universal Feast from each of the seven Liturgical Cycles of the Mysteries of Christ of the previous three (3) years, being *Immanent, Filial, Eucharistic, Transcendent, Sacred Heart, Redemption* and *Apostolic*, unless a special exemption is granted by the local Ordinary.

XXX.V – CELEBRATION OF RITE OF ELDERITY

1. Only a legitimately and validly ordained minister may minister the Rite of Elderity.

Celebration of Rite of Elderity

2. The Ordinary Rite of Elderity may be celebrated on any Day, except those reserved for Holy Feast Days of Good Friday, Easter Sunday and Christmas Day. The Extraordinary Rite of Elderity may not be celebrated on any day reserved for any of the sixty-six (66) Holy Feast Days of the Liturgical Season of the Seven Mysteries of Christ.

Valid days of celebration

The Sacred Colour for the Liturgy of Mass shall be **Purple** if three (3) or more Supplicants or Sponsors are present for the Rite. Otherwise, the Sacred Colour for the Liturgy of Mass shall remain the same for the liturgical season that the particular Mass is celebrated.

XXX.VI – ORDINARY RITE OF ELDERITY

1. The *Ordinary Rite of Elderity* conferred by a competent minister upon an adult having reached the age of seventy-seven (77) years, shall be as follows:

Ordinary Rite of Elderity

LITURGY OF CHRISTIAN LIFE

Liturgy of Christian Life

(Purple sashes are prepared for each Supplicant to be placed over their head and shoulder upon the anointing ceremony.)

PETITION

CELEBRANT
(To all assembled)

I call upon those who seek to make their humble and solemn petition today in the name of Christ our Saviour to now come forward and make their presence and prayer known.

CELEBRANT
What Holy Rite then is it you ask in the name of the Father and of the Son and of the Holy Spirit today?

INITIATE(S)
Elderity

CELEBRANT
The Rite of Elderity you ask is a most solemn and important blessing recognising those of our community having reached an age and vital wisdom of faith, that they rightly be honoured as our most respected guides and mentors as our beloved elders.

Not everyone lives to an older age. No matter what age we achieve, ultimately every one of us will physically die. Such is the fact of our species and natural life. Sometimes, great age may be seen as if a terrible burden on account of the trials and tribulations of a long life. Yet none who have not tasted bitterness know what sweetness truly is. For others, with age may come great regrets on account of the mistakes of life. Yet no wisdom is more precious than what is gained through the many failures in trying.

Christ does not discard nor ignore the elderly. Some of his greatest teachings and wisdom is accounted with his discourse with older people of his community at the time. Nowhere in the Good News of Christ does he speak negatively of those who achieve a greater age. Instead, Christ makes clear that our Heavenly Father considers older age as no excuse not to live the best life we can at the time.

God has given our elders one of the most precious gifts – time. Time to reflect carefully and deeply on all who have hurt us and injured us over our life and to summons the courage and spirit to forgive and make amends. Time to reach out to others or their families whom we have hurt and injured and to earnestly express our remorse and seek appropriate penance. Time to reach out to our family, even if they have less time to be with us, find the means to record a legacy of our deepest love for them. Many people do not get such gifts before they pass. Yet our elders have an opportunity every day they receive as a gift to help shape the course of the future. Remember, the legacy of a person is not wealth or fame but consists of goodness, their deeds, love and compassion.

Today we are witnesses to the living words of Christ. As Christ himself taught us, the last shall be first and the first last. As Scripture teaches us many times, there are some in every generation who find it impossible to humble themselves before their Divine Creator. By your presence and humility today, you allow God to raise you up and embrace you and help you and show his unquenchable love for you in fulfilment of his promises to you of Divine Forgiveness, Mercy and everlasting life. Do each of you understand these sacred responsibilities?

ALL

Yes.

OBLIGATION

Ordinary Elderity Obligation

CELEBRANT

I call upon the Supplicants to kneel and give their solemn vows to their family, their community and the Divine Creator.

CELEBRANT

(Opens his palms before all present before briefly looking to Heaven and then back to all present)

Will you provide and pledge generous and wise support to those of your own family and friends that depend on you?

Do you promise to forgive those that have hurt you and make amends with those you yourself have hurt?

SUPPLICANT(S)

I do.

CELEBRANT

Will you provide and pledge a full commitment and interest in the health and well being of your friends and community? Do you promise to be compassionate and kind without having to accept other peoples burdens and life lessons that are not your own?

ALL

I do.

CELEBRANT

Will you provide and pledge regular contributions to the life of your local church? Do you promise to continue to be a loyal and active member of your community and your faith?

ALL

I do.

OBSIGNATION

CELEBRANT

Then truly this is a joyous day, for we welcome into our Christian community a new elder member. Upon the strength of faith of all here present.

CELEBRANT

(Gently makes the sign of the cross on the forehead of each supplicant with Holy Water)

I now gently trace the sign ✠ of the cross upon the forehead of each of you as a sign and seal of the promise made in the name of our Divine Father.

CELEBRANT

Dear Brothers and Sisters, let us ask that all of Heaven look lovingly upon this person who is about to be anointed and upon all here present as an embodiment of his holy Church. We ask this in the name of Christ.

ALL

Amen.

WILL OF THE PEOPLE

CELEBRANT

Let us pray.

Jesus, through your teachings and sacrifice we have come to no longer fear death, for you have given us eternal life so we can never die.

Heavenly Father, it is our Will and true intention in gratitude for your gifts of healing and our reconciliation into your presence, that we seek to dedicate our lives more fully to enacting your teachings.

We pray you will accept our humble petition and promises as a sign of the truth of our intentions, through Jesus Christ your son.

ALL

Amen.

SPONSOR(S)

By the mystery of your death and resurrection, bathe these sons and daughters in light, give them renewed strength, courage and wisdom of life as valued members of your Church that is your Living Body.

ALL

Christ hear our prayer.

SPONSOR(S)

Through anointing, make these sons and daughters your faithful followers and witnesses to your gospel.

ALL

Christ hear our prayer.

SPONSOR(S)

Lead them by a holy life to the joys of God's kingdom.

ALL

Christ hear our prayer.

SPONSOR(S)
Make the lives of their parents and godparents examples of faith to inspire them.

ALL
Christ hear our prayer.

SPONSOR(S)
Keep all the families here always in your love.

ALL
Christ hear our prayer.

SPONSOR(S)
Renew the grace of our baptism in each one of us.

ALL
Christ hear our prayer.

HOLY OIL ANOINTING

Ordinary Elderity Holy Oil Anointing

CELEBRANT
We anoint you with the most sacred Oil of Christ in the name of our Lord and our Saviour; may he strengthen you with his power, who lives and reigns for ever and ever.

CELEBRANT
(He anoints each elder on the forehead with Chrism Oil)

Be sealed with the gift Divination of the Holy Spirit. May you have strength in the power of Christ our Saviour, who lives and reigns for ever and ever.

ALL
Amen.

UNIVERSAL PROFESSION OF FAITH

Ordinary Elderity Universal Profession of Faith

CELEBRANT
My dear brothers and sisters, Our faith is borne of trust in

the truth of the Good News of the Risen Christ; and nurtured through our concrete actions as Christians. It is not a message of fear or superstition, but one of genuine certainty in the divine love, mercy and forgiveness of our Eternal Father and Creator. So it is as Christians, we freely and joyfully proclaim by our own will the Good News of Christ. In the spirit of this occasion then, I invite each of you once more to consent and make the seven solemn professions of Christian Faith with a loud and clear voice:

CELEBRANT

First, Do you accept that God the one true Divine Creator exists?; and that everything is part of the divine laws of creation, even if we do not always understand?

ALL

I do.

CELEBRANT

Second, Do you agree that our Eternal Father made humanity in his image?; and that everything in life has a purpose?; and that he has a divine plan for us, even if sometimes we reject his laws?

ALL

I do.

CELEBRANT

Third, Do you reject all forms of evil in this world? and all that seeks to confuse us?; and all forms of wickedness that seeks to entrap our minds and harden our hearts, especially all forms of addiction, exploitation, nihilism and cruelty?

ALL

I do.

CELEBRANT

Fourth, Do you recognise Christ as your Saviour?; and as the embodiment of every person who has lived or will ever live?; and that as a Divine singularity, He truly was borne of flesh; and lived and suffered in life as we do?; and that He willingly sacrificed himself to free all of us, without condition, from the bondage of our transgressions?; and that through such an act of Divine Redemption of Divine Mercy and love, He did make it possible so that all may rise from the death of transgressions and have eternal life?

ALL

I do.

CELEBRANT

Fifth, Do you trust in the true teachings and Good News of the Risen Christ? That our Divine Creator is a loving god, who is merciful and loves us, despite our weaknesses? And that because of the gift of the universal law of free will, God does not seek to condemn us, or punish us, or directly cause us pain? And that no person has the right to curse or abuse or kill in the name of God?

ALL

I do.

CELEBRANT

Sixth, Do you welcome the Holy Spirit, the bringer of light and hope? Who illuminated the hearts and minds of the apostles at Pentecost and today is present with us through the celebration of this holy sacrament?

ALL

I do.

CELEBRANT

Seventh, Do you have faith in the one, holy apostolic Universal Ecclesia of Christ? As the one true living apostolic body of Christ and of all Christians?

ALL

I do.

CELEBRANT

This is our faith. This is the same faith of the disciples and Christian Founders. We joyfully profess it in the name of Christ our Saviour.

ALL

Amen.

BLESSING

Ordinary Elderity
Blessing

CELEBRANT

Father, you give us grace through sacramental signs, which tell us of the wonders of your unseen power. In baptism we used your gift of water, which you have made a rich symbol of the grace you give us in this sacrament. At the very dawn of creation your Spirit breathed on the waters, making them the wellspring of all holiness.

Now with you most Holy Oil, we recognise the newest equal members of our family, who have demonstrated their capacity to discern and choose their faith unto you.

God the Father of our Lord Jesus Christ has freed you from spiritual transgression, given you a new birth by water and oil, and welcomed you into his holy people. As Christ was anointed Priest, Prophet, and King, so may you live always as a member of his body, sharing everlasting life.

ALL

Amen.

XXX.VII – EXTRAORDINARY RITE OF ELDERITY

Extraordinary Rite of Elderity

1. The *Extraordinary Rite of Elderity* conferred by a competent minister in formal dedication to the spirit of a still-born infant, or deceased child or youth or adult or senior upon the calculation of what would have been their seventy-seventh birthday, shall be as follows:

LITURGY OF CHRISTIAN LIFE

Liturgy of Christian Life

(Appropriate memorial pictures of the deceased as adults around the age of thirty three if they passed before the age of 44 years or a picture of their age when they died before the age of 77 years are positioned on display around the altar so that the whole congregation may observe. A Purple Ribbon is tied to the side of each picture as a sign of the Rite of Elderity.)

PETITION

Extraordinary Elderity
Petition

CELEBRANT

(To the Sponsors)

Are you Parent(s) or Relative(s) of a unique life and spirit that has reunited with God and continues their journey in the hereafter?

SPONSOR(S)

Yes

CELEBRANT

(To each Sponsor)

What is the name of your Beloved?

SPONSOR(S)

N.

CELEBRANT

(To the Sponsors)

What then is it you ask in the name of the Father and of the Son and of the Holy Spirit for N. today?

SPONSOR(S)

Elderity.

CELEBRANT

The Rite of Elderity you ask for is a significant blessing. It is a foundation of our faith in our Divine Creator as the doorway to eternal life. As Parent(s) and Relative(s) here assembled, you have been called by God our Father to demonstrate to all here present your commitment to a fundamental article of Christian faith that our saviour Jesus Christ has opened the door to eternal life for all of us; and our life does not end with physical death; and that we continue to grow and learn and evolve as unique spiritual beings in the hereafter. Do each of you understand this sacred responsibility?

SPONSOR(S)

Yes.

RECITALS

CELEBRANT

Very well, before we proceed, I ask all of you three simple questions of faith and trust in the name of Christ:

CELEBRANT

(Opens his palms before all present before briefly looking to Heaven and then back to all present)

Do you solemnly promise to always keep the memory of your beloved in your hearts and to care for the needs of those still with us in flesh? And to continue to live, experience and give thanks for life to the best of your abilities?

ALL

We do (promise).

CELEBRANT

And do you solemnly promise to trust Christ and your faith in the one true Apostolic Universal Ecclesia that your beloved can never truly die and are always with you? And to honour their memory by accepting the mystery of faith that they may continue to grow and experience a new life in Heaven as we continue to grow and learn and experience life on Earth?

ALL

We do (promise).

CELEBRANT

And do you solemnly promise to uphold the Christian values of care for one another, and not to shut yourself off from life or others? And that you look to express your love and care and respect of all whom we love, by helping those in our community who still need our love and support?

ALL

We do (promise).

OBSIGNATION

Extraordinary
Elderity
Obsignation

CELEBRANT

Then truly this is a joyous day, for we recognise in our spiritual Christian community the continued experiences, growth and life of our beloved in Heaven. Upon the strength of faith of all here present.

CELEBRANT

(Gently makes the sign of the cross on each picture of the departed at the front of the church)

I now gently trace the sign ✠ of the cross upon the memorial of each of our beloved as a sign and seal of the promise made in the name of our Divine Father that all Baptised in the faith are saved and none be condemned.

CELEBRANT

I invite the Family and Sponsors if you so choose, as a mark of your solemn commitment to the promises made here today to gently do the same.

PARENT(S) AND SPONSOR(S)

(Each gently make the sign of the cross on the memory of their beloved)

CELEBRANT

Dear Brothers and Sisters, let us ask that all of Heaven look lovingly upon this person who is about to be anointed and all here present as an embodiment of his holy Church. We ask this in the name of Christ.

ALL

Amen.

WILL OF THE PEOPLE

Extraordinary Elderity
Will of the People

CELEBRANT

Let us pray.

Jesus, through your teachings and sacrifice we have come to no longer fear death, for you have given us eternal life so we can never die.

Heavenly Father, it is our Will and true intention in gratitude for your gifts of healing and our reconciliation into your presence, that we seek to dedicate our lives more fully to enacting your teachings.

We pray you will accept our humble petition and promises as a sign of the truth of our intentions, through Jesus

Christ your son.

ALL

Amen.

SPONSOR(S)

By the mystery of your death and resurrection, bathe these sons and daughters in light, give them new life and welcome them as equals into your Church that is the fulfilment of your Living Body.

ALL

Christ hear our prayer.

SPONSOR(S)

Through anointing, make these sons and daughters your faithful followers and witnesses to your gospel.

ALL

Christ hear our prayer.

SPONSOR(S)

Lead them by a holy life to the joys of God's kingdom.

ALL

Christ hear our prayer.

SPONSOR(S)

Make the lives of their parents and godparents examples of faith to inspire all people.

ALL

Christ hear our prayer.

SPONSOR(S)

Keep all the families here always in your love.

ALL

Christ hear our prayer.

SPONSOR(S)

Renew the grace of our baptism in each one of us.

ALL

Christ hear our prayer.

HOLY OIL ANOINTING

Extraordinary Elderity
Holy Oil Anointing

CELEBRANT

We anoint the memory of each of our beloved with the oil of salvation in the name of Christ our Saviour; may he strengthen you with his power, who lives and reigns for ever and ever.

CELEBRANT

(Gently makes the sign of the cross on each picture of the departed with anointing oil at the front of the church)

May you have strength in the power of Christ our Saviour, who lives and reigns for ever and ever.

ALL

Amen.

UNIVERSAL PROFESSION OF FAITH

Extraordinary Elderity
Universal Profession of Faith

CELEBRANT

My dear brothers and sisters, Our faith is borne of trust in the truth of the Good News of the Risen Christ; and nurtured through our concrete actions as Christians. It is not a message of fear or superstition, but one of genuine certainty in the divine love, mercy and forgiveness of our Eternal Father and Creator. So it is as Christians, we freely and joyfully proclaim by our own will the Good News of Christ. In the spirit of this occasion then, I invite each of you once more to consent and make the seven solemn professions of Christian Faith with a loud and clear voice:

CELEBRANT

First, Do you accept that God the one true Divine Creator exists?; and that everything is part of the divine laws of creation, even if we do not always understand?

ALL

I do.

CELEBRANT

Second, Do you agree that our Eternal Father made humanity in his image?; and that everything in life has a purpose?; and that he has a divine plan for us, even if sometimes we reject his laws?

ALL

I do.

CELEBRANT

Third, Do you reject all forms of evil in this world? and all that seeks to confuse us?; and all forms of wickedness that seeks to entrap our minds and harden our hearts, especially all forms of addiction, exploitation, nihilism and cruelty?

ALL

I do.

CELEBRANT

Fourth, Do you recognise Christ as your Saviour?; and as the embodiment of every person who has lived or will ever live?; and that as a Divine singularity, He truly was borne of flesh; and lived and suffered in life as we do?; and that He willingly sacrificed himself to free all of us, without condition, from the bondage of our transgressions?; and that through such an act of Divine Redemption of Divine Mercy and love, He did make it possible so that all may rise from the death of transgressions and have eternal life?

ALL

I do.

CELEBRANT

Fifth, Do you trust in the true teachings and Good News of the Risen Christ? That our Divine Creator is a loving god, who is merciful and loves us, despite our weaknesses? And that because of the gift of the universal law of free will, God does not seek to condemn us, or punish us, or directly cause us pain? And that no person has the right to curse or abuse or kill in the name of God?

ALL

I do.

CELEBRANT

Sixth, Do you welcome the Holy Spirit, the bringer of light and hope? Who illuminated the hearts and minds of the apostles at Pentecost and today is present with us through the celebration of this holy sacrament?

ALL

I do.

CELEBRANT

Seventh, Do you have faith in the one, holy apostolic Universal Ecclesia of Christ? As the one true living apostolic body of Christ and of all Christians?

ALL

I do.

CELEBRANT

This is our faith. This is the same faith of the disciples and Christian Founders. We joyfully profess it in the name of Christ our Saviour.

ALL

Amen.

BLESSING

CELEBRANT

Father, you give us grace through sacramental signs, which tell us of the wonders of your unseen power. In baptism we used your gift of water, which you have made a rich symbol of the grace you give us in this sacrament. At the very dawn of creation your Spirit breathed on the waters, making them the wellspring of all holiness.

Now with you most Holy Oil, we recognise the newest equal members of our family, who have demonstrated their capacity to discern and choose their faith unto you.

God the Father of our Lord Jesus Christ has freed you from spiritual transgression, given you a new birth by water and oil, and welcomed you into his holy people. As Christ was anointed Priest, Prophet, and King, so may you live always as a member of his body, sharing everlasting life.

ALL

Amen.

Title XXXI – Sacrament of Visitation & Rite of Unction

XXXI.I – SACRAMENT OF VISITATION

1. **Visiation (*Ritus Sacramentum Visitatio*) is the ninth of the twelve (12) Apostolic Life Sacraments**, also known as "The Twelve", "The Twelve Apostles" and "The Means". Sacrament of Visitation (Ritus Sacramentum Visitatio)

The Sacrament of Visitation shall be granted and administered within months of most certain death in accordance with the most sacred Covenants *Pactum De Singularis Caelum*, *Pactum De Singularis Christus*, and *Missale Christus* and associated approved liturgy.

2. It is the natural order of life and the universe that we are borne, we live and our bodies age and become less reliable until the day that we must leave our bodies behind and return to our eternal Heavenly Home. Divine Purpose of the Sacrament of Visitation

Thus, it is not the natural order, but profoundly unnatural and supremely arrogant to consider that such order should be suspended and that Homo Sapiens live according to an undetermined lifespan. For while it is perfectly reasonable to aspire to a world without debilitating and painful disease, it is encumbered upon all men and women with heroic virtue to protect the boundaries of life of our species, so that we do not become consumed and assume ourselves to be greater than the Universal Divine Creator.

The Holy Spirit reveals through the Risen Christ the true nature of God and the Divine Creator of all Existence and all Heaven and Earth to be Divine Mercy, Divine Forgiveness and Divine Love. Thus, it is not the nature or wish of the Father, nor Christ or the Holy Spirit that any man or woman suffer. The Sacrament therefore stands as a crucial reminder of such Divine Mercy, Divine Forgiveness and Divine Love; and to ease the suffering and pain of the sick; and aid in spiritual and mental healing as well as any physical healing.

3. A pastor of any Christian congregation must remember above all that the care of the sick is one of the most important duties of their ministry. Immediately upon learning that a parishioner is ill, without waiting to be summoned, a pastor ought to visit them of their own accord; and this not only once but frequently throughout the duration of the illness. Moreover, a pastor should request that parishioners inform the parish when one of them takes ill, especially if the case is serious. Mission of care of the sick

When a man or woman approaches such a trial, ordained clergy of the Universal Ecclesia of One Christ have an ecclesiastical and moral obligation as the true Disciples of Christ to do everything within their power to support the sick and vulnerable.

4. Dying with dignity is a fundamental determination of an enlightened society under God and the Divine Creator. Visitation is a celebration that enables those people who have some time before the point of death to seek resolution and peace before death; and before a loss of consciousness deprives the person of the full appreciation of the sacrament. Dignity and Grace when Dying

XXXI.II – DIVINE GRACE AND ACTION OF VISITATION

1. The Divine Grace and Action of *Visitation* is the supernatural effect of the proper ministration of the Rite of Unction to support the dignity of the seriously ill, disabled or dying. Divine Grace and Action of Visitation
2. *Visitation* is a wholly Divine and unmerited action, warranted by God and the Divine Creator. It is not an action effected within the temporal realm, nor can it be equated to physical terms or constructs. Understanding of action and Divine Grace of Visitation
3. The Divine Grace and Supernatural Action of *Visitation* is central to the proper effect of the Holy Rite of Unction. Such supernatural presence and grace is made manifest *first* by the suitable qualification of the recipient; and *second* by the proper authority of one administering the sacrament; and *third* by the constituent parts and order that must be established in order to effect the sacrament. Divine Grace and Action of Sacrament of Visitation

   In accord with sacred liturgy, in the absence of one or more of these central requisites, no legitimate manifestation of such Divine Grace and Action can occur.

XXXI.III – RITE OF UNCTION

1. The Holy Rite of Unction represents the constituent parts and their order that must be established in order to effect the Divine and Supernatural Sacrament of Visitation. In the absence of one or more of these central requisites, no legitimate manifestation or imprint of the Divine Grace and Action of Visitation can occur. Rite of Unction
2. There is only one form of the Sacrament of Visitation as defined by the most sacred *Missale Christus* and associated approved liturgy. One form.

XXXI.IV – CONDITIONS OF RITE OF UNCTION

1. Conditions of the Rite of Unction are those requisite qualifications and contingencies permitted in the proper ministration of the Rite. Conditions of Rite of Unction

   The Rite of Unction is similar to the Rite of Reconciliation (Last Rites)

in placing the absolute minimum conditions for the proper conferral of the Rite:-

(i) *Ordinary* are the Conditions necessary for the conferral of the Rite of Unction upon a conscious patient still with the faculties of reason; and

(ii) *Extraordinary* are the Conditions necessary for the conferral of the Rite of Unction upon an unconscious patient or patient without the necessary faculties of reason.

2. The Ordinary conditions for the Rite of Unction are:- Ordinary Conditions

(i) The patient in question has been baptised, christened and confirmed, or if not, is willing to profess the faith prior to the Rite of Unction and first accept the Rite of Baptism; and

(ii) The patient is sincere in their calling for the Rite; and earnest in accepting the Rite of Confession as part of the Rite.

3. The Extraordinary conditions for the Rite of Unction are:- Extraordinary Conditions

(i) The legal guardians and family of the patient in question have been baptised, christened and confirmed, or if not, are willing to profess the faith prior to any Rite of Unction and first accept the Rite of Baptism; and

(ii) The legal guardians and family of the patient are sincere in their calling for the Rite; and that they truly believe this is what the patient wishes; and that no other legal or moral impediment exists to confer the Rite.

XXXI.V – MINISTER OF RITE OF UNCTION

1. Only an ordained minister may confer the Rite of Unction Minister of Rite of Unction

2. When ordained clergy visit the sick, their demeanour should be sincere and dignified, so that they edify by word and example, not the sick alone, but the relatives and others who are witnesses. Dignity and Care

XXXI.VI – ORDINARY RITE OF UNCTION

1. The *Ordinary Rite of Unction* conferred by a competent minister, shall be as follows: Ordinary Rite of Unction

Ordinary Unction Salutation

SALUTATION

(Ordained minister enters the room where the sick person is resting.)

CELEBRANT

In the name of ✠ the Father, and of the Son, and of the Holy Spirit.

ALL

Amen.

CELEBRANT

(C. joins his hands, then extends his right arm outward his and makes the sign of the cross at the top corner of each of the corners of the room.)

✠ May the healing love and the abiding strength of the angels and saints of Heaven be ever present in this Space.

ALL

Amen.

PETITION

Ordinary Unction Petition

(Ordained minister places holy oil and holy water on a nearby table and vests in stole. Minister may also bring sacred object such as rosary, or saints medal as gift for sick person and also places it on the table)

CELEBRANT

What Holy Rite then is it you ask in the name of the Father and of the Son and of the Holy Spirit today?

PATIENT (OR FAMILY)

Unction (or the healing rite)

CELEBRANT

The Rite of Holy Unction you ask is a most solemn and ancient blessing instituted by Christ himself in recognising the spiritual, mental and physical needs and easing the suffering of those who are very sick or disabled.

Our Heavenly Father wishes none of us suffer and especially none of us suffer in isolation. Pain is a natural function of our physical form and body behaviour. The design of a Universe that enables all things to be as they are and the expression of free will means that it is inevitable by the laws of nature that our body will break down and cease to be. But when parts of our body do not work as they should, it can create crippling and unimaginable pain and suffering.

Christ also seeks to remind us that we are spiritual and mental beings and that sometimes our own memories of life of regrets, unresolved issues and trauma can manifestly amplify illness and pain. It is no coincidence that we live at a time of great mental anguish as well as a great rise in chronic illness.

Thus, while we pray for the inspiration and joy that miracles may bring to our faith and our community, first and foremost the Rite of Unction you seek is to bestow every spiritual and mental blessing to aid in the soothing of pain and suffering and the promotion of healing. Do each of you understand these sacred responsibilities?

PATIENT (OR FAMILY)

Yes.

BLESSING

Ordinary
Unction
Blessing

CELEBRANT

(Minister sprinkles holy water in the form of a cross at the four corners of the room.)

✠In the name of God our Heavenly Father and Christ his son and the Holy Spirit, I bless this Space as Sacred Circumscribed Space, so that it be a place of spiritual, physical and mental healing; and that any and all lingering negativity or regrets or negative spirits of the past be banished from this Sacred Space; and that no negative spirit or force may enter this space to impede its heavenly purpose as a healing space.

ALL

Amen.

CELEBRANT

(Minister sprinkles holy water in the form of a cross on the patient and on all others in the room.)

✠I bless you in the name of the Father, and of the Son, and of the Holy Spirit, that you be free of any sense of fear or negativity or distracting thoughts; and that your love, your intentions and prayers be directed to thoughts of spiritual well being, compassion and healing.

CELEBRANT

(Minister sprinkles holy water in the form of a cross on the rosary or saint medal.)

✠I bless this object in the name of the Father, and of the Son, and of the Holy Spirit, that it be a manifest symbol and power of healing.

(Minister hands blessed object, or puts it around the neck of the patient if possible.)

RITE OF CONFESSION

Ordinary Unction Confession

(Ordained minister offers the Patient the Rite of Confession in privacy if they wish. See Ordinary Rite of Confession.)

RITE OF EUCHARIST

Ordinary Unction Eucharist

(Ordained minister offers the Patient the optional Rite of Eucharist)

UNIVERSAL PROFESSION OF FAITH

Ordinary Maturity Universal Profession of Faith

CELEBRANT

My dear brothers and sisters, Our faith is borne of trust in the truth of the Good News of the Risen Christ; and nurtured through our concrete actions as Christians. It is not a message of fear or superstition, but one of genuine certainty in the divine love, mercy and forgiveness of our Eternal Father and Creator. So it is as Christians, we freely and joyfully proclaim by our own will the Good News of Christ. In the spirit of this occasion then, I invite each of you once more to consent and make the seven solemn professions of Christian Faith with a loud and clear voice:

CELEBRANT

First, Do you accept that God the one true Divine Creator exists?; and that everything is part of the divine laws of creation, even if we do not always understand?

ALL

I do.

CELEBRANT

Second, Do you agree that our Eternal Father made humanity in his image?; and that everything in life has a purpose?; and that he has a divine plan for us, even if sometimes we reject his laws?

ALL

I do.

CELEBRANT

Third, Do you reject all forms of evil in this world? and all that seeks to confuse us?; and all forms of wickedness that seeks to entrap our minds and harden our hearts, especially all forms of addiction, exploitation, nihilism and cruelty?

ALL

I do.

CELEBRANT

Fourth, Do you recognise Christ as your Saviour?; and as the embodiment of every person who has lived or will ever live?; and that as a Divine singularity, He truly was borne of flesh; and lived and suffered in life as we do?; and that He willingly sacrificed himself to free all of us, without condition, from the bondage of our transgressions?; and that through such an act of Divine Redemption of Divine Mercy and love, He did make it possible so that all may rise from the death of transgressions and have eternal life?

ALL

I do.

CELEBRANT

Fifth, Do you trust in the true teachings and Good News of the Risen Christ? That our Divine Creator is a loving god, who is merciful and loves us, despite our weaknesses? And that because of the gift of the universal law of free will, God does not seek to condemn us, or punish us, or directly cause us pain? And that no person has the right to curse or abuse or kill in the name of God?

ALL

I do.

CELEBRANT

Sixth, Do you welcome the Holy Spirit, the bringer of light and hope? Who illuminated the hearts and minds of the apostles at Pentecost and today is present with us through the celebration of this holy sacrament?

ALL

I do.

CELEBRANT

Seventh, Do you have faith in the one, holy apostolic Universal Ecclesia of Christ? As the one true living apostolic body of Christ and of all Christians?

ALL

I do.

CELEBRANT

This is our faith. This is the same faith of the disciples and Christian Founders. We joyfully profess it in the name of Christ our Saviour.

ALL

Amen.

HOLY OIL ANOINTING

Ordinary Unction Holy Oil Anointing

CELEBRANT

I anoint you with the most sacred Oil of Christ in the name of our Lord and our Saviour; may he strengthen your recovery and healing with his power, who lives and reigns for ever and ever.

CELEBRANT

(He anoints the patient on the forehead with Chrism Oil)

Be sealed with the gift of Healing of the Holy Spirit. May you have strength in the power of Christ our Saviour, who lives and reigns for ever and ever.

ALL

Amen.

BLESSING

Ordinary Unction Blessing

CELEBRANT

Father, you give us grace through sacramental signs, which tell us of the wonders of your unseen power. In baptism we used your gift of water, which you have made a rich symbol of the grace you give us in this sacrament. At the very dawn of creation your Spirit breathed on the waters, making them the wellspring of all holiness.

Now with your most Holy Oil, we anoint our brother (sister) that through the intercession of Heaven their pain and suffering be eased and their healing continue.

God the Father of our Lord Jesus Christ has freed you from every spiritual transgression, given you a new birth by water and oil. As Christ was anointed Priest, Prophet, and King, so may you live always as a member of his body, sharing everlasting life.

ALL

Amen.

XXXI.VII – EXTRAORDINARY RITE OF UNCTION

1. The *Extraordinary Rite of Unction* conferred by a competent minister, shall be as follows:-

Extraordinary Rite of Unction

SALUTATION

Extraordinary Unction Salutation

(Ordained minister enters the room where the sick person is resting.)

CELEBRANT

In the name of ✠ the Father, and of the Son, and of the Holy Spirit.

ALL

Amen.

CELEBRANT

(C. joins his hands, then extends his right arm outward his and makes the sign of the cross at the top corner of each of the corners of the room.)

✠ May the healing love and the abiding strength of the angels and saints of Heaven be ever present in this Space.

ALL

Amen.

BLESSING

Extraordinary Unction Blessing

(Ordained minister places holy oil and holy water on a nearby table and vests in stole.)

CELEBRANT

(Minister sprinkles holy water in the form of a cross at the four corners of the room.)

✠ In the name of God our Heavenly Father and Christ his son and the Holy Spirit, I bless this Space as Sacred Circumscribed Space, so that it be a place of spiritual, physical and mental healing; and that any and all lingering negativity or regrets or negative spirits of the past be banished from this Sacred Space; and that no negative spirit or force may enter this space to impede its heavenly purpose as a healing space.

ALL

Amen.

CELEBRANT

(Minister sprinkles holy water in the form of a cross on the patient and on all others in the room.)

✠I bless you in the name of the Father, and of the Son, and of the Holy Spirit, that you be free of any sense of fear or negativity or distracting thoughts; and that your love, your intentions and prayers be directed to thoughts of spiritual well being, compassion and healing.

HOLY OIL ANOINTING

Extraordinary Unction
Holy Oil Anointing

CELEBRANT

I anoint you with the most sacred Oil of Christ in the name of our Lord and our Saviour; may he strengthen your recovery and healing with his power, who lives and reigns for ever and ever.

CELEBRANT

(He anoints the patient on the forehead with Chrism Oil)

Be sealed with the gift of Healing of the Holy Spirit. May you have strength in the power of Christ our Saviour, who lives and reigns for ever and ever.

ALL

Amen.

Title XXXII – Sacrament of Salvation & Reconciliation

XXXII.I – SACRAMENT OF SALVATION

1. Salvation (*Ritus Sacramentum Salvatio*) and Rite of Reconciliation is the tenth of the twelve (12) Apostolic Life Sacraments, also known as "The Twelve", "The Twelve Apostles" and "The Means". Sacrament of Salvation (Ritus Sacramentum Salvatio)

   The Sacrament of Salvation and Rite of Reconciliation shall be granted and administered within days of imminent death in accordance with the most sacred Covenants *Pactum De Singularis Caelum*, *Pactum De Singularis Christus*, and *Missale Christus* and associated approved liturgy.

2. The purpose of the Sacrament of Salvation and Rite of Reconciliation is the formal final (last) rites of bestowal or presentation of a possessory or prescriptive right to an incumbent in accordance with the most sacred Covenants *Pactum De Singularis Caelum*, *Pactum De Singularis Christus*, and *Missale Christus* and associated approved liturgy. Divine Purpose of the Sacrament of Salvation and Rite of Reconciliation

   The Sacrament of Salvation and Rite of Reconciliation is the special celebration of blessing and cleansing to help an individual in the final stages of death to find a point of peace and resolution to their life in the hope of evoking the care of other minds already crossed to help guide the person safely.

XXXII.II – DIVINE GRACE AND ACTION OF SALVATION

1. The Divine Grace and Action of *Salvation* is the supernatural effect of the proper ministration of *Rite of Reconciliation* as the special celebration of blessing and cleansing to help an individual in the final stages of death to find a point of peace and resolution to their life in the hope of evoking the care of other minds already crossed to help guide the person safely. Divine Grace and Action of Salvation

2. *Salvation* is a wholly Divine and unmerited action, warranted by God and the Divine Creator. It is not an action effected within the temporal realm, nor can it be equated to physical terms or constructs. Understanding of action and Divine Grace of Salvation

3. The Divine Grace and Supernatural Action of *Salvation* is central to the proper effect of *Rite of Reconciliation*. Such supernatural presence and grace is made manifest *first* by the suitable qualification of the recipient; and *second* by the proper authority of one administering the sacrament; and *third* by the constituent parts and order that must be established in order to effect the sacrament. Divine Grace and Action of Sacrament of Salvation

In accord with sacred liturgy, in the absence of one or more of these central requisites, no legitimate manifestation of such Divine Grace and Action can occur.

XXXII.III – RITE OF RECONCILIATION

1. Rite of Reconciliation represents the constituent parts and their order that must be established in order to effect the Divine and Supernatural Sacrament of Salvation. In the absence of one or more of these central requisites, no legitimate manifestation or imprint of the Divine Grace and Action of Salvation can occur. Rite of Reconciliation

2. There are only three (3) valid and licit forms for the Rite of Reconciliation as defined by the most sacred *Missale Christus* and associated approved liturgy being Ordinary and Extraordinary:- Form of the Rite of Reconciliation

   (i) "**Ordinary Reconciliation**" is conferred by a competent minister upon a person who is still conscious and in imminent but not immediate danger of death; and

   (ii) "**Extraordinary Reconciliation**" is conferred by a competent minister upon a person who is in the last stages of dying and is not conscious or capable of adequate communication; and

   (iii) "**Special Reconciliation**" is conferred by a competent minister upon a group of people who are about to face the imminent possibility of death.

XXXII.IV – CONDITIONS OF RITE OF RECONCILIATION

1. Conditions of the Rite of Reconciliation are those requisite qualifications and contingencies permitted in the proper ministration of the Rite. Conditions of Rite of Reconciliation

   The Rite of Reconciliation is similar to the Rite of Unction in placing the absolute minimum conditions for the proper conferral of the Rite:-

   (i) *Ordinary* are the Conditions necessary for the conferral of the Ordinary Rite of Reconciliation upon a person who is still conscious and in imminent but not immediate danger of death; and

   (ii) *Extraordinary* are the Conditions necessary for the conferral of the Rite of Reconciliation upon a person who is in the last stages of dying and is not conscious or capable of adequate communication; and

(iii) *Special* are the Conditions necessary for the conferral of the Rite of Reconciliation upon a group of people who are about to face the imminent possibility of death,

2. The conditions for the Ordinary Rite of Reconciliation are:- Ordinary Conditions

(i) The person in question has been baptised, christened and confirmed, or if not, is willing to profess the faith prior to the Rite of Reconciliation and first accept the Rite of Baptism; and

(ii) The person is sincere in their calling for the Rite; and earnest in accepting the Rite of Confession.

3. The conditions for the Extraordinary Rite of Reconciliation are:- Extraordinary Conditions

(i) The minister possesses the legal or moral authority at that time and place to confer the Rite of Reconciliation; and

(ii) The person is in the last stages of dying.

4. The conditions for the Special Rite of Reconciliation are:- Special Conditions

(i) The minister possesses the legal or moral authority at that time and place to confer the Rite of Reconciliation; and

(i) The people assembled in question have been baptised, christened and confirmed, or if not, are willing to profess the faith prior to the Rite of Reconciliation and first accept the Rite of Baptism.

XXXII.V – MINISTER OF RITE OF RECONCILIATION

1. The competent minister for the Rite of Reconciliation may be one ordained to holy orders, or an officer delegated ecclesiastical powers by virtue of their commission to office, such as the roles of deacons and chaplains. Minister of Rite of Reconciliation

---

XXXII.VI – ORDINARY RITE OF RECONCILIATION

1. The *Ordinary Rite of Reconciliation* conferred by a competent minister, upon a person who is still conscious and in imminent but not immediate danger of death shall be as follows:- Ordinary Rite of Reconciliation

BLESSING

Ordinary Reconciliation Blessing

CELEBRANT

(Minister sprinkles holy water in the form of a cross on the dying person)

✠I bless you in the name of the Father, and of the Son,

and of the Holy Spirit, that you be free of any sense of fear or regret or anguish; and that you are supported and comforted now by the love and presence of your guardian angels and the saints of Heaven.

RITE OF CONFESSION

Ordinary Reconciliation Confession

(Ordained minister offers the dying person the Rite of Confession in privacy if they wish. See Ordinary Rite of Confession.)

RITE OF EUCHARIST (VIATICUM)

Ordinary Reconciliation Eucharist

(Ordained minister offers the dying person the optional Rite of Eucharist as Viaticum)

HOLY OIL ANOINTING

Ordinary Reconciliation Holy Oil Anointing

CELEBRANT

(Minister anoints the dying on the forehead with Chrism Oil)

I anoint you with the most sacred Oil of Christ in the name of our Lord and our Saviour. Be sealed with the gift of Reconciliation of the Holy Spirit. May Christ and all the angels and saints of Heaven receive you and protect you from any spiritual harm during your transition to life eternal.

ALL

Amen.

FINAL BLESSING

Ordinary Reconciliation Final Blessing

CELEBRANT

Father, you give us grace through sacramental signs, which tell us of the wonders of your unseen power. In baptism we used your gift of water, which you have made a rich symbol of the grace you give us in this sacrament. At the very dawn of creation your Spirit breathed on the waters, making them the wellspring of all holiness.

Now with your most Holy Oil, we anoint our brother (sister) with the sacred gift of Reconciliation.

God the Father of our Lord Jesus Christ has freed you from every spiritual transgression, given you a new birth by water and oil. As Christ was anointed Priest, Prophet, and King, so may you live always as a member of his body, sharing everlasting life.

XXXII.VII – EXTRAORDINARY RITE OF RECONCILIATION

1. The *Extraordinary Rite of Reconciliation* conferred by a competent minister upon a person who is in the last stages of dying and is not conscious or capable of communication shall be as follows:- Extraordinary Rite of Reconciliation

BLESSING

Extraordinary Reconciliation Blessing

CELEBRANT

(Minister sprinkles holy water in the form of a cross on the dying person.)

✠I bless you in the name of the Father, and of the Son, and of the Holy Spirit, that you be free of any sense of fear or regret or anguish; and that you are supported and comforted now by the love and presence of your guardian angels and the saints of Heaven.

HOLY OIL ANOINTING

Extraordinary Reconciliation Holy Oil Anointing

CELEBRANT

(Minister anoints the dying on the forehead with Chrism Oil)

I anoint you with the most sacred Oil of Christ in the name of our Lord and our Saviour. Be sealed with the gift of Reconciliation of the Holy Spirit. May Christ and all the angels and saints of Heaven receive you and protect you from any spiritual harm during your transition to life eternal. Amen.

FINAL BLESSING

Extraordinary Reconciliation Final Blessing

CELEBRANT

Father, you give us grace through sacramental signs, which tell us of the wonders of your unseen power. In baptism we used your gift of water, which you have made a rich symbol of the grace you give us in this sacrament. At the very dawn of creation your Spirit breathed on the waters, making them the wellspring of all holiness.

Now with your most Holy Oil, we anoint our brother (sister) that through the intercession of Heaven they be sealed with the gift of Reconciliation of the Holy Spirit.

God the Father of our Lord Jesus Christ has freed you from every spiritual transgression, given you a new birth by water and oil. As Christ was anointed Priest, Prophet, and King, so may you live always as a member of his body, sharing everlasting life. Amen.

XXXII.VIII – SPECIAL RITE OF RECONCILIATION

1. The *Special Rite of Reconciliation* conferred by a competent minister, upon a group of people who are about to face the imminent possibility of death shall be as follows:- Special Rite of Reconciliation

SALUTATION

Special Reconciliation Salutation

CELEBRANT

In the name of ✠ the Father, and of the Son, and of the Holy Spirit.

ALL

Amen.

PETITION

Special Reconciliation Petition

CELEBRANT

The Rite of Reconciliation remembers both the approaching hours of the great trial of our Saviour Jesus Christ, when he was in the Gardens of Gethsemane, as well as his last moments of forgiveness and resolution before his death on the cross.

Death comes to us all. Not that we should wish or seek it. But that in the midst of its shadow we might be resolute and find the courage as Christ did, to honour our mission and purpose.

The Rite of Reconciliation reminds us that we are never abandoned or alone. We are loved by God and by our ancestors and guardian angels. That if we indeed must soon face our final fate, then we shall indeed be supported and comforted in those moments by the love of our guardian angels and the saints of Heaven.

Thus, while we pray for every protection, first and foremost the Rite of Reconciliation is to grant us the sacred gift of certainty of our ultimate future; and to be at peace with the past; and to be calm and resolute as to the present, even if all around us the world appears to be crumbling.

BLESSING

Special Reconciliation Blessing

CELEBRANT

(Minister sprinkles holy water in the form of a cross on each present.)

✠I bless you in the name of the Father, and of the Son, and of the Holy Spirit, that you be free of any sense of fear or negativity or distracting thoughts; and that you will be supported and protected by the love and presence of your guardian angels and the saints of Heaven.

PENITENTIAL RITE

Special Reconciliation Penitential Rite

CELEBRANT

As we prepare to celebrate the mystery of Christ's love, let us acknowledge our failures and ask the Lord for pardon and strength.

ALL

I confess before God and the Divine Creator of all Existence, that I have transgressed from your teachings and laws, by my thoughts and through my words and actions; and in what I have done and what I have failed to do.
Before all here present as witness, I admit that I am truly sorry and remorseful for my thoughts, my words and my actions and call out to our Mother Blessed Mary in Heaven, to all the angels and saints and our ancestors, to intercede for me.

CELEBRANT

May God have mercy on us, forgive us our transgressions, and bring us to everlasting life.

ALL

Amen.

CELEBRANT

Jesus, we have earnestly confessed before all here present that we have transgressed against your teachings and rules. Jesus have mercy.

ALL

Jesus have mercy.

CELEBRANT

Christ sacrificed his own holy life, to forever end all forms of blood sacrifice; and to raise the dead to life; and to wash away our sins and the sins of every generation. Christ have mercy.

ALL

Christ have mercy.

CELEBRANT

Jesus you bring pardon and peace to transgressors. Accept our sincere contrition and help reconcile us to your love. Jesus have Mercy.

ALL

Jesus have mercy.

CELEBRANT

Christ, through your Divine Authority you gave us the Gift of the Holy Sacrament of Penance, that through the demonstration of genuine remorse and contrition, your servants might administer the Rite of Absolution. Rise up then my Brother and Sisters!

[Congregation stand.]

CELEBRANT

In witness to the forgiveness and absolution of our Transgressions in the name of the ✠Father and the Son and the Holy Spirit, in union with our Blessed Mother Mary and all the angels, saints and ancestors, let us proclaim to the world the joy of such healing and peace and give glory to our Eternal Father.

GLORIA

ALL

Glory to God and all in Heaven,
And peace to all people on Earth.
Divine Creator of all Existence,
Our loving God and Father,

We worship you, we give you thanks,
We praise you for your mercy.
Glory be unto our Saviour Jesus Christ,
The Son of Man and the Lamb of God.
For you take away the sins of the world,
And set all us free from the bonds of slavery.
Have mercy upon all of us,
And receive our prayers.
For you alone are the Holy One,
You alone are the Absolute Sovereign Lord,
You alone are the most high Jesus Christ,
With the Holy Spirit in the glory of God our Father,
Amen.

UNIVERSAL PROFESSION OF FAITH

Special Reconciliation
Universal Profession of Faith

CELEBRANT

My dear brothers and sisters, Our faith is borne of trust in the truth of the Good News of the Risen Christ; and nurtured through our concrete actions as Christians. It is not a message of fear or superstition, but one of genuine certainty in the divine love, mercy and forgiveness of our Eternal Father and Creator. So it is as Christians, we freely and joyfully proclaim by our own will the Good News of Christ. In the spirit of this occasion then, I invite each of you once more to consent and make the seven solemn professions of Christian Faith with a loud and clear voice:

CELEBRANT

First, Do you accept that God the one true Divine Creator exists?; and that everything is part of the divine laws of creation, even if we do not always understand?

ALL

I do.

CELEBRANT

Second, Do you agree that our Eternal Father made humanity in his image?; and that everything in life has a purpose?; and that he has a divine plan for us, even if sometimes we reject his laws?

ALL

I do.

CELEBRANT

Third, Do you reject all forms of evil in this world? and all that seeks to confuse us?; and all forms of wickedness that seeks to entrap our minds and harden our hearts, especially all forms of addiction, exploitation, nihilism and cruelty?

ALL

I do.

CELEBRANT

Fourth, Do you recognise Christ as your Saviour?; and as the embodiment of every person who has lived or will ever live?; and that as a Divine singularity, He truly was borne of flesh; and lived and suffered in life as we do?; and that He willingly sacrificed himself to free all of us, without condition, from the bondage of our transgressions?; and that through such an act of Divine Redemption of Divine Mercy and love, He did make it possible so that all may rise from the death of transgressions and have eternal life?

ALL

I do.

CELEBRANT

Fifth, Do you trust in the true teachings and Good News of the Risen Christ? That our Divine Creator is a loving god, who is merciful and loves us, despite our weaknesses? And that because of the gift of the universal law of free will, God does not seek to condemn us, or punish us, or directly cause us pain?

ALL

I do.

CELEBRANT

Sixth, Do you welcome the Holy Spirit, the bringer of light and hope? Who illuminated the hearts and minds of the apostles at Pentecost and today is present with us through the celebration of this holy sacrament?

ALL

I do.

CELEBRANT

Seventh, Do you have faith in the one, holy apostolic Universal Ecclesia of Christ? As the one true living apostolic body of Christ and of all Christians?

ALL

I do.

CELEBRANT

This is our faith. This is the same faith of the disciples and Christian Founders. We joyfully profess it in the name of Christ our Saviour.

ALL

Amen.

HOLY OIL ANOINTING

Special Reconciliation Holy Oil Anointing

CELEBRANT

(Minister anoints each person present on the forehead with Chrism Oil)

I anoint you with the most sacred Oil of Christ in the name of our Lord and our Saviour. Be sealed with the gift of Reconciliation of the Holy Spirit. May you have strength in the power of Christ our Saviour, who lives and reigns for ever and ever.

ALL

Amen.

RITE OF EUCHARIST (VIATICUM)

Special Reconciliation Eucharist

(Ordained minister offers the group the optional Rite of Eucharist as Viaticum)

FINAL BLESSING

Special Reconciliation Final Blessing

CELEBRANT

Father, you give us grace through sacramental signs, which tell us of the wonders of your unseen power. In baptism we used your gift of water, which you have made a rich symbol of the grace you give us in this sacrament. At the very dawn of creation your Spirit breathed on the waters, making them the wellspring of all holiness.

Now with your most Holy Oil, we anoint our brothers and sisters that through the intercession of Heaven they be sealed with the gift of Reconciliation of the Holy Spirit.

God the Father of our Lord Jesus Christ has freed you from every spiritual transgression, given you a new birth by water and oil. As Christ was anointed Priest, Prophet, and King, so may you live always as a member of his body, sharing everlasting life.

ALL

Amen.

Title XXXIII – Sacrament of Emancipation & Funerary Rites

XXXIII.I – SACRAMENT OF EMANCIPATION

1. Emancipation (*Ritus Sacramentum Emancipatio*) and Funerary Rites is the eleventh of the twelve (12) Apostolic Life Sacraments, also known as "The Twelve", "The Twelve Apostles" and "The Means".

Sacrament of Emancipation (Ritus Sacramentum Emancipatio)

The Sacrament of Emancipation and Funerary Rites shall be granted and administered after death and prior to the sacrament of Veneration and the burial or disposal of the body in accordance with the most sacred Covenants *Pactum De Singularis Caelum, Pactum De Singularis Christus*, and *Missale Christus* and associated approved liturgy.

2. The purpose of the Sacrament of Emancipation and Funerary Rites is the formal funeral rites to an incumbent in accordance with the present sacred Covenant and associated approved liturgy.

Divine Purpose of the Sacrament of Emancipation and Funerary Rites

The Sacrament of Emancipation and Funerary Rites is both the sacrament and ceremony that remembers the deceased, their life and provides an opportunity for those in attendance to speak, celebrate and honour the memory of the departed.

XXXIII.II – DIVINE GRACE AND ACTION OF EMANCIPATION

1. The Divine Grace and Action of *Emancipation* is the supernatural effect of the proper ministration of Funerary Rites as the sacrament and ceremony that remembers the deceased, their life and provides an opportunity for those in attendance to speak, celebrate and honour the memory of the departed.

Divine Grace and Action of Emancipation

2. *Emancipation* is a wholly Divine and unmerited action, warranted by God and the Divine Creator. It is not an action effected within the temporal realm, nor can it be equated to physical terms or constructs.

Understanding of action and Divine Grace of Emancipation

3. The Divine Grace and Supernatural Action of *Emancipation* is central to the proper effect of Funerary Rites. Such supernatural presence and grace is made manifest *first* by the suitable qualification of the recipient; and *second* by the proper authority of one administering the sacrament; and *third* by the constituent parts and order that must be established in order to effect the sacrament.

Divine Grace and Action of Sacrament of Emancipation

In accord with sacred liturgy, in the absence of one or more of these central requisites, no legitimate manifestation of such Divine Grace and Action can occur.

XXXIII.III – FUNERARY RITES

1. Funerary Rites represent the constituent parts and their order that must be established in order to effect the Divine and Supernatural Sacrament of Emancipation. In the absence of one or more of these central requisites, no legitimate manifestation or imprint of the Divine Grace and Action of Resurrection can occur. Qualification of Sacrament of Emancipation

2. There are only four (4) valid and licit forms for the Sacrament of Emancipation as defined by the most sacred *Missale Christus* and associated approved liturgy being Ordinary, Public, Sovereign and Extraordinary:- Form of the Sacrament of Emancipation and Funerary Rites

   (i) "**Ordinary Funerary Rites**" is conferred by at least one competent minister; and

   (ii) "**Public Funerary Rites**" is conferred by at least three (3) competent ministers as a public act of honour and respect upon the death of a notable person; and

   (iii) "**Sovereign Funerary Rites**" is conferred by a Patriarch and at least two (2) competent ministers assisting upon the death of a sovereign; and

   (iv) "**Extraordinary Funerary Rites**" is conferred by at least three (3) Bishops upon the death of a Bishop or three (3) Patriarchs on the death of a Patriarch.

XXXIII.IV – CONDITIONS OF FUNERARY RITES

1. Conditions of Funerary Rites are those requisite qualifications and contingencies permitted in the proper ministration of the Rite. There shall exist only five (5) possible Conditions for the ministration of Funerary Rites being *Universal, Ordinary, Public, Sovereign and Extraordinary*:- Conditions of Funerary Rites

   (i) *Universal* are the Universal Conditions applicable to all sacred Funerary Rites; and

   (ii) *Ordinary* are the Conditions necessary for the conferral of the Ordinary Funerary Rite; and

   (iii) *Public* are the Conditions necessary for the conferral of the Public Funerary Rite; and

   (iv) *Sovereign* are the Conditions necessary for the conferral of the Sovereign Funerary Rite; and

(v) *Extraordinary* are the Conditions necessary for the conferral of the Extraordinary Funerary Rite; and

2. A deceased person is considered impeded by law of the Universal Ecclesia of One Christ at the time of their death from receiving an ecclesiastical funeral:-

Conditions of Impediment to Funerary Rites

(i) If at the time of their death they remained a notorious and unrepentant apostate, heretic or schismatic; and

(ii) If at the time of their death they remained a notorious and unrepentant transgressor of profound criminal transgressions against the norms of law and public faith.

3. Christ himself made clear the Law of his father that no person be condemned. Thus, all clergy and faithful must obey the *Word of God* and cease any such contradictions against Heaven through erroneous doctrines of persistent condemnation and injury against those who choose to take their own life.

Suicide of deceased alone not a legitimate Impediment

The cause of death by suicide shall not be a just cause alone for claiming a legitimate impediment for receiving an ecclesiastical funeral:-

(i) Christ himself demonstrates that those who choose to take their own life require greater love, care and attention, not less, given the unresolved pain, regret and anguish that may still linger after the act; and

(ii) The notions that suicide is a form of property delict against God, or that suicide is an attack against Divine Law, are an abomination against the Primacy of Free Will as taught by Christ himself. Consequently, any such arguments in error of the true teachings of Christ must be forbidden and suppressed, never to be revived; and

(iii) Any ordained clergy that persist in condemning those who have taken their own lives do condemn themselves tenfold in the eyes of Christ; and automatically induces upon themselves a grave spiritual impediment that renders such unfaithful and belligerent ministers incapable of legitimately administering the Holy Sacraments or Rites of Sacred Liturgy.

4. The Universal conditions for all forms of Funerary Rites are:-

Universal Conditions

(i) All members of the faithful who have been baptised and not otherwise impeded by law possess the right to an ecclesiastical funeral; and

(ii) Infants of baptised parents who died before the Rite of Baptism or Rite of Christening are fully entitled to receive an ecclesiastical funeral; and

(iii) An ecclesiastical funeral for any deceased member of the faithful should generally be celebrated in their local church, unless another is chosen for reasonable cause and with the consent of the person who governs it; and

(iv) Everyone is permitted to choose the cemetery of burial, or place of cremation unless prohibited by law; and

(v) The form of an ecclesiastical funeral is always a Special Mass of the Tripartite form.

5. The conditions for Ordinary Funerary Rites are:- Ordinary Conditions

(i) The choice of cremation shall not be a legitimate or valid cause to claim the presence of an impediment denying a deceased person an ecclesiastical funeral; and

(ii) If a local church has its own cemetery, the deceased members of the faithful should be buried in it unless the deceased or those competent to take care of the burial of the deceased have chosen another cemetery legitimately.

6. The conditions for Public Funerary Rites are:- Public Conditions

(i) The funerals of religious or members of a society of apostolic life are generally to be celebrated in their own church or oratory by the superior if the institute or society is clerical; otherwise by the chaplain.

7. The conditions for Sovereign Funerary Rites are:- Sovereign Conditions

(i) The funerals of sovereigns must confirm to the Tripartite form of Holy Mass and be celebrated in the main church of the realm, unless necessary cause prevents it.

8. The conditions for Extraordinary Funerary Rites are:- Extraordinary Conditions

(i) The funeral of a diocesan bishop is to be celebrated in his own cathedral church unless he has chosen another church.

XXXIII.V – CELEBRATION OF FUNERARY RITES

1. Only a legitimately and validly ordained minister may minister Funerary Rites. Furthermore, in respect of specific Rites:- Celebration of Funerary Rites

(i) Only an ordained bishop consistent with the norms of the faith may confer the Sovereign Funerary Rite; and

(ii) Only ordained bishops consistent with the norms of the faith may confer the Extraordinary Funerary Rite if the deceased is a bishop; and

(iii) Only ordained patriarchs consistent with the norms of the faith may confer the Extraordinary Funerary Rite if the deceased is a patriarch.

2. Funerary Rites may not be celebrated on any day reserved for any of the sixty-six (66) Holy Feast Days of the Liturgical Season of the Seven Mysteries of Christ. Valid days of celebration

---

XXXIII.VI – FUNERARY RITE

xx. The *Funerary Rite* conferred by a competent minister, shall be as follows: Funerary Rite

LITURGY OF DIVINE REDEMPTION

Liturgy of Christian Redemption

OFFERTORY ANTIPHON

Psalm 50: 4-6

ALL

He shall call to the heavens from above, and to the earth, that he may judge his people. Let all the saints be gathered unto him; and all who have sealed his new covenant of mercy and forgiveness by their sacrifice. For the heavens shall declare his glory according to his Will.

PRESENTATION OF OFFERING

Funerary Rite
Presentation of Offering

CELEBRANT

Blessed are you, God of all creation. Through your goodness we have this bread to offer, that the earth has given and human hands have made. It will become for us the bread of life.

ALL

Blessed be God for ever.

CELEBRANT

Blessed are you, God of all creation. Through your goodness we have this wine to offer, fruit of the vine and work of human hands. It will become for us a spiritual drink.

ALL

Blessed be God for ever.

CELEBRANT

Pray, my brothers and sisters, that our offerings may be acceptable to God, our heavenly Father.

[Congregation stand.]

ALL

May God our Father accept these offerings through your hands, for the praise and glory of his name, for our good, and the good of the one true apostolic Universal Church.

PREFACE

CELEBRANT

Christ be with us!

ALL

And through you.

CELEBRANT

Open then our hearts!

ALL

We open them to the truth!

CELEBRANT

Let us remember and give thanks to our Saviour Jesus Christ.

ALL

It is right we give him our thanks and praise!

CELEBRANT

It is right and proper that we give thanks and praise to our Saviour Jesus Christ as we contemplate the life of N.

Through the Crucified and Risen Christ, God our Father makes all things new again, re-affirming our forgiveness and redemption; and breathing the rejuvenating strength and life of the Holy Spirit into the Holy Vine that is your Ecclesia.

And so with the Angels and all the Saints, we praise you and acclaim:

ALL

Holy, Holy, Holy Christ,
God of all Powers and Majesty,
Heaven and Earth are full of your Glory,
Hosanna in the highest.
Blessed are they who come
In the name of the Risen Christ.
Hosanna in the Highest.

[Congregation kneel.]

EUCHARISTIC PRAYER

Funerary Rite
Eucharistic Prayer

CELEBRANT

We come before you, Father, with humility and thanksgiving, through Jesus Christ your Son.

CELEBRANT (cont.)

(C. joins his hands, making the sign of the cross over both bread and chalice:)

Through him, we ask you to accept and bless ✠ these gifts we offer you as a manifest symbol of our own personal sacrifice.

CELEBRANT (cont.)

(C. Extends outward his hands:)

We offer them for your one true and holy Apostolic Universal Ecclesia. Watch over us; and guide us; grant us the grace and unity of being one living body of your son Jesus Christ, through our good works in this world. We offer them for N.; and for all who hold true and teach the authentic Christian faith that comes to us from your apostles.

Funerary Rite
Remembrance

CELEBRANT (cont.)

(C. joins hands briefly, before bowing head in moment of silence after the reciting of names:)

Remember your faithful servants, especially N. for whom we now pray.

CELEBRANT (cont.)

(C. lifts his head and extends his arms and hands outward in gesture toward the whole congregation:)

Heavenly Father, remember all of us gathered here before you. You know how firmly we trust in you and dedicate ourselves to you. We offer you our personal sacrifice and praise for our well-being and redemption and for all those who are dear to us.

CELEBRANT (cont.)

(C. lifts his head and eyes upward whilst also tilting upward his already extended hands:)

In union with all members of the Universal Ecclesia of Christ, we honour Mary, the blessed mother of Jesus and our universal mother. We honour Joseph, her husband, the apostles and martyrs Peter and Paul and all the apostles and saints. May their merits and prayers grant us your constant help and protection. Father, please accept our authentic offering. Bestow upon us your peace and good graces in this life; as we ask to be granted nothing more than the same mercy and forgiveness in death as we have shown to others in our lifetime.

CELEBRANT (cont.)

(C. lowers his head and eyes to the congregation and rotates his palms and hand to them whilst arms remain outstretched:)

We ask all this in the name of Christ, our Saviour.

ALL

Amen.

CELEBRANT (cont.)

(C. takes the bread and, raising it a little above the altar, continues:)

The day before he suffered, Jesus took some bread in his own hands,

CELEBRANT (cont.)

(C. looks upward:)

And looking up to Heaven, to you, our Divine Father, he gave you thanks and praise. He then broke the bread, gave it to each of his disciples, saying,

CELEBRANT (cont.)

(C. shows the consecrated host to the people.)

Take this, all of you, and eat it: this is my flesh that will be given up for you.

(C. places the consecrated host on the paten, and genuflects in adoration.)

CELEBRANT (cont.)

(C. takes the chalice, and raising it a little above the altar, continues.)

Jesus then took a cup of wine. Again he gave you thanks and praise, before giving the cup to his disciples, saying.

CELEBRANT (cont.)

(C. shows the consecrated chalice to the people.)

Take this all of you and drink from it. This is the cup of my blood, the blood of the new and everlasting covenant. It will be shed for you and for all mankind so that every sin may be forgiven.

(C. places it on the corporal, and genuflects in adoration.)

ACCLAMATION

Funerary Rite
Acclamation

(C. extends his arms:)

In honour of the memory of the sacrifice of our Saviour and our own humble offerings, let us rise up and proclaim the mystery of our faith:

[Congregation stand.]

ALL

Christ suffered and died for us; Christ is risen for us; Christ has returned through us as his united living body.

CELEBRANT (cont.)

(C. with hands extended, the priest says:)

Divine Father, we celebrate the memory of Christ, your Son. We, your people and your ministers, recall his passion, his resurrection from the dead, and his ascension into Heaven; and from the many gifts you have given us we offer to you, this, our humble and heartfelt personal sacrifice: symbolised by these, the bread of life and the cup of merciful salvation. We trust you look favourably upon our reverent and faithful offerings and accept them.

CELEBRANT (cont.)

(C. bows, with hands joined:)

In your name Heavenly Father, in honour of the will of your son, and through the power and authority of the Holy Spirit, we pray these perfect symbols of your New Covenant are transformed into the Bread and Fruits of Eternal Spiritual Life as the spiritual manifestation of the most sacred body of the Risen Christ,

CELEBRANT (cont.)

(C. stands up straight and makes the sign of the cross, saying:)

✠That as disciples of Christ, and in partaking in the blessed Eucharist, we too may be filled with the strength and grace of the Holy Spirit,

CELEBRANT (cont.)

(C. joins his hands:)

As the one true living Body of Christ.

ALL

Amen.

DOXOLOGY

Funerary Rite
Doxology

CELEBRANT (cont.)

(C. joins his hands:)

Through him, with him, and in him. In unity with the Holy Spirit, all glory and honour is your our Heavenly Father, for ever and ever.

ALL

Amen.

CHRISTS' PRAYER

Funerary Rite
Christs' Prayer

[Congregation stand.]

CELEBRANT

It is Christ that taught us to call the Divine Creator of all Existence our Father. Let us pray with confidence to our Father in the manner and Spirit our Saviour taught us.

ALL

Our Father of All Creation,

We beseech thee and honour your name,
For your Rule be united as One,
And your Laws be equal to All,
On Earth as it is in Heaven,
Grant us the means to sustenance,
As we shall give alms to those in need.
Save us from trickery and false oaths,
As our vows and our oaths shall be true.
Forgive us our debits and transgressions,
As we shall forgive the debits and transgressions of others.
Release us from any curse and ills,
As we shall not curse nor wish ill upon another.
We ask most humbly and with deep gratitude,
For let then your will be done.
Amen.

CELEBRANT

Deliver us, Jesus, from every evil, and grant us peace in our day. In your mercy help us to free ourselves from transgressions and protect us from all fear as we defend and proclaim the authentic mysteries of our Christian Faith.

ALL

For the kingdom, the power, and the glory are yours, now and forever.

SIGN OF PEACE

CELEBRANT

Jesus, you said to your apostles: I leave you peace, my peace I give you. Look not on our transgressions, but on the courage and faith of your Church, and grant us the peace and unity of your kingdom where you live for ever and ever.

ALL

Amen.

CELEBRANT

The Peace of Jesus Christ be with you always.

ALL

And also with you.

CELEBRANT

As true Christians, let us express to one another, the signs of peace and goodwill.

[The ministers and all the people exchange an embrace, handshake, or other appropriate gesture of peace with those near them, according to local custom.]

BREAKING OF BREAD

Funerary Rite
Breaking of Bread

ALL

Lamb of God, you take away the transgressions of the world: have mercy on us.
Lamb of God, you take away the transgressions of the world: have mercy on us.
Lamb of God, you take away the transgressions of the world: grant us peace.

[Congregation kneel.]

COMMUNION

Funerary Rite
Communion

CELEBRANT

This is the Lamb of God who takes away the transgressions of the world. Happy are those who are called to his supper.

ALL

Jesus, though I am not worthy to receive you, I trust in your promise that none be turned away and all shall be healed.

COMMUNION MINISTER

The Bread of Eternal Life

COMMUNICANT

Amen.

COMMUNION MINISTER

The Water of Spiritual Renewal

COMMUNICANT

Amen.

COMMUNION ANTIPHON

4 Esdr 2: 34-35

[Congregation sit.]

Let perpetual light shine upon them,
with your Saints for ever, for you are merciful.
Eternal rest grant unto them, O Lord,
and let perpetual light shine upon them,
with your Saints for ever, for you are merciful.

PRAYER AFTER COMMUNION

Funerary Rite
Prayer after Communion

CELEBRANT
[Announcements, etc.]

[If there are any announcements, acknowledgements, reflections, eulogies, or similar actions, these are best included here, after the Prayer after Communion and before the Concluding Rite. The people may remain standing, or may be invited to sit, depending on the length of the announcements or activity.]

CELEBRANT
Let us pray.

[Congregation stand.]

(A prayer chosen by the Celebrant, or members of the Congregation relevant to the life of the community and the feast.)

CELEBRANT
We humbly petition and ask for your help, through your son, Jesus Christ.

ALL
Amen.

BLESSING OF THE BODY

Funerary Rite
Blessing of the Body

(Before the casket is picked up by the pall bearers to be taken from the church, the minister(s) may bless the body with Holy Water and Incense.)

AT THE GRAVESITE

RECITALS OF THREE TRUTHS

Funerary Rite
Recitals of the Three Truths

CELEBRANT
In the name of ✠ the Father, and of the Son, and of the

Holy Spirit.

ALL

Amen.

CELEBRANT

Let us pray and recite the Three Truths of Eternal Life as Christ did teach us.

ALL

I am the resurrection. All who trust in me can never die.

I am the life. One who keeps faith shall have eternal life.

I am the truth. One who holds my commands is a light unto this world and the next.

ALL

Amen.

Funerary Rite
Final Blessing

CELEBRANT

May God our true Father grant N. freedom from all that may bind us upon this Earth and plain of existence.

ALL

Let your perpetual light shine upon him (her).

CELEBRANT

May your Son and our saviour Jesus Christ bestow N. your infinite mercy and forgiveness so that he/she be fully emancipated in mind and spirit.

ALL

Grant his (her) spirit safe passage unto your presence. Amen

CONCLUDING RITES

Funerary Rite
Concluding Rite

CELEBRANT

May Jesus always be with you.

ALL

And also with you.

CELEBRANT

Just as God our Father has forgiven us of our transgressions and his son Jesus Christ has healed us with his love and mercy and the Holy Spirit has filled us with renewed strength and courage to do better, let us make a firm promise now, before we depart, to live and act in each moment of our lives as true and authentic Christians.

ALL

We do honestly and sincerely promise.

CELEBRANT

May our God and Divine Creator bless you, ✠ the Father, and the Son and the Holy Spirit.

ALL

Amen

CELEBRANT

Go forth with the peace and love of Christ.

ALL

Thanks be to God!

Title XXXIV – Sacrament of Veneration & Rite of Beatification

XXXIV.I – SACRAMENT OF VENERATION

1. Veneration (*Ritus Sacramentum Veneratio*) is the twelfth of the twelve (12) Apostolic Life Sacraments, also known as "The Twelve", "The Twelve Apostles" and "The Means". Sacrament of Veneration (Ritus Sacramentum Veneratio)

The Sacrament of Veneration shall be granted and administered by a valid Minister following the Rite of Beatification in accordance with the most sacred Covenants *Pactum De Singularis Caelum*, *Pactum De Singularis Christus*, and *Missale Christus* and associated approved liturgy.

2. The purpose of the sacrament of Veneration is a formal rite of blessing and remembrance in favour of the formal recognition, honour and trust of an incumbent in Heaven in accordance with the most sacred Covenant *Pactum De Singularis Caelum* and associated approved liturgy. Divine Purpose of the Sacrament of Veneration

XXXIV.II – DIVINE GRACE AND ACTION OF VENERATION

1. The Divine Grace and Action of Veneration is the supernatural effect of the proper ministration of the Rite of Beatification as a formal rite of blessing and remembrance in favour of the formal recognition, honour and trust of an incumbent in Heaven. Divine Grace and Action of Veneration

2. *Veneration* is a wholly Divine and unmerited action, warranted by God and the Divine Creator. It is not an action effected within the temporal realm, nor can it be equated to physical terms or constructs. Understanding of action and Divine Grace of Veneration

3. The Divine Grace and Supernatural Action of Veneration is central to the proper effect of the Rite of Beatification. Such supernatural presence and grace is made manifest *first* by the suitable qualification of the recipient; and *second* by the proper authority of one administering the sacrament; and *third* by the constituent parts and order that must be established in order to effect the sacrament. Divine Grace and Action of Sacrament of Veneration

In accord with sacred liturgy, in the absence of one or more of these central requisites, no legitimate manifestation of such Divine Grace and Action can occur.

XXXIV.III – RITE OF BEATIFICATION

1. The Holy Rite of Beatification represents the constituent parts and their order that must be established in order to effect the Divine and Rite of Beatification

Supernatural Sacrament of Veneration. In the absence of one or more of these central requisites, no legitimate manifestation or imprint of the Divine Grace and Action of Veneration can occur.

2. There are only four (4) valid and licit forms for the Rite of Beatification as defined by the most sacred *Missale Christus* and associated approved liturgy being Exemplary, Heroic, Beatific (Venerable) and Blessed:- Form of the Rite of Beatification

   (i) "**Exemplary Beatification**" is when the title and sacramental grace of Exemplary is conferred upon the memory, name and relics of a deceased person; and

   (ii) "**Heroic Beatification**" is when the title and sacramental grace of Heroic is conferred upon the memory, name and relics of a deceased person; and

   (iii) "**Beatific (Venerable) Beatification**" is when the title and sacramental grace of Beatific is conferred upon the memory, name and relics of a deceased person; and

   (iv) "**Blessed Beatification**" is when the title and sacramental grace of Blessed is conferred upon the memory, name and relics of a deceased person.

3. The Rite of Exemplary Beatification is when the life and works of a deceased person have been thoroughly investigated and unequivocal evidence exists of an extraordinary and exemplary life of faith, piety and compassion. Once declared, such a person is entitled to be known as "Exemplary" and a servant of God. Exemplary Beatification

4. The Rite of Heroic Beatification is when sufficient evidence has been gathered to unequivocally confirm that the deceased person in question died in the service of their faith; and that the deceased person had previously demonstrated a deep love, piety and loyalty to their faith in Christ. Once declared, such a person is entitled to be known as "Honored" or "Hon." Heroic Beatification

5. The Rite of Beatific (Venerable) Beatification is when the life and works of the deceased person have been thoroughly investigated and unequivocal evidence exists of an extraordinary and heroic life of faith, piety and compassion, against significant obstacles and challenges. Once declared, such a person is entitled to be known as "Heroic in Virtue" and "Venerable" or "Ven." Beatific (Venerable) Beatification

6. The Rite of Blessed Beatification is when the life and works of the deceased person have been thoroughly investigated and demonstrates a deep, personal and mystical relation with the Divine Creator and Blessed Beatification

Heaven, whereby there is unequivocal evidence of an extraordinary and heroic life of faith, piety and compassion; and significantly a life of revelation and deep connection with the Divine and Heaven. Because of this deep connection, such deceased persons are worthy of veneration in the pleading for causes and intercessions including miracles.

Once declared, such a person is entitled to be known as "Blessed" and "Worthy of Belief".

XXXIV.IV – CONDITIONS OF RITE OF BEATIFICATION

1. Conditions of the Rite of Beatification are those requisite qualifications and contingencies permitted in the proper ministration of the Rite. There shall exist only four (4) possible Conditions for the ministration of Rite of Beatification being *Exemplary, Heroic, Beatific (Venerable) and Blessed*:- Conditions of Rite of Beatification

(i) *Exemplary* are the Conditions necessary for the conferral of the Exemplary Rite of Beatification upon the memory, name and relics of a deceased person; and

(ii) *Heroic* are the Conditions necessary for the conferral of the Heroic Rite of Beatification upon the memory, name and relics of a deceased person; and

(iii) *Beatific (Venerable)* are the Conditions necessary for the conferral of the Beatific Rite of Beatification upon the memory, name and relics of a deceased person; and

(iv) *Blessed* are the Conditions necessary for the conferral of the Blessed Rite of Beatification upon the memory, name and relics of a deceased person.

2. The conditions for the Exemplary Rite of Beatification are:- Exemplary Conditions

(i) That the deceased person was baptised in faith with Christ; and

(ii) Sufficient evidence exists of an extraordinary and exemplary life of faith, piety and compassion.

3. The conditions for the Heroic Rite of Beatification are:- Heroic Conditions

(i) That the deceased person was baptised in faith with Christ; and

(ii) That the deceased person had previously demonstrated a deep love, piety and loyalty to their faith in Christ; and

(iii) Sufficient evidence exists that the deceased person died in the service and defense of their faith.

4. The conditions for the Beatific (Venerable) Rite of Beatification are:- Beatific Conditions

(i) That the deceased person was baptised in faith with Christ; and

(ii) Sufficient evidence exists of an extraordinary and heroic life of faith, piety and compassion, against significant obstacles and challenges.

5. The conditions for the Blessed Rite of Beatification are:- Blessed Conditions

(i) That the deceased person was baptised in faith with Christ; and

(ii) Sufficient evidence exists of an extraordinary and heroic life of faith, piety and compassion; and significantly a life of revelation and deep connection with the Divine and Heaven; and

(iii) That credible evidence exists that two or more miracles were granted pleading for causes and intercessions in the name of the deceased person.

XXXIV.V – CELEBRATION OF RITE OF BEATIFICATION

1. Only a legitimately and validly ordained minister may confer the Rite of Beatification. Furthermore, in respect of specific Rites:- Celebration of Beatification Rites

(i) Only an ordained bishop or patriarch consistent with the norms of the faith may confer the Beatification Rites; and

(ii) Only ordained patriarchs consistent with the norms of the faith may confer the Beatification Rite if the deceased is a bishop; and

(iii) Only ordained patriarchs consistent with the norms of the faith may confer the Beatification Rite if the deceased is a patriarch.

2. The Rite of Beatification may not be celebrated on any day reserved for any of the sixty-six (66) Holy Feast Days of the Liturgical Season of the Seven Mysteries of Christ. Valid days of celebration

XXXIV.VI – BEATIFICATION RITE

1. The *Beatification Rite* conferred by a competent minister, shall be as follows: Beatification Rite

LITURGY OF CHRISTIAN REDEMPTION

Liturgy of Christian Redemption

OFFERTORY ANTIPHON

Lk 4: 18

ALL

The Spirit of the Lord is upon me, for he has anointed me and sent me to preach good news to the poor, to heal the broken-hearted and to let the oppressed go free.

PRESENTATION OF OFFERING

Beatification
Presentation of Offering

CELEBRANT

Blessed are you, God of all creation. Through your goodness we have this bread to offer, that the earth has given and human hands have made. It will become for us the bread of life.

ALL

Blessed be God for ever.

CELEBRANT

Blessed are you, God of all creation. Through your goodness we have this wine to offer, fruit of the vine and work of human hands. It will become for us a spiritual drink.

ALL

Blessed be God for ever.

CELEBRANT

Pray, my brothers and sisters, that our offerings may be acceptable to God, our heavenly Father.

[Congregation stand.]

ALL

May God our Father accept these offerings through your hands, for the praise and glory of his name, for our good, and the good of the one true apostolic Universal Church.

PREFACE

Beatification
Preface

CELEBRANT

Christ be with us!

ALL

And through you.

CELEBRANT
Open then our hearts!

ALL
We open them to the truth!

CELEBRANT
Let us remember and give thanks to our Saviour Jesus Christ.

ALL
It is right we give him our thanks and praise!

CELEBRANT
It is right and proper that we give thanks and praise to our Saviour Jesus Christ as we contemplate the life of your [Exemplary/Heroic/Venerable/Blessed] Servant N.

Through the Crucified and Risen Christ, God our Father makes all things new again, re-affirming our forgiveness and redemption; and breathing the rejuvenating strength and life of the Holy Spirit into the Holy Vine that is your Ecclesia.

And so with the Angels and all the Saints, we praise you and acclaim:

ALL
Holy, Holy, Holy Christ,
God of all Powers and Majesty,
Heaven and Earth are full of your Glory,
Hosanna in the highest.
Blessed are they who come
In the name of the Risen Christ.
Hosanna in the Highest.

[Congregation kneel.]

EUCHARISTIC PRAYER

Beatification
Eucharistic Prayer

CELEBRANT
We come before you, Father, with humility and thanksgiving, through Jesus Christ your Son.

CELEBRANT (cont.)
(C. joins his hands, making the sign of the cross over both bread and chalice:)

Through him, we ask you to accept and bless ✠ these gifts

we offer you as a manifest symbol of our own personal sacrifice.

CELEBRANT (cont.)

(C. Extends outward his hands:)

We offer them for your one true and holy Apostolic Universal Ecclesia. Watch over us; and guide us; grant us the grace and unity of being one living body of your son Jesus Christ, through our good works in this world. We offer them for your [Exemplary/ Heroic/Venerable/Blessed] Servant N.; and for all who hold true and teach the authentic Christian faith that comes to us from your apostles.

CELEBRANT (cont.)

(C. joins hands briefly, before bowing head in moment of silence after the reciting of names:)

Remember your faithful servants, especially N. for whom we now pray.

Beatification
Remembrance

CELEBRANT (cont.)

(C. lifts his head and extends his arms and hands outward in gesture toward the whole congregation:)

Heavenly Father, remember all of us gathered here before you. You know how firmly we trust in you and dedicate ourselves to you. We offer you our personal sacrifice and praise for our well-being and redemption and for all those who are dear to us.

CELEBRANT (cont.)

(C. lifts his head and eyes upward whilst also tilting upward his already extended hands:)

In union with all members of the Universal Ecclesia of Christ, we honour Mary, the blessed mother of Jesus and our universal mother. We honour Joseph, her husband, the apostles and martyrs Peter and Paul and all the apostles and saints. May their merits and prayers grant us your constant help and protection. Father, please accept our authentic offering. Bestow upon us your peace and good graces in this life; as we ask to be granted nothing more than the same mercy and forgiveness in death as we have shown to others in our lifetime.

CELEBRANT (cont.)

(C. lowers his head and eyes to the congregation and rotates his palms and hand to them whilst arms remain outstretched:)

We ask all this in the name of Christ, our Saviour.

ALL

Amen.

Beatification
Consecration

CELEBRANT (cont.)

(C. takes the bread and, raising it a little above the altar, continues:)

The day before he suffered, Jesus took some bread in his own hands,

CELEBRANT (cont.)

(C. looks upward:)

And looking up to Heaven, to you, our Divine Father, he gave you thanks and praise. He then broke the bread, gave it to each of his disciples, saying,

CELEBRANT (cont.)

(C. shows the consecrated host to the people.)

Take this, all of you, and eat it: this is my flesh that will be given up for you.

(C. places the consecrated host on the paten, and genuflects in adoration.)

CELEBRANT (cont.)

(C. takes the chalice, and raising it a little above the altar, continues.)

Jesus then took a cup of wine. Again he gave you thanks and praise, before giving the cup to his disciples, saying.

CELEBRANT (cont.)

(C. shows the consecrated chalice to the people.)

Take this all of you and drink from it. This is the cup of my blood, the blood of the new and everlasting covenant. It will be shed for you and for all mankind so that every sin may be forgiven.

(C. places it on the corporal, and genuflects in

adoration.)

ACCLAMATION

Beatification
Acclamation

(C. extends his arms:)

In honour of the memory of the sacrifice of our Saviour and our own humble offerings, let us rise up and proclaim the mystery of our faith:

[Congregation stand.]

ALL

Christ suffered and died for us; Christ is risen for us; Christ has returned through us as his united living body.

CELEBRANT (cont.)

(C. with hands extended, the priest says:)

Divine Father, we celebrate the memory of Christ, your Son. We, your people and your ministers, recall his passion, his resurrection from the dead, and his ascension into Heaven; and from the many gifts you have given us we offer to you, this, our humble and heartfelt personal sacrifice: symbolised by these, the bread of life and the cup of merciful salvation. We trust you look favourably upon our reverent and faithful offerings and accept them.

CELEBRANT (cont.)

(C. bows, with hands joined:)

In your name Heavenly Father, in honour of the will of your son, and through the power and authority of the Holy Spirit, we pray these perfect symbols of your New Covenant are transformed into the Bread and Fruits of Eternal Spiritual Life as the spiritual manifestation of the most sacred body of the Risen Christ,

CELEBRANT (cont.)

(C. stands up straight and makes the sign of the cross, saying:)

✠That as disciples of Christ, and in partaking in the blessed Eucharist, we too may be filled with the strength and grace of the Holy Spirit,

CELEBRANT (cont.)

(C. joins his hands:)

As the one true living Body of Christ.

ALL

Amen.

DOXOLOGY

Beatification
Doxology

CELEBRANT (cont.)

(C. joins his hands:)

Through him, with him, and in him. In unity with the Holy Spirit, all glory and honour is yours our Heavenly Father, for ever and ever.

ALL

Amen.

CHRISTS' PRAYER

Beatification
Christs' Prayer

[Congregation stand.]

CELEBRANT

It is Christ that taught us to call the Divine Creator of all Existence our Father. Let us pray with confidence to our Father in the manner and Spirit our Saviour taught us.

ALL

Our Father of All Creation,
We beseech thee and honour your name,
For your Rule be united as One,
And your Laws be equal to All,
On Earth as it is in Heaven,
Grant us the means to sustenance,
As we shall give alms to those in need.
Save us from trickery and false oaths,
As our vows and our oaths shall be true.
Forgive us our debits and transgressions,
As we shall forgive the debits and transgressions of others.
Release us from any curse and ills,
As we shall not curse nor wish ill upon another.
We ask most humbly and with deep gratitude,
For let then your will be done.
Amen.

CELEBRANT

Deliver us, Jesus, from every evil, and grant us peace in our day. In your mercy help us to free ourselves from transgressions and protect us from all fear as we defend and proclaim the authentic mysteries of our Christian Faith.

ALL

For the kingdom, the power, and the glory are yours, now and forever.

SIGN OF PEACE

Beatification
Sign of Peace

CELEBRANT

Jesus, you said to your apostles: I leave you peace, my peace I give you. Look not on our transgressions, but on the courage and faith of your Church, and grant us the peace and unity of your kingdom where you live for ever and ever.

ALL

Amen.

CELEBRANT

The Peace of Jesus Christ be with you always.

ALL

And also with you.

CELEBRANT

As true Christians, let us express to one another, the signs of peace and goodwill.

[The ministers and all the people exchange an embrace, handshake, or other appropriate gesture of peace with those near them, according to local custom.]

BREAKING OF BREAD

Beatification
Breaking of Bread

ALL

Lamb of God, you take away the transgressions of the world: have mercy on us.
Lamb of God, you take away the transgressions of the world: have mercy on us.
Lamb of God, you take away the transgressions of the world: grant us peace.

[Congregation kneel.]

COMMUNION

Beatification
Communion

CELEBRANT

This is the Lamb of God who takes away the transgressions of the world. Happy are those who are called to his supper.

ALL

Jesus, though I am not worthy to receive you, I trust in your promise that none be turned away and all shall be healed.

COMMUNION MINISTER

The Bread of Eternal Life

COMMUNICANT

Amen.

COMMUNION MINISTER

The Water of Spiritual Renewal

COMMUNICANT

Amen.

COMMUNION ANTIPHON

Beatification
Communion
Antiphon

[Congregation sit.]

Let perpetual light shine upon them,
with your Saints for ever, for you are merciful.
Eternal rest grant unto them, O Lord,
and let perpetual light shine upon them,
with your Saints for ever, for you are merciful.

PRAYER AFTER COMMUNION

Beatification
Prayer after
Communion

CELEBRANT

[Announcements, etc.]

[If there are any announcements, acknowledgements, reflections, eulogies, or similar actions, these are best included here, after the Prayer after Communion and before the Concluding Rite. The people may remain standing, or may be invited to sit, depending on the length of the announcements or activity.]

CELEBRANT

Let us pray.

[Congregation stand.]

(A prayer chosen by the Celebrant, or members of the Congregation relevant to the life of the community and the feast.)

CELEBRANT

We humbly petition and ask for your help, through your son, Jesus Christ.

ALL

Amen.

BLESSING OF THE NAME

Beatification
Blessing of the Name

(Blessing of the picture of the Venerated whereby the minister(s) may bless the picture with Holy Water and Incense.)

RECITALS OF THREE TRUTHS

Beatification
Recitals of the Three Truths

CELEBRANT

In the name of ✠ the Father, and of the Son, and of the Holy Spirit.

ALL

Amen.

CELEBRANT

Let us pray and recite the Three Truths of Eternal Life as Christ did teach us.

ALL

I am the resurrection. All who trust in me can never die.

I am the life. One who keeps faith shall have eternal life.

I am the truth. One who holds my commands is a light unto this world and the next.

ALL

Amen.

CONCLUDING RITES

Beatification
Concluding Rite

CELEBRANT
May Jesus always be with you.

ALL
And also with you.

CELEBRANT
Just as God our Father has forgiven us of our transgressions and his son Jesus Christ has healed us with his love and mercy and the Holy Spirit has filled us with renewed strength and courage to do better, let us make a firm promise now, before we depart, to live and act in each moment of our lives as true and authentic Christians in the name of your [Exemplary/Heroic/Venerable/Blessed] Servant N.

ALL
We do honestly and sincerely promise.

CELEBRANT
May our God and Divine Creator bless you, ✠ the Father, and the Son and the Holy Spirit.

ALL
Amen

CELEBRANT
Go forth with the peace and love of Christ

ALL
Thanks be to God!

Title XXXV – Rite of Dedication

XXXV.I – RITE OF DEDICATION

1. **Dedication, also known as the Rite of Dedicatory Consecration** shall be when the Sacrament of Sanctification is imparted through the authority and character of Holy Orders of one who is properly ordained, to then solemnly dedicate a place, object or thing and set it apart for religious purposes. Rite of Dedication

   The Rite of Dedication (Dedicatory Consecration) shall be granted and conferred in accordance with the most sacred Covenants *Pactum De Singularis Caelum* and *Pactum De Singularis Christus* and associated approved liturgy.

2. A place, object or thing worthy and suitable to be set apart for dedicated religious service, function or use, requires the formation of a special and significant form of Sacred Circumscribed Space, wherein the full effect of such intention and ceremony may be protected, preserved and respected. This is the purpose and function of the Rite of Dedication. Divine Purpose of the Rite of Dedication

   The Rite of Dedication creates original Sacred Circumscribed Space of a place, object or thing. Such space is either defined and recognised by its customary presence and existence or is recognised during the time of its construction or near completion.

3. There are only twelve (12) valid and licit forms for the Rite of Dedication as defined by the most sacred *Missale Christus* and associated approved liturgy being Sacred Site, Foundation Stone, Chapel, Church, Cathedral, Altar, Shrine, Cemetery, Crematorium, Religious House, Registry and Oratory:- Form of the Rite of Dedication

   (i) "**Sacred Site**" is when the Rite of Dedication is imparted to consecrate a place; and

   (ii) "**Foundation Stone**" is when the Rite of Dedication is imparted to consecrate a foundation stone; and

   (iii) "**Chapel**" is when the Rite of Dedication is imparted to consecrate a chapel; and

   (iv) "**Church**" is when the Rite of Dedication is imparted to consecrate a church; and

   (v) "**Cathedral**" is when the Rite of Dedication is imparted to consecrate a cathedral; and

   (vi) "**Altar**" is when the Rite of Dedication is imparted to consecrate an altar; and

(vii) "**Shrine**" is when the Rite of Dedication is imparted to consecrate a shrine; and

(viii) "**Cemetery**" is when the Rite of Dedication is imparted to consecrate a cemetery; and

(ix) "**Crematorium**" is when the Rite of Dedication is imparted to consecrate a crematorium; and

(x) "**Religious House**" is when the Rite of Dedication is imparted to consecrate a religious house; and

(xi) "**Registry**" is when the Rite of Dedication is imparted to consecrate a registry; and

(xii) "**Oratory**" is when the Rite of Dedication is imparted to consecrate a oratory.

XXXV.II – CONDITIONS OF RITE OF DEDICATION

1. Conditions of the Rite of Dedication are those requisite qualifications and contingencies permitted in the proper ministration of the Rite. There shall exist only twelve (12) possible Conditions for the ministration of Rite of Dedication being *Sacred Site, Foundation Stone, Chapel, Church, Cathedral, Altar, Shrine, Cemetery, Crematorium, Religious House, Registry* and *Oratory*:- Conditions of Rite of Dedication

(i) *Sacred Site* are the Conditions necessary for the conferral of the Rite of Dedication of Sacred Site; and

(ii) *Foundation Stone* are the Conditions necessary for the conferral of the Rite of Dedication of Foundation Stone; and

(iii) *Chapel* are the Conditions necessary for the conferral of the Rite of Dedication of Chapel; and

(iv) *Church* are the Conditions necessary for the conferral of the Rite of Dedication of Church; and

(v) *Cathedral* are the Conditions necessary for the conferral of the Rite of Dedication of Cathedral; and

(vi) *Altar* are the Conditions necessary for the conferral of the Rite of Dedication of Altar; and

(vii) *Shrine* are the Conditions necessary for the conferral of the Rite of Dedication of Shrine; and

(viii) *Cemetery* are the Conditions necessary for the conferral of the Rite of Dedication of Cemetery; and

(ix) *Crematorium* are the Conditions necessary for the conferral of the Rite of Dedication of Crematorium; and

(x) *Religious House* are the Conditions necessary for the conferral of the Rite of Dedication of Religious House; and

(xi) *Registry* are the Conditions necessary for the conferral of the Rite of Dedication of Registry; and

(xii) *Oratory* are the Conditions necessary for the conferral of the Rite of Dedication of Oratory.

2. The conditions for the Rite of Dedication of Sacred Site are:- Sacred Site Conditions

(i) That a Decree of Exemplification (*Decretum Ecclesiae Exemplificatio*) and an Ecclesiastical Original Writ of Entry (*Recto Ecclesiae Originalis*) were duly issued by the proper Ecclesiastical Authority concerning the Site in question; and

(ii) That no motion to appeal the Decree and Writ were properly filed by a party possessing a valid interest within forty (40) days of issuance and notice; or that a validly constituted tribunal ruled in favour of the original Decree and Writ after having heard a valid appeal; and

(iii) That the Rite of Dedication of Sacred Site was duly performed under the authority of the Decree of Exemplification (*Decretum Ecclesiae Exemplificatio*) and an Ecclesiastical Original Writ of Entry (*Recto Ecclesiae Originalis*); and

(iv) That the Ecclesiastical Original Writ of Entry (*Recto Ecclesiae Originalis*) was executed and fulfilled and a record of the event of the proper performance of the Rite of Dedication of Sacred Site was entered into the *Register of Ecclesiastical Sacred Places* of the *Great Register of Title and Rights* of the Universal Ecclesia.

3. The conditions for the Rite of Dedication of Foundation Stone are:- Foundation Stone Conditions

(i) That a Decree of Exemplification (*Decretum Ecclesiae Exemplificatio*) and an Ecclesiastical Original Writ of Entry (*Recto Ecclesiae Originalis*) were duly issued by the proper Ecclesiastical Authority concerning the Foundation Stone in question; and

(ii) That no motion to appeal the Decree and Writ were properly filed by a party possessing a valid interest within forty (40) days of issuance and notice; or that a validly constituted tribunal ruled in favour of the original Decree and Writ after having heard a valid appeal; and

(iii) That the Rite of Dedication of Foundation Stone was duly performed under the authority of the Decree of Exemplification (*Decretum Ecclesiae Exemplificatio*) and an Ecclesiastical Original Writ of Entry (*Recto Ecclesiae Originalis*); and

(iv) That the Ecclesiastical Original Writ of Entry (*Recto Ecclesiae Originalis*) was executed and fulfilled and a record of the event of the proper performance of the Rite of Dedication of Foundation Stone was entered into the *Register of Ecclesiastical Sacred Places* of the *Great Register of Title and Rights* of the Universal Ecclesia.

4. The conditions for the Rite of Dedication of Chapel are:- Chapel Conditions

(i) That a Decree of Exemplification (*Decretum Ecclesiae Exemplificatio*) and an Ecclesiastical Original Writ of Entry (*Recto Ecclesiae Originalis*) were duly issued by the proper Ecclesiastical Authority concerning the Chapel in question; and

(ii) That no motion to appeal the Decree and Writ were properly filed by a party possessing a valid interest within forty (40) days of issuance and notice; or that a validly constituted tribunal ruled in favour of the original Decree and Writ after having heard a valid appeal; and

(iii) That the Rite of Dedication of Chapel and Holy Mass was duly performed under the authority of the Decree of Exemplification (*Decretum Ecclesiae Exemplificatio*) and an Ecclesiastical Original Writ of Entry (*Recto Ecclesiae Originalis*); and

(iv) That the Ecclesiastical Original Writ of Entry (*Recto Ecclesiae Originalis*) was executed and fulfilled and a record of the event of the proper performance of the Rite of Dedication of Chapel was entered into the *Register of Ecclesiastical Places of Worship* of the *Great Register of Title and Rights* of the Universal Ecclesia.

5. The conditions for the Rite of Dedication of Church are:- Church Conditions

(i) That a Decree of Exemplification (*Decretum Ecclesiae Exemplificatio*) and an Ecclesiastical Original Writ of Entry (*Recto Ecclesiae Originalis*) were duly issued by the proper

Ecclesiastical Authority concerning the Church in question; and

(ii) That no motion to appeal the Decree and Writ were properly filed by a party possessing a valid interest within forty (40) days of issuance and notice; or that a validly constituted tribunal ruled in favour of the original Decree and Writ after having heard a valid appeal; and

(iii) That the Rite of Dedication of Church and Holy Mass was duly performed under the authority of the Decree of Exemplification (*Decretum Ecclesiae Exemplificatio*) and an Ecclesiastical Original Writ of Entry (*Recto Ecclesiae Originalis*); and

(iv) That the Ecclesiastical Original Writ of Entry (*Recto Ecclesiae Originalis*) was executed and fulfilled and a record of the event of the proper performance of the Rite of Dedication of Church was entered into the *Register of Ecclesiastical Places of Worship* of the *Great Register of Title and Rights* of the Universal Ecclesia.

6. The conditions for the Rite of Dedication of Cathedral are:- Cathedral Conditions

(i) That a Decree of Exemplification (*Decretum Ecclesiae Exemplificatio*) and an Ecclesiastical Original Writ of Entry (*Recto Ecclesiae Originalis*) were duly issued by the proper Ecclesiastical Authority concerning the Cathedral in question; and

(ii) That no motion to appeal the Decree and Writ were properly filed by a party possessing a valid interest within forty (40) days of issuance and notice; or that a validly constituted tribunal ruled in favour of the original Decree and Writ after having heard a valid appeal; and

(iii) That the Rite of Dedication of Cathedral and Holy Mass was duly performed under the authority of the Decree of Exemplification (*Decretum Ecclesiae Exemplificatio*) and an Ecclesiastical Original Writ of Entry (*Recto Ecclesiae Originalis*); and

(iv) That the Ecclesiastical Original Writ of Entry (*Recto Ecclesiae Originalis*) was executed and fulfilled and a record of the event of the proper performance of the Rite of Dedication of Cathedral was entered into the *Register of Ecclesiastical Places of Worship* of the *Great Register of Title and Rights* of the Universal Ecclesia.

7. The conditions for the Rite of Dedication of Altar are:- Altar Conditions

(i) That a Decree of Exemplification (*Decretum Ecclesiae Exemplificatio*) and an Ecclesiastical Original Writ of Entry (*Recto Ecclesiae Originalis*) were duly issued by the proper Ecclesiastical Authority concerning the Altar in question; and

(ii) That no motion to appeal the Decree and Writ were properly filed by a party possessing a valid interest within forty (40) days of issuance and notice; or that a validly constituted tribunal ruled in favour of the original Decree and Writ after having heard a valid appeal; and

(iii) That the Rite of Dedication of Altar and Holy Mass was duly performed under the authority of the Decree of Exemplification (*Decretum Ecclesiae Exemplificatio*) and an Ecclesiastical Original Writ of Entry (*Recto Ecclesiae Originalis*); and

(iv) That the Ecclesiastical Original Writ of Entry (*Recto Ecclesiae Originalis*) was executed and fulfilled and a record of the event of the proper performance of the Rite of Dedication of Altar was entered into the *Register of Ecclesiastical Altars and Shrines* of the *Great Register of Title and Rights* of the Universal Ecclesia.

8. The conditions for the Rite of Dedication of Shrine are:- Shrine Conditions

(i) That a Decree of Exemplification (*Decretum Ecclesiae Exemplificatio*) and an Ecclesiastical Original Writ of Entry (*Recto Ecclesiae Originalis*) were duly issued by the proper Ecclesiastical Authority concerning the Shrine in question; and

(ii) That no motion to appeal the Decree and Writ were properly filed by a party possessing a valid interest within forty (40) days of issuance and notice; or that a validly constituted tribunal ruled in favour of the original Decree and Writ after having heard a valid appeal; and

(iii) That the Rite of Dedication of Shrine and Holy Mass was duly performed under the authority of the Decree of Exemplification (*Decretum Ecclesiae Exemplificatio*) and an Ecclesiastical Original Writ of Entry (*Recto Ecclesiae Originalis*); and

(iv) That the Ecclesiastical Original Writ of Entry (*Recto Ecclesiae Originalis*) was executed and fulfilled and a record of the event of the proper performance of the Rite of Dedication of Shrine was entered into the *Register of Ecclesiastical Altars and Shrines* of the *Great Register of Title and Rights* of the

Universal Ecclesia.

9. The conditions for the Rite of Dedication of Cemetery are:- Cemetery Conditions

(i) That a Decree of Exemplification (*Decretum Ecclesiae Exemplificatio*) and an Ecclesiastical Original Writ of Entry (*Recto Ecclesiae Originalis*) were duly issued by the proper Ecclesiastical Authority concerning the Cemetery in question; and

(ii) That no motion to appeal the Decree and Writ were properly filed by a party possessing a valid interest within forty (40) days of issuance and notice; or that a validly constituted tribunal ruled in favour of the original Decree and Writ after having heard a valid appeal; and

(iii) That the Rite of Dedication of Cemetery was duly performed under the authority of the Decree of Exemplification (*Decretum Ecclesiae Exemplificatio*) and an Ecclesiastical Original Writ of Entry (*Recto Ecclesiae Originalis*); and

(iv) That the Ecclesiastical Original Writ of Entry (*Recto Ecclesiae Originalis*) was executed and fulfilled and a record of the event of the proper performance of the Rite of Dedication of Cemetery was entered into the *Register of Cemeteries and Crematoriums* of the *Great Register of Title and Rights* of the Universal Ecclesia.

10. The conditions for the Rite of Dedication of Crematorium are:- Crematorium Conditions

(i) That a Decree of Exemplification (*Decretum Ecclesiae Exemplificatio*) and an Ecclesiastical Original Writ of Entry (*Recto Ecclesiae Originalis*) were duly issued by the proper Ecclesiastical Authority concerning the Crematorium in question; and

(ii) That no motion to appeal the Decree and Writ were properly filed by a party possessing a valid interest within forty (40) days of issuance and notice; or that a validly constituted tribunal ruled in favour of the original Decree and Writ after having heard a valid appeal; and

(iii) That the Rite of Dedication of Crematorium was duly performed under the authority of the Decree of Exemplification (*Decretum Ecclesiae Exemplificatio*) and an Ecclesiastical Original Writ of Entry (*Recto Ecclesiae Originalis*); and

(iv) That the Ecclesiastical Original Writ of Entry (*Recto Ecclesiae*

Originalis) was executed and fulfilled and a record of the event of the proper performance of the Rite of Dedication of Crematorium was entered into the *Register of Cemeteries and Crematoriums* of the *Great Register of Title and Rights* of the Universal Ecclesia.

11. The conditions for the Rite of Dedication of Religious House are:- Religious House Conditions

(i) That a Decree of Exemplification (*Decretum Ecclesiae Exemplificatio*) and an Ecclesiastical Original Writ of Entry (*Recto Ecclesiae Originalis*) were duly issued by the proper Ecclesiastical Authority concerning the Religious House in question; and

(ii) That no motion to appeal the Decree and Writ were properly filed by a party possessing a valid interest within forty (40) days of issuance and notice; or that a validly constituted tribunal ruled in favour of the original Decree and Writ after having heard a valid appeal; and

(iii) That the Rite of Dedication of Religious House was duly performed under the authority of the Decree of Exemplification (*Decretum Ecclesiae Exemplificatio*) and an Ecclesiastical Original Writ of Entry (*Recto Ecclesiae Originalis*); and

(iv) That the Ecclesiastical Original Writ of Entry (*Recto Ecclesiae Originalis*) was executed and fulfilled and a record of the event of the proper performance of the Rite of Dedication of Religious House was entered into the *Register of Ecclesiastical Houses and Monasteries* of the *Great Register of Title and Rights* of the Universal Ecclesia.

12. The conditions for the Rite of Dedication of Registry are:- Registry Conditions

(i) That a Decree of Exemplification (*Decretum Ecclesiae Exemplificatio*) and an Ecclesiastical Original Writ of Entry (*Recto Ecclesiae Originalis*) were duly issued by the proper Ecclesiastical Authority concerning the Registry in question; and

(ii) That no motion to appeal the Decree and Writ were properly filed by a party possessing a valid interest within forty (40) days of issuance and notice; or that a validly constituted tribunal ruled in favour of the original Decree and Writ after having heard a valid appeal; and

(iii) That the Rite of Dedication of Registry was duly performed under the authority of the Decree of Exemplification (*Decretum*

Ecclesiae Exemplificatio) and an Ecclesiastical Original Writ of Entry (*Recto Ecclesiae Originalis*); and

(iv) That the Ecclesiastical Original Writ of Entry (*Recto Ecclesiae Originalis*) was executed and fulfilled and a record of the event of the proper performance of the Rite of Dedication of Registry was entered into the *Register of Ecclesiastical Places of Worship* of the *Great Register of Title and Rights* of the Universal Ecclesia.

13. The conditions for the Rite of Dedication of Oratory are:- Oratory Conditions

(i) That a Decree of Exemplification (*Decretum Ecclesiae Exemplificatio*) and an Ecclesiastical Original Writ of Entry (*Recto Ecclesiae Originalis*) were duly issued by the proper Ecclesiastical Authority concerning the Oratory in question; and

(ii) That no motion to appeal the Decree and Writ were properly filed by a party possessing a valid interest within forty (40) days of issuance and notice; or that a validly constituted tribunal ruled in favour of the original Decree and Writ after having heard a valid appeal; and

(iii) That the Rite of Dedication of Oratory was duly performed under the authority of the Decree of Exemplification (*Decretum Ecclesiae Exemplificatio*) and an Ecclesiastical Original Writ of Entry (*Recto Ecclesiae Originalis*); and

(iv) That the Ecclesiastical Original Writ of Entry (*Recto Ecclesiae Originalis*) was executed and fulfilled and a record of the event of the proper performance of the Rite of Dedication of Oratory was entered into the *Register of Ecclesiastical Places of Worship* of the *Great Register of Title and Rights* of the Universal Ecclesia.

XXXV.III – RITE OF DEDICATION OF SACRED SITE

1. The *Rite of Dedication of Sacred Site* conferred by a competent minister, shall be as follows:- Rite of Dedication of Sacred Site

Dedication Sacred Site Approach

APPROACH

(Ordained minister approaches the site but does not cross the threshold and enter the site but remains at the boundary of the site.)

CELEBRANT

In the name of ✠ the Father, and of the Son, and of the Holy Spirit. Amen.

✠ May the healing love and the abiding strength of the angels and saints of Heaven be ever present to this Space. Amen.

BLESSING OF THE HANDS

Dedication
Sacred Site
Blessing of the Hands

(Minister in vestments begins a clockwise circumscription of the boundary of the site, stopping only at each corner or significant change in the direction of the boundary and reciting the invocation below whilst clapping his hands together in a loud and definitive gesture.)

CELEBRANT

(Minister clapping his hands at each location.)

✠ In the name of God our Heavenly Father. In the name of Christ his son and our saviour. In the name of the Holy Spirits and all the angels and saints of Heaven, I invoke and awaken the spirits and memories of this place. So that all that is good and pure may be made present; and that any past sadness, regret or negativity of this place be made visible and known to us.

For we come in the name and authority of our Divine Creator to forgive and to heal, not to harm; and to bring peace to any past sadness, regret or negativity. Awaken then! Hear our sacred invocation in the name of Christ. Amen.

BLESSING OF THE HOLY INCENSE

Dedication
Sacred Site
Blessing of the Holy Incense

(Minister begins a clockwise circumscription of the boundary of the site for a second time, stopping only at each corner or significant change in the direction of the boundary and reciting the invocation below whilst swinging the incense burner (brazier) at the site.)

CELEBRANT

(Minister smudging with holy incense in the form of a cross at each location.)

✠In the name of God our Heavenly Father. In the name of Christ his son and our saviour. In the name of the Holy Spirits and all the angels and saints of Heaven, I invoke and release into this sacred smoke any and all past sadness, regret or negativity of this place; and any spirit that does not serve the intentions of the Divine Creator upon this place; and any last negativity or fear or limitation.

By the authority of our Divine Creator let this place be free of any impurities or impediments to its sacred purpose. We do this in the name of Christ our saviour and Mary, our Heavenly mother. Amen.

BLESSING OF THE HOLY WATER

Dedication Sacred Site Blessing of the Holy Water

(Minister begins a clockwise circumscription of the boundary of the site for a third and final time, stopping only at each corner or significant change in the direction of the boundary and reciting the invocation below whilst sprinkling holy water.)

CELEBRANT

(Minister sprinkles holy water in the form of a cross at each location.)

✠In the name of God our Heavenly Father and Christ his son and the Holy Spirit, I bless this Space as Sacred Space, so that it be a place of spiritual, physical and mental healing; and I seal the boundary of this place so that any and all lingering negativity or regrets or negative spirits of the past be banished from this Sacred Space; and that no negative spirit or force may enter this space to impede its heavenly purpose. Amen.

XXXV.IV – RITE OF DEDICATION OF FOUNDATION STONE

Rite of Dedication of Foundation Stone

1. The *Rite of Dedication of Foundation Stone* conferred by a competent minister assumes the Rite of Dedication of Sacred Site has already been performed. The Rite of Dedication of Foundation Stone shall be as follows:-

ENTRANCE

Dedication Foundation Stone Entrance

(Ordained minister approaches the site and crosses the threshold to enter the site and then immediately stops, kneels and then kisses the ground at a designated clean and suitable space)

CELEBRANT

(After arising to their feet having kissed the Sacred Ground of the Sacred Space.)

In the name of ✠ the Father, and of the Son, and of the Holy Spirit. Amen.

✠ May the healing love and the abiding strength of the angels and saints of Heaven be ever present throughout this Space. Amen.

PETITION

Dedication Foundation Stone Petition

CELEBRANT

The Rite of Dedication of a Foundation Stone is a most sacred and ancient rite dating back to even before the time of Christ. The Foundation Stone or "Corner Stone" has always been considered to be the key stone in the formation of buildings since the first civilisations.

The three primary elements of such a dedication has always been: a dedicatory blessing of the stone; and the recitation of a formal invocation prayer; and then the binding of the sacred stone and the invocation prayer by placing the prayer within a designated space within the stone itself.

Christ himself was well aware of the ancient significance of this Rite and the purpose and function of ancient temples and buildings. On more than one occasion he referred to himself as a stone discarded by the builders that his Heavenly Father would raise up to become the "foundation stone". Thus, this dedication rite has held a special significance for Christians since the first times, as the rite represents not only the consecration of a foundation stone for a new building, but a sacred foundation for the whole community.

RECITALS

Dedication Foundation Stone

Recitals

CELEBRANT

I now call upon those present to come forward and demonstrate their authority and prove their vows before God concerning the dedication of this Foundation Stone. By what proper authority is the Rite of Dedication of Foundation Stone called to be performed today?

REPRESENTATIVE(S)

(Handing the Celebrant a copy of the Decree of Exemplification and Original Writ.)

Decree of Exemplification and Original Writ.

CELEBRANT

And are you the proper representatives of the congregation for this sacred site?

REPRESENTATIVE(S)

Yes (we are).

CELEBRANT

And have you prepared a proper Dedication Prayer in accord with the norms of the Universal Ecclesia?

REPRESENTATIVE(S)

(Handing the Celebrant a copy of the Dedication Prayer.)

Yes (we have).

CELEBRANT

And are you prepared to come forward and answer three vows of faith and trust in the name of Christ in honour and respect to the intentions of use of this Sacred Space?

REPRESENTATIVE(S)

Yes (we will).

CELEBRANT

First, do you solemnly promise to always keep this sacred place only for sacred and consecrated acts? And to ensure this place is not used for profane or sordid acts, contrary to the norms of the Universal Ecclesia?

REPRESENTATIVE(S)

We do (promise).

CELEBRANT

And do you solemnly promise to obey the laws, prescripts, doctrines, rules and liturgy of the Universal Ecclesia of One Christ in the proper conduct of all sacraments and rites within this sacred place?

REPRESENTATIVE(S)

We do (promise).

CELEBRANT

And do you solemnly promise to uphold the Christian values of care for one another and the community? And that you will support and defend those in our community who are in genuine need?

REPRESENTATIVE(S)

We do (promise).

OBSIGNATION

CELEBRANT

Then truly this is a joyous day, for we recognise in our midst the wellspring of a true spiritual Christian community. Upon the strength of faith of all here present.

CELEBRANT

(Gently makes the sign of the cross over the foundation stone.)

I now gently trace the sign ✠ of the cross upon this foundation stone as a sign and seal of the promises made in the name of our Divine Father.

Dear Brothers and Sisters, let us ask that all of Heaven look lovingly upon this moment and all here present as an embodiment of his holy Church. We ask this in the name of Christ.

ALL

Amen.

WILL OF THE PEOPLE

Stone
Will of the People

CELEBRANT

Let us pray.

Jesus, through your teachings and sacrifice we have come to no longer fear death, for you have given us eternal life so we can never die.

Heavenly Father, it is our Will and true intention in gratitude for your gifts of healing and our reconciliation into your presence, that we seek to dedicate this sacred place fully to enacting your teachings.

We pray you will accept our humble petition and promises as a sign of the truth of our intentions, through Jesus Christ your son.

ALL

Amen.

(NOTE: Dedication Prayer is then read out aloud to all gathered by the officials of the congregation.)

HOLY BLESSING

Dedication Foundation Stone
Holy Blessing

CELEBRANT

Dear Brothers and Sisters, may this Special Holy Water of Healing and Sanctity, that was consecrated and dedicated in the presence of the Holy Spirit and a Company of Guardian Angels of Heaven, for the express purpose that when dispensed it should be for such intentions and needs of healing, consecration and reconciliation as we have already pronounced. Let this Special Blessing also be a reminder to us all of our Baptism into the one, apostolic and united Universal Ecclesia of Christ.

CELEBRANT

(Celebrant opens his arms and looks up)

God our Father, your gift of pure water brings life and abundance to the Earth; it washes away our transgressions and brings us to eternal life. With this Special Holy Water of Healing and Sanctity, help us rid and cleanse ourselves of all negativity and profanity that may cloak our mortal frames, and seek to prevent us from opening our hearts more fully to your forgiveness and healing.

CELEBRANT

(Celebrant brings his hands over the water in the aspersorium (sacramental bowl):)

We now bind our healing intentions and dedications to this Holy Water in the name ✠ of the Father, the Son and the Holy Spirit.

We do this in the name of Jesus Christ, the Ruler of all Heaven and Earth and the Lord of Hosts whom no spirit can deny.

ALL

Amen.

(The Celebrant now moves and sprinkles Holy Water on Foundation Stone:)

CELEBRANT

I Bless this Foundation Stone in the ✠ name of the Father and of the Son and of the Holy Spirit.

ALL

Amen.

CHRISTS' PRAYER

CELEBRANT

It is Christ that taught us to call the Divine Creator of all Existence our Father. Let us pray with confidence to our Father in the manner and Spirit our Saviour taught us.

ALL

Our Father of All Creation,
We beseech thee and honour your name,
For your Rule be united as One,
And your Laws be equal to All,
On Earth as it is in Heaven,
Grant us the means to sustenance,
As we shall give alms to those in need.
Save us from trickery and false oaths,
As our vows and our oaths shall be true.
Forgive us our debits and transgressions,
As we shall forgive the debits and transgressions of others.
Release us from any curse and ills,
As we shall not curse nor wish ill upon another.
We ask most humbly and with deep gratitude,
For let then your will be done.
Amen.

CELEBRANT
Deliver us, Jesus, from every evil, and grant us peace in our day. In your mercy help us to free ourselves from transgressions and protect us from all fear as we defend and proclaim the authentic mysteries of our Christian Faith.

ALL
For the kingdom, the power, and the glory are yours, now and forever.

CONCLUDING RITES

Dedication Foundation Stone
Concluding Rite

CELEBRANT
May Jesus always be with you.

ALL
And also with you.

CELEBRANT
Just as God our Father has forgiven us of our transgressions and his son Jesus Christ has healed us with his love and mercy and the Holy Spirit has filled us with renewed strength and courage to do better, let us make a firm promise now, before we depart, to live and act in each moment of our lives as true and authentic Christians.

ALL
We do honestly and sincerely promise.

CELEBRANT
May our God and Divine Creator bless you, ✠ the Father, and the Son and the Holy Spirit.

ALL
Amen

CELEBRANT
Go forth with the peace and love of Christ.

ALL
Thanks be to God!

XXXV.V – RITE OF DEDICATION OF CHAPEL

1. The *Rite of Dedication of Chapel* conferred by a competent minister assumes the Rite of Dedication of Sacred Site has already been performed. The Rite of Dedication of Chapel shall be as follows:-

Rite of Dedication of Chapel

ENTRANCE

Dedication Chapel Entrance

(Ordained minister enters the Chapel and then immediately stops, kneels and then kisses the ground at a designated clean and suitable space.)

CELEBRANT

(After arising to their feet having kissed the Sacred Ground of the Chapel.)

In the name of ✠ the Father, and of the Son, and of the Holy Spirit. Amen.

✠ May the healing love and the abiding strength of the angels and saints of Heaven be ever present throughout this Sacred Place. Amen.

BLESSING OF THE HOLY INCENSE

Dedication Chapel Blessing of the Holy Incense

(Minister begins a clockwise circumscription of the interior of the building for a first time, stopping only at each corner or significant change in the direction of the interior walls and reciting the invocation below whilst swinging the incense burner (brazier) at the site.)

CELEBRANT

(Minister smudging with holy incense in the form of a cross at each location.)

✠ In the name of God our Heavenly Father. In the name of Christ his son and our saviour. In the name of the Holy Spirits and all the angels and saints of Heaven, I invoke and release into this sacred fragrant smoke our purest intentions to honour thy name through your Holy Sacraments and Actions.

By the authority of our Divine Creator let this place be free of any impurities or impediments to its sacred purpose. We do this in the name of Christ our saviour and Mary, our

Heavenly mother. Amen.

BLESSING OF THE HOLY WATER

Dedication Chapel Blessing of the Holy Water

(Minister moves in a clockwise circumscription of the interior of the building for a second time, stopping only at each corner or significant change in the direction of the interior walls and reciting the invocation below whilst sprinkling holy water.)

CELEBRANT

(Minister sprinkles holy water in the form of a cross at each location.)

✠In the name of God our Heavenly Father and Christ his son and the Holy Spirit, I bless this Space as Sacred Space, so that it be a place of spiritual, physical and mental healing; and I seal the boundary of this place so that any and all lingering negativity or regrets or negative spirits of the past be banished from this Sacred Space; and that no negative spirit or force may enter this space to impede its heavenly purpose. Amen.

BLESSING OF THE LIGHT

Dedication Chapel Blessing of the Light

(A Lantern is lit and raised on a pole, so all can see. Other Lanterns may also be lit and handed to supporters of the Minister to follow in procession. The Minister moves in a clockwise circumscription of the interior of the building for a third and final time, stopping with the Lantern only at each corner or significant change in the direction of the interior walls and reciting the invocation.)

CELEBRANT

✠In the name of God our Heavenly Father, I invoke the light of Christ in all its glory. That it fill this sacred place with your radiance and your love, mercy and compassion for all life and all persons; and that evil and ignorance shall find no shelter in this sacred place; and that all who come to this sacred place will have their eyes opened to your revelation and the gifts you have bestowed upon the Universal Ecclesia as the Living Body of Christ. Amen.

HOLY MASS

Dedication Chapel Holy Mass

(NOTE: The Rite of Dedication of Chapel is considered incomplete until Holy Mass is conducted within the Chapel immediately after the above Dedication Rites.)

XXXV.VI – RITE OF DEDICATION OF CHURCH

Rite of Dedication of Church

1. The *Rite of Dedication of Church* conferred by a competent minister assumes the Rite of Dedication of Sacred Site has already been performed. The Rite of Dedication of Church shall be as follows:-

ENTRANCE

Dedication Church Entrance

(Ordained minister enters the Church and then immediately stops, kneels and then kisses the ground at a designated clean and suitable space.)

CELEBRANT

(After arising to their feet having kissed the Sacred Ground of the Church.)

In the name of ✠ the Father, and of the Son, and of the Holy Spirit. Amen.

✠ May the healing love and the abiding strength of the angels and saints of Heaven be ever present throughout this Revered Sacred Place. Amen.

BLESSING OF THE HOLY INCENSE

Dedication Church Blessing of the Holy Incense

(Minister begins a clockwise circumscription of the interior of the building for a first time, stopping only at each corner or significant change in the direction of the interior walls and reciting the invocation below whilst swinging the incense burner (brazier) at the site.)

CELEBRANT

(Minister smudging with holy incense in the form of a cross at each location.)

✠ In the name of God our Heavenly Father. In the name of Christ his son and our saviour. In the name of the Holy Spirits and all the angels and saints of Heaven, I invoke and release into this sacred fragrant smoke our purest intentions to honour thy name through your Holy Sacraments and Actions.

By the authority of our Divine Creator let this place be free of any impurities or impediments to its sacred purpose. We do this in the name of Christ our saviour and Mary, our Heavenly mother. Amen.

BLESSING OF THE HOLY WATER

Dedication
Church
Blessing of the Holy Water

(Minister moves in a clockwise circumscription of the interior of the building for a second time, stopping only at each corner or significant change in the direction of the interior walls and reciting the invocation below whilst sprinkling holy water.)

CELEBRANT

(Minister sprinkles holy water in the form of a cross at each location.)

✠In the name of God our Heavenly Father and Christ his son and the Holy Spirit, I bless this Space as Sacred Space, so that it be a place of spiritual, physical and mental healing; and I seal the boundary of this place so that any and all lingering negativity or regrets or negative spirits of the past be banished from this Sacred Space; and that no negative spirit or force may enter this space to impede its heavenly purpose. Amen.

BLESSING OF THE LIGHT

Dedication
Church
Blessing of the Light

(A Lantern is lit and raised on a pole, so all can see. Other Lanterns may also be lit and handed to supporters of the Minister to follow in procession. The Minister moves in a clockwise circumscription of the interior of the building for a third and final time, stopping with the Lantern only at each corner or significant change in the direction of the interior walls and reciting the invocation.)

CELEBRANT

✠In the name of God our Heavenly Father, I invoke the light of Christ in all its glory. That it fill this sacred place with your radiance and your love, mercy and compassion for all life and all persons; and that evil and ignorance shall find no shelter in this sacred place; and that all who come to this sacred place will have their eyes opened to your revelation and the gifts you have bestowed upon the Universal Ecclesia as the Living Body of Christ. Amen.

NAMING

Dedication Church Naming

(A wooden crozier is handed to the Celebrant who returns to the centre of the Church in front of the Altar)

CELEBRANT

Christ himself did speak of the Great Divine Register in Heaven where all that is Holy is recorded for all eternity. In respect and honour of his teachings we now proclaim the name of this most holy place of worship to be N. and humbly inscribe it in the language of the prophets and saints, so that the angels and saints of Heaven may take these signs and symbols to Heaven and enter them into your most Holy of Registers.

(Celebrant then uses the crozier to trace the name of the Church in Latin or Greek on the floor.)

HOLY MASS

Dedication Church Holy Mass

(NOTE: The Rite of Dedication of Church is considered incomplete until Holy Mass is conducted within the Church immediately after the above Dedication Rites.)

XXXV.VII – RITE OF DEDICATION OF CATHEDRAL

Rite of Dedication of Cathedral

1. The *Rite of Dedication of Cathedral* conferred by a competent minister assumes the Rite of Dedication of Sacred Site has already been performed. The Rite of Dedication of Cathedral shall be as follows:-

ENTRANCE

Dedication Cathedral Entrance

(Ordained minister enters the Cathedral and then immediately stops, kneels and then kisses the ground at a designated clean and suitable space.)

CELEBRANT

(After arising to their feet having kissed the Sacred Ground of the Cathedral.)

In the name of ✠ the Father, and of the Son, and of the Holy Spirit. Amen.

✠ May the healing love and the abiding strength of the angels and saints of Heaven be ever present throughout this Most Sacred Place. Amen.

BLESSING OF THE HOLY INCENSE

Dedication Cathedral
Blessing of the Holy Incense

(Minister begins a clockwise circumscription of the interior of the building for a first time, stopping only at each corner or significant change in the direction of the interior walls and reciting the invocation below whilst swinging the incense burner (brazier) at the site.)

CELEBRANT

(Minister smudging with holy incense in the form of a cross at each location.)

✠ In the name of God our Heavenly Father. In the name of Christ his son and our saviour. In the name of the Holy Spirits and all the angels and saints of Heaven, I invoke and release into this sacred fragrant smoke our purest intentions to honour thy name through your Holy Sacraments and Actions.

By the authority of our Divine Creator let this place be free of any impurities or impediments to its sacred purpose. We do this in the name of Christ our saviour and Mary, our Heavenly mother. Amen.

BLESSING OF THE HOLY WATER

Dedication Cathedral
Blessing of the Holy Water

(Minister moves in a clockwise circumscription of the interior of the building for a second time, stopping only at each corner or significant change in the direction of the interior walls and reciting the invocation below whilst sprinkling holy water.)

CELEBRANT

(Minister sprinkles holy water in the form of a

cross at each location.)

✠In the name of God our Heavenly Father and Christ his son and the Holy Spirit, I bless this Space as Sacred Space, so that it be a place of spiritual, physical and mental healing; and I seal the boundary of this place so that any and all lingering negativity or regrets or negative spirits of the past be banished from this Sacred Space; and that no negative spirit or force may enter this space to impede its heavenly purpose. Amen.

BLESSING OF THE LIGHT

Dedication Cathedral
Blessing of the Light

(A Lantern is lit and raised on a pole, so all can see. Other Lanterns may also be lit and handed to supporters of the Minister to follow in procession. The Minister moves in a clockwise circumscription of the interior of the building for a third and final time, stopping with the Lantern only at each corner or significant change in the direction of the interior walls and reciting the invocation.)

CELEBRANT

✠In the name of God our Heavenly Father, I invoke the light of Christ in all its glory. That it fill this sacred place with your radiance and your love, mercy and compassion for all life and all persons; and that evil and ignorance shall find no shelter in this sacred place; and that all who come to this sacred place will have their eyes opened to your revelation and the gifts you have bestowed upon the Universal Ecclesia as the Living Body of Christ. Amen.

NAMING

Dedication Cathedral
Naming

(A wooden crozier is handed to the Celebrant who returns to the centre of the Cathedral in front of the Altar)

CELEBRANT

Christ himself did speak of the Great Divine Register in Heaven where all that is Holy is recorded for all eternity. In respect and honour of his teachings we now proclaim the name of this most holy place of worship to be N. and humbly inscribe it in the language of the prophets and saints, so that the angels and saints of Heaven may take these signs and symbols to Heaven and enter them into your most Holy of Registers.

(Celebrant then uses the crozier to trace the name of the Cathedral in Latin or Greek on the floor.)

HOLY MASS

Dedication Cathedral Holy Mass

(NOTE: The Rite of Dedication of Cathedral is considered incomplete until Holy Mass is conducted within the Cathedral immediately after the above Dedication Rites.)

XXXV.VIII – RITE OF DEDICATION OF ALTAR

Rite of Dedication of Altar

1. The *Rite of Dedication of Altar* conferred by a competent minister assumes the Rite of Dedication of Sacred Site has already been performed. The Rite of Dedication of Altar shall be as follows:-

ENTRANCE

Dedication Altar Entrance

(Ordained minister kisses the Altar)

CELEBRANT

In the name of ✠ the Father, and of the Son, and of the Holy Spirit. Amen.

✠ May the healing love and the abiding strength of the angels and saints of Heaven be ever present upon this Sacred Space. Amen.

BLESSING OF THE HOLY INCENSE

Dedication Altar Blessing of the Holy Incense

(Minister begins a clockwise circumscription of the Altar for a first time whilst swinging the incense burner (brazier) at the site.)

CELEBRANT

(Minister smudging with holy incense in the form of a cross at each location.)

✠ In the name of God our Heavenly Father. In the name of Christ his son and our saviour. In the name of the Holy Spirits and all the angels and saints of Heaven, I invoke and release into this sacred fragrant smoke our purest intentions to honour thy name through your Holy Sacraments and Actions.

By the authority of our Divine Creator let this place be free of any impurities or impediments to its sacred purpose. We do this in the name of Christ our saviour and Mary, our Heavenly mother. Amen.

BLESSING OF THE HOLY WATER

Dedication Altar
Blessing of the Holy Water

(Minister moves in a clockwise circumscription of the Altar for a second time reciting the invocation below whilst sprinkling holy water.)

CELEBRANT

(Minister sprinkles holy water in the form of a cross at each location.)

✠In the name of God our Heavenly Father and Christ his son and the Holy Spirit, I bless this Space as Sacred Space, so that it be a place of spiritual, physical and mental healing; and I seal the boundary of this space so that any and all lingering negativity or regrets or negative spirits of the past be banished from this Sacred Space; and that no negative spirit or force may enter this space to impede its heavenly purpose. Amen.

BLESSING OF THE LIGHT

Dedication Altar
Blessing of the Light

(A Candle is lit, so all can see. Other Candles may also be lit and handed to supporters of the Minister to follow in procession. The Minister moves in a clockwise circumscription of the Altar for a third and final time and reciting the invocation.)

CELEBRANT

✠In the name of God our Heavenly Father, I invoke the light of Christ in all its glory. That it fill this sacred place with your radiance and your love, mercy and compassion for all life and all persons; and that evil and ignorance shall find no shelter in this sacred place; and that all who come to this sacred place will have their eyes opened to your revelation and the gifts you have bestowed upon the Universal Ecclesia as the Living Body of Christ. Amen.

HOLY MASS

Dedication Altar
Holy Mass

(NOTE: The Rite of Dedication of Altar is

considered incomplete until Holy Mass is conducted with the Altar immediately after the above Dedication Rites.)

XXXV.IX – RITE OF DEDICATION OF SHRINE

Rite of Dedication of Shrine

1. The *Rite of Dedication of Shrine* conferred by a competent minister assumes the Rite of Dedication of Sacred Site has already been performed. The Rite of Dedication of Shrine shall be as follows:-

Dedication Shrine
Entrance

ENTRANCE

(Ordained minister approaches the Shrine and then immediately stops, kneels and then kisses the base of the Shrine.)

CELEBRANT

(After arising to their feet having kissed the Sacred Ground of the Shrine.)

In the name of ✠ the Father, and of the Son, and of the Holy Spirit. Amen.

✠ May the healing love and the abiding strength of the angels and saints of Heaven be ever present throughout this Sacred Place. Amen.

Dedication Shrine
Blessing of the Holy Incense

BLESSING OF THE HOLY INCENSE

(Minister begins a clockwise circumscription of the Shrine for a first time, stopping only at each corner or significant change in the direction of the structure and reciting the invocation below whilst swinging the incense burner (brazier) at the site.)

CELEBRANT

(Minister smudging with holy incense in the form of a cross at each location.)

✠ In the name of God our Heavenly Father. In the name of Christ his son and our saviour. In the name of the Holy Spirits and all the angels and saints of Heaven, I invoke and release into this sacred fragrant smoke our purest intentions to honour thy name through your Holy Sacraments and Actions.

By the authority of our Divine Creator let this place be free of any impurities or impediments to its sacred purpose. We do this in the name of Christ our saviour and Mary, our Heavenly mother. Amen.

BLESSING OF THE HOLY WATER

Dedication Shrine
Blessing of the Holy Water

(Minister moves in a clockwise circumscription of the Shrine for a second time, stopping only at each corner or significant change in the direction of the structure and reciting the invocation below whilst sprinkling holy water.)

CELEBRANT

(Minister sprinkles holy water in the form of a cross at each location.)

✠In the name of God our Heavenly Father and Christ his son and the Holy Spirit, I bless this Space as Sacred Space, so that it be a place of spiritual, physical and mental healing; and I seal the boundary of this place so that any and all lingering negativity or regrets or negative spirits of the past be banished from this Sacred Space; and that no negative spirit or force may enter this space to impede its heavenly purpose. Amen.

BLESSING OF THE LIGHT

Dedication Shrine
Blessing of the Light

(A Lantern is lit and raised on a pole, so all can see. Other Lanterns may also be lit and handed to supporters of the Minister to follow in procession. The Minister moves in a clockwise circumscription of the Shrine for a third and final time, stopping with the Lantern only at each corner or significant change in the direction of the structure and reciting the invocation.)

CELEBRANT

✠In the name of God our Heavenly Father, I invoke the light of Christ in all its glory. That it fill this sacred place with your radiance and your love, mercy and compassion for all life and all persons; and that evil and ignorance shall find no shelter in this sacred place; and that all who come to this sacred place will have their eyes opened to your revelation and the gifts you have bestowed upon the

Universal Ecclesia as the Living Body of Christ. Amen.

HOLY MASS

Dedication Shrine Holy Mass

(NOTE: The Rite of Dedication of Shrine is considered incomplete until Holy Mass is conducted at the Shrine immediately after the above Dedication Rites.)

XXXV.X – RITE OF DEDICATION OF CEMETERY

Rite of Dedication of Cemetery

1. The *Rite of Dedication of Cemetery* conferred by a competent minister assumes the Rite of Dedication of Sacred Site has already been performed. The Rite of Dedication of Cemetery shall be as follows:-

ENTRANCE

Dedication Cemetery Entrance

(Ordained minister approaches the Cemetery and crosses the threshold and then immediately stops, kneels and then kisses the ground at a designated clean and suitable space)

CELEBRANT

(After arising to their feet having kissed the Sacred Ground of the Cemetery.)

In the name of ✠ the Father, and of the Son, and of the Holy Spirit. Amen.

✠ May the healing love and the abiding strength of the angels and saints of Heaven be ever present throughout this Sacred Place. Amen.

BLESSING OF THE HOLY INCENSE

Dedication Cemetery Blessing of the Holy Incense

(Minister begins a clockwise circumscription of the interior boundary of the site for a first time, stopping only at each corner or significant change in the direction and reciting the invocation below whilst swinging the incense burner (brazier) at the site.)

CELEBRANT

(Minister smudging with holy incense in the form of a cross at each location.)

✠ In the name of God our Heavenly Father. In the name of

Christ his son and our saviour. In the name of the Holy Spirits and all the angels and saints of Heaven, I invoke and release into this sacred fragrant smoke our purest intentions to honour thy name through your Holy Sacraments and Actions.

By the authority of our Divine Creator let this place be free of any impurities or impediments to its sacred purpose. We do this in the name of Christ our saviour and Mary, our Heavenly mother. Amen.

BLESSING OF THE HOLY WATER

Dedication Cemetery Blessing of the Holy Water

(Minister moves in a clockwise circumscription of the interior boundary of the site for a second time, stopping only at each corner or significant change in the direction of the boundary and reciting the invocation below whilst sprinkling holy water.)

CELEBRANT

(Minister sprinkles holy water in the form of a cross at each location.)

✠In the name of God our Heavenly Father and Christ his son and the Holy Spirit, I bless this Space as Sacred Space, so that it be a place of spiritual, physical and mental healing; and I seal the boundary of this place so that any and all lingering negativity or regrets or negative spirits of the past be banished from this Sacred Space; and that no negative spirit or force may enter this space to impede its heavenly purpose. Amen.

BLESSING OF THE LIGHT

Dedication Cemetery Blessing of the Light

(A Lantern is lit and raised on a pole, so all can see. Other Lanterns may also be lit and handed to supporters of the Minister to follow in procession. The Minister moves in a clockwise circumscription of the interior boundary of the site for a third and final time, stopping with the Lantern only at each corner or significant change in the direction of the interior walls and reciting the invocation.)

CELEBRANT

✠In the name of God our Heavenly Father, I invoke the light of Christ in all its glory. That it fill this sacred place with your radiance and your love, mercy and compassion for all life and all persons; and that evil and ignorance shall find no shelter in this sacred place; and that all who come to this sacred place will have their eyes opened to your revelation and the gifts you have bestowed upon the Universal Ecclesia as the Living Body of Christ. Amen.

XXXV.XI – RITE OF DEDICATION OF CREMATORIUM

1. The *Rite of Dedication of Crematorium* conferred by a competent minister assumes the Rite of Dedication of Sacred Site has already been performed. The Rite of Dedication of Crematorium shall be as follows:- Rite of Dedication of Crematorium

ENTRANCE

Dedication Crematorium Entrance

(Ordained minister approaches the Crematorium and crosses the threshold and then immediately stops, kneels and then kisses the ground at a designated clean and suitable space)

CELEBRANT

(After arising to their feet having kissed the Sacred Ground of the Crematorium.)

In the name of ✠the Father, and of the Son, and of the Holy Spirit. Amen.

✠May the healing love and the abiding strength of the angels and saints of Heaven be ever present throughout this Sacred Space. Amen.

BLESSING OF THE HOLY INCENSE

Dedication Crematorium Blessing of the Holy Incense

(Minister begins a clockwise circumscription of the interior boundary of the site for a first time, stopping only at each corner or significant change in the direction of the interior walls and reciting the invocation below whilst swinging the incense burner (brazier) at the site.)

CELEBRANT

(Minister smudging with holy incense in the form of a cross at each location.)

✠In the name of God our Heavenly Father. In the name of Christ his son and our saviour. In the name of the Holy Spirits and all the angels and saints of Heaven, I invoke and release into this sacred fragrant smoke our purest intentions to honour thy name through your Holy Sacraments and Actions.

By the authority of our Divine Creator let this place be free of any impurities or impediments to its sacred purpose. We do this in the name of Christ our saviour and Mary, our Heavenly mother. Amen.

BLESSING OF THE HOLY WATER

Dedication Crematorium
Blessing of the Holy Water

(Minister moves in a clockwise circumscription of the interior boundary of the site for a second time, stopping only at each corner or significant change in the direction of the interior walls and reciting the invocation below whilst sprinkling holy water.)

CELEBRANT

(Minister sprinkles holy water in the form of a cross at each location.)

✠In the name of God our Heavenly Father and Christ his son and the Holy Spirit, I bless this Space as Sacred Space, so that it be a place of spiritual, physical and mental healing; and I seal the boundary of this place so that any and all lingering negativity or regrets or negative spirits of the past be banished from this Sacred Space; and that no negative spirit or force may enter this space to impede its heavenly purpose. Amen.

BLESSING OF THE LIGHT

Dedication Crematorium
Blessing of the Light

(A Lantern is lit and raised on a pole, so all can see. Other Lanterns may also be lit and handed to supporters of the Minister to follow in procession. The Minister moves in a clockwise circumscription of the interior boundary of the site for a third and final time, stopping with the Lantern only at each corner or significant change in the direction of the interior walls and reciting the invocation.)

CELEBRANT

✠In the name of God our Heavenly Father, I invoke the light of Christ in all its glory. That it fill this sacred place with your radiance and your love, mercy and compassion for all life and all persons; and that evil and ignorance shall find no shelter in this sacred place; and that all who come to this sacred place will have their eyes opened to your revelation and the gifts you have bestowed upon the Universal Ecclesia as the Living Body of Christ. Amen.

XXXV.XII – RITE OF DEDICATION OF RELIGIOUS HOUSE

1. The *Rite of Dedication of Religious House* conferred by a competent minister assumes the Rite of Dedication of Sacred Site has already been performed. The Rite of Dedication of Religious House shall be as follows:-

Rite of Dedication of Religious House

ENTRANCE

Dedication Religious House Entrance

(Ordained minister approaches the Religious House and crosses the threshold and then immediately stops, kneels and then kisses the ground at a designated clean and suitable space)

CELEBRANT

(After arising to their feet having kissed the Sacred Ground of the Religious House.)

In the name of ✠the Father, and of the Son, and of the Holy Spirit. Amen.

✠May the healing love and the abiding strength of the angels and saints of Heaven be ever present throughout this Sacred Space. Amen.

BLESSING OF THE HOLY INCENSE

Dedication Religious House Blessing of the Holy Incense

(Minister begins a clockwise circumscription of the interior of the building for a first time, stopping only at each corner or significant change in the direction of the interior walls and reciting the invocation below whilst swinging the incense burner (brazier) at the site.)

CELEBRANT

(Minister smudging with holy incense in the

form of a cross at each location.)

✠In the name of God our Heavenly Father. In the name of Christ his son and our saviour. In the name of the Holy Spirits and all the angels and saints of Heaven, I invoke and release into this sacred fragrant smoke our purest intentions to honour thy name through your Holy Sacraments and Actions.

By the authority of our Divine Creator let this place be free of any impurities or impediments to its sacred purpose. We do this in the name of Christ our saviour and Mary, our Heavenly mother. Amen.

BLESSING OF THE HOLY WATER

Dedication Religious House
Blessing of the Holy Water

(Minister moves in a clockwise circumscription of the interior of the building for a second time, stopping only at each corner or significant change in the direction of the interior walls and reciting the invocation below whilst sprinkling holy water.)

CELEBRANT

(Minister sprinkles holy water in the form of a cross at each location.)

✠In the name of God our Heavenly Father and Christ his son and the Holy Spirit, I bless this Space as Sacred Space, so that it be a place of spiritual, physical and mental healing; and I seal the boundary of this place so that any and all lingering negativity or regrets or negative spirits of the past be banished from this Sacred Space; and that no negative spirit or force may enter this space to impede its heavenly purpose. Amen.

BLESSING OF THE LIGHT

Dedication Religious House
Blessing of the Light

(A Lantern is lit so all can see. Other Lanterns may also be lit and handed to supporters of the Minister to follow in procession. The Minister moves in a clockwise circumscription of the interior of the building for a third and final time, stopping with the Lantern only at each corner or significant change in the direction of the interior walls and reciting the invocation.)

CELEBRANT

✠In the name of God our Heavenly Father, I invoke the light of Christ in all its glory. That it fill this sacred place with your radiance and your love, mercy and compassion for all life and all persons; and that evil and ignorance shall find no shelter in this sacred place; and that all who come to this sacred place will have their eyes opened to your revelation and the gifts you have bestowed upon the Universal Ecclesia as the Living Body of Christ. Amen.

XXXV.XIII – RITE OF DEDICATION OF REGISTRY

1. The *Rite of Dedication of Registry* conferred by a competent minister assumes the Rite of Dedication of Sacred Site has already been performed. The Rite of Dedication of Registry shall be as follows:- Rite of Dedication of Registry

ENTRANCE

Dedication Registry Entrance

(Ordained minister approaches the Registry and crosses the threshold and then immediately stops, kneels and then kisses the ground at a designated clean and suitable space)

CELEBRANT

(After arising to their feet having kissed the Sacred Ground of the Registry.)

In the name of ✠the Father, and of the Son, and of the Holy Spirit. Amen.

✠May the healing love and the abiding strength of the angels and saints of Heaven be ever present throughout this Sacred Space. Amen.

BLESSING OF THE HOLY INCENSE

Dedication Registry Blessing of the Holy Incense

(Minister begins a clockwise circumscription of the interior of the building for a first time, stopping only at each corner or significant change in the direction of the interior walls and reciting the invocation below whilst swinging the incense burner (brazier) at the site.)

CELEBRANT

(Minister smudging with holy incense in the form of a cross at each location.)

✠In the name of God our Heavenly Father. In the name of Christ his son and our saviour. In the name of the Holy Spirits and all the angels and saints of Heaven, I invoke and release into this sacred fragrant smoke our purest intentions to honour thy name through your Holy Sacraments and Actions.

By the authority of our Divine Creator let this place be free of any impurities or impediments to its sacred purpose. We do this in the name of Christ our saviour and Mary, our Heavenly mother. Amen.

BLESSING OF THE HOLY WATER

Dedication Registry
Blessing of the Holy Water

(Minister moves in a clockwise circumscription of the interior of the building for a second time, stopping only at each corner or significant change in the direction of the interior walls and reciting the invocation below whilst sprinkling holy water.)

CELEBRANT

(Minister sprinkles holy water in the form of a cross at each location.)

✠In the name of God our Heavenly Father and Christ his son and the Holy Spirit, I bless this Space as Sacred Space, so that it be a place of spiritual, physical and mental healing; and I seal the boundary of this place so that any and all lingering negativity or regrets or negative spirits of the past be banished from this Sacred Space; and that no negative spirit or force may enter this space to impede its heavenly purpose. Amen.

BLESSING OF THE LIGHT

Dedication Registry
Blessing of the Light

(A Lantern is lit and raised on a pole, so all can see. Other Lanterns may also be lit and handed to supporters of the Minister to follow in procession. The Minister moves in a clockwise circumscription of the interior of the building for a third and final time, stopping with the Lantern only at each corner or significant change in the direction of the interior walls and reciting the invocation.)

CELEBRANT

✠In the name of God our Heavenly Father, I invoke the light of Christ in all its glory. That it fill this sacred place with your radiance and your love, mercy and compassion for all life and all persons; and that evil and ignorance shall find no shelter in this sacred place; and that all who come to this sacred place will have their eyes opened to your revelation and the gifts you have bestowed upon the Universal Ecclesia as the Living Body of Christ. Amen.

XXXV.XIV – RITE OF DEDICATION OF ORATORY

1. The *Rite of Dedication of Oratory* conferred by a competent minister assumes the Rite of Dedication of Sacred Site has already been performed. The Rite of Dedication of Oratory shall be as follows:-

Rite of Dedication of Oratory

ENTRANCE

Dedication Oratory Entrance

(Ordained minister approaches the Oratory and crosses the threshold and then immediately stops, kneels and then kisses the ground at a designated clean and suitable space)

CELEBRANT

(After arising to their feet having kissed the Sacred Ground of the Oratory.)

In the name of ✠the Father, and of the Son, and of the Holy Spirit. Amen.

✠May the healing love and the abiding strength of the angels and saints of Heaven be ever present throughout this Sacred Space. Amen.

BLESSING OF THE HOLY INCENSE

Dedication Oratory Blessing of the Holy Incense

(Minister begins a clockwise circumscription of the interior of the building for a first time, stopping only at each corner or significant change in the direction of the interior walls and reciting the invocation below whilst swinging the incense burner (brazier) at the site.)

CELEBRANT

(Minister smudging with holy incense in the form of a cross at each location.)

✠In the name of God our Heavenly Father. In the name of

Christ his son and our saviour. In the name of the Holy Spirits and all the angels and saints of Heaven, I invoke and release into this sacred fragrant smoke our purest intentions to honour thy name through your Holy Sacraments and Actions.

By the authority of our Divine Creator let this place be free of any impurities or impediments to its sacred purpose. We do this in the name of Christ our saviour and Mary, our Heavenly mother. Amen.

BLESSING OF THE HOLY WATER

Dedication Oratory
Blessing of the Holy Water

(Minister moves in a clockwise circumscription of the interior of the building for a second time, stopping only at each corner or significant change in the direction of the interior walls and reciting the invocation below whilst sprinkling holy water.)

CELEBRANT

(Minister sprinkles holy water in the form of a cross at each location.)

✠In the name of God our Heavenly Father and Christ his son and the Holy Spirit, I bless this Space as Sacred Space, so that it be a place of spiritual, physical and mental healing; and I seal the boundary of this place so that any and all lingering negativity or regrets or negative spirits of the past be banished from this Sacred Space; and that no negative spirit or force may enter this space to impede its heavenly purpose. Amen.

BLESSING OF THE LIGHT

Dedication Oratory
Blessing of the Light

(A Lantern is lit and raised on a pole, so all can see. Other Lanterns may also be lit and handed to supporters of the Minister to follow in procession. The Minister moves in a clockwise circumscription of the interior of the building for a third and final time, stopping with the Lantern only at each corner or significant change in the direction of the interior walls and reciting the invocation.)

CELEBRANT

✠In the name of God our Heavenly Father, I invoke the light of Christ in all its glory. That it fill this sacred place with your radiance and your love, mercy and compassion for all life and all persons; and that evil and ignorance shall find no shelter in this sacred place; and that all who come to this sacred place will have their eyes opened to your revelation and the gifts you have bestowed upon the Universal Ecclesia as the Living Body of Christ. Amen.

Title XXXVI – Rite of Deconsecration

XXXVI.I – RITE OF DECONSECRATION

1. Deconsecration shall be when a person, place, object or thing set aside for religious purposes through a form of the Sacrament of Sanctification and Rite of Consecration is formally removed from such service or purpose and ecclesiastical status. The Rite for deconsecration of persons of the ecclesial state is the Rite of Secularisation. Rite of Deconsecration

The Rite of Deconsecration shall be granted and conferred in accordance with the most sacred Covenants *Pactum De Singularis Caelum* and *Pactum De Singularis Christus* and associated approved liturgy.

2. Only the Rite of Consecration properly conferred creates Sacred Circumscribed Space. Once the Sacrament of Sanctification and Rite of Consecration forms certain Sacred Circumscribed Space, such space cannot be dissolved or destroyed, only set aside. Divine Purpose of the Rite of Deconsecration

Thus the Rite of Deconsecration is the temporary suppression of Sacred Circumscribed Space dedicated to Divine purpose or service. The Rite itself does not create any new character, nor does it taint, defile or diminish the original Sacrament of Sanctification and Rite of Consecration. Instead, the Rite of Deconsecration properly imparts a valid ecclesial impediment upon a sacred place.

A person, place, object or thing properly deconsecrated has its ecclesiastical character, purpose and service temporarily suppressed, thus constricting its ability to perform or be used for certain licit ecclesiastical acts.

Deconsecration does not create, nor infer the formation of "unholy" space, as such a notion is an abomination and a defiance of the logic and articles of the most sacred Covenants *Pactum De Singularis Caelum* and *Pactum De Singularis Christus*. Instead, Deconsecration inserts an intentional impediment into a previously consecrated space, preventing such space from being used legitimately and authentically for authorised sacred rites and acts.

3. There are only nine (9) valid and licit forms for the Rite of Deconsecration as defined by the most sacred *Missale Christus* and associated approved liturgy being *Chapel, Church, Cathedral, Shrine, Cemetery, Crematorium, Religious House, Registry* and *Oratory*:- Forms of the Rite of Deconsecration

   (i) "**Rite of Deconsecration of Chapel**" is when the Rite of Deconsecration is imparted upon a Chapel once such a place fulfils the conditions for such a Rite; and

(ii) "**Rite of Deconsecration of Church**" is when the Rite of Deconsecration is imparted upon a Church once such a place fulfils the conditions for such a Rite; and

(iii) "**Rite of Deconsecration of Cathedral**" is when the Rite of Deconsecration is imparted upon a Cathedral once such a place fulfils the conditions for such a Rite; and

(iv) "**Rite of Deconsecration of Shrine**" is when the Rite of Deconsecration is imparted upon a Shrine once such a place fulfils the conditions for such a Rite; and

(v) "**Rite of Deconsecration of Cemetery**" is when the Rite of Deconsecration is imparted upon a Cemetery once such a place fulfils the conditions for such a Rite; and

(vi) "**Rite of Deconsecration of Crematorium**" is when the Rite of Deconsecration is imparted upon a Crematorium once such a place fulfils the conditions for such a Rite; and

(vii) "**Rite of Deconsecration of Religious House**" is when the Rite of Deconsecration is imparted upon a Religious House once such a place fulfils the conditions for such a Rite; and

(viii) "**Rite of Deconsecration of Registry**" is when the Rite of Deconsecration is imparted upon a Registry once such a place fulfils the conditions for such a Rite; and

(ix) "**Rite of Deconsecration of Oratory**" is when the Rite of Deconsecration is imparted upon a Oratory once such a place fulfils the conditions for such a Rite.

XXXVI.II – CONDITIONS OF RITE OF DECONSECRATION

1. Conditions of the Rite of Deconsecration are those requisite qualifications and contingencies permitted in the proper ministration of the Rite. There shall exist only nine (9) possible Conditions for the ministration of Rite of Deconsecration being *Chapel, Church, Cathedral, Shrine, Cemetery, Crematorium, Religious House, Registry and Oratory*:- Conditions of Rite of Deconsecration

(i) *Chapel* are the Conditions necessary for the conferral of the Rite of Deconsecration of Chapel; and

(ii) *Church* are the Conditions necessary for the conferral of the Rite of Deconsecration of Church; and

(iii) *Cathedral* are the Conditions necessary for the conferral of the Rite of Deconsecration of Cathedral; and

(iv) *Shrine* are the Conditions necessary for the conferral of the Rite of Deconsecration of Shrine; and

(v) *Cemetery* are the Conditions necessary for the conferral of the Rite of Deconsecration of Cemetery; and

(vi) *Crematorium* are the Conditions necessary for the conferral of the Rite of Deconsecration of Crematorium; and

(vii) *Religious House* are the Conditions necessary for the conferral of the Rite of Deconsecration of Religious House; and

(viii) *Registry* are the Conditions necessary for the conferral of the Rite of Deconsecration of Registry; and

(ix) *Oratory* are the Conditions necessary for the conferral of the Rite of Deconsecration of Oratory.

2. The conditions for the Rite of Deconsecration of Chapel are:- Chapel Conditions

(i) That a Decree of Suppression (*Decretum Ecclesiae Annullas*) and an Ecclesiastical Writ of Annulment (*Recto Ecclesiae Abrogationis*) were duly issued by the proper Ecclesiastical Authority concerning the Chapel in question; and

(ii) That no motion to appeal the Decree and Writ were properly filed by a party possessing a valid interest within forty (40) days of issuance and notice; or that a validly constituted tribunal ruled in favour of the original Decree and Writ after having heard a valid appeal; and

(iii) That the Ecclesiastical Writ of Annulment (*Recto Ecclesiae Abrogationis*) was executed and fulfilled and the record of the former Chapel in question was struck out of the *Register of Ecclesiastical Places of Worship* of the *Great Register of Title and Rights* of the Universal Ecclesia; and

(iv) That the Decree of Suppression (*Decretum Ecclesiae Annullas*) was honoured and any Altar, Tabernacle or Shrine was removed from the former Chapel, including any and all sacred statues and movable sacred objects; and

(v) That a formal visitation of the building completed the Rite of Deconsecration of Chapel.

3. The conditions for the Rite of Deconsecration of Church are:- Church Conditions

(i) That a Decree of Suppression (*Decretum Ecclesiae Annullas*) and an Ecclesiastical Writ of Annulment (*Recto Ecclesiae Abrogationis*) were duly issued by the proper Ecclesiastical Authority concerning the Church in question; and

(ii) That no motion to appeal the Decree and Writ were properly filed by a party possessing a valid interest within forty (40) days of issuance and notice; or that a validly constituted tribunal ruled in favour of the original Decree and Writ after having heard a valid appeal; and

(iii) That the Ecclesiastical Writ of Annulment (*Recto Ecclesiae Abrogationis*) was executed and fulfilled and the record of the former Church in question was struck out of the *Register of Ecclesiastical Places of Worship* of the *Great Register of Title and Rights* of the Universal Ecclesia; and

(iv) That the Decree of Suppression (*Decretum Ecclesiae Annullas*) was honoured and any Altar, Tabernacle or Shrine or Relics were removed from the former Church, including any and all sacred statues and movable sacred objects; and

(v) That a formal visitation of the building completed the Rite of Deconsecration of Church.

4. The conditions for the Rite of Deconsecration of Cathedral are:- Cathedral Conditions

(i) That a Decree of Suppression (*Decretum Ecclesiae Annullas*) and an Ecclesiastical Writ of Annulment (*Recto Ecclesiae Abrogationis*) were duly issued by the proper Ecclesiastical Authority concerning the Cathedral in question; and

(ii) That no motion to appeal the Decree and Writ were properly filed by a party possessing a valid interest within forty (40) days of issuance and notice; or that a validly constituted tribunal ruled in favour of the original Decree and Writ after having heard a valid appeal; and

(iii) That the Ecclesiastical Writ of Annulment (*Recto Ecclesiae Abrogationis*) was executed and fulfilled and the record of the former Cathedral in question was struck out of the *Register of Ecclesiastical Places of Worship* of the *Great Register of Title and Rights* of the Universal Ecclesia; and

(iv) That the Decree of Suppression (Decretum Ecclesiae Annullas) was honoured and all Altars, Tabernacles, Shrines, Relics or Bodies were removed from the former Cathedral, including any and all sacred statues and movable sacred objects; and

(v) That a formal visitation of the building completed the Rite of Deconsecration of Cathedral.

5. The conditions for the Rite of Deconsecration of Shrine are:- Shrine Conditions

(i) That a Decree of Suppression (*Decretum Ecclesiae Annullas*) and an Ecclesiastical Writ of Annulment (*Recto Ecclesiae Abrogationis*) were duly issued by the proper Ecclesiastical Authority concerning the Shrine in question; and

(ii) That no motion to appeal the Decree and Writ were properly filed by a party possessing a valid interest within forty (40) days of issuance and notice; or that a validly constituted tribunal ruled in favour of the original Decree and Writ after having heard a valid appeal; and

(iii) That the Ecclesiastical Writ of Annulment (*Recto Ecclesiae Abrogationis*) was executed and fulfilled and the record of the former Shrine in question was struck out of the *Register of Ecclesiastical Altars and Shrines* of the *Great Register of Title and Rights* of the Universal Ecclesia; and

(iv) That the Decree of Suppression (*Decretum Ecclesiae Annullas*) was honoured and that the Shrine was disassembled from any Altar, Tabernacle or Relics were removed from the former Shrine, including any and all sacred statues and movable sacred objects; and

(v) That a formal visitation of the site of former Shrine completed the Rite of Deconsecration of Shrine.

6. The conditions for the Rite of Deconsecration of Cemetery are:- Cemetery Conditions

(i) That a Decree of Suppression (*Decretum Ecclesiae Annullas*) and an Ecclesiastical Writ of Annulment (*Recto Ecclesiae Abrogationis*) were duly issued by the proper Ecclesiastical Authority concerning the Cemetery in question; and

(ii) That no motion to appeal the Decree and Writ were properly filed by a party possessing a valid interest within forty (40) days of issuance and notice; or that a validly constituted tribunal ruled in favour of the original Decree and Writ after having heard a valid appeal; and

(iii) That the Ecclesiastical Writ of Annulment (*Recto Ecclesiae Abrogationis*) was executed and fulfilled and the record of the former Cemetery in question was struck out of the *Register of*

Cemeteries and Crematoriums of the *Great Register of Title and Rights* of the Universal Ecclesia; and

(iv) That the Decree of Suppression (*Decretum Ecclesiae Annullas*) was honoured and all bodies and ashes were exhumed and re-buried in a new consecrated location, so that no bodily remains exist at the former Cemetery site; and any Chapels, Shrines or Altars were likewise dismantled; and

(v) That a formal visitation of the site of former Cemetery completed the Rite of Deconsecration of Cemetery.

7. The conditions for the Rite of Deconsecration of Crematorium are:- Crematorium Conditions

(i) That a Decree of Suppression (*Decretum Ecclesiae Annullas*) and an Ecclesiastical Writ of Annulment (*Recto Ecclesiae Abrogationis*) were duly issued by the proper Ecclesiastical Authority concerning the Crematorium in question; and

(ii) That no motion to appeal the Decree and Writ were properly filed by a party possessing a valid interest within forty (40) days of issuance and notice; or that a validly constituted tribunal ruled in favour of the original Decree and Writ after having heard a valid appeal; and

(iii) That the Ecclesiastical Writ of Annulment (*Recto Ecclesiae Abrogationis*) was executed and fulfilled and the record of the former Crematorium in question was struck out of the *Register of Cemeteries and Crematoriums* of the *Great Register of Title and Rights* of the Universal Ecclesia; and

(iv) That the Decree of Suppression (*Decretum Ecclesiae Annullas*) was honoured and any ashes or remains were removed from the former Crematorium site, including the dismantling of any and all Chapels, Shrines or Altars, including any and all sacred statues and movable sacred objects; and

(v) That a formal visitation of the site of former Crematorium completed the Rite of Deconsecration of Crematorium.

8. The conditions for the Rite of Deconsecration of Religious House are:- Religious House Conditions

(i) That a Decree of Suppression (*Decretum Ecclesiae Annullas*) and an Ecclesiastical Writ of Annulment (*Recto Ecclesiae Abrogationis*) were duly issued by the proper Ecclesiastical Authority concerning the Religious House in question; and

(ii) That no motion to appeal the Decree and Writ were properly filed by a party possessing a valid interest within forty (40) days of issuance and notice; or that a validly constituted tribunal ruled in favour of the original Decree and Writ after having heard a valid appeal; and

(iii) That the Ecclesiastical Writ of Annulment (*Recto Ecclesiae Abrogationis*) was executed and fulfilled and the record of the former Religious House in question was struck out of the *Register of Ecclesiastical Houses and Monasteries* of the *Great Register of Title and Rights* of the Universal Ecclesia; and

(iv) That the Decree of Suppression (*Decretum Ecclesiae Annullas*) was honoured and any Altar, Tabernacle or Shrine was removed from the former Religious House, including any and all sacred statues and movable sacred objects; and

(v) That a formal visitation of the site of former Religious House completed the Rite of Deconsecration of Religious House.

9. The conditions for the Rite of Deconsecration of Registry are:- Registry Conditions

(i) That a Decree of Suppression (*Decretum Ecclesiae Annullas*) and an Ecclesiastical Writ of Annulment (*Recto Ecclesiae Abrogationis*) were duly issued by the proper Ecclesiastical Authority concerning the Registry in question; and

(ii) That no motion to appeal the Decree and Writ were properly filed by a party possessing a valid interest within forty (40) days of issuance and notice; or that a validly constituted tribunal ruled in favour of the original Decree and Writ after having heard a valid appeal; and

(iii) That the Ecclesiastical Writ of Annulment (*Recto Ecclesiae Abrogationis*) was executed and fulfilled and the record of the former Registry in question was struck out of the *Register of Ecclesiastical Places of Worship* of the *Great Register of Title and Rights* of the Universal Ecclesia; and

(iv) That the Decree of Suppression (*Decretum Ecclesiae Annullas*) was honoured and any sacred statues and movable sacred objects and registers were removed from the former registry; and

(v) That a formal visitation of the site of former Registry completed the Rite of Deconsecration of Registry.

10. The conditions for the Rite of Deconsecration of Oratory are:- Oratory Conditions

(i) That a Decree of Suppression (*Decretum Ecclesiae Annullas*) and an Ecclesiastical Writ of Annulment (*Recto Ecclesiae*

Abrogationis) were duly issued by the proper Ecclesiastical Authority concerning the Oratory in question; and

(ii) That no motion to appeal the Decree and Writ were properly filed by a party possessing a valid interest within forty (40) days of issuance and notice; or that a validly constituted tribunal ruled in favour of the original Decree and Writ after having heard a valid appeal; and

(iii) That the Ecclesiastical Writ of Annulment (*Recto Ecclesiae Abrogationis*) was executed and fulfilled and the record of the former Oratory in question was struck out of the *Register of Ecclesiastical Places of Worship* of the *Great Register of Title and Rights* of the Universal Ecclesia; and

(iv) That the Decree of Suppression (*Decretum Ecclesiae Annullas*) was honoured and any Altar, Tabernacle or Shrine was removed from the former Oratory, including any and all sacred statues and movable sacred objects; and

(v) That a formal visitation of the site of former Oratory completed the Rite of Deconsecration of Oratory.

XXXVI.III – RITE OF DECONSECRATION OF CHAPEL

1. The *Rite of Deconsecration of Chapel* conferred by a competent minister shall be as follows:- Rite of Deconsecration of Chapel

FINAL VISITATION Final Visitation

(Minister visits former Chapel, holding a thin wooden rod at least 5ft in length. The Minister checks that the site has been properly prepared.)

CELEBRANT

(Striking the ground three times with the Rod within the former Chapel then speaking the words.)

It is ended.

(Minister leaves the former Chapel and outside breaks the wooden rod into two or more pieces)

XXXVI.IV – RITE OF DECONSECRATION OF CHURCH

1. The *Rite of Deconsecration of Church* conferred by a competent minister shall be as follows:- Rite of Deconsecration of Church

FINAL VISITATION Final Visitation

(Minister visits former Church, holding a thin wooden rod at least 5ft in length. The Minister checks that the site has been properly prepared.)

CELEBRANT

(Striking the ground three times with the Rod within the former Church then speaking the words.)

It is complete.

(Minister leaves the former Church and outside breaks the wooden rod into two or more pieces)

XXXVI.V – RITE OF DECONSECRATION OF CATHEDRAL

1. The *Rite of Deconsecration of Cathedral* conferred by a competent minister shall be as follows:- Rite of Deconsecration of Cathedral

FINAL VISITATION Final Visitation

(Minister visits former Cathedral, holding a thin wooden rod at least 5ft in length. The Minister checks that the site has been properly prepared.)

CELEBRANT

(Striking the ground three times with the Rod within the former Cathedral then speaking the words.)

It is finished.

(Minister leaves the former Cathedral and outside breaks the wooden rod into two or more pieces)

XXXVI.VI – RITE OF DECONSECRATION OF SHRINE

1. The *Rite of Deconsecration of Shrine* conferred by a competent minister shall be as follows:- Rite of Deconsecration of Shrine

FINAL VISITATION Final Visitation

(Minister visits former Shrine, holding a thin wooden rod at least 5ft in length. The Minister checks that the site has been properly prepared.)

CELEBRANT

(Striking the former base of the Shrine three times with the Rod then speaking the words.)

It is done.

(Minister breaks the wooden rod into two or more pieces)

XXXVI.VII – RITE OF DECONSECRATION OF CEMETERY

1. The *Rite of Deconsecration of Cemetery* conferred by a competent minister shall be as follows:- Rite of Deconsecration of Cemetery

FINAL VISITATION Final Visitation

(Minister visits former Cemetery, holding a thin wooden rod at least 5ft in length. The Minister checks that the site has been properly prepared.)

CELEBRANT

(Striking the ground three times with the Rod within the former Cemetery then speaking the words.)

It is complete.

(Minister leaves the former Cemetery and outside breaks the wooden rod into two or more pieces)

XXXVI.VIII – RITE OF DECONSECRATION OF CREMATORIUM

1. The *Rite of Deconsecration of Crematorium* conferred by a competent minister shall be as follows:- Rite of Deconsecration of Crematorium

FINAL VISITATION Final Visitation

(Minister visits former Crematorium, holding a thin wooden rod at least 5ft in length. The Minister checks that the site has been properly prepared.)

CELEBRANT

(Striking the ground three times with the Rod within the former Crematorium then speaking the words.)

It is complete.

(Minister leaves the former Crematorium and outside breaks the wooden rod into two or more pieces)

XXXVI.IX – RITE OF DECONSECRATION OF RELIGIOUS HOUSE

1. The *Rite of Deconsecration of Religious House* conferred by a competent minister shall be as follows:- Rite of Deconsecration of Religious House

FINAL VISITATION Final Visitation

(Minister visits former Religious House, holding a thin wooden rod at least 5ft in length. The Minister checks that the site has been properly prepared.)

CELEBRANT

(Striking the ground three times with the Rod within the former Religious House then speaking the words.)

It is closed.

(Minister leaves the former Religious House and outside breaks the wooden rod into two or more pieces)

XXXVI.X – RITE OF DECONSECRATION OF REGISTRY

1. The *Rite of Deconsecration of Registry* conferred by a competent minister shall be as follows:- Rite of Deconsecration of Registry

FINAL VISITATION Final Visitation

(Minister visits former Registry, holding a thin wooden rod at least 5ft in length. The Minister checks that the site has been properly prepared.)

CELEBRANT

(Striking the ground three times with the Rod within the former Registry then speaking the words.)

It is done.

(Minister leaves the former Registry and outside breaks the wooden rod into two or more pieces)

XXXVI.XI – RITE OF DECONSECRATION OF ORATORY

1. The *Rite of Deconsecration of Oratory* conferred by a competent minister shall be as follows:- Rite of Deconsecration of Oratory

FINAL VISITATION Final Visitation

(Minister visits former Oratory, holding a thin wooden rod at least 5ft in length. The Minister checks that the site has been properly prepared.)

CELEBRANT

(Striking the ground three times with the Rod within the former Oratory then speaking the words.)

It is done.

(Minister leaves the former Oratory and outside breaks the wooden rod into two or more pieces)

Title XXXVII – Rite of Restoration

XXXVII.I – RITE OF RESTORATION

1. Restoration shall be when a place, object or thing previously Deconsecrated has its original character restored through the lifting of any previous suppression. The proper Rite to restore the Ecclesial state of Deconsecrated clergy or officials is the Rite of Reformation. Rite of Restoration

The Rite of Restoration shall be granted and conferred in accordance with the most sacred Covenant *Pactum De Singularis Caelum* and *Pactum De Singularis Christus* and associated approved liturgy.

2. By their nature, some things are capable of being restored to a proper Ecclesial state. Previously dedicated buildings are generally capable of being restored to their original sacred state. Divine Purpose of the Rite of Restoration

The Rite of Restoration removes any impediment to a building and sacred space that it may be returned to its sacred purpose.

3. There are only six (6) valid and licit forms for the Rite of Restoration as defined by the most sacred *Missale Christus* and associated approved liturgy being *Chapel, Church, Cathedral, Religious House, Registry* and *Oratory*:- Forms of the Rite of Deconsecration

(i) "**Rite of Restoration of Chapel**" is when the Rite of Restoration is imparted upon a Chapel once such a place fulfils the conditions for such a Rite; and

(ii) "**Rite of Restoration of Church**" is when the Rite of Restoration is imparted upon a Church once such a place fulfils the conditions for such a Rite; and

(iii) "**Rite of Restoration of Cathedral**" is when the Rite of Restoration is imparted upon a Cathedral once such a place fulfils the conditions for such a Rite; and

(iv) "**Rite of Restoration of Religious House**" is when the Rite of Restoration is imparted upon a Religious House once such a place fulfils the conditions for such a Rite; and

(v) "**Rite of Restoration of Registry**" is when the Rite of Restoration is imparted upon a Registry once such a place fulfils the conditions for such a Rite; and

(vi) "**Rite of Restoration of Oratory**" is when the Rite of Restoration is imparted upon a Oratory once such a place fulfils the conditions for such a Rite.

XXXVII.II – CONDITIONS OF RITE OF RESTORATION

1. Conditions of the Rite of Restoration are those requisite qualifications and contingencies permitted in the proper ministration of the Rite. There shall exist only six (6) possible Conditions for the ministration of Rite of Restoration being *Chapel, Church, Cathedral, Religious House, Registry and Oratory*:- Conditions of Rite of Restoration

(i) *Chapel* are the Conditions necessary for the conferral of the Rite of Restoration of Chapel; and

(ii) *Church* are the Conditions necessary for the conferral of the Rite of Restoration of Church; and

(iii) *Cathedral* are the Conditions necessary for the conferral of the Rite of Restoration of Cathedral; and

(iv) *Religious House* are the Conditions necessary for the conferral of the Rite of Restoration of Religious House; and

(v) *Registry* are the Conditions necessary for the conferral of the Rite of Restoration of Registry; and

(vi) *Oratory* are the Conditions necessary for the conferral of the Rite of Restoration of Oratory.

2. The conditions for the Rite of Restoration of Chapel are:- Chapel Conditions

(i) That a Decree of Restoration (*Decretum Ecclesiae Levationis*) and an Ecclesiastical Writ of Restitution (*Recto Ecclesiae Restitutio*) were duly issued by the proper Ecclesiastical Authority concerning the former Chapel in question; and

(ii) That no motion to appeal the Decree and Writ were properly filed by a party possessing a valid interest within forty (40) days of issuance and notice; or that a validly constituted tribunal ruled in favour of the original Decree and Writ after having heard a valid appeal; and

(iii) That the interior of the Chapel was restored for sacred use with the return of necessary sacred objects; and

(iv) That the **Rite of Dedication of Chapel** and Holy Mass was duly performed under the authority of the Decree of Restoration (*Decretum Ecclesiae Levationis*) and an Ecclesiastical Writ of Restitution (*Recto Ecclesiae Restitutio*); and

(v) That the Ecclesiastical Writ of Restitution (*Recto Ecclesiae Restitutio*) was executed and fulfilled and the record of the event of the proper performance of the Rite of Restoration of Chapel was entered into the *Register of Ecclesiastical Places of Worship* of the *Great Register of Title and Rights* of the Universal Ecclesia.

3. The conditions for the Rite of Restoration of Church are:- Church Conditions

(i) That a Decree of Restoration (*Decretum Ecclesiae Levationis*) and an Ecclesiastical Writ of Restitution (*Recto Ecclesiae Restitutio*) were duly issued by the proper Ecclesiastical Authority concerning the Church in question; and

(ii) That no motion to appeal the Decree and Writ were properly filed by a party possessing a valid interest within forty (40) days of issuance and notice; or that a validly constituted tribunal ruled in favour of the original Decree and Writ after having heard a valid appeal; and

(iii) That the interior of the Church was restored for sacred use with the return of necessary sacred objects; and

(iv) That the **Rite of Dedication of Church** and Holy Mass was duly performed under the authority of the Decree of Restoration (*Decretum Ecclesiae Levationis*) and an Ecclesiastical Writ of Restitution (*Recto Ecclesiae Restitutio*); and

(v) That the Ecclesiastical Writ of Restitution (*Recto Ecclesiae Restitutio*) was executed and fulfilled and the record of the event of the proper performance of the Rite of Restoration of Church was entered into the *Register of Ecclesiastical Places of Worship* of the *Great Register of Title and Rights* of the Universal Ecclesia.

4. The conditions for the Rite of Restoration of Cathedral are:- Cathedral Conditions

(i) That a Decree of Restoration (*Decretum Ecclesiae Levationis*) and an Ecclesiastical Writ of Restitution (*Recto Ecclesiae Restitutio*) were duly issued by the proper Ecclesiastical Authority concerning the Cathedral in question; and

(ii) That no motion to appeal the Decree and Writ were properly filed by a party possessing a valid interest within forty (40) days of issuance and notice; or that a validly constituted tribunal ruled in favour of the original Decree and Writ after having heard a valid appeal; and

(iii) That the interior of the Cathedral was restored for sacred use with the return of necessary sacred objects; and

(iv) That the **Rite of Dedication of Cathedral** and Holy Mass was duly performed under the authority of the Decree of Restoration (*Decretum Ecclesiae Levationis*) and an Ecclesiastical Writ of Restitution (*Recto Ecclesiae Restitutio*); and

(v) That the Ecclesiastical Writ of Restitution (*Recto Ecclesiae Restitutio*) was executed and fulfilled and the record of the event of the proper performance of the Rite of Restoration of Cathedral was entered into the *Register of Ecclesiastical Places of Worship* of the *Great Register of Title and Rights* of the Universal Ecclesia.

5. The conditions for the Rite of Restoration of Religious House are:- Religious House Conditions

(i) That a Decree of Restoration (*Decretum Ecclesiae Levationis*) and an Ecclesiastical Writ of Restitution (*Recto Ecclesiae Restitutio*) were duly issued by the proper Ecclesiastical Authority concerning the Religious House in question; and

(ii) That no motion to appeal the Decree and Writ were properly filed by a party possessing a valid interest within forty (40) days of issuance and notice; or that a validly constituted tribunal ruled in favour of the original Decree and Writ after having heard a valid appeal; and

(iii) That the interior of the Religious House was restored for sacred use with the return of necessary sacred objects; and

(iv) That the **Rite of Dedication of Religious House** was duly performed under the authority of the Decree of Restoration (*Decretum Ecclesiae Levationis*) and an Ecclesiastical Writ of Restitution (*Recto Ecclesiae Restitutio*); and

(v) That the Ecclesiastical Writ of Restitution (*Recto Ecclesiae Restitutio*) was executed and fulfilled and the record of the event of the proper performance of the Rite of Restoration of Religious House was entered into the *Register of Ecclesiastical Places of Worship* of the *Great Register of Title and Rights* of the Universal Ecclesia.

6. The conditions for the Rite of Restoration of Registry are:- Registry Conditions

(i) That a Decree of Restoration (*Decretum Ecclesiae Levationis*) and an Ecclesiastical Writ of Restitution (*Recto Ecclesiae Restitutio*) were duly issued by the proper Ecclesiastical Authority concerning the Registry in question; and

(ii) That no motion to appeal the Decree and Writ were properly filed by a party possessing a valid interest within forty (40) days of issuance and notice; or that a validly constituted tribunal ruled in favour of the original Decree and Writ after having heard a valid appeal; and

(iii) That the interior of the Registry was restored for sacred use with the return of necessary sacred objects; and

(iv) That the **Rite of Dedication of Registry** was duly performed under the authority of the Decree of Restoration (*Decretum Ecclesiae Levationis*) and an Ecclesiastical Writ of Restitution (*Recto Ecclesiae Restitutio*); and

(v) That the Ecclesiastical Writ of Restitution (*Recto Ecclesiae Restitutio*) was executed and fulfilled and the record of the event of the proper performance of the Rite of Restoration of Registry was entered into the *Register of Ecclesiastical Places of Worship* of the *Great Register of Title and Rights* of the Universal Ecclesia.

7. The conditions for the Rite of Restoration of Oratory are:- Oratory Conditions

(i) That a Decree of Restoration (*Decretum Ecclesiae Levationis*) and an Ecclesiastical Writ of Restitution (*Recto Ecclesiae Restitutio*) were duly issued by the proper Ecclesiastical Authority concerning the Oratory in question; and

(ii) That no motion to appeal the Decree and Writ were properly filed by a party possessing a valid interest within forty (40) days of issuance and notice; or that a validly constituted tribunal ruled in favour of the original Decree and Writ after having heard a valid appeal; and

(iii) That the interior of the Oratory was restored for sacred use with the return of necessary sacred objects; and

(iv) That the **Rite of Dedication of Oratory** was duly performed under the authority of the Decree of Restoration (*Decretum Ecclesiae Levationis*) and an Ecclesiastical Writ of Restitution (*Recto Ecclesiae Restitutio*); and

(v) That the Ecclesiastical Writ of Restitution (*Recto Ecclesiae Restitutio*) was executed and fulfilled and the record of the event of the proper performance of the Rite of Restoration of Oratory was entered into the *Register of Ecclesiastical Places of Worship* of the *Great Register of Title and Rights* of the Universal Ecclesia.

Title XXXVIII – Rite of Ordination

XXXVIII.I – RITE OF ORDINATION

1. By divine institution, the Rite of Ordination, also known as Holy Orders shall establish a distinct and unique form of Sacred Circumscribed Space possessing an indelible sacred and religious character, through the Sacrament of Sanctification and Rite of Consecration. The formation of the unique Sacred Circumscribed Space shall also be known as the Clerical State. Rite of Ordination

The Rite of Ordination shall be granted and conferred in accordance with the most sacred Covenant *Pactum De Singularis Caelum* and *Pactum De Singularis Christus* and associated approved liturgy.

2. The Universal Ecclesia as the Living Body of Christ has the solemn obligation and exclusive right to form the character of those who are properly designated to become consecrated and ordained Clerics. Formation of Clerics

The obligation of fostering vocations rests with the entire united Christian and Jewish community so that the needs of the sacred ministry in the Universal Ecclesia of One Christ are provided for sufficiently.

This obligation especially binds Christian families, educators, and in a special way priests, particularly pastors. Diocesan bishops, who most especially are to be concerned for promoting vocations, are to teach the people entrusted to them of the importance of the sacred ministry and of the need for ministers in the Universal Ecclesia and are to encourage and support endeavours to foster authentic vocations.

3. Whilst a member of equals, a Cleric may be characterised by their sacramental authority and pastoral duties as an Acolyte, Presbyter, Deacon, Bishop and Patriarch:- Characteristics of Cleric

(i) *Acolyte* is a Cleric consecrated and ordained in the Key Sacraments; and

(ii) *Presbyter* is a Cleric consecrated and ordained in the Key Sacraments, the Apostolic Life Sacraments and the Cardinal Sacraments of the Eucharist, Matrimony, Union, Penance and Mercy; and

(iii) *Deacon* is a Cleric consecrated and ordained in the Key Sacraments, the Apostolic Life Sacraments and the Cardinal Sacraments of the Eucharist, Matrimony, Union, Penance, Mercy, Record, Oath and Vow; and

(iv) *Bishop* is a Cleric fully consecrated and ordained in the Key

Sacraments, the Apostolic Life Sacraments and the Cardinal Sacraments having Pastoral Care of a Diocese or Community of a Customary and Traditional Rite; and

(v) *Patriarch* is a Cleric fully consecrated and ordained in the Key Sacraments, the Apostolic Life Sacraments and the Cardinal Sacraments having Pastoral Care of a University and Patriarchal See or the See of a Customary and Traditional Rite.

Celebration and Minister of Ordination

4. The minister of sacred Rite of Ordination shall be a consecrated bishop. Ordination, through the Sacred Rite of Ordinary Consecration is ideally to be celebrated within the solemnities of the Mass on a Sunday or holy day of obligation. Ordination generally is to be celebrated in the cathedral church, with Clerics and other members of the Christian faithful invited to the Ordination so that as large an assembly as possible is present at the celebration:-

(i) For the celebration of the *Rite of Presbyterial Consecration*, the minister of sacred ordination is a consecrated bishop; and

(ii) For the celebration of a *Rite of Diaconal Consecration*, the ministers of sacred ordination is a consecrated bishop and at least two (2) Deacons; and

(iii) For the celebration of a *Rite of Episcopal Consecration*, the ministers of sacred ordination is a consecrated patriarch and at least two (2) bishops; and

(iv) For the celebration of a *Rite of Patriarchal Consecration*, the ministers of sacred ordination is the Supreme Patriarch and at least two (2) other patriarchs.

XXXVIII.II – CONDITIONS OF RITE OF ORDINATION

Conditions of Rite of Ordination

1. The path of Holy Orders is reserved for those specially touched by the Holy Spirit to enter into the service of their community and all of humanity; and to devote their lives to the fulfilment of the propositions of the Universal Ecclesia of One Christ.

It is why the first of two special sections of liturgy concerning Ordination is called "The Liturgy of Divine Revelation" precisely because men and women who choose such a life are considered to have been "called by the Divine Creator".

In leading their lives, Clerics are bound in a special way to pursue holiness, since having been consecrated to God and the Divine Creator of all Heaven and Earth by a new title in the reception of orders, they are dispensers of Divine Mercy and Redemption through the most

Holy Sacraments.

It is why the second of two special sections of liturgy concerning Ordination is called "The Liturgy of Divine Mission" because of the sacred and solemn mission each and every person who receives Holy Orders freely and willingly binds themselves to fulfil. The Divine Mission given to them by Christ himself through the Rite of Holy Ordination.

2. Without dispute, the calling to witness the Revelation of God and the Divine Creator of Heaven and Earth through the Holy Spirit is open equally to men and women, regardless of race or economic status or faith. The Universal Ecclesia of One Christ is bestowed a supreme and unique position, yet is not qualified nor permitted to judge a calling to Consecrated Life as more or less worthy based upon gender alone. Gender and Clerical Life

In accord with the most sacred Covenants *Pactum De Singularis Caelum* and *Pactum De Singularis Christus*, the Holy Liturgy recognises those customary and traditional rites that hold to the historic roles of men and women consecrated and ordained to religious life. Those that choose to celebrate and worship through those sacred customary and traditional rites are acknowledged as having a Divine Mandate to honour such distinctions.

However, without prejudice to those acknowledged Customary and Traditional Rites, the Universal Ecclesia of One Christ is compelled to full equality of gender during its sacred lifetime.

3. Celibacy is a state of voluntary abstinence from any form of sexual relations, stimulation or activity. Celibacy is enacted as one of the Three Sacred Vows of an Exemplary Consecrated Life and is one of the greatest demonstrations of universal love, self sacrifice and objective service to humanity in maintaining the union of the Covenant uniting Heaven and Earth as one. Celibacy and Clerical Life

So precious, important and profound is the sacred vow of Celibacy and dedication to a Celibate Life, that such a vow cannot be imposed or demanded without grossly damaging its sacredness and integrity. Furthermore, implied universal requirements of permanent Celibacy has the consequence of not only completely negating the effectiveness and holiness of such sacred Vows, but cleaving the true Spirit from the body of Christ.

Therefore, universal demands for Celibacy across all Clerics is an abomination, profane, sacrilegious, reprobate and to be suppressed and never revived. Instead, the most sacred vow of Celibacy shall be reserved for those consecrated and ordained Clerics of suitable temperament and competence to strengthen and guide the Living Body of One Christ.

In accord with the sacred Covenant *Pactum De Singularis Christus*, Presbyters, Deacons and Bishops living within the general community and entrusted with the pastoral care of a community of faithful to One Christ, shall be free to enter into and maintain Matrimonial vows through the sacrament of Matrimony, without impediment to their See. Furthermore, Clerics living a full and secular life in the fulfilment of their Holy Orders and Commission shall be free to enter into and maintain Matrimonial vows through the sacrament of Matrimony.

However, Bishops fulfilling Cardinalate obligations and Patriarchs are expected to have taken the sacred vow of Celibacy for the duration of their encumbancy.

In respect of religious communities of consecrated life seeking to live an exemplary and holy existence, it is expected that all members of such a fraternity take the sacred vow of Celibacy.

Furthermore, in respect of secular communities of consecrated life, possessing the Divine Commission of sovereign or military orders, the sacred vow of Celibacy is regarded as a condition of such a high sacred calling.

4. A male or female of age eighteen years or older, in seeking to enter the Consecrated Life of the Living Body of One Christ shall be called at first a Supplicant, in reflection of their outward and inward sincere and genuine humility and prayerful yearning to such a life.

Supplicants for Ordination and Key Conditions

Whilst not seeking to dampen the heartfelt and earnest actions of a Supplicant that sincerely feels a calling to Consecrated Life, the Universal Ecclesia of One Christ must first be a wise and objective guide and counsel to its most fervent Members, before seeking to regard the passion of a Supplicant as ground alone to be accepted as a Novice.

Thus, all Supplicants must be interviewed over a period of not less than nine months, to discern their competency in seven core qualities being:-

(i) Scholastic Respect, means that the Supplicant has completed higher studies or is committed to completing higher studies upon being accepted to a Novitiate; and

(ii) Emotional Honesty, means that the Supplicant has undergone thorough psychological and emotional interview to gauge their emotional maturity and suitability for the form of consecrated life they seek; and

(iii) Courageous Commitment, means the Supplicant demonstrates a willingness and ability to remain focused and disciplined and to restore their dedication in the event of challenges or doubts; and

(iv) Heartfelt Enthusiasm, means the Supplicant is passionate and enthusiastic as to their request and sense of calling; and

(v) Authentic Compassion, means the Supplicant possesses and demonstrates authentic compassion, mercy and care towards others as an outward focus of their calling, beyond any inward calling for a scholastic or meditative form of consecrated life; and

(vi) Humble Cheerfulness, means the Supplicant possesses a joyous and happy disposition and is not grossly affected by senses of ego, or pride; and

(vii) Objective Discernment, means the Supplicant demonstrates an objective discernment of themselves, the Universal Ecclesia and the world around them.

Religious Profession

5. By Religious Profession, members assume the observance of the Doctrines and Rules of the Universal Ecclesia of One Christ by public Oath and Vows; and are therefore consecrated to God and the Divine Creator of Heaven and Earth through the ministry of the Universal Ecclesia; and are incorporated into their Association, Institute or Society with the rights and duties defined by law.

Upon acceptance, a new Cleric makes a Temporary Profession for a period defined in proper law; it is not to be less than three years nor longer than six. For the validity of temporary profession it is required that:-

(i) The person who is to make it has completed at least eighteen years of age; and

(ii) The novitiate has been validly completed; and

(iii) Admission has been given freely by the competent superior with the vote of the council according to the norm of law; and

(iv) The profession is expressed and made without force, grave fear, or malice; and

(v) The profession is received by a legitimate superior personally or through another.

6. All living Persons possessing the valid character and impression of Consecrated and Holy Orders are listed within the Directory of Ecclesiastical Persons of Christ, also known as *Directorium Ecclesiam Christus* upon proof of the existence of a valid document of Oath of Holy Orders. Directorium Ecclesiam Christus

A living man or woman not being properly listed within the Directorium Ecclesiam Christus shall not have the authority to act as Cleric or Celebrant of religious ceremony.

XXXVIII.III – RITE OF PRESBYTERIAL CONSECRATION

1. The *Ordinary Rite of Presbyterial Consecration* conferred by a consecrated bishop, shall be as follows:- Rite of Presbyterial Consecration

LITURGY OF THE PEOPLE OF GOD

Liturgy of the People of God

(NOTE: See the relevant Liturgy within the Proper of Life & Mysteries of Christ for a Special Mass of Consecration)

LITURGY OF THE GOOD NEWS OF CHRIST

Liturgy of Good News

(NOTE: See the relevant Liturgy within the Proper of Life & Mysteries of Christ for a Special Mass of Consecration)

LITURGY OF DIVINE REVELATION

Liturgy of Divine Revelation

PETITION

Presbyterial Petition

CELEBRANT

(To all assembled)

I call upon those who seek to make their solemn petition today in the name of Christ our Saviour to now stand and make their presence and prayer known.

(The supplicant clergy come forward and stand before the celebrant)

CELEBRANT

What then is it you ask in the name of the Father and of the Son and of the Holy Spirit today?

SUPPLICANT(S)

Presbyterial Consecration.

CELEBRANT
(Turning to Supplicants.)

The Rite of Presbyterial Consecration that you ask is a moment of great significance, not only for you and your family and this community, but our wider community of the People of God.

Christ, the eternal High Priest and ultimate mediator between God and the Divine Creator did redeem the sacred character of holy vows and clerical devotion by humbling Himself to be a servant of the People of God; and through his suffering, sacrifice and resurrection.

It is Christ and no other that first instituted both the Sacred Liturgy of the Mass through the Last Supper and the Christian fraternal order of brothers and sisters united in the Light of Christ and his Sacred Mission.

To all who are called by Divine Revelation to unite with Him more completely in the order of the Society of Christ of the Universal Ecclesia, such a Divine Mission demands great personal self sacrifice, persistence and patience. Our Heavenly Father does not expect every person he calls to Holy Orders to immediately forsake themselves to a life of extreme austerity and holiness, as exemplified by many beloved saints. Nor does God and the Divine Creator expect those newly called to a life of clerical devotion not to make mistakes. Rather, it is how we overcome through our faith and courage; and how we persist and grow as true followers of Christ that is the greatest example we can give to our community and the People of God.

Remember always, those who are about to take their solemn vows and oath, that they who stand at the Altar representing Christ and the intercessions of the faithful are not Him nor the ultimate mediator between God and the Divine Creator and his people.

Remember always to be careful in matters of the Divine and mystical; and that it is not for men and women to decide when the Divine chooses to speak, but the Divine Creator, through his Son and all the angels and saints of

Heaven who choose when it be the time and the place.

Finally, remember always thou art mortal in this temporal realm and to be gentle and compassionate of your soul and mind; and to be wise in your discernments and decisions; and to always be on guard against the hardening of your heart or the creeping wilful ignorance of narrow doctrinal rigidity. Do each of you understand these sacred responsibilities?

SUPPLICANTS

Yes.

INQUISITION

Presbyterial Inquisition

CELEBRANT

Very well, I call upon a trusted soul to speak on your behalf as to the Inquisition of whether you are adequately prepared and ready for your new clerical life.

(Religious instructor of the supplicants comes forward)

CELEBRANT

N., are you prepared to testify before God and the Divine Creator that these supplicants are suitable and worthy candidates for such a sacred Rite?

RELIGIOUS INSTRUCTOR

Yes, [your grace/eminence], I testify on my oath and office that those before you are indeed suitable and worthy to join the ranks of the fraternal order of brothers and sisters in Christ.

CELEBRANT

Thanks be to God.

OBLIGATION

Presbyterial Obligation

CELEBRANT

I call then for the Supplicants to come forward and kneel before Heaven so that they may perfect their Holy Orders in a humble and clear voice.

VOWS

Presbyterial Vows

(Supplicants now kneel before the Celebrant)

CELEBRANT

I call upon the Supplicants knelt before us to each give

their solemn vows.

CELEBRANT

(To Supplicants)

Do you take your fraternity of brothers and sisters in Christ to be your new friends and family? Do you promise to always be truthful to them in good times and bad, and in times of sickness and distress?

SUPPLICANTS

I do.

CELEBRANT

Do you take this sacred calling to be your life journey? Do you promise to be trusting in your faith, and to always be gentle and kind to your soul throughout this journey with Christ?

SUPPLICANTS

I do.

CELEBRANT

Do you take your Ordinary as your instructor and guide? Do you promise always to be respectful and obedient and support your leaders and the order of hierarchy of clergy of the most holy Universal Ecclesia every day of your life?

SUPPLICANTS

I do.

HOLY OATH

Presbyterial
Holy Oath

CELEBRANT

I now call upon each Supplicant to individually stand and make their Oath of Holy Orders before signing the record.

SUPPLICANT

(Each Supplicant in turn stands facing the congregation, whilst having right hand upon the Holy Gospel)

In the Name of God the Father, Christ the Son and the Holy Spirit, I, N. do solemnly and humbly promise before all Heaven and Earth that all I have here before avowed, I will perform and keep in sacred trust for the benefit of all the People of God; and for the bishops and hierarchy of all the clergy of this country; and for the Holy Father and all the fraternal brothers and sisters of the One Holy Apostolic Universal Ecclesia of One Christ.

(Each Supplicant then kisses the sacred text and then signs their name to an original document of the previous Vows and Oath representing the Original Deed of a new sacred trust of Holy Orders. They then return to their position of kneeling.)

LITURGY OF DIVINE MISSION

Liturgy of Divine Mission

CONSECRATION

Presbyterial Consecration

CELEBRANT

(The Supplicants bow their heads whilst kneeling as Celebrant circumscribes the Supplicants using his crozier.)

✠In the name of God our Heavenly Father. In the name of Christ his son and our saviour. In the name of the Holy Spirits and all the angels and saints of Heaven, I invoke your blessings in the formation of new Persons of God, within your Holy Family of brothers and sisters. Watch over them and help them stay upon the right path of Light.

CELEBRANT

(The Celebrant now circumscribes the kneeling Supplicants for a second time, now using Holy Incense)

✠In the name of God and the Divine Creator. In the name of the Alpha and Omega, I purify with sacred smoke these worthy supplicants of any lingering sadness, doubt or negativity to their new Persons and Office.

CELEBRANT

(The Celebrant now circumscribes the kneeling Supplicants for a third time, now Sprinkling Holy Water.)

✠In the Name of God the Father, Christ the Son and the Holy Spirit, I bless these Persons as Priests of your fraternal order of brothers and sisters of the One Holy Apostolic Universal Ecclesia of One Christ.

INVESTITURE

Presbyterial Investiture

(After the Presbyterial Consecration, the newly ordained priests stand, accompanied by the priests who will help the newly ordained to arrange the stole in the manner proper to priests and to put on the chasuble)

CELEBRANT

You are a priest for ever according to the order of the Light of Christ. Our Lord has made His Testament as a Promise he will not break. We Pray to God and the Divine Creator that we may always honour His Trust.

ANOINTING

Presbyterial Anointing

(After the newly ordained Priests are vested, they each go to the Bishop and kneel before him. The Bishop then anoints each of their palms of the newly ordained Priests with holy Chrism.)

CELEBRANT

We anoint you with the most sacred Oil of Christ in the name of our Lord and our Saviour; may he strengthen you with his power, who lives and reigns for ever and ever.

CELEBRANT

(The Bishop then anoints their lips with the sign of the cross and each of the palms of the newly ordained Priests with holy Chrism.)

Be sealed with the gift of the Holy Spirit. May you serve and sanctify the People of God in the power of Christ our Saviour, who lives and reigns for ever and ever.

PRIEST

Amen.

CELEBRANT

(The Bishop then hands a paten holding the bread and a chalice holding the wine mixed with water to each kneeling Priest.)

Receive your oblation to be offered to God as a symbol of your unity with Christ. Remember always the purpose of what you do. Imitate what you celebrate and conform your life to the Seven Sacred Mysteries of Christ.

PRIEST

Amen.

(The new Priests stand and join in the Liturgy of the Eucharist.)

LITURGY OF THE EUCHARIST

Liturgy of the Eucharist

(NOTE: See the relevant Liturgy within the Proper of Life & Mysteries of Christ for a Special Mass of Consecration)

XXXVIII.IV – RITE OF DIACONAL CONSECRATION

1. The *Ordinary Rite of Diaconal Consecration* conferred by a consecrated bishop and at least two (2) Deacons, shall be as follows:-

Rite of Diaconal Consecration

LITURGY OF THE PEOPLE OF GOD

Liturgy of the People of God

(NOTE: See the relevant Liturgy within the Proper of Life & Mysteries of Christ for a Special Mass of Consecration)

LITURGY OF THE GOOD NEWS OF CHRIST

Liturgy of Good News

(NOTE: See the relevant Liturgy within the Proper of Life & Mysteries of Christ for a Special Mass of Consecration)

LITURGY OF DIVINE REVELATION

Liturgy of Divine Revelation

PETITION

Diaconal Petition

CELEBRANT

(To all assembled)

I call upon those who seek to make their solemn petition today in the name of Christ our Saviour to now stand and make their presence and prayer known.

(The Supplicant Deacon come forward and stand before the celebrant)

CELEBRANT

What then is it you ask in the name of the Father and of the Son and of the Holy Spirit today?

SUPPLICANT (DEACON)

Diaconal Consecration.

CELEBRANT

(Turning to Supplicants.)

The Rite of Diaconal Consecration that you ask is a moment of pastoral significance, not only for you and your family and this community, but our wider community of the People of God.

Christ, the eternal High Priest and ultimate mediator between God and the Divine Creator did redeem the sacred character of holy vows and clerical devotion by humbling Himself to be a servant of the People of God; and through his suffering, sacrifice and resurrection.

It is Christ and no other that first instituted both the Sacred Liturgy of the Mass through the Last Supper and the Christian fraternal order of brothers and sisters united in the Light of Christ and his Sacred Mission.

To all who are called by Divine Revelation to unite with Him more completely in the order of the Society of Christ of the Universal Ecclesia, such a Divine Mission demands great personal self sacrifice, persistence and patience. Our Heavenly Father does not expect every person he calls to Holy Orders to immediately forsake themselves to a life of extreme austerity and holiness, as exemplified by many beloved saints. Nor does God and the Divine Creator expect those newly called to a life of clerical devotion not to make mistakes. Rather, it is how we overcome through our faith and courage; and how we persist and grow as true followers of Christ that is the greatest example we can give to our community and the People of God.

Remember always, those who are about to take their solemn vows and oath, that they who stand at the Altar representing Christ and the intercessions of the faithful are not Him nor the ultimate mediator between God and the Divine Creator and his people.

Remember always to be careful in matters of the Divine and mystical; and that it is not for men and women to decide when the Divine chooses to speak, but the Divine Creator, through his Son and all the angels and saints of Heaven who choose when it be the time and the place.

Finally, remember always thou art mortal in this temporal realm and to be gentle and compassionate of your soul and mind; and to be wise in your discernments and decisions; and to always be on guard against the hardening of your heart or the creeping wilful ignorance of narrow doctrinal rigidity. Do each of you understand these sacred responsibilities?

SUPPLICANT (DEACON)

Yes.

INQUISITION

Diaconal Inquisition

CELEBRANT

Very well, I call upon a trusted Advocate to speak on your behalf as to the Inquisition of whether you are adequately prepared and ready to accept the obligations and new personage of Deacon.

(Advocate of the supplicant comes forward)

CELEBRANT

N., are you prepared to testify before God and the Divine Creator that this supplicant is suitable and worthy candidates for such a sacred Rite?

ADVOCATE

Yes, [your grace/eminence], I testify on my oath and office that the supplicant before you is indeed suitable and worthy to join the rank of Deacon of the fraternal order of brothers and sisters in Christ.

CELEBRANT

N., does the supplicant have a proper mandate approved by the Holy Mother Church? If so, let it be read.

ADVOCATE

Yes, [your grace/eminence]. The Mandate reads as follows...

(Advocate reads mandate.)

CELEBRANT

Thanks be to God.

OBLIGATION

Diaconal

Obligation

CELEBRANT

I call then for the Supplicant to come forward and kneel before Heaven so that they may perfect their Holy Orders to Office in a humble and clear voice.

VOWS

Diaconal Vows

(Supplicant now kneels before the Celebrant)

CELEBRANT

I call upon the Supplicant knelt before us to give his (her) solemn vows.

CELEBRANT

(To Supplicant)

Do you solemnly vow a life of frugality, self restraint and humility? And do you promise to forsake your own personal wants and desires for the sake of the sacred office and mission you shall hold?

SUPPLICANT (DEACON)

I do.

CELEBRANT

Do you solemnly vow to always uphold the gift of charity and alms to those in need? And do you promise to act with mercy, compassion and forgiveness of others, as you yourself are forgiven by God?

SUPPLICANT (DEACON)

I do.

CELEBRANT

Do you solemnly vow to respect and protect the rule of law, fairness and the equality of rights of all? And do you promise to pursue every remedy, relief and reform against injustice, or moral repugnancy or corruption of the laws and institutions of the Universal Ecclesia and all its bodies, institutions and fraternities?

SUPPLICANT (DEACON)

I do.

CELEBRANT

Do you solemnly vow to absolute obedience to the Mission and the Powers delegated to you by Christ through his Holy Universal Ecclesia with dignity, grace and the gift of wise discernment?

SUPPLICANT (DEACON)

I do.

HOLY OATH

Diaconal Holy Oath

CELEBRANT

I now call upon the Supplicant to stand and make their Oath of Holy Orders before signing the record.

SUPPLICANT (DEACON)

(The Supplicant stands facing the congregation, whilst having right hand upon the Holy Gospel)

In the Name of God the Father, Christ the Son and the Holy Spirit, I, N. do solemnly and humbly promise before all Heaven and Earth that all I have here before avowed, I will perform and keep in sacred trust for the benefit of all the People of God; and for the bishops and hierarchy of all the clergy of this country; and for the Holy Father and all the fraternal brothers and sisters of the One Holy Apostolic Universal Ecclesia of One Christ.

(The Supplicant then kisses the sacred text and then signs his (her) name to an original document of the previous Vows and Oath representing the Original Deed of a new sacred trust of Holy Orders of Office. They then return to their position of kneeling.)

LITURGY OF DIVINE MISSION

Liturgy of Divine Mission

CONSECRATION

Diaconal Consecration

CELEBRANT

(The Supplicant Deacon bows his (her) head whilst kneeling as Celebrant circumscribes the Supplicants three times, first with the crozier.)

✠In the name of God our Heavenly Father. In the name of Christ his son and our saviour. In the name of the Holy Spirits and our Mother Mary and all the angels and saints of Heaven, I invoke your blessings in the formation of a new Person of God, within your Holy Family of brothers and sisters. Watch over them, guide them and help them stay upon the path of Light.

CELEBRANT

(The Celebrant now circumscribes the kneeling Supplicant Deacon for a second time, now using Holy Incense)

✠In the name of God and the Divine Creator. In the name of the Alpha and Omega, I purify with sacred smoke this worthy supplicant; and remove any doubt as to the sacred sweetness of the calling to their new Person and Office.

CELEBRANT

(The Celebrant now circumscribes the kneeling Supplicant Deacon for a third time, now Sprinkling Holy Water.)

✠In the Name of God the Father, Christ the Son and the Holy Spirit, I bless this Person as a Deacon of your fraternal order of brothers and sisters of the One Holy Apostolic Universal Ecclesia of One Christ.

INVESTITURE

Diaconal Investiture

(After the Diaconal Consecration, the newly consecrated Deacon stands, accompanied by the priests who will help them arrange new vestments signifying their new personage.)

CELEBRANT

Remember you are a priest for ever according to the order of the Light of Christ. Our Lord has made His Testament as a Promise he will not break. We Pray to God and the Divine Creator that we may always honour His Trust.

ANOINTING

Diaconal Anointing

(After the newly consecrated Deacon is vested, he (she) goes to the Bishop and kneels before him. The Bishop then anoints the forehead as cross, lips with a cross with holy Chrism.)

CELEBRANT

We anoint you with the most sacred Oil of Christ in the name of our Lord and our Saviour; may he strengthen you with his power, who lives and reigns for ever and ever.

CELEBRANT

(The Bishop then anoints each of their palms of the newly ordained Deacons with holy Chrism.)

Be sealed with the gift of the Holy Spirit. May you serve and sanctify the People of God in the power of Christ our Saviour, who lives and reigns for ever and ever.

NEW DEACON

Amen.

CELEBRANT

Remember always the purpose of what you do. Imitate what you celebrate and conform your life to the Seven Sacred Mysteries of Christ.

NEW DEACON

Amen.

(The new Deacon stands and joins in the Liturgy of the Eucharist.)

LITURGY OF THE EUCHARIST

Liturgy of the Eucharist

(NOTE: See the relevant Liturgy within the Proper of Life & Mysteries of Christ for a Special Mass of Consecration)

XXXVIII.V – RITE OF EPISCOPAL CONSECRATION

1. The *Ordinary Rite of Episcopal Consecration* conferred by a consecrated patriarch and at least two (2) bishops, shall be as follows:-

Rite of Episcopal Consecration

LITURGY OF THE PEOPLE OF GOD

Liturgy of the People of God

(NOTE: See the relevant Liturgy within the Proper of Life & Mysteries of Christ for a Special Mass of Consecration)

LITURGY OF THE GOOD NEWS OF CHRIST

Liturgy of Good News

(NOTE: See the relevant Liturgy within the Proper of Life & Mysteries of Christ for a Special Mass of Consecration)

LITURGY OF DIVINE REVELATION

Liturgy of Divine Revelation

PETITION

Episcopal Petition

PATRIARCH

(To all assembled)

I call upon those who seek to make their solemn petition today in the name of Christ our Saviour to now stand and make their presence and prayer known.

(The Supplicant Bishop comes forward and stands before the Patriarch.)

PATRIARCH

What then is it you ask in the name of the Father and of the Son and of the Holy Spirit today?

SUPPLICANT (BISHOP)

Episcopal Consecration.

PATRIARCH

(Turning to Supplicant Bishop.)

The Rite of Episcopal Consecration that you ask is a moment of great spiritual significance, not only for you and your family and this community, but as a living symbol of our continued faithfulness to the Mission of Christ.

It is our Lord and Saviour Jesus Christ who was sent by the Creator of all Existence and all Heaven and Earth to redeem humanity. Christ Himself, as eternal High Priest and ultimate mediator between God and the Divine Creator, did consecrate the first Apostles, through the power of the Holy Spirit, to go forth and proclaim the Good News of the sacred gifts and true nature of the Divine as being one of love, mercy and wisdom, not wrath and harsh judgement.

Illuminated by the Holy Spirit, the Apostles knew clearly the Mission of Christ did not rest solely upon their shoulders, but with those men and women of each subsequent generation who are called by God to join them as Disciples. The Apostles themselves consecrated others in a special way with the gifts of the Holy Spirit by the laying on of hands, conferring unto the first Disciples the sacraments they themselves had received from Christ.

This method of succession of authority and the special way of conferring the gifts of the Holy Spirit by the laying on of hands is what the Holy Mother Church truly means by the notion of Apostolic Succession. To preserve its integrity and sanctity, the Universal Ecclesia of One Christ reserves such succession of the Mission of Christ to the Person of Bishop.

In the Person of Bishop, in a special way, the powers of the first Disciples and the Apostles are ever present. Aided by his Priests, a Bishop and local clergy continue to embody in a very real sense the essence of the very first Christian Communities. When we as Christians recognise a Bishop as first Priest, we means it as Christ intended to be the first to serve.

Remember always, those who are about to take the garments and honours of Bishop, that they are called to such office to be a living embodiment of the first Apostles and Disciples, by demonstrating such temporal symbols of status and power cannot corrupt the heart or mind when it is bound by a deep love of Christ and his Divine Message.

Remember always to be discerning in matters in the civil and political affairs of men and women; and to never forget that the path towards nihilism is defined not by a great loss of faith, but incremental compromises. In choosing the extravagances that are frequently permitted to high office, instead of humility and frugality. In choosing the comforts of luxury and the finest of meals, instead of choosing to frequently dine with those who have nothing but are closest to Christ.

Finally, remember always to be discerning in matters of the Divine and mystical; and that it is not for men and women to decide when the Divine chooses to speak, but the Divine Creator, through his Son and all the angels and saints of Heaven who choose when it be the time and the place. Do each of you understand these sacred responsibilities?

SUPPLICANT (BISHOP)

Yes.

INQUISITION

Episcopal Inquisition

PATRIARCH

Very well, I call upon a trusted Advocate to speak on your behalf as to the Inquisition of whether you are adequately prepared and ready to accept the obligations and new personage of Bishop.

(Advocate of the Supplicant Bishop comes forward)

PATRIARCH

N., are you prepared to testify before God and the Divine Creator that these supplicants are suitable and worthy candidates for such a sacred Rite?

ADVOCATE

Yes, [title], I testify on my oath and office that those before you are indeed suitable and worthy to join the ranks of the fraternal order of brothers and sisters in Christ.

PATRIARCH

N., does the supplicant have a proper mandate approved by the Holy Mother Church? If so, let it be read.

ADVOCATE

Yes, [title]. The Mandate reads as follows...

(Advocate reads mandate.)

PATRIARCH

Thanks be to God.

OBLIGATION

Episcopal Obligation

PATRIARCH

I call then for the Supplicant to come forward and kneel before Heaven so that they may perfect their Holy Orders of Office in a humble and clear voice.

VOWS

Episcopal Vows

(Supplicant Bishop now kneels before the Patriarch.)

PATRIARCH

I call upon the Supplicant knelt before us to give his solemn vows.

PATRIARCH

(To Supplicant Bishop)

Do you solemnly vow a life of poverty, chastity and humility? And do you promise to forsake your own personal wants and desires for the sake of the sacred office and mission you shall hold?

SUPPLICANT (BISHOP)

I do.

PATRIARCH

Do you solemnly vow to always uphold the gift of charity and alms to those in need? And do you promise to act with mercy, compassion and forgiveness of others, as you yourself are forgiven by God?

SUPPLICANT (BISHOP)

I do.

PATRIARCH

Do you solemnly vow to respect and protect the rule of law, fairness and the equality of rights of all? And do you promise to pursue every remedy, relief and reform against injustice, or moral repugnancy or corruption of the laws and institutions of the Universal Ecclesia and all its bodies, institutions and fraternities?

SUPPLICANT (BISHOP)

I do.

PATRIARCH

Do you solemnly vow to absolute obedience to the Mission and the Powers delegated to you by Christ through the Supreme Patriarch of the Holy Universal Ecclesia with dignity, grace and the gift of wise discernment?

SUPPLICANT (BISHOP)

I do.

HOLY OATH

Episcopal Holy Oath

PATRIARCH

I now call upon the Supplicant to stand and make their Oath of Holy Orders before signing the record.

SUPPLICANT (BISHOP)

(The Supplicant stands facing the congregation, whilst having right hand upon the Holy Gospel)

In the Name of God the Father, Christ the Son and the Holy Spirit, I, N. do solemnly and humbly promise before all Heaven and Earth that all I have here before avowed, I will perform and keep in sacred trust for the benefit of all the People of God; and for the hierarchy of all the clergy of this country; and for the Holy Father and all the fraternal brothers and sisters of the One Holy Apostolic Universal Ecclesia of One Christ.

(The Supplicant then kisses the sacred text and then signs their name to an original document of the previous Vows and Oath representing the Original Deed of a new sacred trust of Holy Orders. They then return to their position of kneeling.)

LITURGY OF DIVINE MISSION

Liturgy of Divine Mission

CONSECRATION

Episcopal Consecration

PATRIARCH

(The Supplicant Bishop bows his (her) head whilst kneeling as Celebrant circumscribes the Supplicants three times, first with the crozier.)

✠In the name of God our Heavenly Father. In the name of Christ his son and our saviour. In the name of the Holy Spirits and our Mother Mary and all the angels and saints of Heaven, I invoke your blessings in the formation of a new Person of God, within your Holy Family of brothers and sisters. Watch over them, guide them and help them stay upon the path of the Light of Christ.

PATRIARCH

(The Celebrant now circumscribes the kneeling Supplicant Bishop for a second time, now using Holy Incense)

✠In the name of God and the Divine Creator. In the name of the Alpha and Omega, I purify with this sacred smoke this worthy supplicant; and remove any doubt as to the sacred sweetness of the calling to their new Person and Office.

PATRIARCH

(The Celebrant now circumscribes the kneeling Supplicant Bishop for a third time, now Sprinkling Holy Water.)

✠In the Name of God the Father, Christ the Son and the Holy Spirit, I bless this Person as a Bishop of your fraternal order of brothers and sisters of the One Holy Apostolic Universal Ecclesia of One Christ.

ANOINTING

Episcopal Anointing

(After the Episcopal Consecration, he/she goes to the Patriarch and kneels before him. The Patriarch then anoints the Bishop on the forehead, the lips and on each of his palms with holy Chrism.)

PATRIARCH

We anoint you with the most sacred Oil of Christ in the name of our Lord and our Saviour; may he strengthen you with his power, who lives and reigns for ever and ever.

PATRIARCH

(The Patriarch then anoints each palm of the newly ordained Bishop with holy Chrism.)

Be sealed with the gift of the Holy Spirit. May you serve and sanctify the People of God in the power of Christ our Saviour, who lives and reigns for ever and ever.

NEW BISHOP

Amen.

INVESTITURE

Episcopal Investiture

(After the Episcopal Anointing, the newly consecrated Bishop stands, accompanied by the priests who will help the newly consecrated to arrange their vestments and miter.)

PATRIARCH

Remember you are a priest for ever according to the order of the Light of Christ. Our Lord has made His Testament as a Promise he will not break. We Pray to God and the Divine Creator that we may always honour His Trust.

PATRIARCH

(The Patriarch places the ring on the ring finger of the new Bishop's right hand.)

Take this ring, the seal of your fidelity and binding to Christ. Remember always the purpose of what you do. Imitate what you celebrate and conform your life to the

Seven Sacred Mysteries of Christ.

NEW BISHOP

I will.

PATRIARCH

(The Patriarch places the miter on the head of the new bishop, in silence. Lastly he gives the pastoral staff to the bishop.)

Take this staff as a sign of your pastoral office: keep watch over all those members entrusted to your care, especially the marginalised, the sick and the forgotten as a Good Shepherd in the footsteps of Christ.

NEW BISHOP

I will.

PATRIARCH

Thanks Be to God.

(The New Bishop rises and participates in the Eucharist).

LITURGY OF THE EUCHARIST

Liturgy of the Eucharist

(NOTE: See the relevant Liturgy within the Proper of Life & Mysteries of Christ for a Special Mass of Consecration)

XXXVIII.VI – RITE OF PATRIARCHAL CONSECRATION

1. The *Ordinary Rite of Patriarchal Consecration* conferred by the Supreme Patriarch and at least two (2) other patriarchs, shall be as follows:-

Rite of Patriarchal Consecration

LITURGY OF THE PEOPLE OF GOD

Liturgy of the People of God

(NOTE: See the relevant Liturgy within the Proper of Life & Mysteries of Christ for a Special Mass of Consecration)

LITURGY OF THE GOOD NEWS OF CHRIST

Liturgy of Good News

(NOTE: See the relevant Liturgy within the Proper of Life & Mysteries of Christ for a Special Mass of Consecration)

LITURGY OF DIVINE REVELATION

Liturgy of Divine Revelation

PETITION

SUPREME PATRIARCH

(To all assembled)

I call upon those who seek to make their solemn petition today in the name of Christ our Saviour to now stand and make their presence and prayer known.

(The Supplicant Patriarch comes forward and stand before the celebrant)

SUPREME PATRIARCH

What then is it you ask in the name of the Father and of the Son and of the Holy Spirit today?

SUPPLICANT (PATRIARCH)

Patriarchal Consecration.

SUPREME PATRIARCH

(Turning to Supplicant Patriarch)

The Rite of Patriarchal Consecration that you ask is a moment of great historical significance, not only for you and your family and this community, but our wider community of the People of God.

To the faithful, a Patriarch is a living symbol of the power and majesty of Christ on earth. They are by their rank a member of the leaders of the Living Body of Christ. It is their piety, wisdom and strength that helps guide the People of God and all those clerical brothers and sisters professed to Holy Orders.

Indeed, the Rite of Patriarchal Consecration shares many similarities to the Rite of Coronation, especially in the Vows, the Holy Oath and Sacred Anointing. Only a proper Monarch and a Patriarch share the same formality of Anointing in Christ and God through the Holy Spirit. This is because only a true Monarch and a true Patriarch are called by God to accept such a heavy burden of Office.

An individual called to the Office of Patriarch is called to Sacrifice their individual person, personal wants and desires, to accept and become entirely the Person of Patriarch. While the Divine Creator does not will pain or suffering upon anyone, the responsibility of Patriarch demands the greatest test of humility, austerity, celibacy, persistence, courage, compassion and faith.

To be human is to err. Thus Christ does not expect perfection or the confection of a false image of piety and dignity by each Patriarch. Rather, it is how we overcome through our faith and courage; and how we persist and grow as true followers of Christ that is the greatest example we can give to our community and the People of God.

Remember always, those who are about to take their solemn vows and oath, that they who stand at the Altar representing Christ and the intercessions of the faithful are not Him nor the ultimate mediator between God and the Divine Creator and his people.

Remember always to be careful in matters of the Divine and mystical; and that it is not for men and women to decide when the Divine chooses to speak, but the Divine Creator, through his Son and all the angels and saints of Heaven who choose when it be the time and the place.

Finally, remember always thou art mortal in this temporal realm and to be gentle and compassionate of your soul and mind; and to be wise in your discernments and decisions; and to always be on guard against the hardening of your heart or the creeping wilful ignorance of narrow doctrinal rigidity. Do each of you understand these sacred responsibilities?

SUPPLICANT (PATRIARCH)

Yes.

INQUISITION

Patriarchal Inquisition

SUPREME PATRIARCH

Very well, I call upon a trusted Advocate to speak on your behalf as to the Inquisition of whether you are adequately prepared and ready to accept the obligations and new personage of Patriarch.

(Advocate of the Supplicant Patriarch comes forward)

SUPREME PATRIARCH

N., are you prepared to testify before God and the Divine Creator that these supplicants are suitable and worthy candidates for such a sacred Rite?

ADVOCATE

Yes, your Holiness, I testify on my oath and office that those before you are indeed suitable and worthy to join the ranks of the fraternal order of brothers and sisters in Christ.

SUPREME PATRIARCH

N., does the supplicant have a proper mandate approved by the Holy Mother Church? If so, let it be read.

ADVOCATE

Yes, [title]. The Mandate reads as follows...

(Advocate reads mandate.)

SUPREME PATRIARCH

Thanks be to God.

OBLIGATION

Patriarchal Obligation

SUPREME PATRIARCH

I call then for the Supplicant to come forward and kneel before Heaven so that they may perfect their Holy Orders of Office in a humble and clear voice.

VOWS

Patriarchal Vows

(Supplicant Patriarch now kneels before the Supreme Patriarch.)

SUPREME PATRIARCH

I call upon the Supplicant knelt before us to give his solemn vows.

SUPREME PATRIARCH

(To Supplicant Patriarch)

Do you solemnly vow a life of poverty, chastity and humility? And do you promise to forsake your own personal wants and desires for the sake of the sacred office and mission you shall hold?

SUPPLICANT (PATRIARCH)

I do.

SUPREME PATRIARCH

Do you solemnly vow to always uphold the gift of charity

and alms to those in need? And do you promise to act with mercy, compassion and forgiveness of others, as you yourself are forgiven by God?

SUPPLICANT (PATRIARCH)

I do.

SUPREME PATRIARCH

Do you solemnly vow to respect and protect the rule of law, fairness and the equality of rights of all? And do you promise to pursue every remedy, relief and reform against injustice, or moral repugnancy or corruption of the laws and institutions of the Universal Ecclesia and all its bodies, institutions and fraternities?

SUPPLICANT (PATRIARCH)

I do.

SUPREME PATRIARCH

Do you solemnly vow to absolute obedience to the Mission and the Powers delegated to you by Christ through the Office of Supreme Patriarch of the Holy Universal Ecclesia with dignity, grace and the gift of wise discernment?

SUPPLICANT (PATRIARCH)

I do.

HOLY OATH

Patriarchal Holy Oath

SUPREME PATRIARCH

I now call upon the Supplicant to stand and make their Oath of Holy Orders before signing the record.

SUPPLICANT (PATRIARCH)

(The Supplicant stands facing the congregation, whilst having right hand upon the Holy Gospel)

In the Name of God the Father, Christ the Son and the Holy Spirit, I, N. do solemnly and humbly promise before all Heaven and Earth that all I have here before avowed, I will perform and keep in sacred trust for the benefit of all the People of God; and for the hierarchy of all the clergy; and for the Holy Father and all the fraternal brothers and sisters of the One Holy Apostolic Universal Ecclesia of One Christ.

(The Supplicant then kisses the sacred text and then signs their name to an original document of the previous Vows and Oath representing the Original Deed of a new sacred trust of Holy Orders. They then return to their position of kneeling.)

LITURGY OF DIVINE MISSION

Liturgy of Divine Mission

CONSECRATION

Patriarchal Consecration

SUPREME PATRIARCH

(The Supplicant Patriarch bows his head whilst kneeling as Supreme Patriarch circumscribes the Supplicant Patriarch first with his staff.)

✠In the name of God our Heavenly Father. In the name of Christ his son and our saviour. In the name of the Holy Spirits and our Mother Mary and all the angels and saints of Heaven, I invoke your blessings in the formation of a new Person of God, within your Holy Family of brothers and sisters. Watch over them, guide them and help them stay upon the path of a Society of Light.

SUPREME PATRIARCH

(The Supreme Patriarch now circumscribes the kneeling Supplicant Patriarch for a second time, now using Holy Incense.)

✠In the name of God and the Divine Creator. In the name of the Alpha and Omega, I purify with this sacred smoke this worthy supplicant; and remove any doubt as to the sacred sweetness of the calling to their new Person and Office.

SUPREME PATRIARCH

(The Celebrant now circumscribes the kneeling Supplicants for a third time, now Sprinkling Holy Water.)

✠In the Name of God the Father, Christ the Son and the Holy Spirit, I bless this Person as a Patriarch of your fraternal order of brothers and sisters of the One Holy Apostolic Universal Ecclesia of One Christ.

ANOINTING

Patriarchal

Anointing

(After the Patriarchal Consecration, the new Patriarch kneels before the Supreme Patriarch. The Supreme Patriarch then anoints his forehead, his lips, his chest and each of his palms with holy Chrism.)

SUPREME PATRIARCH

We anoint you with the most sacred Oil of Christ in the name of our Lord and our Saviour; may he strengthen you with his power, who lives and reigns for ever and ever.

SUPREME PATRIARCH

(The Supreme Patriarch then anoints each palm of the newly ordained Patriarch with holy Chrism.)

Be sealed with the gift of the Holy Spirit. May you serve and sanctify the People of God in the power of Christ our Saviour, who lives and reigns for ever and ever.

NEW PATRIARCH

Amen.

INVESTITURE

Patriarchal Investiture

(After the Patriarchal Anointing, the new Patriarch stands, accompanied by the priests who will help him.)

SUPREME PATRIARCH

Remember you are a priest for ever according to the order of the Light of Christ. Our Lord has made His Testament as a Promise he will not break. We Pray to God and the Divine Creator that we may always honour His Trust.

SUPREME PATRIARCH

(The Supreme Patriarch places the ring on the ring finger of the new Patriarchs right hand.)

Take this ring, the seal of your absolute fidelity and binding to Christ. Remember always the purpose of what you do. Imitate what you celebrate and conform your life to the Seven Sacred Mysteries of Christ.

NEW PATRIARCH

I will.

SUPREME PATRIARCH

(The Supreme Patriarch places the miter or other ceremonial hat on the head of the new Patriarch, in silence. Lastly he gives the pastoral staff to the Patriarch.)

Take this staff as a sign of your pastoral office: keep watch over all those members entrusted to your care, especially the marginalised, the sick and the forgotten as a Good Shepherd in the footsteps of Christ.

NEW PATRIARCH

I will.

SUPREME PATRIARCH

Thanks Be to God.

(The new Patriarch stand and join in the Liturgy of the Eucharist.)

LITURGY OF THE EUCHARIST

Liturgy of the Eucharist

(NOTE: See the relevant Liturgy within the Proper of Life & Mysteries of Christ for a Special Mass of Consecration)

Title XXXIX – Rite of Secularisation

XXXIX.I – RITE OF SECULARISATION

1. Secularisation is when the Clerical State (Sacred Circumscribed Space) of a person is set aside for religious purposes through a form of the Sacrament of Sanctification and Rite of Consecration and formally removed from such service or purpose and ecclesiastical status. The Rite for deconsecration of buildings and places of the ecclesial state is the Rite of Deconsecration. Rite of Secularisation

   The Rite of Secularisation is granted and conferred in accordance with the most sacred Covenants *Pactum De Singularis Caelum*, *Pactum De Singularis Christus* and associated approved liturgy.

2. Only the Rite of Ordination properly conferred creates the Cleric State through Ordinary Consecration. Once the Sacrament of Sanctification and Rite of Consecration forms certain Sacred Circumscribed Space as the Clerical State, such space cannot be dissolved or destroyed, only set aside. Divine Purpose of the Rite of Secularisation

   Thus the Rite of Secularisation is the temporary suppression of Sacred Circumscribed Space dedicated to the Clerical State. The Rite itself does not create any new character, nor does it taint, defile or diminish the original Sacrament of Sanctification and Rite of Consecration.

   The person deprived of their character does not have to be present during the Rite. However, a person called upon to be present who then refuses a formal summons, may not in the future be considered nor granted the Rite of Reformation as a restoration of Clerical State.

   A person deconsecrated has their ecclesiastical character, purpose and service temporarily suppressed, by depriving them of their authorised Sacred Circumscribed Space or Clerical State, thus constricting their ability to perform certain licit ecclesiastical acts.

   Secularisation does not create, nor infer the formation of "unholy" character, as such a notion is an abomination and a defiance of the logic and articles of the most sacred Covenants *Pactum De Singularis Caelum* and *Pactum De Singularis Christus.*

3. There are only four (4) valid and licit forms for the Rite of Secularisation as defined by the most sacred *Missale Christus* and associated approved liturgy being Presbyterial, Diaconal, Episcopal and Patriarchal:- Form of the Rite of Secularisation

   (i) "**Rite of Presbyterial Secularisation**" is when the Rite of Secularisation is imparted upon ordinary clergy once the conditions are fulfilled for such a Rite; and

(ii) "**Rite of Diaconal Secularisation**" is when the Rite of Secularisation is imparted upon deacons or senior diocese and religious clergy once the conditions are fulfilled for such a Rite; and

(iii) "**Rite of Episcopal Secularisation**" is when the Rite of Secularisation is imparted upon bishops, archbishops or cardinals once the conditions are fulfilled for such a Rite; and

(iv) "**Rite of Patriarchal Secularisation**" is when the Rite of Secularisation is imparted upon a patriarch once the conditions are fulfilled for such a Rite.

XXXIX.II – CONDITIONS OF RITE OF SECULARISATION

1. Conditions of the Rite of Secularisation are those requisite qualifications and contingencies permitted in the proper ministration of the Rite. There shall exist only four (4) possible Conditions for the ministration of Rite of Secularisation being *Presbyterial, Diaconal, Episcopal* and *Patriarchal*:- Conditions of Rite of Secularisation

(i) *Presbyterial* are the Conditions necessary for the conferral of the Rite of Presbyterial Secularisation concerning the secularisation of ordinary clergy; and

(ii) *Diaconal* are the Conditions necessary for the conferral of the Rite of Diaconal Secularisation concerning the secularisation of deacons and senior diocese or religious clergy; and

(iii) *Episcopal* are the Conditions necessary for the conferral of the Rite of Episcopal Secularisation concerning the secularisation of bishops, archbishops or cardinals; and

(iv) *Patriarchal* are the Conditions necessary for the conferral of the Rite of Patriarchal Secularisation concerning the secularisation of patriarchs.

2. The conditions for the Rite of Presbyterial Secularisation are:- Presbyterial Conditions

(i) That a Decree of Interdiction (*Decretum Ecclesiae Interdictum*) and an Ecclesiastical Writ of Prohibition (*Recto Ecclesiae Interdico*) were duly issued by the proper Ecclesiastical Authority concerning the former cleric in question; and

(ii) That no motion to appeal the Decree and Writ were properly filed by the former cleric in question within forty (40) days of issuance and notice; or that a validly constituted tribunal ruled in favour of the original Decree and Writ after having heard a valid appeal; and

(iii) That the Ecclesiastical Writ of Prohibition (*Recto Ecclesiae Interdico*) was executed and fulfilled and that the record of the Oath of Holy Orders of the former cleric was struck out of the *Directory of Ecclesiastical Oaths;* and that all relevant secular legal and financial authorities notified of the cancellation and removal of the former cleric from any accounts, benefits, insurances or privileges in any official or ecclesiastical capacity; and

(iv) That the Decree of Interdiction (*Decretum Ecclesiae Interdictum*) was honoured and that the record of the former cleric in question was struck out of the *Directory of Ecclesiastical Persons of Christ (Directorium Ecclesiam Christus)* of the *Great Register of Title and Rights* of the Universal Ecclesia; and formal notice to the former cleric, requiring signed acknowledgement of the interdict from performing any Holy Sacraments or Rites or functioning in any proper ecclesiastical capacity; and

(v) If the convicted is a belligerent and refuses to freely sign and acknowledge the interdict or to attend the Rite before the Bishop, then for the issuance of a *Presbyterial Secularisation*, that the minister of the Rite of Secularisation shall be a consecrated bishop and all the clergy of the diocese in attendance, where the convicted shall be excommunicated; and

(vi) If the convicted is an authentic penitent and has demonstrated clear remorse to both secular and ecclesial authorities, and has freely signed and acknowledged the interdict and attend the Rite before the Bishop, then for the issuance of a *Presbyterial Secularisation*, that the minister of the Rite of Secularisation shall be the Rite of Confession by a consecrated bishop with the authentic penitent.

3. The conditions for the Rite of Diaconal Secularisation are:- Diaconal Conditions

(i) That a Decree of Interdiction (*Decretum Ecclesiae Interdictum*) and an Ecclesiastical Writ of Prohibition (*Recto Ecclesiae Interdico*) were duly issued by the proper Ecclesiastical Authority concerning the former cleric in question; and

(ii) That no motion to appeal the Decree and Writ were properly filed by the former cleric in question within forty (40) days of issuance and notice; or that a validly constituted tribunal ruled in favour of the original Decree and Writ after having heard a valid appeal; and

(iii) That the Ecclesiastical Writ of Prohibition (*Recto Ecclesiae Interdico*) was executed and fulfilled and that the record of the Oath of Holy Orders of the former cleric was struck out of the *Directory of Ecclesiastical Oaths;* and that all relevant secular legal and financial authorities notified of the cancellation and removal of the former cleric from any accounts, benefits, insurances or privileges in any official or ecclesiastical capacity; and

(iv) That the Decree of Interdiction (*Decretum Ecclesiae Interdictum*) was honoured and that the record of the former cleric in question was struck out of the *Directory of Ecclesiastical Persons of Christ (Directorium Ecclesiam Christus)* of the *Great Register of Title and Rights* of the Universal Ecclesia; and formal notice to the former cleric, requiring signed acknowledgement of the interdict from performing any Holy Sacraments or Rites or functioning in any proper ecclesiastical capacity; and

(v) If the convicted is a belligerent and refuses to freely sign and acknowledge the interdict or to attend the Rite before the Bishop, then for the issuance of a *Diaconal Secularisation*, that the ministers of the Rite of Secularisation shall be a consecrated bishop and at least two (2) Deacons and all the clergy of the diocese in attendance, where the convicted shall be excommunicated; and

(vi) If the convicted is an authentic penitent and has demonstrated clear remorse to both secular and ecclesial authorities, and has freely signed and acknowledged the interdict and attend the Rite before the Bishop, then for the issuance of a *Diaconal Secularisation*, that the minister of the Rite of Secularisation shall be the Rite of Confession by a consecrated bishop with the authentic penitent.

4. The conditions for the Rite of Episcopal Secularisation are:- Episcopal Conditions

(i) That a Decree of Interdiction (*Decretum Ecclesiae Interdictum*) and an Ecclesiastical Writ of Prohibition (*Recto Ecclesiae Interdico*) were duly issued by the proper Ecclesiastical Authority concerning the former cleric in question; and

(ii) That no motion to appeal the Decree and Writ were properly filed by the former cleric in question within forty (40) days of issuance and notice; or that a validly constituted tribunal ruled in favour of the original Decree and Writ after having heard a valid appeal; and

(iii) That the Ecclesiastical Writ of Prohibition (*Recto Ecclesiae Interdico*) was executed and fulfilled and that the record of the Oath of Holy Orders of the former cleric was struck out of the *Directory of Ecclesiastical Oaths;* and that all relevant secular legal and financial authorities notified of the cancellation and removal of the former cleric from any accounts, benefits, insurances or privileges in any official or ecclesiastical capacity; and

(iv) That the Decree of Interdiction (*Decretum Ecclesiae Interdictum*) was honoured and that the record of the former cleric in question was struck out of the *Directory of Ecclesiastical Persons of Christ (Directorium Ecclesiam Christus)* of the *Great Register of Title and Rights* of the Universal Ecclesia; and formal notice to the former cleric, requiring signed acknowledgement of the interdict from performing any Holy Sacraments or Rites or functioning in any proper ecclesiastical capacity; and

(v) If the convicted is a belligerent and refuses to freely sign and acknowledge the interdict or to attend the Rite before the Patriarch, then for the issuance of an *Episcopal Secularisation*, that the ministers of the Rite of Secularisation shall be a consecrated patriarch and at least two (2) bishops and all the cardinals, bishops and deacons of the conference in attendance, where the convicted shall be excommunicated; and

(vi) If the convicted is an authentic penitent and has demonstrated clear remorse to both secular and ecclesial authorities, and has freely signed and acknowledged the interdict and attend the Rite before the Supreme Patriarch, then for the issuance of an *Episcopal Secularisation*, that the minister of the Rite of Secularisation shall be the Rite of Confession by a Patriarch with the authentic penitent.

5. The conditions for the Rite of Patriarchal Secularisation are:- Patriarchal Conditions

(i) That a Decree of Interdiction (*Decretum Ecclesiae Interdictum*) and an Ecclesiastical Writ of Prohibition (*Recto Ecclesiae Interdico*) were duly issued by the proper Ecclesiastical Authority concerning the former cleric in question; and

(ii) That no motion to appeal the Decree and Writ were properly filed by the former cleric in question within forty (40) days of issuance and notice; or that a validly constituted tribunal ruled in favour of the original Decree and Writ after having heard a valid appeal; and

(iii) That the Ecclesiastical Writ of Prohibition (*Recto Ecclesiae Interdico*) was executed and fulfilled and that the record of the Oath of Holy Orders of the former cleric was struck out of the *Directory of Ecclesiastical Oaths;* and that all relevant secular legal and financial authorities notified of the cancellation and removal of the former cleric from any accounts, benefits, insurances or privileges in any official or ecclesiastical capacity; and

(iv) That the Decree of Interdiction (*Decretum Ecclesiae Interdictum*) was honoured and that the record of the former cleric in question was struck out of the *Directory of Ecclesiastical Persons of Christ (Directorium Ecclesiam Christus)* of the *Great Register of Title and Rights* of the Universal Ecclesia; and formal notice to the former cleric, requiring signed acknowledgement of the interdict from performing any Holy Sacraments or Rites or functioning in any proper ecclesiastical capacity; and

(v) If the convicted is a belligerent and refuses to freely sign and acknowledge the interdict or to attend the Rite before the Supreme Patriarch, then for the issuance of a *Patriarchal Secularisation*, the ministers of the Rite of Secularisation shall be the Supreme Patriarch and at least two (2) other patriarchs and all the patriarchs in attendance, where the convicted shall be excommunicated; and

(vi) If the convicted is an authentic penitent and has demonstrated clear remorse to both secular and ecclesial authorities, and has freely signed and acknowledged the interdict and attend the Rite before the Supreme Patriarch, then for the issuance of a *Patriarchal Secularisation*, that the minister of the Rite of Secularisation shall be the Rite of Confession by the Supreme Patriarch with the authentic penitent.

XXXIX.III – EXTRAORDINARY RITE OF SECULARISATION

1. The *Extraordinary Rite of Secularisation* when the convicted is belligerent and refuses to freely sign and acknowledge the interdict or to attend the Rite, shall be conferred as follows:-

Extraordinary Rite of Secularisation

INTROIT

Introit

(Celebrant is only one in vestments, holding a thin wooden rod at least 5ft in length.)

CELEBRANT

In the name of ✠ the Father, and of the Son, and of the Holy Spirit.

ALL

Amen.

CELEBRANT

It is with no joy that I summons you here to pray for the soul of our brother (sister) N., lost to the faith by their rejection of the admission of the truth and that God and the Divine Creator sees everything; and their rejection of the Divine Grace of forgiveness and mercy; and their rejection of the Living Body of Christ as represented by the clerical authority of the Universal Ecclesia of One Christ.

The Divine Creator of all Existence and all Heaven and Earth so loves the Homo Sapien species and specifically each and every living and deceased member, that he brought forth a "singularity" of all human beings that have lived or will ever live, in the form of our Lord and Saviour Jesus Christ, who chose to sacrifice himself, to end forever all forms of ritual blood sacrifice, to forgive the transgressions of our first forefathers as well as our future descendants, so that we might learn that the true nature of God and the Divine Creator is love and wisdom, not wrath and
harsh judgement.

In truth, Christ himself has repeatedly reminded us and admonished us that He and our Heavenly Father be the final arbiter in the affairs of souls, not men or women consecrated to holy orders – no matter how pious or respected they may be.

Indeed, when we do fail our faith and our promise to God and choose to usurp the Liturgy and Divine Revelation of our Saviour to judge and condemn others, it is ultimately only we whom we condemn. We come together not to condemn but to bear witness to a necessary and solemn rite. To acknowledge both as pastors and shepherds to Heaven when one of our flock is lost and does not yet want to be found.

Therefore, let us first pray for the healing strength of the Holy Spirit to purify our hearts of any animus against our lost brother (sister) N. Instead, let us ask that the angels and saints find a way to open the heart of N., that they may see the truth and consequences of their actions and seek forgiveness and redemption. We ask this in the name of Christ the eternal redeemer.

ALL

Amen.

ANATHEMA

Anathema

CELEBRANT

Mother Mary, Queen of Heaven your family on Earth has been injured by the actions of N., yet who refuses to take accountability for their actions or demonstrate genuine remorse and atonement.

ALL

Pray for N.

CELEBRANT

Beloved Saints, Martyrs and Heroes, the good name of your faith has been damaged by the scandalous behaviour of N., and their refusal and lack of courage to accept their penance and forgiveness.

ALL

Pray for N.

CELEBRANT

O Lord and saviour, your gifts of salvation and redemption have been rejected by N., by his (her) refusal to obey your One Holy Apostolic Church.

ALL

Pray for N.

CELEBRANT

Heavenly Father, N has by his (her) own volition and acts caused their own Anathema. We pray that you find a way to help bring all those who wish to be lost, back into the hold. We ask this in the name of your only son and our Lord Jesus Christ.

ALL

Amen.

FINAL VISITATION

Final Visitation

CELEBRANT

My brothers and sisters it is time to conclude this most solemn ceremony with the symbol of the rod and your support.

The rod represents the authority once given unto our brother (sister) N. The rod also represents the sacred trust that our brother (sister) N. entered through consecration. Finally, the rod represents the connection we once had with our brother (sister) N, now lost to us.

I shall now strike the ground with three deliberate blows, symbolising the final act of deconsecration. I ask you to aid in this act by your feet and your hands in time with each strike. Let us begin.

CELEBRANT

(Celebrant slowly raises the rod and strikes the ground with three deliberate strikes, aided by the stomping of feet and hands to increase the sound.

ALL

It is ended.

(Celebrant breaks the wooden rod into two or more pieces in front of the witness and all leave.)

Title XL – Rite of Reformation

XL.I – RITE OF REFORMATION

1. Reformation shall be when a person previously deprived of their Clerical State (Sacred Circumscribed Space) has their original character restored through the lifting of any previous suppression. The proper Rite to restore the Ecclesiastical state of Deconsecrated persons is the Rite of Reformation. Rite of Reformation

The Rite of Reformation shall be granted and conferred in accordance with the most sacred Covenant *Pactum De Singularis Caelum* and *Pactum De Singularis Christus* and associated approved liturgy.

2. The loss of Clerical State (Sacred Circumscribed Space) is an extreme sanction of the Universal Ecclesia. Thus, the grounds for its restoration through the Rite of Reformation must be equally compelling. Divine Purpose of the Rite of Reformation

Unlike places, objects and things, human beings that have undergone the significant life changing events of the loss of Clerical State; and through authentic remorse, prayer and deep personal discernment, with continual acts of penance and charity, a person may merit in their lifetime a restoration of such a state.

Under clear and unmistakable circumstances of remorse, reform and redemption, the term "reformation" more appropriately describes the accumulative lessons of such a soul being more than simply a "restoration", but an enlarging of experience as to the eternal presence of Divine Mercy and Forgiveness.

However, a person who previously refused to acknowledge their culpability; and refused to attend on summons the Rite of Secularisation shall be forbidden from receiving the Rite of Reformation by their own actions. Such a person may still seek restoration through a posthumous Reformation following their death.

3. There are only four (4) valid and licit forms for the Rite of Reformation as defined by the most sacred *Missale Christus* and associated approved liturgy being Presbyterial, Diaconal, Episcopal and Patriarchal:- Form of the Rite of Reformation

(i) "**Rite of Presbyterial Reformation**" is when the Rite of Reformation is imparted upon former ordinary clergy once the conditions are fulfilled for such a Rite; and

(ii) "**Rite of Diaconal Reformation**" is when the Rite of Reformation is imparted upon former deacons or former senior diocese and religious clergy once the conditions are fulfilled for such a Rite; and

(iii) "**Rite of Episcopal Reformation**" is when the Rite of Reformation is imparted upon former bishops, archbishops or former cardinals once the conditions are fulfilled for such a Rite; and

(iv) "**Rite of Patriarchal Reformation**" is when the Rite of Reformation is imparted upon a former patriarch once the conditions are fulfilled for such a Rite.

XL.II – CONDITIONS OF RITE OF REFORMATION

1. Conditions of the Rite of Reformation are those requisite qualifications and contingencies permitted in the proper ministration of the Rite. Previous belligerent ex-communicants under the Rite of Secularisation can never qualify for the Rite of Reformation. Conditions of Rite of Reformation

There shall exist only four (4) possible Conditions for the ministration of Rite of Reformation being *Presbyterial, Diaconal, Episcopal* and *Patriarchal*:-

(i) *Presbyterial* are the Conditions necessary for the conferral of the Rite of Presbyterial Reformation concerning the redemption of former ordinary clergy; and

(ii) *Diaconal* are the Conditions necessary for the conferral of the Rite of Diaconal Reformation concerning the redemption of deacons and senior diocese or religious clergy; and

(iii) *Episcopal* are the Conditions necessary for the conferral of the Rite of Episcopal Reformation concerning the redemption of bishops, archbishops or cardinals; and

(iv) *Patriarchal* are the Conditions necessary for the conferral of the Rite of Patriarchal Reformation concerning the redemption of patriarchs.

2. The conditions for the Rite of Presbyterial Reformation are:- Presbyterial Conditions

(i) That no Extraordinary Rite of Secularisation was issued against the candidate seeking the Rite; and

(ii) That a minimum of seven years have passed since the conclusion of any civil or criminal sentences and punishments; and

(iii) That an independent Inquisitor has investigated the behaviour, reformed actions and conduct of the candidate during and since their civil or criminal sentences were finished and concluded that the candidate is suitable for the Rite of Reformation; and

(iv) That a Decree of Restoration (*Decretum Ecclesiae Levationis*) and an Ecclesiastical Writ of Restitution (*Recto Ecclesiae Restitutio*) were duly issued by the proper Ecclesiastical Authority concerning the former cleric in question; and

(v) That no motion to appeal the Decree and Writ were properly filed by a party possessing a valid interest within forty (40) days of issuance and notice; or that a validly constituted tribunal ruled in favour of the original Decree and Writ after having heard a valid appeal; and

(vi) That the **Rite of Presbyterial Consecration** and Holy Mass was duly performed, without the consecration or anointing, under the authority of the Decree of Restoration (*Decretum Ecclesiae Levationis*) and an Ecclesiastical Writ of Restitution (*Recto Ecclesiae Restitutio*); and

(vii) That the Ecclesiastical Writ of Restitution (*Recto Ecclesiae Restitutio*) was executed and fulfilled and that the record of the Oath of Holy Orders of the fully restored cleric was entered into the *Directory of Ecclesiastical Oaths* of the *Great Register of Title and Rights* of the Universal Ecclesia; and

(viii) That the Decree of Restoration (*Decretum Ecclesiae Levationis*) was honoured and that the record of the fully restored cleric in question was entered into the *Directory of Ecclesiastical Persons of Christ (Directorium Ecclesiam Christus)* of the *Great Register of Title and Rights* of the Universal Ecclesia.

3. The conditions for the Rite of Diaconal Reformation are:- Diaconal Conditions

(i) That no Extraordinary Rite of Secularisation was issued against the candidate seeking qualification; and that only the Ordinary Rite of Diaconal Secularisation was issued against the candidate; and

(ii) That a minimum of five years have passed since the conclusion of any ecclesial, civil or criminal sentences and punishments; and

(iii) That an independent Inquisitor has investigated the behaviour, reformed actions and conduct of the candidate during and since their civil or criminal sentences were finished and concluded that the candidate is suitable for the Rite of Reformation; and

(iv) That a Decree of Restoration (*Decretum Ecclesiae Levationis*) and an Ecclesiastical Writ of Restitution (*Recto Ecclesiae Restitutio*) were duly issued by the proper Ecclesiastical Authority concerning the former Deacon in question; and

(v) That no motion to appeal the Decree and Writ were properly filed by a party possessing a valid interest within forty (40) days of issuance and notice; or that a validly constituted tribunal ruled in favour of the original Decree and Writ after having heard a valid appeal; and

(vi) That the **Rite of Diaconal Consecration** and Holy Mass was duly performed, without the consecration or anointing, under the authority of the Decree of Restoration (*Decretum Ecclesiae Levationis*) and an Ecclesiastical Writ of Restitution (*Recto Ecclesiae Restitutio*); and

(vii) That the Ecclesiastical Writ of Restitution (*Recto Ecclesiae Restitutio*) was executed and fulfilled and that the record of the Oath of Holy Orders of the fully restored Deacon was entered into the *Directory of Ecclesiastical Oaths* of the *Great Register of Title and Rights* of the Universal Ecclesia; and

(viii) That the Decree of Restoration (*Decretum Ecclesiae Levationis*) was honoured and that the record of the fully restored Deacon in question was entered into the *Directory of Ecclesiastical Persons of Christ (Directorium Ecclesiam Christus)* of the *Great Register of Title and Rights* of the Universal Ecclesia.

4. The conditions for the Rite of Episcopal Reformation are:- Episcopal Conditions

(i) That no Extraordinary Rite of Secularisation was issued against the candidate seeking qualification; and that only the Ordinary Rite of Episcopal Secularisation was issued against the candidate; and

(i) That a minimum of five years have passed since the conclusion of any ecclesial, civil or criminal sentences and punishments; and

(ii) That an independent Inquisitor has investigated the behaviour, reformed actions and conduct of the candidate during and since their civil or criminal sentences were finished and concluded that the candidate is suitable for the Rite of Reformation; and

(iii) That a Decree of Restoration (*Decretum Ecclesiae Levationis*) and an Ecclesiastical Writ of Restitution (*Recto Ecclesiae Restitutio*) were duly issued by the proper Ecclesiastical Authority concerning the former Bishop or Cardinal in question; and

(iv) That no motion to appeal the Decree and Writ were properly filed by a party possessing a valid interest within forty (40) days of issuance and notice; or that a validly constituted tribunal ruled in favour of the original Decree and Writ after having heard a valid appeal; and

(v) That the **Rite of Episcopal Consecration** and Holy Mass was duly performed, without the consecration or anointing, under the authority of the Decree of Restoration (*Decretum Ecclesiae Levationis*) and an Ecclesiastical Writ of Restitution (*Recto Ecclesiae Restitutio*); and

(vi) That the Ecclesiastical Writ of Restitution (*Recto Ecclesiae Restitutio*) was executed and fulfilled and that the record of the Oath of Holy Orders of the fully restored Bishop or Cardinal was entered into the *Directory of Ecclesiastical Oaths* of the *Great Register of Title and Rights* of the Universal Ecclesia; and

(vii) That the Decree of Restoration (*Decretum Ecclesiae Levationis*) was honoured and that the record of the fully restored Bishop or Cardinal in question was entered into the *Directory of Ecclesiastical Persons of Christ (Directorium Ecclesiam Christus)* of the *Great Register of Title and Rights* of the Universal Ecclesia.

5. The conditions for the Rite of Patriarchal Reformation are:- Patriarchal Conditions

(i) That no Extraordinary Rite of Secularisation was issued against the candidate seeking qualification; and that only the Ordinary Rite of Patriarchal Secularisation was issued against the candidate; and

(i) That a minimum of five years have passed since the conclusion of any ecclesial, civil or criminal sentences and punishments; and

(ii) That an independent Inquisitor has investigated the behaviour, reformed actions and conduct of the candidate during and since their civil or criminal sentences were finished and concluded that the candidate is suitable for the Rite of Reformation; and

(iii) That a Decree of Restoration (*Decretum Ecclesiae Levationis*) and an Ecclesiastical Writ of Restitution (*Recto Ecclesiae Restitutio*) were duly issued by the proper Ecclesiastical Authority concerning the former Patriarch in question; and

(iv) That no motion to appeal the Decree and Writ were properly filed by a party possessing a valid interest within forty (40) days of issuance and notice; or that a validly constituted tribunal ruled in favour of the original Decree and Writ after having heard a valid appeal; and

(v) That the **Rite of Patriarchal Consecration** and Holy Mass was duly performed, without the consecration or anointing, under the authority of the Decree of Restoration (*Decretum Ecclesiae Levationis*) and an Ecclesiastical Writ of Restitution (*Recto Ecclesiae Restitutio*); and

(vi) That the Ecclesiastical Writ of Restitution (*Recto Ecclesiae Restitutio*) was executed and fulfilled and that the record of the Oath of Holy Orders of the fully restored Patriarch was entered into the *Directory of Ecclesiastical Oaths* of the *Great Register of Title and Rights* of the Universal Ecclesia; and

(vii) That the Decree of Restoration (*Decretum Ecclesiae Levationis*) was honoured and that the record of the fully restored Patriarch in question was entered into the *Directory of Ecclesiastical Persons of Christ (Directorium Ecclesiam Christus)* of the *Great Register of Title and Rights* of the Universal Ecclesia.

Title XLI – Rite of Blessing

XLI.I – RITE OF BLESSING

1. Blessing is an Incantation and formula of words and specific actions to consecrate a person, or object or place or thing; or to summons an authentic spiritual presence; or to anoint a person and dedicate them to God and the Divine Creator of all Heaven and Earth; or to bestow the expectation and experience of divine favour. Thus, Blessing may refer to a formal procedure of Consecration, or Invocation or Anointing or Dispensation. Rite of Blessing

Blessing is a fundamental set of formal rituals and acts of the Living Body of Christ, with holy water replacing blood as to the origin of the word and rituals. The conduct of any form of ritual in blood is hereby profane, sacrilegious, reprobate, forbidden and to be suppressed now and forever, in honour of the sacred Covenants *Pactum De Singularis Caelum* and *Pactum De Singularis Christus*.

All formula and actions of Blessing are subject to the liturgical norms of the Universal Ecclesia of One Christ in accord with the most sacred *Missale Christus* and associated approved liturgical texts.

2. Excluding specific forms pertaining to Sacramental Rites, all forms of valid Blessing may be characterised as *Universal, Magisterial, Patriarchal, Apostolic, Episcopal* or *Ordinary*:- Forms of Blessing

(i) *Universal Blessing* is a form of Blessing as prescribed by Scriptural Revelation and/or ancient custom and tradition; and

(ii) *Magisterial Blessing* is a form of Blessing prescribed and reserved to the Office of Supreme Patriarch; and

(iii) *Patriarchal Blessing* is a form of Blessing prescribed and reserved to authentic Office of Patriarch of the Universal Ecclesia of Christ; and

(iv) *Apostolic Blessing* is a form of Blessing acknowledged and prescribed either by venerated members or by custom and tradition, not otherwise Plenary or Apostolic; and

(v) *Episcopal Blessing* is a form of Blessing prescribed and reserved to the Office of Episcopal Bishop; and

(vi) *Ordinary Blessing* is a form of Blessing as prescribed by the present sacred liturgy not otherwise Universal, Magisterial, Patriarchal, Apostolic or Episcopal.

XLI.II – CONDITIONS OF RITE OF BLESSING

Conditions of Rite of Blessing

1. In accord with the norms of Liturgy and reservations of certain Blessings to rank and rite:-

   (i) Any priest may confer the blessings of the Universal Ecclesia, except those reserved to the Supreme Patriarch, to bishops, or to others; and

   (ii) A reserved blessing that is conferred by a priest who does not have the required delegation is valid, but illicit, unless the Universal Ecclesia has declared otherwise in the reservation; and

   (iii) Deacons can give validly and licitly only those blessings expressly allowed by law; and

   (iv) Both constitutive and invocative blessings are invalid if the forms prescribed by the Church are not observed; and

   (v) Objects that have received the constitutive blessing should be treated reverently, and should never be put to profane or improper use, even though they may be personal possessions.

Title XLII – Rite of Exorcism

XLII.I – RITE OF EXORCISM

1. Exorcism, is a Sacred Rite reserved exclusively for competent Clergy to bind any and every form of malevolent spirit, form, ghost or presence under *Holy Writ*; and thus remove them from any further temporal negative influence, using the full coercive plenary authority of Heaven and Earth, from any and every place, or space, or person, or animal, or object or thing. Rite of Exorcism

2. A fundamental and immutable Law of the Universe, as sealed permanently and irrevocable through the most sacred Covenant *Pactum De Singularis Caelum*, is that every spirit and mind entrusted with a physical body is entitled to its use and enjoyment without malevolent and vexatious interference or haunting or possession by some disembodied spirit or ghost. Therefore, such a malevolent and vexatious spirit, form or ghost is a trespasser and in contempt of the laws of Heaven and Earth. Divine Purpose of the Rite of Exorcism

   Through the most sacred Covenants *Pactum De Singularis Caelum* and *Pactum De Singularis Christus*, the Universal Ecclesia of One Christ is entrusted to protect the Living Members from any and all forms of spirits, forms and ghosts that refuse to accept the Rule of Law, Decency and the Law of Sanctity of Spirit. The rite of Exorcism is therefore a most potent and dreadful action of last resort; and not to be administered unless the conditions and form is followed in accord with the most sacred Missale Christus and associated approved liturgical texts.

3. To ensure the integrity of the Rite of Exorcism and to avoid gross error or ignorance in presuming most or all cases submitted for the Extraordinary Rite of Exorcism of Persons warrant the need for Exorcism, each Diocese of the Universal Ecclesia of One Christ shall maintain a juridic body known as the Sacred Court of the Exorcist. Sacred Court of the Exorcist

   The Sacred Court of the Exorcist shall only apply for cases requesting the Extraordinary Rite of Exorcism of Persons. All other forms of Exorcism may be approved by the Exorcist, subject to the oversight of the Ordinary. Whenever a case having sufficient merit arises requesting an Extraordinary Rite of Exorcism of Persons:-

   (i) A qualified member of the clergy shall be appointed on an interim or permanent basis as the Logicist with the express purpose of investigating and rationally arguing against the case for Exorcism; and

   (ii) The Exorcist or their Associate shall then be required to investigate and reasonably argue that sufficient grounds exists for an Exorcism; and

(iii) If both the Logicist and Exorcist agree that insufficient grounds exist, then the case shall be closed and referred to suitable professional practitioners; and

(iv) If the Logicist and Exorcist develop opposing views, then the Ordinary shall be the Jurist who ultimately decides if an Exorcism should proceed.

Form of the Rite of Exorcism

4. There are only eleven (11) valid and licit forms for the Rite of Exorcism as defined by the most sacred *Missale Christus* and associated approved liturgy being Earth, Water, Wilderness, Foreshores, Buildings, Vessels, Structures, Animals, Objects, Ordinary Rite and Extraordinary Rite:-

(i) "**Rite of Exorcism of Earth**" is when the Rite of Exorcism is imparted to enforce the cleansing of earth, land and fields of all forms of malevolent spirits, ghosts or negative elemental presence; and

(ii) "**Rite of Exorcism of Water**" is when the Rite of Exorcism is imparted to enforce the cleansing of pools, ponds, lakes, streams and rivers of all forms of malevolent spirits, ghosts or negative elemental presence; and

(iii) "**Rite of Exorcism of Wilderness**" is when the Rite of Exorcism is imparted to enforce the cleansing of dense, sparse and barren wilderness of all forms of malevolent spirits, ghosts or negative elemental presence; and

(iv) "**Rite of Exorcism of Foreshores**" is when the Rite of Exorcism is imparted to enforce the cleansing of foreshores, headlands and embankments of all forms of malevolent spirits, ghosts or negative elemental presence; and

(v) "**Rite of Exorcism of Buildings**" is when the Rite of Exorcism is imparted to enforce the cleansing of buildings of all forms of malevolent spirits, ghosts or negative elemental presence; and

(vi) "**Rite of Exorcism of Vessels**" is when the Rite of Exorcism is imparted to enforce the cleansing of water, air and space vessels of all forms of malevolent spirits, ghosts or negative elemental presence; and

(vii) "**Rite of Exorcism of Structures**" is when the Rite of

Exorcism is imparted to enforce the cleansing of structures and infrastructure of all forms of malevolent spirits, ghosts or negative elemental presence; and

(viii) "**Rite of Exorcism of Animals**" is when the Rite of Exorcism is imparted to enforce the cleansing of animals of all forms of malevolent spirits, ghosts or negative elemental presence; and

(ix) "**Rite of Exorcism of Objects**" is when the Rite of Exorcism is imparted to enforce the cleansing of movable and immovable objects of malevolent spirits, ghosts or negative elemental presence; and

(x) "**Ordinary Rite of Exorcism of Persons**" is when the Rite of Exorcism is imparted to enforce the cleansing of persons of all forms of malevolent spirits, ghosts or negative elemental presence; and

(xi) "**Extraordinary Rite of Exorcism of Persons**" is when the Rite of Exorcism is imparted to enforce the cleansing of persons of all forms of persistent malevolent and diabolical spirits, ghosts or negative elemental presence.

XLII.II – CONDITIONS OF RITE OF EXORCISM

1. Conditions of the Rite of Exorcism are those requisite qualifications and contingencies permitted in the proper ministration of the Rite. Conditions of Rite of Exorcism

There exists specific conditions associated with each Type of Rite of Exorcism necessary to proceed; and universal conditions relating to the investigation and approval of the Ordinary and the Exorcist in relation to the Extraordinary Rite.

2. The conditions of the Exorcist are:- Conditions of the Exorcist

(i) That the Exorcist is an authorised cleric bound by austere vows, having been approved into the role of Exorcist; and not having served as an Exorcist greater than twelve (12) years. No clerical person is permitted to continue as an Exorcist beyond twelve (12) years without special approval of the Supreme Patriarch; and

(ii) That the Exorcist is highly intelligent and with a sound knowledge and understanding of forensic investigation and psychological techniques, particularly in discerning the merit of cases that may warrant the Rite; and

(iii) That the Exorcist continues to demonstrate a natural gift of compassion, care, love and sanctity towards others and especially to lost souls, confused spirits and ghosts and individuals suffering severe mental trauma; and

(iv) That the Exorcist, despite their experience on cases, remains professionally objective with each case and each request; and not prone to personal superstition, paranoia or obsession in the most extremes of personal cases and whether they are overwhelmingly affected by demonic possessions; and

(v) That the Exorcist has not personally performed more than nine (9) Extraordinary Rites of Exorcism of Persons in a given twelve month period, unless granted a special dispensation by the Supreme Patriarch.

3. The *Rite of Exorcism of Earth* is the Rite of Dedication of Sacred Site as approved under the following conditions:- Rite of Exorcism of Earth Conditions

(i) That the site in question is developed or undeveloped earth, or land or field; and

(ii) That a formal petition for the Rite was submitted to the Diocese, using the proper form; and containing the necessary affidavits, historical research of the site in question and witness testimony from two (2) or more persons; and

(iii) That the petitioners for the Rite have written permission from the current owners and custodians, managers or occupiers of the site to file the formal petition for the Rite; and

(iv) That the current owners and custodians, managers or occupiers of the site do not currently engage in, or propose in the future to engage in, any form of sordid use of the site; and

(v) That the historical research provided within the petition concerning the site indicates clear evidence of previous trauma concerning death, or severe psychological distress, or sordid or profoundly wicked and diabolical acts; and

(vi) That the necessary affidavits within the petition for the Rite testifies to two (2) or more separate events indicating a lingering and persistent presence of malevolent spirits, or ghosts or other form of strong negative presence; and

(vii) That the Petition was approved as extraordinary relief.

4. The *Rite of Exorcism of Water* is the Rite of Dedication of Sacred Site as approved under the following conditions:- Rite of Exorcism of Water Conditions

(i) That the site in question is a pool, or pond, or lake, or stream or river; and

(ii) That a formal petition for the Rite was submitted to the Diocese, using the proper form; and containing the necessary affidavits, historical research of the site in question and witness testimony from two (2) or more persons; and

(iii) That the petitioners for the Rite have written permission from the current owners and custodians, managers or occupiers of the site to file the formal petition for the Rite; and

(iv) That the current owners and custodians, managers or occupiers of the site do not currently engage in, or propose in the future to engage in, any form of sordid use of the site; and

(v) That the historical research provided within the petition concerning the site indicates clear evidence of previous trauma concerning death, or severe psychological distress, or sordid or profoundly wicked and diabolical acts; and

(vi) That the necessary affidavits within the petition for the Rite testifies to two (2) or more separate events indicating a lingering and persistent presence of malevolent spirits, or ghosts or other form of strong negative presence; and

(vii) That the Petition was approved as extraordinary relief.

5. The *Rite of Exorcism of Wilderness* is the Rite of Dedication of Sacred Site as approved under the following conditions:- Rite of Exorcism of Wilderness Conditions

(i) That the site in question is dense, or sparse or barren wilderness; and

(ii) That a formal petition for the Rite was submitted to the Diocese, using the proper form; and containing the necessary affidavits, historical research of the site in question and witness testimony from three (3) or more persons; and

(iii) That the petitioners for the Rite have written permission from the current owners and custodians, managers or occupiers of the site to file the formal petition for the Rite; and

(iv) That the current owners and custodians, managers or occupiers of the site do not currently engage in, or propose in the future to engage in, any form of sordid use of the site; and

(v) That the historical research provided within the petition concerning the site indicates clear evidence of previous trauma concerning death, or severe psychological distress, or sordid or profoundly wicked and diabolical acts; and

(vi) That the necessary affidavits within the petition for the Rite testifies to three (3) or more separate events indicating a lingering and persistent presence of malevolent spirits, or ghosts or other form of strong negative presence; and

(vii) That the Petition was approved as extraordinary relief.

6. The *Rite of Exorcism of Foreshores* is the Rite of Dedication of Sacred Site as approved under the following conditions:- Rite of Exorcism of Foreshores Conditions

(i) That the site in question is a foreshore, or headland or embankment; and

(ii) That a formal petition for the Rite was submitted to the Diocese, using the proper form; and containing the necessary affidavits, historical research of the site in question and witness testimony from three (3) or more persons; and

(iii) That the petitioners for the Rite have written permission from the current owners and custodians, managers or occupiers of the site to file the formal petition for the Rite; and

(iv) That the current owners and custodians, managers or occupiers of the site do not currently engage in, or propose in the future to engage in, any form of sordid use of the site; and

(v) That the historical research provided within the petition concerning the site indicates clear evidence of previous trauma concerning death, or severe psychological distress, or sordid or profoundly wicked and diabolical acts; and

(vi) That the necessary affidavits within the petition for the Rite testifies to three (3) or more separate events indicating a lingering and persistent presence of malevolent spirits, or ghosts or other form of strong negative presence; and

(vii) That the Petition was approved as extraordinary relief.

7. The *Rite of Exorcism of Buildings* is the Rite of Dedication of Chapel without a concluding Holy Mass, as approved under the following conditions:- Rite of Exorcism of Buildings Conditions

(i) That the site in question is a building, whether inhabited or uninhabited, or complete, or damaged or in ruins; and

(ii) That a formal petition for the Rite was submitted to the Diocese, using the proper form; and containing the necessary affidavits, historical research of the site in question and witness testimony from three (3) or more persons; and

(iii) That the petitioners for the Rite have written permission from the current owners and custodians, managers or occupiers of the site to file the formal petition for the Rite; and

(iv) That the current owners and custodians, managers or occupiers of the site do not currently engage in, or propose in the future to engage in, any form of sordid use of the site; and

(v) That the historical research provided within the petition concerning the site indicates clear evidence of previous trauma concerning death, or severe psychological distress, or sordid or profoundly wicked and diabolical acts; and

(vi) That the necessary affidavits within the petition for the Rite testifies to three (3) or more separate events indicating a lingering and persistent presence of malevolent spirits, or ghosts or other form of strong negative presence; and

(vii) That the Petition was approved as extraordinary relief.

Rite of Exorcism of Vessels Conditions

8. The *Rite of Exorcism of Vessels* is the Rite of Dedication of Chapel without a concluding Holy Mass, as approved under the following conditions:-

(i) That the site in question is a water, or air or space vessel; and

(ii) That a formal petition for the Rite was submitted to the Diocese, using the proper form; and containing the necessary affidavits, historical research of the site in question and witness testimony from three (3) or more persons; and

(iii) That the petitioners for the Rite have written permission from the current owners and custodians, managers or occupiers of the site to file the formal petition for the Rite; and

(iv) That the current owners and custodians, managers or occupiers of the site do not currently engage in, or propose in the future to engage in, any form of sordid use of the site; and

(v) That the historical research provided within the petition concerning the site indicates clear evidence of previous trauma concerning death, or severe psychological distress, or sordid or profoundly wicked and diabolical acts; and

(vi) That the necessary affidavits within the petition for the Rite testifies to three (3) or more separate events indicating a lingering and persistent presence of malevolent spirits, or ghosts or other form of strong negative presence; and

(vii) That the Petition was approved as extraordinary relief.

9. The *Rite of Exorcism of Structures* is the Rite of Dedication of Chapel without a concluding Holy Mass, as approved under the following conditions:- Rite of Exorcism of Structures Conditions

(i) That the site in question is a form of permanent structure or infrastructure, including but not limited to a highway, or road, or footpath, or bridge, or underpass, or tower, or pipeline or pole; and

(ii) That a formal petition for the Rite was submitted to the Diocese, using the proper form; and containing the necessary affidavits, historical research of the site in question and witness testimony from three (3) or more persons; and

(iii) That the petitioners for the Rite have written permission from the current owners and custodians, managers or occupiers of the site to file the formal petition for the Rite; and

(iv) That the current owners and custodians, managers or occupiers of the site do not currently engage in, or propose in the future to engage in, any form of sordid use of the site; and

(v) That the historical research provided within the petition concerning the site indicates clear evidence of previous trauma concerning death, or severe psychological distress, or sordid or profoundly wicked and diabolical acts; and

(vi) That the necessary affidavits within the petition for the Rite testifies to three (3) or more separate events indicating a lingering and persistent presence of malevolent spirits, or ghosts or other form of strong negative presence; and

(vii) That the Petition was approved as extraordinary relief.

10. The conditions for the *Rite of Exorcism of Animals* are:- Rite of Exorcism of Animals Conditions

(i) That the case concerns domestic animals or livestock; and

(ii) That a formal petition for the Rite was submitted to the Diocese, using the proper form; and containing the necessary affidavits, historical research of the site in question and witness testimony from three (3) or more persons; and

(iii) That the petitioners for the Rite have written permission from the current owners and custodians, managers or occupiers of the site where the animals are located to file the formal petition for the Rite; and

(iv) That the current owners and custodians, managers or occupiers of the site where the animals are located do not currently engage in, or propose in the future to engage in, any form of sordid use of the site; and

(v) That the historical research provided within the petition concerning the site where the animals are located indicates clear evidence of previous trauma concerning death, or severe psychological distress, or sordid or profoundly wicked and diabolical acts. If any person tending or connected to the animals has a strong history of death, personal trauma or previous engagement in wicked and diabolical acts, see Rite of Exorcism of Person; and

(vi) That the necessary affidavits within the petition for the Rite testifies to three (3) or more separate events indicating a lingering and persistent presence of malevolent spirits, or ghosts or other form of strong negative presence; and

(vii) That the Petition was approved as extraordinary relief; and if the animals are permanently outdoors, that the Rite of Dedication of Sacred Site is first performed; or if indoor animals, that the Rite of Dedication of Chapel without Holy Mass was first performed on the barn or dedicated animal accommodation.

11. The conditions for the *Rite of Exorcism of Objects* is the Rite of Dedication of Sacred Site as applied to the consecration of an Object; and approved under the following conditions:- Rite of Exorcism of Objects Conditions

(i) That the object is a movable or immovable object; and

(ii) That a formal petition for the Rite was submitted to the Diocese, using the proper form; and containing the necessary affidavits, historical research of the site in question and witness testimony from three (3) or more persons; and

(iii) That the petitioners for the Rite have written permission from the current owners and custodians, managers or occupiers of the site where the object is located to file the formal petition for the Rite; and

(iv) That the current owners and custodians, managers or occupiers of the site where the object is located do not currently engage in, or propose in the future to engage in, any form of sordid use of the site; and

(v) That the historical research provided within the petition concerning the object indicates clear evidence of previous trauma concerning death, or severe psychological distress, or sordid or profoundly wicked and diabolical acts, or cultural theft; and

(vi) That the research of the provenance of the object demonstrates that it does not need to be repatriated by law or moral obligation to a culture or location that it originates; and

(vii) That the necessary affidavits within the petition for the Rite testifies to three (3) or more separate events indicating a lingering and persistent presence of malevolent spirits, or ghosts or other form of strong negative presence; and

(viii) That the Petition was approved as extraordinary relief.

12. The conditions for the Ordinary Rite of Exorcism of Persons are:- Ordinary Rite of Exorcism of Persons Conditions

(i) That a formal petition for the Rite was submitted to the Diocese, using the proper form; and containing the necessary affidavits, historical research of the site in question and witness testimony from four (4) or more persons; and

(ii) That the petitioners for the Rite have written permission from the immediate family of the person in question; and written permission from the current owners and custodians, managers of the property where the person currently resides to file the formal petition for the Rite; and

(iii) That the current owners and custodians, managers or occupiers of the site where the person in question currently resides do not currently engage in, or propose in the future to engage in, any form of sordid use of the site; and

(iv) That the historical research concerning the person indicates clear evidence and pattern of previous mental trauma concerning death, or severe psychological distress, or sordid or profoundly wicked and diabolical acts; and

(v) That the person in question has been a user in the past of narcotics or hallucinogens, but is no longer a user of such substances and has undergone a minimum period of detoxification; and

(vi) That the person in question is not on any significant anti-psychotic medication or regularly supervised psychological treatment program; and

(vii) That the necessary affidavits within the petition for the Rite testifies to three (3) or more separate events indicating a presence of malevolent spiritual and supernatural possession, including but not limited to actual manifestations of definitively malevolent supernatural force separate from any claimed possession of the person in question; and

(viii) That the Petition was approved as extraordinary relief; and

(ix) That the *Rite of Dedication of Sacred Site* and *Rite of Dedication of Chapel* without Holy Mass, were first performed before any further Rites.

13. The conditions for the Extraordinary Rite of Exorcism of Persons are:- Extraordinary Rite of Exorcism of Persons Conditions

(i) That a formal petition for the Rite was submitted to the Diocese, using the proper form; and containing the necessary affidavits, historical research of the site in question and witness testimony from four (4) or more persons; and

(ii) That the petitioners for the Rite have written permission from the immediate family of the person in question; and written permission from the current owners and custodians, managers of the property where the person currently resides to file the formal petition for the Rite; and

(iii) That the current owners and custodians, managers or occupiers of the site where the person in question currently resides do not currently engage in, or propose in the future to engage in, any form of sordid use of the site; and

(iv) That the historical research concerning the person indicates clear evidence and pattern of previous mental trauma concerning death, or severe psychological distress, or sordid or profoundly wicked and diabolical acts; and

(v) That the person in question has been a user in the past of narcotics or hallucinogens, but is no longer a user of such substances and has undergone a minimum period of detoxification; and

(vi) That the person in question is not on any significant anti-psychotic medication or regularly supervised psychological treatment program; and

(vii) That the necessary affidavits within the petition for the Rite testifies to six (6) or more separate events indicating a lingering, persistent and unmistakably belligerent presence of malevolent spiritual and supernatural possession, including but not limited to actual manifestations of definitively malevolent supernatural force separate from any claimed persistent belligerent malevolent possession of the person in question; and

(viii) That the Petition was approved by the Sacred Court of the Exorcist as extraordinary relief; and

(ix) That a doctor, preferably with knowledge of the medical history of the person in question will be present for the final stages of the Rite; and

(x) That the *Rite of Dedication of Sacred Site* and *Rite of Dedication of Chapel* without Holy Mass, were first performed before any further Rites.

XLII.III – MINISTER OF RITE OF EXORCISM

1. Only a cleric consecrated under austere vows, registered and authorised as an Exorcist may perform any Rite of Exorcism. Any attempt by any party not authorised to perform one or more acts concerning the Rite of Exorcism shall have no spiritual force or effect, but shall constitute a profound sacrilege and transgression.

Minister of Rite of Exorcism

2. Of all the elements essential to the successful conduct of the rite of Exorcism, wise discernment in the form of Intelligent Research is essential – both in terms of the state of mind, experience and events that may have affected the candidate for Exorcism, as well as the domicile, friends, family and activities.

Intelligence as a key weapon to defeat Evil

Every element in detailed research into the past events, circumstances and people is essential, particularly as the vast majority of malevolent experiences are due to ghosts of people previously known to the family, or place or the victim.

Without Intelligence and knowledge of the precise context, the Rite of Exorcism is defective and in error, even if performed in accord with sacred liturgy. Evil as wilful ignorance and arrogance, cannot be defeated by the same demonstration of such wilful ignorance and prejudice. Thus, all clergy are forbidden to perform the rite of Exorcism, except in clear and unmistakable signs of supernatural malevolence and the immediate and dire threat against the life of the victim.

3. Contrary to ignorant presumptions, the greatest power of the

Manifest Compassion as a

competent Exorcist is their ability to manifest intelligent and authentic compassion not only for the victim, but the malevolent spirits and ghosts in breach of the Laws of Heaven.

key weapon to defeat Evil

It is only in this ability to confidently name the contributing factors and influences through proper research and the qualities of Mercy, Love and Forgiveness, does the Exorcist become the embodiment of the Spirit of Christ and a beacon of the purest light that none in spirit can hide.

When the heart of the Exorcist is truly open, they create the doorway necessary to effect the proper binding of the malevolent spirit or ghost through the full and complete spiritual forces of Heaven as the final weapon to defeat evil.

4. By the power of the present Rite and its binding to the most sacred *Pactum De Singularis Christus*, a certified Exorcist shall have such instruments of supreme power and authority that no malevolent spirit shall prevail in defiance. These shall be known as the Keys of the Exorcist include:

The Keys of the Exorcist

   (i) A physical copy of the *Pactum De Singularis Caelum*; and

   (ii) A physical copy of the *Pactum De Singularis Christus*; and

   (iii) A Holy Cross in the form of the Risen Christ (without the body); and

   (iv) The Official certificate of authority of the Exorcist as approved by a proper higher authority; and

   (v) Incense, candles and holy water all blessed by the Supreme Patriarch for the specific function of Exorcism ceremonies; and

   (vi) The saints and angels assigned to the Exorcist to protect them and assist in combating malevolent and evil spirits.

5. While the Keys of the Exorcist validate the power and authority of the Exorcist to command any malevolent and evil spirit to vacate property or person, a further set of instruments of power shall be known collectively as the Sword of the Exorcist and relate directly to compelling the evil spirit to account and to recognise the authority and command of the Exorcist. These include (and are not limited to):

The Sword of the Exorcist

   (i) The presence of a living owner of the property during the Rite of Exorcism, who has previously undergone the Sacrament of Penance; and

   (ii) The written name of the alleged malevolent spirit and/or clothing, possessions or furniture most frequently associated with the malevolent spirits influence; and

(iii) The presence of a living blood relative of the possessed person during the Rite of Exorcism, who has previously undergone the Sacrament of Penance.

XLII.IV – RITE OF EXORCISM OF ANIMALS

1. The *Rite of Exorcism of Animals* conferred by a competent minister, upon meeting the necessary strict qualification of the Conditions for such a Rite, shall be as follows:- Rite of Exorcism of Animals

RITE OF DEDICATION

Rite of Exorcism of Animals Dedication

(The appropriate Rite of Dedication as per Conditions must be performed first and a minimum of three days lapse before the following Rite is conducted.)

ENTRANCE

Rite of Exorcism of Animals Entrance

(Ordained Exorcist approaches the site where the animals in question are located and crosses the threshold to enter the site and then immediately stops, kneels and then kisses the ground at a designated clean and suitable space)

EXORCIST

(After arising to their feet having kissed the Sacred Ground of the Sacred Space.)

In the name of ✠ the Father, and of the Son, and of the Holy Spirit.

ALL

Amen.

✠ May the healing love and the abiding strength of the angels and saints of Heaven be ever present throughout this Sacred Consecrated Space.

ALL

Amen.

PETITION

Rite of Exorcism of Animals Petition

EXORCIST

The Rite of Exorcism is a most sacred and ancient rite dating back to even before the time of Christ. Trust in the existence of higher powers capable of effecting the eviction of malevolent spiritual entities from a person or place is a common belief shared by many ancient communities dating back to the very first civilisations of humanity.

The word "exorcism" itself comes from Ancient Greek meaning "binding by oath". Thus, the meaning of the sacred Rite of Exorcism itself literally refers to two key powers of Heaven. The first being the power of spiritual binding and the second being the significance of authentic oaths and vows in forcing belligerent and malevolent spirits from leaving the possession of animals or places or persons.

Christ himself made it abundantly clear through his teachings and his actions what constitutes the extraordinary powers and weapons behind the authentic Christian Rite of Exorcism. These are Love, Compassion and Forgiveness that drive effective spiritual bindings, vows and oaths. Real love, the kind of love demonstrated by the actions of Christ is the most powerful binding of all existence. Love is the essence of existence, the glue that keeps parents with their children and members with their communities and God and the Divine Creator connected with humanity. Compassion is the true ability to acknowledge and understand the pain and anguish of others and the most powerful first part of any meaningful healing. Forgiveness, especially when emulating the Divine Mercy of our Creator upon all our failings is the power that has the capacity to transform any situation into one of profound healing and emancipation. Are all of you prepared then to trust in the healing words and authentic wisdom of Christ?

ALL

Yes.

RECITALS

Rite of Exorcism of Animals
Recitals

EXORCIST

I now call upon those present to come forward and demonstrate their authority and prove their vows before God concerning these beloved animals. By what proper authority is the Rite of Exorcism called to be performed today?

REPRESENTATIVE(S)

(Handing the Exorcist a copy of the Decree of Exemplification and Original Writ.)

Decree of Exemplification and Original Holy Writ.

EXORCIST

And are you the proper representatives for these beautiful animals and for this community?

REPRESENTATIVE(S)

Yes we are.

EXORCIST

And can you testify as your own witnesses that the land where we stand has now been consecrated? And that no malevolent force or ill may find safe harbour or defy the laws of the Divine Creator of all existence?

REPRESENTATIVE(S)

Yes we can.

EXORCIST

(Turns around to everyone present with his hands open)

Very well, are all of you present now prepared to kneel as a mark of respect to God and the Divine Creator and all of Heaven; and answer three vows of faith and trust in the name of Christ in honour of our intentions and petition through this sacred Rite?

ALL

Yes we will.

(All kneel.)

VOWS

EXORCIST

First, do you accept and love these animals as part of your family and community? Do you solemnly promise to always keep this sacred place only for good and respectful acts? And to ensure this place is not used for sordid or cruel acts, contrary to the norms of the Universal Ecclesia?

ALL

We do (promise).

EXORCIST

Do you accept and understand with heartfelt compassion the terrible unresolved torment, pain and anguish must be at the root of the malevolent and disturbed forces you have witnessed? Do you solemnly promise to forgive such forces with all your heart and mind and spirit so that authority of the *Holy Writ* may be properly given over to the angels and saints of Heaven to help bring final healing and peace and resolution?

ALL

We do (promise).

EXORCIST

Finally, do you solemnly promise to pray now and into the future for the continued well being of all the souls helped by the angels and saints of Heaven to transition to a final state of peace and resolution through this sacred Rite?

ALL

We do (promise).

(All stand.)

OBSIGNATION

EXORCIST

Then truly this is a Divine teaching moment, for we recognise in our midst the wellspring of a true spiritual Christian community. Upon the strength of faith of all here present.

EXORCIST

(Gently makes the sign of the cross over the animals.)

I now gently trace the sign ✠ of the cross over these beloved animals as a sign and seal of the promises made in the name of our Divine Father.

Dear Brothers and Sisters, let us ask that all of Heaven look lovingly upon this moment and all here present as an embodiment of his holy Church. We ask this in the name of Christ.

ALL

Amen.

WILL OF THE PEOPLE

Rite of Exorcism of Animals
Will of the People

EXORCIST

Let us pray.

Jesus, through your teachings and sacrifice we have come to no longer fear death, for you have given us eternal life so we can never die.

Heavenly Father, it is our Will and true intention in gratitude for your gifts of healing and our reconciliation into your presence, that we seek to dedicate this sacred Rite fully to enacting your teachings.

We pray you will accept our humble petition and promises as a sign of the truth of our intentions; and that your angels and saints will now take up the execution of the *Holy Writ* of binding in spirit what is spirit and in flesh what is flesh, through Jesus Christ your son.

ALL

Amen.

HOLY BLESSING

Rite of Exorcism of Animals
Holy Blessing

EXORCIST

Dear Brothers and Sisters, may this Special Holy Water of Healing and Sanctity, that was consecrated and dedicated in the presence of the Holy Spirit and a Company of Guardian Angels of Heaven, for the express purpose that when dispensed it should be for such intentions and needs of healing, consecration and reconciliation as we have already pronounced. Let this Special Blessing also be a reminder to us all of our Baptism into the one, apostolic and united Universal Ecclesia of Christ.

EXORCIST

(Exorcist opens his arms and looks up)

God our Father, your gift of pure water bring life and abundance to the Earth; it washes away our transgressions and brings us to eternal life. With this Special Holy Water of Healing and Sanctity, help us rid and cleanse ourselves of all negativity and profanity that may cloak our mortal frames, and seek to prevent us from opening our hearts more fully to your forgiveness and healing.

EXORCIST

(Exorcist brings his hands over the water in the aspersorium (sacramental bowl):)

We now bind our healing intentions and dedications to this Holy Water in the name ✠ of the Father, the Son and the Holy Spirit.

We do this in the name of Jesus Christ, the Ruler of all Heaven and Earth and the Lord of Hosts whom no spirit can deny.

ALL

Amen.

(The Exorcist now moves and sprinkles Holy Water on and around the animals)

EXORCIST

I Bless these Animals in the ✠ name of the Father and of the Son and of the Holy Spirit.

ALL

Amen.

CHRISTS' PRAYER

Rite of Exorcism of Animals
Christs' Prayer

EXORCIST

It is Christ that taught us to call the Divine Creator of all Existence our Father. Let us pray with confidence to our Father in the manner and Spirit our Saviour taught us.

ALL

Our Father of All Creation,
We beseech thee and honour your name,
For your Rule be united as One,
And your Laws be equal to All,
On Earth as it is in Heaven,
Grant us the means to sustenance,
As we shall give alms to those in need.
Save us from trickery and false oaths,
As our vows and our oaths shall be true.
Forgive us our debits and transgressions,
As we shall forgive the debits and transgressions of others.
Release us from any curse and ills,
As we shall not curse nor wish ill upon another.
We ask most humbly and with deep gratitude,

For let then your will be done.
Amen.

EXORCIST

Deliver us, Jesus, from every evil, and grant us peace in our day. In your mercy help us to free ourselves from transgressions and protect us from all fear as we defend and proclaim the authentic mysteries of our Christian Faith.

ALL

For the kingdom, the power, and the glory are yours, now and forever.

CONCLUDING RITE

EXORCIST

May Jesus always be with you.

ALL

And also with you.

EXORCIST

Just as God our Father has forgiven us of our transgressions and his son Jesus Christ has healed us with his love and mercy and the Holy Spirit has filled us with renewed strength and courage, so through this most ancient and sacred Rite a profound healing occurred both here on Earth and in Heaven. Let us make a firm promise now, before we depart this extraordinary event, to live and act in each moment of our lives as true and authentic Christians.

ALL

We do honestly and sincerely promise.

EXORCIST

May our God and Divine Creator bless you, ✠ the Father, and the Son and the Holy Spirit.

ALL

Amen

EXORCIST

Go forth with the peace and love of Christ.

ALL
Thanks be to God!

XLII.V – ORDINARY RITE OF EXORCISM OF PERSONS

1. The *Ordinary Rite of Exorcism of Persons* conferred by a competent minister, upon meeting the necessary strict qualification of the Conditions for such a Rite, shall be as follows:- Ordinary Rite of Exorcism of Persons

RITE OF DEDICATION

Ordinary Rite of Exorcism of Persons Dedication

(The *Rite of Dedication of Sacred Site* and *Rite of Dedication of Chapel* without Mass as per Conditions must be performed first and a minimum of three days lapse before the following Rite is conducted.)

ENTRANCE

Ordinary Rite of Exorcism of Persons Entrance

(Ordained Exorcist approaches the site and crosses the threshold to enter the site where the person in question is located and then immediately stops, kneels and then kisses the ground at a designated clean and suitable space in sight of the person in question.)

EXORCIST
(After arising to their feet having kissed the Sacred Ground of the Sacred Space.)

In the name of ✠ the Father, and of the Son, and of the Holy Spirit. Amen.

✠ May the healing love and the abiding strength of the angels and saints of Heaven be ever present throughout this Sacred Consecrated Space. Amen.

PETITION

Ordinary Rite of Exorcism of Persons Petition

EXORCIST
The Rite of Exorcism is a most sacred and ancient rite dating back to even before the time of Christ. Trust in the existence of higher powers capable of effecting the eviction of malevolent spiritual entities from a person or place is a common belief shared by many ancient communities dating back to the very first civilisations of humanity.

The word "exorcism" itself comes from Ancient Greek meaning "binding by oath". Thus, the meaning of the sacred Rite of Exorcism itself literally refers to two key powers of Heaven. The first being the power of spiritual binding and the second being the significance of authentic oaths and vows in forcing belligerent and malevolent spirits from leaving the possession of a place or person.

Christ himself made it abundantly clear through his teachings and his actions what constitutes the extraordinary powers and weapons behind the authentic Christian Rite of Exorcism. These are Love, Compassion and Forgiveness that drive effective spiritual bindings, vows and oaths. Real love, the kind of love demonstrated by the actions of Christ is the most powerful binding of all existence. Love is the essence of existence, the glue that keeps parents with their children and members with their communities and God and the Divine Creator connected with humanity. Compassion is the true ability to acknowledge and understand the pain and anguish of others and the most powerful first part of any meaningful healing. Forgiveness, especially when emulating the Divine Mercy of our Creator upon all our failings is the power that has the capacity to transform any situation into one of profound healing and emancipation. Are all of you prepared then to trust in the healing words and authentic wisdom of Christ?

ALL

Yes.

RECITALS

EXORCIST

I now call upon those present to come forward and demonstrate their authority and prove their vows before God concerning our beloved son (daughter) N. By what proper authority is the Rite of Exorcism called to be performed today?

REPRESENTATIVE(S)

(Handing the Exorcist a copy of the Decree of Exemplification and Original Writ.)

Decree of Exemplification and Original Holy Writ.

EXORCIST

And are you the proper representatives for the family of N.

and for this community?

REPRESENTATIVE(S)

Yes we are.

EXORCIST

And can you testify as your own witnesses that the land where we stand has now been consecrated? And that this building has now been sanctified as a sacred place where no malevolent force or ill may find safe harbour or defy the laws of the Divine Creator of all existence?

REPRESENTATIVE(S)

Yes we can.

EXORCIST

(Turns around to everyone in the room with his hands open)

Very well, are all of you present now prepared to kneel as a mark of respect to God and the Divine Creator and all of Heaven; and answer three vows of faith and trust in the name of Christ in honour of our intentions and petition through this sacred Rite?

ALL

Yes we will.

(All kneel.)

VOWS

EXORCIST

First, do you accept and welcome with open arms N. as a beloved and worthy member of your family and community? Do you solemnly promise to always be truthful and kind to N. in good times and in bad, in times of sickness and distress?

ALL

We do (promise).

EXORCIST

Do you accept and forgive N. for any past faults, disappointments and transgressions as God has forgiven you? Do you solemnly promise to be gentle and slow to judge in the future and to always show N. by your actions that they are truly loved, valued and accepted for who they are and not judged as others might wish them to be?

ALL

We do (promise).

EXORCIST

Finally, do you accept and understand with heartfelt compassion the terrible unresolved torment, pain and anguish must have been at the root of the malevolent and disturbed forces you have witnessed? Do you solemnly promise to forgive with all your heart and mind and spirit so that such pain and suffering may be properly given over to the angels and saints of Heaven to help bring final healing peace, protection and resolution?

ALL

We do (promise).

(All stand.)

OBSIGNATION

Ordinary Rite of Exorcism of Persons Obsignation

EXORCIST

Then truly this is a Divine teaching moment, for we recognise in our midst the wellspring of a true spiritual Christian community. Upon the strength of faith of all here present.

EXORCIST

(Gently makes the sign of the cross over the person.)

I now gently trace the sign ✠ of the cross over our beloved N. as a sign and seal of the promises made in the name of our Divine Father.

Dear Brothers and Sisters, let us ask that all of Heaven look lovingly upon this moment and all here present as an embodiment of his holy Church. We ask this in the name of Christ.

ALL

Amen.

WILL OF THE PEOPLE

Ordinary Rite of Exorcism of Persons Will of the People

EXORCIST

Let us pray.

Jesus, through your teachings and sacrifice we have come to no longer fear death, for you have given us eternal life so we can never die.

Heavenly Father, it is our Will and true intention in gratitude for your gifts of healing and our reconciliation into your presence, that we seek to dedicate this sacred Rite fully to enacting your teachings.

We pray you will accept our humble petition and promises as a sign of the truth of our intentions; and that your angels and saints will now take up the execution of the *Holy Writ* of binding in spirit what is spirit and in flesh what is flesh, through Jesus Christ your son.

ALL

Amen.

HOLY BLESSING

Ordinary Rite of Exorcism of Persons
Holy Blessing

EXORCIST

Dear Brothers and Sisters, may this Special Holy Water of Healing and Sanctity, that was consecrated and dedicated in the presence of the Holy Spirit and a Company of Guardian Angels of Heaven, for the express purpose that when dispensed it should be for such intentions and needs of healing, consecration and reconciliation as we have already pronounced. Let this Special Blessing also be a reminder to us all of our Baptism into the one, apostolic and united Universal Ecclesia of Christ.

EXORCIST

(Exorcist opens his arms and looks up)

God our Father, your gift of pure water bring life and abundance to the Earth; it washes away our transgressions and brings us to eternal life. With this Special Holy Water of Healing and Sanctity, help us rid and cleanse ourselves of all negativity and profanity that may cloak our mortal frames, and seek to prevent us from opening our hearts more fully to your forgiveness and healing.

EXORCIST

(Exorcist brings his hands over the water in the aspersorium (sacramental bowl):)

We now bind our healing intentions and dedications to this Holy Water in the name ✠ of the Father, the Son and the Holy Spirit.

We do this in the name of Jesus Christ, the Ruler of all Heaven and Earth and the Lord of Hosts whom no spirit can deny.

ALL

Amen.

(The Exorcist now moves and sprinkles Holy Water on the person and around the person)

EXORCIST

I Bless N. in the ✠ name of the Father and of the Son and of the Holy Spirit.

ALL

Amen.

CONCLUDING RITE

EXORCIST

May Jesus always be with you.

ALL

And also with you.

EXORCIST

Just as God our Father has forgiven us of our transgressions and his son Jesus Christ has healed us with his love and mercy and the Holy Spirit has filled us with renewed strength and courage, so through this most ancient and sacred Rite a profound healing occurred both here on Earth and in Heaven. Let us make a firm promise now, before we depart this extraordinary event, to live and act in each moment of our lives as true and authentic Christians.

ALL

We do honestly and sincerely promise.

EXORCIST

May our God and Divine Creator bless you, ✠ the Father, and the Son and the Holy Spirit.

ALL

Amen

EXORCIST

Go forth with the peace and love of Christ.

ALL

Thanks be to God!

XLII.VI – EXTRAORDINARY RITE OF EXORCISM OF PERSONS

1. The *Extraordinary Rite of Exorcism of Persons* conferred by a competent minister, upon meeting the necessary strict qualification of the Conditions for such a Rite, shall be as follows:-

Extraordinary Rite of Exorcism of Persons

RITE OF DEDICATION

(The *Rite of Dedication of Sacred Site* and *Rite of Dedication of Chapel* without Mass as per Conditions must be performed first and a minimum of three days lapse before the following Rite is conducted.)

Extraordinary Rite of Exorcism of Persons Dedication

ENTRANCE

(Ordained Exorcist approaches the site and crosses the threshold to enter the site where the person in question is located and then immediately stops, kneels and then kisses the ground at a designated clean and suitable space in sight of the person in question.)

Extraordinary Rite of Exorcism of Persons Entrance

EXORCIST

(After arising to their feet having kissed the Sacred Ground of the Sacred Space.)

In the name of ✠ the Father, and of the Son, and of the Holy Spirit. Amen.

✠ May the healing love and the abiding strength of the angels and saints of Heaven be ever present throughout this Sacred Consecrated Space. Amen.

PENITENTIAL RITE

Extraordinary Rite of Exorcism of Persons Penitential Rite

EXORCIST

We gather together at this moment of great distress and trial, let us all honestly acknowledge our failures and ask the Lord for pardon and strength.

ALL

I confess before God and the Divine Creator of all Existence, that I have transgressed from your teachings and laws, by my thoughts and through my words and actions; and in what I have done

and what I have failed to do.
Before all here present as witness, I admit that I am truly sorry and remorseful for my thoughts, my words and my actions and call out to our Mother Blessed Mary in Heaven, to all the angels and saints and our ancestors, to intercede for me.

(All kneel)

EXORCIST
May God have mercy on us, forgive us our sins, and bring us to everlasting life.

ALL
Amen.

EXORCIST
Jesus, we have earnestly confessed before all here present that we have transgressed against your teachings and rules. Jesus have mercy.

ALL
Jesus have mercy.

EXORCIST
Christ sacrificed his own holy life, to forever end all forms of blood sacrifice; and to raise the dead to life; and to wash away our transgressions and the transgressions of every generation. Christ have mercy.

ALL
Christ have mercy.

EXORCIST
Jesus you bring pardon and peace to the transgressor. Accept our sincere contrition and help reconcile us to your love. Jesus have Mercy.

ALL
Jesus have mercy.

EXORCIST
Christ, through your Divine Authority you gave us the Gift of the Holy Sacrament of Penance, that through the demonstration of genuine remorse and contrition, your servants might administer the Rite of Absolution. Rise up then my Brother and Sisters!

(All kneel)

EXORCIST

In witness to the forgiveness and absolution of our Transgressions in the name of the Father and the Son and the Holy Spirit, in union with our Blessed Mother Mary and all the angels, saints and ancestors, let us proclaim to the world the joy of such healing and peace and give glory to our Eternal Father.

GLORIA

Extraordinary Rite of Exorcism of Persons
Gloria

ALL

Glory to God and all in Heaven,
And peace to all people on Earth.
Divine Creator of all Existence,
Our loving God and Father,
We worship you, we give you thanks,
We praise you for your mercy.
Glory be unto our Saviour Jesus Christ,
The Son of Man and the Lamb of God.
For you take away the transgressions of the world,
And set all us free from the bonds of slavery.
Have mercy upon all of us,
And receive our prayers.
For you alone are the Holy One,
You alone are the Absolute Sovereign Lord,
You alone are the most high Jesus Christ,
With the Holy Spirit in the glory of God our Father,
Amen.

PETITION

Extraordinary Rite of Exorcism of Persons
Petition

EXORCIST

The Rite of Exorcism is a most sacred and ancient rite dating back to even before the time of Christ. Trust in the existence of higher powers capable of effecting the eviction of malevolent spiritual entities from a person or place is a common belief shared by many ancient communities dating back to the very first civilisations of humanity.

The word "exorcism" itself comes from Ancient Greek meaning "binding by oath". Thus, the meaning of the sacred Rite of Exorcism itself literally refers to two key powers of Heaven. The first being the power of spiritual binding and the second being the significance of authentic oaths and vows in forcing belligerent and malevolent spirits from leaving the possession of a place or person.

Christ himself made it abundantly clear through his teachings and his actions what constitutes the extraordinary powers and weapons behind the authentic Christian Rite of Exorcism. These are Love, Compassion and Forgiveness that drive effective spiritual bindings, vows and oaths. Real love, the kind of love demonstrated by the actions of Christ is the most powerful binding of all existence. Love is the essence of existence, the glue that keeps parents with their children and members with their communities and God and the Divine Creator connected with humanity. Compassion is the true ability to acknowledge and understand the pain and anguish of others and the most powerful first part of any meaningful healing. Forgiveness, especially when emulating the Divine Mercy of our Creator upon all our failings is the power that has the capacity to transform any situation into one of profound healing and emancipation. Are all of you prepared then to trust in the healing words and authentic wisdom of Christ?

ALL

Yes.

RECITALS

EXORCIST

I now call upon those present to come forward and demonstrate their authority and prove their vows before God concerning our beloved son (daughter) N. By what proper authority is the Rite of Exorcism called to be performed today?

REPRESENTATIVE(S)

(Handing the Exorcist a copy of the Decree of Exemplification and Original Writ.)

Decree of Exemplification and Original Holy Writ.

EXORCIST

And are you the proper representatives for the family of N. and for this community?

REPRESENTATIVE(S)

Yes we are.

EXORCIST

And can you testify as your own witnesses that the land where we stand has now been consecrated? And that this building has now been sanctified as a sacred place where no malevolent force or ill may find safe harbour or defy the laws of the Divine Creator of all existence?

REPRESENTATIVE(S)

Yes we can.

EXORCIST

(Turns around to everyone in the room with his hands open)

Very well, are all of you present now prepared to kneel as a mark of respect to God and the Divine Creator and all of Heaven; and answer three vows of faith and trust in the name of Christ in honour of our intentions and petition through this sacred Rite?

ALL

Yes we will.

(All kneel.)

VOWS

EXORCIST

First, do you accept and welcome with open arms N. as a beloved and worthy member of your family and community? Do you solemnly promise to always be truthful and kind to N. in good times and in bad, in times of sickness and distress?

ALL

We do (promise).

EXORCIST

Do you accept and forgive N. for any past faults, disappointments and transgressions as God has forgiven you? Do you solemnly promise to be gentle and slow to judge in the future and to always show N. by your actions that they are truly loved, valued and accepted for who they are and not judged as others might wish them to be?

ALL

We do (promise).

EXORCIST

Finally, do you accept and understand with heartfelt compassion the terrible unresolved torment, pain and anguish must have been at the root of the malevolent and disturbed forces we continue witness? Do you solemnly promise to forgive with all your heart and mind and spirit so that such pain and suffering may be properly given over to the angels and saints of Heaven to help bring final healing peace, protection and resolution?

ALL

We do (promise).

(All stand.)

OBSIGNATION

Extraordinary Rite of Exorcism of Persons Obsignation

EXORCIST

Then truly this is a Divine teaching moment, for we recognise in our midst the wellspring of a true spiritual Christian community that so love N. and that they are willing to face such torment, anguish and negativity with the most powerful weapons in the Universe of Divine Love, Compassion and Forgiveness.

EXORCIST

(Gently makes the sign of the cross over the person.)

I now gently trace the sign ✠ of the cross over our beloved N. as a sign and seal of the promises made in the name of our Divine Father.

Dear Brothers and Sisters, let us ask that all of Heaven look lovingly upon this moment and all here present as an embodiment of his holy Church. We ask this in the name of Christ.

ALL

Amen.

WILL OF THE PEOPLE

Extraordinary Rite of Exorcism of Persons Will of the People

EXORCIST

Let us pray.

Jesus, through your teachings and sacrifice we have come to no longer fear death, for you have given us eternal life so we can never die.

Heavenly Father, it is our Will and true intention in gratitude for your gifts of healing and our reconciliation into your presence, that we seek to dedicate this sacred Rite fully to enacting your teachings.

We pray you will accept our humble petition and promises as a sign of the truth of our intentions; and that your angels and saints will now take up the execution of the *Holy Writ* of binding in spirit what is spirit and in flesh what is flesh, through Jesus Christ your son.

ALL

Amen.

(Exorcist reaches out to join hands with others in the room until all are holding hands united)

EXORCIST

Dear Brothers and Sisters strengthened by the angels and saints who have answered our call upon a Holy Writ issued with the full authority of Christ and Heaven, let us invoke every blessing and healing for our beloved N., that they may be filled with the light and strength of Heaven to overcome. Let us also pray with open hearts of love, compassion and forgiveness to help heal and transition the hate and torment and anguish and negativity that may still cling to this sacred and consecrated place.

INVOCATION

Extraordinary Rite of Exorcism of Persons
Invocation

(With hands joined, All repeat each separate line of the invocation after the Exorcist, conscious of the changes of the person and the atmosphere until the Exorcist is clear the malevolent presence is at its weakest.)

E: Bless this house and those within.

E: Bless our beloved N., and deliver them from harm.

E: Bless and forgive the spirits that have broken the Divine Laws of the Universe.

E: Bless our intentions, our petitions and prayers.

E: Bless this family and this community.

E: Bless our member N. and help them accept all our remorse for any harm or hurt we have inflicted on them.

E: Bless this house and those within.

E: Bless and help those spirits that have caused so much distress to find forgiveness and peace in moving on.

E: Bless our beloved N., and free them from any further pain or harm.

E: Bless the names of the angels and saints come to our aid to enforce your Holy Writ.

E: Bless this family and this community.

E: Bless this sacred land and all life.

E: Bless N. as we have forgiven them for any past pain or regrets.

E: Bless your Holy Laws and those that keep them.

HOLY BLESSING

EXORCIST

Dear Brothers and Sisters, may this Special Holy Water of Healing and Sanctity, that was consecrated and dedicated in the presence of the Holy Spirit and a Company of Guardian Angels of Heaven, for the express purpose that when dispensed it should be for such intentions and needs of healing, consecration and reconciliation as we have already pronounced. Let this Special Blessing also be a reminder to us all of our Baptism into the one, apostolic and united Universal Ecclesia of Christ.

EXORCIST

(Exorcist opens his arms and looks up)

God our Father, your gift of pure water bring life and abundance to the Earth; it washes away our transgressions and brings us to eternal life. With this Special Holy Water of Healing and Sanctity, help us rid and cleanse ourselves of all negativity and profanity that may cloak our mortal frames, and seek to prevent us from opening our hearts more fully to your forgiveness and healing.

EXORCIST

(Exorcist brings his hands over the water in the aspersorium (sacramental bowl):)

We now bind our healing intentions and dedications to this Holy Water in the name ✠ of the Father, the Son and the Holy Spirit.

We do this in the name of Jesus Christ, the Ruler of all Heaven and Earth and the Lord of Hosts whom no spirit can deny.

ALL

Amen.

(The Exorcist now moves and sprinkles Holy Water on the person)

EXORCIST

I Bless this N. in the ✠ name of the Father and of the Son and of the Holy Spirit.

ALL

Amen.

TESTAMENT OF UNIVERSAL FAITH

Extraordinary Rite of Exorcism of Persons
Testament of Universal Faith

(All repeat at the direction of the Exorcist until it is clear the room is at peace.)

ALL

By the symbol of the Cross,
I pledge my mind and heart and spirit,
To the Golden Rule of Law,
That all are equal before the same laws,
And that no man or woman be enslaved,
Or be bound against their will.
With the sign of the Cross,
I promise that my word is my bond,
When given with my consent,
And that I shall live my life,
According to the seven Christian Virtues,
Of Respect, Honesty, Courage, Enthusiasm,
Compassion, Joy and Discernment,
And shall only give my word,
To those who do the same.
Through the symbol and sign of the Cross,
I vow to defend others against all evil,
So that no tyrant or false messenger,
Shall prevail against the Light of the Risen Christ.
Amen.

CONCLUDING RITE

Extraordinary Rite of Exorcism

EXORCIST
May Jesus always be with you.

ALL
And also with you.

EXORCIST
Just as God our Father has forgiven us of our transgressions and his son Jesus Christ has healed us with his love and mercy and the Holy Spirit has filled us with renewed strength and courage, so through this most ancient and sacred Rite a profound healing occurred both here on Earth and in Heaven. Let us make a firm promise now, before we depart this extraordinary event, to live and act in each moment of our lives as true and authentic Christians.

ALL
We do honestly and sincerely promise.

EXORCIST
May our God and Divine Creator bless you, ✠ the Father, and the Son and the Holy Spirit.

ALL
Amen

EXORCIST
Go forth with the peace and love of Christ.

ALL
Thanks be to God!

Title XLIII – Rite of Inquisition

XLIII.I – RITE OF INQUISITION

1. Inquisition shall be an ecclesiastical authority conferred by Rite for the proper investigation of any matter of thing within the Jurisdiction of the Universal Ecclesia, in accordance with the most sacred Covenants *Pactum De Singularis Caelum* and *Pactum De Singularis Christus*. Rite of Inquisition

   The Rite of Inquisition shall be granted and conferred in accordance with the most sacred Covenants *Pactum De Singularis Caelum*, *Pactum De Singularis Christus* and associated approved liturgy.

2. The Divine Purpose of the Rite of Inquisition is to confer sufficient powers and authority to enable the investigation of a matter that requires the establishment of one or more truths. Divine Purpose of Rite of Inquisition

   Given the nature of established structures of power and authority, in combination with the potential reluctance of one or more persons to fully co-operate or be fully transparent to inquiries, a body or individual tasked with establishing the truth of a matter requires the assistance of Heaven to remind others that no one is above the law; and all are subject equally to it.

   A person or body without sufficient ecclesiastical authority has no right or power or legitimacy to detain a person for questioning, or to seize goods or property for investigation, or to execute an entry of property against the will of the occupants, or to hold a person considered a danger to the proper operation of the law, or to prosecute a person.

3. A properly formed inquiry under the Rite of Inquisition shall always presume at its core that any accused person is innocent of any allegations. Presumption of Innocence

   The function of the investigator is to find the truth. For a prosecutor it is the presentation of the truth. The question of culpability or innocence is not the jurisdiction of an investigator but a jury under the rules of a trial.

4. The Rite of Inquisition expressly forbids the use of forms of cruel and unusual punishment, or torture as means or methods of attempting to secure a confession or admission of evidence. Forbiddance of Cruel & Unusual Punishment

   Any person or body that is culpable of breaching the conditions of the Rite, automatically has no authority or immunity under such Rite.

5. There exists only one form of the Rite of Inquisition. Forms of Rite of Inquisition

XLIII.II – CONDITIONS OF RITE OF INQUISITION

1. Conditions of the Rite of Inquisition are those requisite qualifications and contingencies permitted in the proper ministration of the Rite. The conditions for the Rite of Inquisition are:- Conditions of Rite of Inquisition

   (i) That information was received by a proper Ecclesiastical Authority as to one or more offences having occurred. Upon reviewing the information received, sufficient probable cause exists for the launch of an Inquisition; and

   (ii) That an Inquisitor with Ecclesial Authority and Powers was appointed to lead the Inquisition; and

   (iii) That an Ecclesiastical Writ of Inquiry and Search (*Recto Ecclesiae Investigationis*) was duly issued by the proper Ecclesiastical Authority concerning the Inquisition in question; and

   (iv) That any subsequent writs including (but not limited to) Writ of Seizure and Return (*Recto Ecclesiae Capionis*) and Writ of Arrest and Custody (*Recto Ecclesiae Custodiae*) were done under the authority of the original Ecclesiastical Writ of Inquiry and Search.

Title XLIV – Rite of Dispensation

XLIV.I – RITE OF DISPENSATION

1. Dispensation, also known as an *Indulgence*, is the mode of proper publication, or distribution of certain rights, usually memorialised in document form. Therefore, Dispensation is usually a derivative of some other sacred act occurring first. Thus, the first forms of instruments of value were the forms of indulgences and instruments themselves called "dispensations". Rite of Dispensation

As all rights come from Divine Rights, all documents and instruments of value must by definition be Dispensations properly conferred and issued in accord with the most sacred Covenants *Pactum De Singularis Caelum, Pactum De Singularis Christus* and associated approved liturgy.

XLIV.II – CONDITIONS OF RITE OF DISPENSATION

1. Conditions of the Rite of Dispensation are those requisite qualifications and contingencies permitted in the proper ministration of the Rite. The conditions for the Rite of Dispensation are:- Conditions of Rite of Dispensation

   (i) That a Dispensation is issued strictly in accord with the most sacred Covenants *Pactum De Singularis Caelum* and *Pactum De Singularis Christus*; and

   (ii) That the Dispensation does not in any way perpetuate the abhorrent, forbidden and suppressed practice of the "monetisation of sin"; and

   (iii) That any associated surety or credit or capital concerning Dispensations are associated with the supreme Ecclesiastical forms of money including the Supreme Credo (Credit), Gold Credo (Credit), Silver Credo (Credit) and Moneta.

2. A Dispensation shall be reprobate, profane, repugnant and therefore invalid and improper and rejected:- Reprobate, Profane and Repugnant forms of Dispensation

   (i) When a personal payment or payment of profit is made to the maker or issuer body, beyond the legitimate recovery of costs; or

   (ii) When the issuance contains such exclusive or restrictive rights that contradict the most sacred Covenants *Pactum De Singularis Caelum* or *Pactum De Singularis Christus*; or

   (iii) When the issuance contains language of promises or benefits contrary to the most sacred Covenants *Pactum De Singularis*

Caelum or *Pactum De Singularis Christus*; or

(iv) If it is motivated or driven by an attempt to shift blame or avoid accepting self-responsibility; or

(v) If it is motivated or driven by a desire, or wish, or worship of money or abundant material wealth.

Title XLV – Rite of Abrogation

XLV.I – RITE OF ABROGATION

1. Abrogation is the formal repeal by Rite and authority of a previously issued edict, act, bill, patent, regulation or instrument. All and any edicts, acts, regulations or instruments found to be contrary to the articles of the most sacred Covenant *Pactum De Singularis Caelum* or the sacred Covenant *Pactum De Singularis Christus*. Any such edict, act, bill, patent, regulation or instrument shall be automatically suppressed, having no force or effect from the date of first publication. Rite of Abrogation

The Rite of Abrogation shall be granted and conferred in accordance with the most sacred Covenants *Pactum De Singularis Caelum* and *Pactum De Singularis Christus* and associated approved liturgy.

2. The corruption of law begins not with rebellion to its precepts, but its incremental decay through the assent of successive edicts, acts, bills, patents, regulations or instruments that are fundamentally unjust and morally repugnant. Divine Purpose of Rite of Abrogation

No law shall be law without the necessary ecclesial authority to deem it so. Similarly, no elected official may possess the power to propose, debate or pass a law without the requisite ecclesial authority bestowed to their office.

Despite such safeguards, history continues to demonstrate that when it comes to the power of making laws, such powers inevitably attract corruption. When it comes to the absolute power of wealthy nations, such power of making laws inevitably corrupts absolutely.

Thus, it is left to the Divine Mandate bestowed to certain ecclesial bodies and persons, in accordance with the most sacred Covenants *Pactum De Singularis Caelum* and *Pactum De Singularis Christus,* to ensure that such corrupt and wicked laws are repealed and/or nullified in all their effects.

3. There exists only one form of the Rite of Abrogation. Form of the Rite of Abrogation

XLV.II – CONDITIONS OF RITE OF ABROGATION

1. Conditions of the Rite of Abrogation are those requisite qualifications and contingencies permitted in the proper ministration of the Rite. The conditions for the Rite of Abrogation are:- Conditions of Rite of Abrogation

   (i) That an edict, act, bill, patent, regulation or instrument has been issued by a body politic that is manifestly unjust and morally repugnant; and

(ii) That no motion to appeal such unjust and morally repugnant laws were properly filed by a party possessing a valid interest within forty (40) days of assent of the improper law; and

(iii) That an Ecclesiastical Writ of Annulment of Previous Laws and Instruments (*Recto Ecclesiae Abrogationis*) was issued from the proper Ecclesiastical Authority to the highest competent forum of law of the body politic, giving notice that such improper law contravenes the Laws of Heaven and the most sacred Covenants *Pactum De Singularis Caelum* and *Pactum De Singularis Christus*.

Title XLVI – Rite of Nullification

XLVI.I – RITE OF NULLIFICATION

1. Nullification is the formal striking and removal of any record, page, leaf, or document or instrument found to be contrary to the articles of the most sacred Covenant *Pactum De Singularis Caelum* or the sacred Covenant *Pactum De Singularis Christus*. Any such record, page, leaf, or document or instrument shall be automatically suppressed, having no force or effect from the date of first publication. Rite of Nullification

The Rite of Nullification shall be granted and conferred in accordance with the most sacred Covenants *Pactum De Singularis Caelum*, *Pactum De Singularis Christus* and associated approved liturgy.

2. By their innate nature, all Registers and Rolls are ecclesiastical, owing their legitimacy and authority upon ultimate provenance to the Great Register and Roll of Heaven in accord with the most sacred Covenants *Pactum De Singularis Caelum*, *Pactum De Singularis Christus* and associated approved liturgy. Divine Purpose of the Rite of Nullification

Thus, subject to the the most sacred Covenants *Pactum De Singularis Caelum*, *Pactum De Singularis Christus* and associated approved liturgy, the Universal Ecclesia shall hold the plenary authority to render a certain record, page, leaf, or document or instrument null and void from the beginning from any Register or Roll under its authority, whether or not such a Register or Roll is under its direct control.

These powers extend into the jurisdiction of all bodies politic administering Registers or Rolls or their equivalent.

3. The Rite of Nullification first and foremost creates two new records in the proper Registers and Rolls of the Universal Ecclesia that an Ecclesiastical Writ of Annulment of Previous Laws and Instruments (*Recto Ecclesiae Abrogationis*) and Ecclesiastical Decree of Annulment (*Decretum Ecclesiae Annullas*) were issued and the circumstances for such issue. Function and Effect of the Rite of Nullification

The entry of such records into the appropriate Registers and Rolls creates both an Ecclesiastical and Divine Impediment to any previously issued record. Thus, the proper effect and function of the Rite of Nullification is not to strike previous records from lesser Registers or Rolls, but to effect the existence of a valid and legitimate Ecclesiastical and Divine Impediment and therefore record ineffective and void, even if the record itself is struck off or not.

This understanding of the proper effect of the Rite of Nullification is particularly important when facing obstinate, or belligerent secular bodies and persons, who may choose to delay or refuse to enact the proper striking of records subject to a Nullification Writ and Decree.

Such a delay or refusal shall have absolutely no effect on the ecclesiastical powers of enforcement of the Universal Ecclesia to fulfil its Divine Mandate.

4. There exists only one form of the Rite of Nullification. Form of the Rite of Nullification

XLVI.II – CONDITIONS OF RITE OF NULLIFICATION

1. Conditions of the Rite of Nullification are those requisite qualifications and contingencies permitted in the proper ministration of the Rite. The conditions for the Rite of Nullification are:- Conditions of Rite of Nullification

(i) That an Ecclesiastical Writ of Annulment of Previous Laws and Instruments (*Recto Ecclesiae Abrogationis*) was issued from the proper Ecclesiastical Authority; and proper notice given; and

(ii) That forty days have passed without any acknowledgement or action from the receiving body or person concerning any required actions to be taken; and

(iii) That a Ecclesiastical Decree of Annulment (*Decretum Ecclesiae Annullas*) was duly recorded and issued by the proper Ecclesiastical Authority concerning the record, page, leaf, or document or instrument in question making clear the presence of both a Divine and Ecclesiastical Impediment to any attempt to continue to claim any form of benefit or use of the annulled record, page, leaf, or document or instrument in question.

Title XLVII – Rite of Inauguration

XLVII.I – RITE OF INAUGURATION

1. Inauguration is the formal Rite and ceremony for the induction and investiture of a proper and eligible candidate into high secular office. Rite of Inauguration

The Rite of Inauguration shall be granted and conferred in accordance with the most sacred Covenants *Pactum De Singularis Caelum*, *Pactum De Singularis Christus* and associated approved liturgy.

2. By the norms of Divine Law, Ecclesiastical Law and Positive Law, all offices are ecclesiastical in origin. Furthermore, all rights, powers and authority ascribed to an office owe their origin to the rights and powers defined in accord with the most sacred Covenants *Pactum De Singularis Caelum* and *Pactum De Singularis Christus*. Divine Purpose of Rite of Inauguration

To deny such norms or proclaim that an office be self made, or powers be self determined is the height of ignorance and arrogance against God and the Divine Creator and the norms of law itself. Any such claimed office and any subsequent claimed powers have no legitimacy or force or effect whatsoever.

The proper Rite of Inauguration therefore is the recognition of the necessary records entered into the Registers and Rolls of the Universal Ecclesia that gives any such office and its rights and powers the force and effect intended by related charters, constitution and bylaws.

3. By definition, the Rite of Inauguration is unique compared to the Rite of Investiture in that a proper candidate duly inaugurated, assumes occupancy of an existing office, without the reconstitution of the trust or property of such Office. Inauguration and Office

The Oath of Office creates unique Sacred Circumscribed Space and Trust that is firmly bound to the character and existing person as occupant of that Office; and remains attached to the person even after leaving office.

4. As a solemn Oath of Office is mandatory and fundamental to the proper formation of the Trust of Office, any failure to repair a defect or failure to properly execute such an Oath shall render such occupancy of Office null and voice, having no legitimacy or validity whatsoever. Inauguration and Oath of Office

5. There exists only one form of the Rite of Inauguration. Form of the Rite of Inauguration

XLVII.II – CONDITIONS OF RITE OF INAUGURATION

Conditions of Rite of Inauguration

1. Conditions of the Rite of Inauguration are those requisite qualifications and contingencies permitted in the proper ministration of the Rite. The conditions for the Rite of Inauguration are:-

(i) That a Decree of Exemplification (*Decretum Ecclesiae Exemplificatio*) or Ratification (*Decretum Ecclesiae Ratificationis*) in accord with the precepts of the relevant body politic have been issued and a copy received by the proper Ecclesiastical Authority; and

(ii) That the designated new incumbent performs the necessary Oath of Office mandatory and fundamental to the proper formation of the Trust of Office; and

(iii) That the proper Ecclesiastical Authority enters the necessary records in its Registers and Rolls and summons the incumbent to participate in Holy Mass to complete the Rite.

Title XLVIII – Rite of Investiture

XLVIII.I – RITE OF INVESTITURE

1. Investiture shall be the formal Rite and ceremony for the induction and investiture of a suitable and proper candidate into high fiduciary office. Rite of Investiture

The Rite of Investiture shall be granted and conferred in accordance with the most sacred Covenants *Pactum De Singularis Caelum*, *Pactum De Singularis Christus* and associated approved liturgy.

2. By the norms of Divine Law, Ecclesiastical Law and Positive Law, all offices are ecclesiastical in origin. Furthermore, all rights, powers and authority ascribed to an office owe their origin to the rights and powers defined in accord with the most sacred Covenants *Pactum De Singularis Caelum* and *Pactum De Singularis Christus*. Divine Purpose of Rite of Investiture

To deny such norms or proclaim that an office be self made, or powers be self determined is the height of ignorance and arrogance against God and the Divine Creator and the norms of law itself. Any such claimed office and any subsequent claimed powers have no legitimacy or force or effect whatsoever.

When a claimed office pertains to a position of public trust, the necessity for ecclesiastical authority and legitimacy is even greater. The proper Rite of Investiture therefore is the recognition of the necessary records entered into the Registers and Rolls of the Universal Ecclesia that gives any such office and its rights and powers the force and effect intended by related charters, constitution and bylaws.

3. By definition, the Rite of Investiture is unique compared to the Rite of Inauguration in that a proper candidate duly invested, assumes occupancy of an existing office, but through the reconstitution of the trust and property of such Office, by their Oath. Investiture and Office

The Oath of Office creates unique Sacred Circumscribed Space and Trust that is firmly bound to the character and existing Office; and dissolves upon gross breach of trust or in leaving such office.

4. As a solemn Oath of Office is mandatory and fundamental to the proper formation of the Trust of Office, any failure to repair a defect or failure to properly execute such an Oath shall render such occupancy of Office null and void, having no legitimacy or validity whatsoever. Investiture and Oath of Office

5. There exists only one form of the Rite of Investiture. Form of the Rite of Investiture

XLVIII.II – CONDITIONS OF RITE OF INVESTITURE

1. Conditions of the Rite of Investiture are those requisite qualifications and contingencies permitted in the proper ministration of the Rite. The conditions for the Rite of Investiture are:- Conditions of Rite of Investiture

(i) That a Decree of Exemplification (*Decretum Ecclesiae Exemplificatio*) or Ratification (*Decretum Ecclesiae Ratificationis*) in accord with the precepts of the relevant body politic have been issued and a copy received by the proper Ecclesiastical Authority; and

(ii) That the designated new incumbent performs the necessary Oath of Office mandatory and fundamental to the proper formation of the Trust of Office; and

(iii) That the proper Ecclesiastical Authority enters the necessary records in its Registers and Rolls and summons the incumbent to participate in Holy Mass to complete the Rite.

Title XLIX – Rite of Coronation

XLIX.I – RITE OF CORONATION

1. Coronation shall be the formal Rite and ceremony for the investiture of a proper royal candidate into the sacred office of sovereign. Rite of Coronation

The Rite of Coronation shall be granted and conferred in accordance with the most sacred Covenants *Pactum De Singularis Caelum*, *Pactum De Singularis Christus* and associated approved liturgy.

2. By definition, the Rite of Coronation is unique compared to the Rite of Inauguration and Investiture in that a proper candidate duly invested, assumes occupancy of an existing office, but through the reconstitution of the trust and property of the Dominion, including all the laws of the Dominion, by their solemn Sacred Oath. Coronation and Office

The Sacred Oath of Sovereign Office creates unique Sacred Circumscribed Space and Trust that is firmly bound to the character and existing Office of Sovereign; and dissolves only upon death or abdication.

3. As a solemn Oath of Office is mandatory and fundamental to the proper formation of the Trust of Office, any failure to repair a defect or failure to properly execute such an Oath shall render such occupancy of Office null and void, having no legitimacy or validity whatsoever. Coronation and Oath of Office

4. While the Vows and Oath of Office forms the Sacred Trust of the Monarch, it is the consecration and anointing that forms the Person of Monarch. Both parts are needed to form an authentic Sovereign and Crown. Consecration and Person of Monarch

5. There exists only one form of the Rite of Coronation. Form of the Rite of Coronation

XLIX.II – CONDITIONS OF RITE OF CORONATION

1. Conditions of the Rite of Coronation are those requisite qualifications and contingencies permitted in the proper ministration of the Rite. The conditions for the Rite of Coronation are:- Conditions of Rite of Coronation

    (i) That a Decree of Succession (*Decretum Ecclesiae Successio*) in accord with the precepts of the relevant body politic have been issued and a copy received by the proper Ecclesiastical Authority; and

    (ii) That the designated monarch performs the necessary Vows and Oath of Office mandatory and fundamental to the proper formation of the Trust of Office of Sovereign; and is then blessed, consecrated and anointed as the Person of Sovereign; and

(iii) That the proper Ecclesiastical Authority enters the necessary records in its Registers and Rolls and summons the incumbent to participate in Holy Mass to complete the Rite.

XLIX.III – ORDINARY RITE OF CORONATION

1. The *Ordinary Rite of Coronation* conferred by a Patriarch and at least two (2) bishops, shall be as follows:- Ordinary Rite of Cororonation

LITURGY OF THE PEOPLE OF GOD

Liturgy of the People of God

(NOTE: See the relevant Liturgy within the Proper of Life & Mysteries of Christ for a Special Mass of Coronation)

LITURGY OF THE GOOD NEWS OF CHRIST

Liturgy of Good News

(NOTE: See the relevant Liturgy within the Proper of Life & Mysteries of Christ for a Special Mass of Coronation)

LITURGY OF DIVINE REVELATION

Liturgy of Divine Revelation

PETITION

Coronation Petition

PATRIARCH

(To all assembled)

I call upon those who seek to make their solemn petition today in the name of Christ our Saviour to now stand and come forward and make their presence and prayer known.

(The Supplicant Monarch arises from the simple seat at the transept comes forward and stands below the altar in front of the Patriarch)

SUPPLICANT (MONARCH)

It is I N., (son/daughter) of [Name without regnal]. A true penitent of faith who comes before these witnesses to humbly petition Heaven and the Divine Creator.

PATRIARCH

What then is it you ask in the name of the Father and of

the Son and of the Holy Spirit today?

SUPPLICANT (MONARCH)

Coronation.

PATRIARCH

(Turning to Supplicant Monarch)

The Holy Rite of Coronation you ask of God and the Divine Creator and all of Heaven is of great historical significance, not only for your subjects and the body politic and all its realms, protectorates and territories, but for all of the People of God.

To the people, a true Sovereign is a living symbol of the power and majesty of Christ on earth. They are by their rank a member of the leaders of the Living Body of Christ. It is their piety, wisdom and strength that helps guide and inspire their subjects and all those clerical brothers and sisters professed to Holy Orders.

Indeed, the Holy Rite of Coronation shares many similarities to the Rite of Patriarchal Consecration, especially in the Vows, the Holy Oath and Sacred Anointing. Only a Patriarch and a proper Monarch share the same formality of Anointing in Christ and God through the Holy Spirit. This is because only a true Monarch and a true Patriarch are called by God to accept such a heavy burden of Office.

An individual called to the Holy Office of Sovereign is called to Sacrifice their individual person, personal wants and desires, to accept and become entirely the Person of the Crown. While the Divine Creator does not will pain or suffering upon anyone, the responsibility of the Monarch demands the greatest test of humility, austerity, persistence, courage, compassion and faith.

To be human is to err. Thus Christ does not expect perfection or the confection of a false image of piety and dignity by a Monarch. Rather, it is how we overcome through our faith and courage; and how we persist and grow as true followers of Christ that is the greatest example we can give to our subjects and the People of God.

Remember always, you, who are about to take your solemn vows and oath, that one who stand at the Altar representing Christ and the intercessions of the faithful are not Him nor the ultimate mediator between God and the Divine Creator and his people.

Remember always to be careful in matters of the Divine and mystical; and that it is not for men and women to decide when the Divine chooses to speak, but the Divine Creator, through his Son and all the angels and saints of Heaven who choose when it be the time and the place.

Finally, remember always thou art mortal in this temporal realm and to be gentle and compassionate of your soul and mind; and to be wise in your discernments and decisions; and to always be on guard against the hardening of your heart or the creeping wilful ignorance of doctrinal rigidity. Do you understand these sacred responsibilities?

SUPPLICANT (MONARCH)

Yes.

INQUISITION

PATRIARCH

Very well, I call upon a trusted Advocate to speak on your behalf as to the Inquisition of whether you are adequately prepared and ready to accept the obligations and new personage of Ruler and Sovereign.

(Advocate of the Supplicant Monarch comes forward)

PATRIARCH

A., are you prepared to testify before God and the Divine Creator that N., is adequately prepared, capable and ready for such a sacred Office?

ADVOCATE

Yes, [title], I testify on my oath and office that N., is indeed adequately prepared, capable and ready for such high and sacred obligation.

PATRIARCH

A., does N.,have a proper mandate approved by the Body Politic of the people and Holy Mother Church? If so, let it be read.

ADVOCATE

Yes, [title]. The Mandate reads as follows...

(Advocate reads mandate.)

PATRIARCH

Thanks be to God.

OBLIGATION

Coronation
Obligation

PATRIARCH

I call then for N. to come forward and kneel before Heaven so that [he/she] may perfect their Holy Orders of Office in a humble and clear voice.

VOWS

Coronation
Vows

(Supplicant Monarch now kneels before the Patriarch.)

PATRIARCH

I call upon the one knelt before us to give their solemn vows.

PATRIARCH

(To Supplicant Monarch)

First, do you take your fraternity of clergy, peers, ministers and officers to be your new family? Do you promise to always be truthful to them in good times and bad, and in times of sickness and distress?

SUPPLICANT (MONARCH)

I do.

PATRIARCH

Do you take this sacred calling to be your life journey? Do you promise to be trusting in your faith, and to always be loyal, trustworthy and dependable to the one true and Holy Universal Church?

SUPPLICANT (MONARCH)

I do.

PATRIARCH

Do you take the Holy Gospel of Christ and the Maxims of Divine Law as your instruction and guide? Do you promise always to be respectful and support the well being of your government and the order of hierarchy of the Body Politic and all its dominions, dependencies, protectorates and territories every day of your life?

SUPPLICANT (MONARCH)

I do.

PATRIARCH

Do you solemnly vow a life of self restraint, frugality and humility? And do you promise to forsake your own personal wants and desires for the sake of the sacred office and mission you shall hold?

SUPPLICANT (MONARCH)

I do.

PATRIARCH

Do you solemnly vow to always uphold the gift of charity and alms to those in need? And do you promise to the act with mercy, compassion and forgiveness of others, as you yourself are forgiven by God?

SUPPLICANT (MONARCH)

I do.

PATRIARCH

Do you solemnly vow to respect and protect the rule of law, fairness and the equality of rights of all? And do you promise to pursue every remedy, relief and reform against injustice, or moral repugnancy or corruption of the laws and institutions of the Body Politic?

SUPPLICANT (MONARCH)

I do.

PATRIARCH

Finally, do you solemnly vow to uphold this sacred Mission and the Powers delegated to you by Christ with dignity, grace and the gift of wise discernment?

SUPPLICANT (MONARCH)

I do.

HOLY OATH

PATRIARCH

I now call upon the Supplicant to stand and make their Oath of Holy Orders before signing the record.

SUPPLICANT (MONARCH)

(The Supplicant stands facing the congregation, whilst having right hand upon the Holy Gospel)

In the Name of God the Father, Christ the Son and the

Holy Spirit, I, N. do solemnly and humbly promise before all Heaven and Earth that all I have here before avowed, I will perform and keep in sacred trust for the benefit of all the people of this realm; and for the Body Politic and all its realms, dependencies, protectorates and territories; and for the crown and all its ministers and officers.

(The Supplicant then kisses the sacred text and then signs their name to an original document of the previous Vows and Oath representing the Original Deed of a new sacred majestic trust for the realm.)

LITURGY OF THE EUCHARIST

Liturgy of the Eucharist

(NOTE: See the relevant Liturgy within the Proper of Life & Mysteries of Christ for a Special Mass of Coronation)

LITURGY OF DIVINE MISSION

Liturgy of Divine Mission

CONSECRATION

Coronation
Consecration

PATRIARCH

(The Supplicant Monarch bows their head whilst kneeling as the Patriarch circumscribes the Supplicant Monarch first with his staff.)

✠In the name of God our Heavenly Father. In the name of Christ his son and our saviour. In the name of the Holy Spirit and our Mother Mary and all the angels and saints of Heaven, I invoke your blessings in the formation of a new Person of God, within your Holy Family of brothers and sisters. Watch over them, guide them and help them stay upon the path of your Society of Light.

PATRIARCH

(The Patriarch now circumscribes the kneeling Supplicant Monarch for a second time, now using Holy Incense.)

✠In the name of God and the Divine Creator. In the name of the Alpha and Omega, I purify with this sacred smoke this worthy supplicant; and remove any doubt as to the sacred sweetness of the calling to their new Person and Holy Office.

PATRIARCH

(The Patriarch now circumscribes the kneeling Supplicant for a third time, now Sprinkling Holy Water.)

✠In the Name of God the Father, Christ the Son and the Holy Spirit, I bless this Person as a true Sovereign and Ruler under your One Holy Apostolic Universal Ecclesia of Christ.

ANOINTING

Coronation
Anointing

(After the Monarch Consecration, the new Sovereign is seated in the Coronation Throne. The Patriarch then anoints the forehead, the lips and the chest of the new Sovereign with holy Chrism.)

PATRIARCH

We anoint you with the most sacred Oil of Christ in the name of our Lord and our Saviour; may he strengthen you with his power, who lives and reigns for ever and ever.

PATRIARCH

(The Patriarch then anoints each palm of the new Monarch with holy Chrism.)

Be sealed with the gift of the Holy Spirit. May you serve and sanctify the People of God in the power of Christ our Saviour, who lives and reigns for ever and ever.

MONARCH

Amen.

INVESTITURE

Coronation
Investiture

(After the Sovereign Anointing, the new Sovereign stands, to receive the vestments of sovereign, assisted by the attendants who will help vest in the sacred robes.)

PATRIARCH

Remember you are a sovereign for ever according to the Society of the Light of Christ. Our Lord has made His Testament as a Promise he will not break. We Pray to God and the Divine Creator that we may always honour His Trust.

(The sovereign sits again and the ceremony of the crown proceeds with the Patriarch crowning the new Monarch.)

PATRIARCH

This crown be a constant symbol of your Divine and Apostolic commission and your solemn vows and oath to your subjects in the name of God and the Divine Creator.

(The Patriarch now places a gold orb adorned with a cross in the left hand of the Monarch.)

PATRIARCH

This sacred globe be a symbol of your lawful custody and possession as a wise steward of all land and all the fruits of the land of all the realms, protectorates and territories of the body politic as one kingdom.

(The Patriarch now places the sword of state in the right hand of the Monarch.)

PATRIARCH

This be the sacred sword of state and destiny and the true sword of Monarchs. It is a symbol of the dreadful power bestowed upon your Person by Divine Authority. You must now choose whether you shall rule by the sword or by the rule of law?

MONARCH

(The new Monarch hands back the sword to Patriarch.)

I choose to rule by law and not by force or fear.

PATRIARCH

Then may Heaven ordain you be known forever as a just and a wise Monarch.

PATRIARCH

(The Patriarch now hands a gold Sceptre to the right hand of the new Monarch.)

By this rod of law, you N., are the living embodiment of our laws. What you assent shall be law and what you decline shall not be law.

PATRIARCH

(The Patriarch now turns to the audience and

opens his arms.)

Heaven and the Divine Creator has ordained that N. be worthy as our Ruler and Sovereign. Yet no king (queen) may rule without the consent of the people. What say you? Shall you elect N. to be your king (queen)?

COLLECTIVE AUDIENCE

Long live the king (queen)! Long live the king (queen)! Long live the king (queen)!

Title L – Rite of Hours

L.I – RITE OF HOURS

1. **Hours**, also known as *Ritus Horarum*, also known as the *Divine Office,* also known as the *Work of God* or *Canonical Hours,* is a sacred Rite that marks the divisions of the day in terms of fixed times of prayer at regular intervals, reflecting the seasons of the Liturgy of the Seven Mysteries of Christ and the Days allocated to honour Saints and Heroes of the Living Body of Christ. Rite of Hours

The official set of prayers of the Universal Ecclesia of One Christ for use according to the Rite of Hours is known as the **Universal Hours** (*Universus Horarum*), in accord with the formula for Prayers defined by the most sacred Covenants *Pactum De Singularis Caelum* and *Pactum De Singularis Christus* and associated approved liturgy.

2. The formal recitation of prayer at periodic intervals of each and every day in honour of The Divine and Heaven and Higher Beings is a practice as old as the first civilisations. Almost every advanced civilisation that has lasted more than a few hundred years did embed within the obligations of its priests and officials some form of regular prayer throughout each day. Ancient Practice of Ritual Daily Prayer

Numerous civilisations recognised the symbiotic and mystical nature of a twenty four hour day representing a microcosm of a year of seasons and indeed of the seasons of life and death. Furthermore, a number of ancient civilisations viewed their collective prosperity and the good fortune of individuals to be intimately connected to the constant connection and respect of the Divine.

3. Over time, the very nature of prescriptive formula for praise, did produce in many ancient cultures and faiths a system of recitation lacking in deeper meaning or importance. Consequently, when rules of obligation and observance were relaxed or even challenged, many practices ceased to exist in a few short decades. Fragmentation and Corruption of Practice of Ritual Daily Prayer

Even in history among the faithful clerical observants of regular Christian prayer, corrosive aspects have arisen over time. In ages past, acceptance was given to forms of negative prayer, calling upon divine or supernatural power to send injury or impediments upon certain enemies. Some prayers accepted into certain liturgies even permitted invocations calling for harm or misfortune or torment of others, in complete contradiction to the teachings of Christ. Even the word *curse*, describing such abominations became accepted in some circles as a valid description for certain forms of claimed ritual daily Christian prayer.

4. Christ fully understands the emptiness and ineffectiveness of hollow prescriptive formula for periodic praise. He warned all who dared open their eyes and ears to the danger of mediocrity and lukewarm doctrinal practices – as an abomination to God and the Divine Creator. That it be better for the soul of those priests, pharisees and lawmakers to say nothing, than to offend Heaven with empty ritual.

Divine Purpose of the Rite of Hours

Christ also warned those who sought to corrupt the process of prayer to invoke curses that by their own intentions and mouths, they condemn themselves and all who support them tenfold. Categorically and unequivocally God and the Divine Creator forbid all forms of curses and the united supernatural and spiritual forces consider such action as an abomination.

Thus Christ instituted clear guidance in his own ministry as to the purpose and practice of the hours. That to remember God and the Divine Creator, as well as the beloved saints and heroes of Heaven, is an act of profound respect and blessing upon the one who remembers. Secondly, the formula for such recognition must always remain personal, visceral and meaningful. The length and time of prayer is far less important than its intent and authentic expression.

The true Hours then is a reflection on the authentic Mysteries of Christ as celebrated across a year, also reflected in the microcosm of a sacred day. In fact, the purpose of the true Hours of Christ is precisely to sanctity each and every day in the name of our Lord and in the name of God and the Divine Creator.

5. The Hours of the Universal Hours (*Universus Horarum*) is the division of a Day into eight (8) sacred Offices of three hours each being: *Lauds*, *Ortus*, *Matins*, *Meridies*, *Dies*, *Occasus*, *Vespers* and *Vigilis*:-

The Hours

(i) *Lauds* (meaning praise and glory) are the hours between 2 a.m. and 5 a.m. symbolising the Office of the *Filial Mystery of Christ* as a time of praise of the birth of the spirit of Light and the Divine; and

(ii) *Ortus* (meaning sunrise) are the hours between 5 a.m. and 8 a.m. symbolising the Office of the *Transcendent Mystery of Christ* as a time of prayer and reflection upon Divine Revelation and the Divine Nature of the Singularity of Christ; and

(iii) *Matins* (meaning morning) are the hours between 8 a.m. and 11 a.m. symbolising the Office of the *Mercy & Redemption Mystery of Christ* as a time of prayer and reflection upon the Divine Love, Compassion and Mercy of God and the Divine

Creator in manifesting himself in physical form upon the earth through Jesus Christ and then through the Universal Ecclesia as his Living Body; and

(iv) *Meridies* (meaning midday) are the hours between 11 a.m. and 2 p.m. symbolising the Office of the *Sacred Heart Mystery of Christ* as a time of prayer and reflection upon the Divine Love, Compassion and Mercy of God and the Divine Creator as revealed through the Sacred Heart of Christ and Mother Mary; and

(v) *Dies* (meaning daytime) are the hours between 2 p.m. and 5 p.m. symbolising the Office of the *Eucharistic Mystery of Christ* as a time of solemn prayer and reflection upon the suffering, death and resurrection of Christ; and

(vi) *Occasus* (meaning sunset) are the hours between 5 p.m. and 8 p.m. symbolising the Office of the *Seven Mysteries of Christ* as a time of prayer and meditation on the symmetry, beauty and perfect expression of Divine Law and Divine Love through the Seven Mysteries of Christ; and

(vii) *Vespers* (meaning evening) are the hours between 8 p.m. and 11 p.m. symbolising the Office of *Apostolic Mystery of Christ* as a time of prayer and thanksgiving for the miracle and fulfilment of prophecy of the One True Apostolic Universal Ecclesia of Christ as the ecumenical living body of Christ; and

(viii) *Vigilis* (meaning the night watch) are the hours between 11 p.m. and 2 a.m. symbolising the Office of the *Immanent Mystery of Christ* as a time of expectant waiting, preparation of the coming Light of Christ.

6. Faithful to Christ not professed to Holy Vows are not obligated to participate in the Rite of Hours. However, such voluntarily recognition at least once a day in respect of one of the eight Sacred Offices is seen as an authentic act of piety to God and the Divine Creator.

Obligation of Faithful not professed to Holy Vows

7. Non-Cloistered Clerical Faithful are by definition in the world. As a consequence, their time per day is to be directed to serving the community through the full range of sacraments, rites and prayers of Sacred Liturgy.

Obligation of Non-Cloistered Clerical Faithful

Despite such demands on time, Non-Cloistered Clerical Faithful are still expected to perform a minimum of two (2) Sacred Offices being Lauds (with permission to extend up to 8 am) and Vespers.

8. Cloistered Clerical Faithful are by definition closed to the direct world.

Obligation of

It is a special calling of service through deep prayer, contemplation and duty. As a consequence, their time per day is bound in a holy way to the Rite of Hours and eight Sacred Offices. Cloistered Clerical Faithful

Title LI – Prayers

LI.I – PRAYERS

1. **P**rayer is a formula of words knowingly and deliberately intended as a communication with the Divine. The word prayer itself originates from the Latin *precari* meaning "to ask earnestly; or beseech; or implore". Prayers

As prayer is by definition a knowing and deliberate intention of communication with the Divine, prayer is a central and vital element of the life of the People of God and the Living Body of Christ.

2. Prayers may be *formal*, according the norms of proper Divine Liturgy, or *informal*, according to the heart, mind and spirit of the one making such a prayer. When spoken, a prayer may be a form of invocation, or incantation. When not vocalised, a prayer is properly defined as a meditation. Form of Prayer

The proper formation and expression of prayer, whether invocation, or incantation or meditation is to be encouraged as a daily and regular occurrence of all people. Indeed, the innate right of every soul to communicate with the Divine is a fundamental pillar of the faith of the one true apostolic Universal Ecclesia of Christ. It was Christ himself that emphasised repeatedly that no academic or religious body may claim a monopoly upon others in respect of impeding, or permitting communication with Heaven.

3. There are three general elements to a formal Prayer being *petitio, precari* and *promissio*: General Elements of Prayer

   (i) *Petitio* (Petition) is the first part of a Prayer being some form of Petition or Invocation to a higher power. Some forms of Prayer (such as Thanksgiving and Blessings) may place the Petition or Invocation at the end of the Prayer; and

   (ii) *Precari* (Prayer) is the body of the Prayer; and

   (iii) *Promissio* (Promise) is an offering as a component to the Prayer (such as frequently found in forms of Prayers such as *Confession, Testification or Unction).*

4. Excluding specific forms pertaining to Sacramental Rites, all forms of valid Prayer may be characterised as *Adoration, Thanksgiving, Promise, Blessing, Incantation, Intercession, Intervention, Lamentation, Confession, Testification, Unction* and *Sanction*: Forms of Prayer

   (i) *Adoration* is a type of Invocation or Meditation used for honouring and praising a higher spiritual presence; and

(ii) *Thanksgiving* is a type of Invocation used for offering gratitude to a higher spiritual presence; and

(iii) *Promise* is a type of Invocation or Meditation

(iv) *Blessing* is a type of Invocation or Meditation used to summons an authentic spiritual presence for another, often consonant with the rite of consecration; and

(v) *Incantation* is a type of Invocation or Meditation within a specific formula of words, often sung or spoken in the context of other rites; and

(vi) *Intercession* is a type of Invocation or Meditation for calling upon spiritual assistance for others; and

(vii) *Intervention* is a type of Invocation or Meditation calling upon direct spiritual assistance for self; and

(viii) *Lamentation* is a type of Invocation or Meditation associated with great distress, grief and suffering in calling upon assistance, or forgiveness or vindication; and

(ix) *Confession* is a type of Invocation or Meditation used for the atonement and repentance of wrongdoing and the asking of forgiveness; and

(x) *Testification* is a type of Invocation concerning the act of vocalising and giving testimony or evidence; and

(xi) *Unction* is a type of Invocation seeking release, forgiveness, clemency, healing or redemption; and

(xii) *Sanction* is a type of Invocation used for the expression of Obligations, Penalties or Condemnations.

LI.II – UNIVERSAL PRAYERS

1. *Universal Prayers* are forms of Prayer as prescribed by Scriptural Revelation or ancient custom and tradition. Such prayers are typically the most well known and loved of the faithful, as well as specific prayers that form an integral part of the sacred liturgy. Universal Prayers

All persons may invoke or meditate on Universal Prayers.

LI.III – MAGISTERIAL PRAYERS

1. *Magisterial Prayers* are forms of Prayers prescribed and reserved to the Office of Supreme Patriarch. Such formal Prayers are reserved for feasts and rites of significance, such as a Patriarchal Blessing. Magisterial Prayers

   Magisterial Prayers are typically short, simple in their nature and universal in application, reflecting the universal nature of the office of Supreme Patriarch.

LI.IV – PATRIARCHAL PRAYERS

1. *Patriarchal Prayers* are forms of Prayers prescribed and reserved to authentic Office of Patriarch of the Universal Ecclesia of Christ. Patriarchal Prayers

   Patriarchal Prayers are similar to Magisterial Prayers in being typically short, simple in their nature and widely applicable, especially at a national, regional and cultural level.

LI.V – APOSTOLIC PRAYERS

1. *Apostolic Prayers* are forms of Prayers acknowledged and prescribed either by venerated members or by custom and tradition, not otherwise Plenary or Apostolic. Apostolic Prayers

   Apostolic Prayers are traditionally the highest form of technical prayers whereby the language, length and substance is usually of a more specific nature in relation to the form of prayer, as well as subject matter detail.

   Apostolic Prayers are distinguished primarily from Universal Prayers in being reserved for special feasts and rites.

LI.VI – EPISCOPAL PRAYERS

1. Episcopal Prayers is a form of Prayers prescribed and reserved to the Office of Episcopal Bishop. Such Prayers share similarities to Patriarchal Prayers, while Episcopal Prayers have a greater focus of detail and obligations of rites and sacraments. Episcopal Prayers

Title LII – Prayers of Adoration

LII.I – PRAYERS OF ADORATION

1. Adoration is a type of Prayer of *Invocation* or *Meditation* for giving honour and praise to a higher spiritual presence or a particular venerated being. Prayer of Adoration

2. Excluding specific forms pertaining to Sacramental Rites, all forms of valid Adoration may be characterised as *Universal, Magisterial, Patriarchal, Apostolic, Episcopal* or *Ordinal*:- Forms of Adoration

   (i) *Universal Adoration* is a form of Adoration as prescribed by Scriptural Revelation and/or ancient custom and tradition; and

   (ii) *Magisterial Adoration* is a form of Adoration prescribed and reserved to the Office of Supreme Patriarch; and

   (iii) *Patriarchal Adoration* is a form of Adoration prescribed and reserved to authentic Office of Patriarch of the Universal Ecclesia of Christ; and

   (iv) *Apostolic Adoration* is a form of Adoration acknowledged and prescribed either by venerated members or by custom and tradition, not otherwise Plenary or Apostolic; and

   (v) *Episcopal Adoration* is a form of Adoration prescribed and reserved to the Office of Episcopal Bishop; and

   (vi) *Ordinal Adoration* is a form of Adoration as prescribed by the present sacred liturgy not otherwise Universal, Magisterial, Patriarchal, Apostolic or Episcopal.

LII.II – UNIVERSAL ADORATIONS

1. *Universal Adorations* are forms of Adoration as prescribed by Scriptural Revelation and/or ancient custom and tradition. Universal Adorations

Adoration of God

Adoration of God

Glory to God in the highest,
And peace to all people on Earth.
Merciful God, heavenly King,
Loving God and Father,
We worship you, we give you thanks,
We praise you for your glory.
Lord Jesus Christ, only son of the Father,
Lord God as the Lamb of God,

You did take away the transgressions of this world:
Have mercy then on us!
As the one seated at the right hand of the Father,
We humbly beg you receive our prayer.
For you alone are the Holy One,
You alone are the Lord,
You alone are the Most High, Jesus Christ,
With the Holy Spirit, in the glory of God the Father.
Amen.

Adoration of Trinity

Adoration of Trinity

Glory be to the Father,
And to the Son,
And to the Holy Spirit.
As it was in the beginning,
Is now, and ever shall be,
Our true Divine Creator without end.
Amen.

Adoration of Divine Father

Adoration of Divine Father

Our Father, who is in Heaven,
Sacred be all your Names.
Your kingdom has come,
Your will be done on Earth as it is in Heaven.
Give us each day our daily bread,
And forgive us our trespasses,
As we forgive those who trespass against us.
And lead us not into temptation,
Or deliberate acts of evil.
Amen.

Adoration of Mary

Adoration of Mary

Hail Mary, full of Grace,
God is with thee.
Blessed are you for all women,
And blessed is the fruit of your womb in Jesus,
Holy Mary, mother of all,
Pray for us now,
And at the hour of our death.
Amen.

Adoration of Divine Annunciation

Adoration of Divine Annunciation

My soul does magnify the Lord,
And my Spirit does rejoice in God my Saviour.
For he has chosen the lowliness of but a handmaiden,
Yet henceforth all generations shall call her blessed.

For he that is mighty has magnified me,
And holy are all His Names.
And mercy is upon them that obey and follow Him,
Throughout all generations.
He that is the Divine Creator of all has shown his wisdom,
For he scatters the proud and the hardened of hearts.
He fills the hungry for truth with great treasures,
Yet leaves the rich in ignorance empty handed.
He remembers always his covenants and promises,
To all the people of God he brings redemption forever.
Amen.

Adoration of Surrender

Adoration of Surrender

Take, O Lord, and receive all my liberty,
my memory, my understanding,
and my entire will,
All I have and call my own.
You have given all to me.
To you, Lord, I return it.
Everything is yours;
do with it what you will.
Give me only your love and your grace,
that is enough for me. Amen.

Adoration of Life

Adoration of Life

Lord, I thank you this day,
For all you have made
And all that you save.
For my family and friends,
My life and my home,
My partner and love.

Adoration of Glory

Adoration of Glory

Glory to you for the feast day of life.
Glory to you for the perfume of lilies and roses.
Glory to you for each different taste of berry and fruit.
Glory to you for the sparkling silver of early morning dew.
Glory to you for the joy of dawn's awakening.
Glory to you for the new life each day brings.

Adoration of Perspective

Adoration of Perspective

I find you, Lord, in all things
and in all my fellow creatures,
pulsing with your life;
as a tiny seed you sleep in what is small
and in the vast you vastly yield yourself.

Come, true light.
Come, eternal life.
Come, hidden mystery.
Come, treasure without name.
Come, rejoicing without end.
Come, light that knows no evening.
Come, raising of the fallen.
Come, resurrection of the dead.
Come, for you are yourself the desire that is within me.
Come, my breath and my life.
Come, the consolation of my humble soul.
Come, my joy, my glory, my endless delight.

Adoration of Light

Adoration of Light

O living Source of Power,
Beautiful is Your dawning.
When You arise in the East,
You fill each land with beauty.
Glittering high above every land,
Your greatness is visible to all.
Though You are far away,
Your rays are upon the Earth.
Though You are high,
Your footprints are the day.
When You arise on the horizon,
You drive the darkness away.
When You send forth Your rays,
The lands are in daily festivity.
When You awaken them,
The cattle stand on their feet.
The trees and plants flourish;
Birds sing along the river.
All the animals dance on their feet
When You shine on them.
Your rays nourish every garden
As You make things live and grow.
Dawning, glittering, going and returning,
You make the season's millions of forms.
Tribes and towns and cities all see You,
For You are the Strength of the Earth.

Adoration of the Lord

Adoration of the Lord

You are holy, Lord, the only God,
and Your deeds are wonderful.
You are strong. You are great.

You are the Most High. You are Almighty.
You, Holy Father are King of heaven and earth.
You are Three and One, Lord God, all Good.
You are Good, all Good, supreme Good,
Lord God, living and true.
You are love. You are wisdom.
You are humility. You are endurance.
You are rest. You are peace.
You are joy and gladness.
You are justice and moderation.
You are all our riches,
and You suffice for us.
You are beauty. You are gentleness.
You are our protector.
You are our guardian and defender.
You are our courage.
You are our haven and our hope.
You are our faith, our great consolation.
You are our eternal life, Great and Wonderful Lord,
God Almighty, Merciful Saviour.
Amen

LII.III – MAGISTERIAL ADORATIONS

1. *Magisterial Adorations* are forms of Adoration prescribed and reserved to the Office of Supreme Patriarch. Magisterial Adorations

Adoration

O praise the Lord,
all you nations: praise him,
all you people.
For his merciful kindness is great toward us:
and the truth of the Lord endures for ever.
Praise you the Lord. Amen.

LII.IV – PATRIARCHAL ADORATIONS

1. *Patriarchal Adorations* are forms of Adoration prescribed and reserved to authentic Office of Patriarch of the Universal Ecclesia of Christ. Patriarchal Adorations

Adoration

O God, give me light in my heart
and light in my tongue and light in my hearing
and light in my sight

and light in my feeling
and light in all body
and light before me
and light behind me.
Give me, I pray Thee,
Light on my right hand
And light on my left hand
And light above me
And light beneath me,
O Lord,
Increase light within me
And give me light
And illuminate me.Amen.

LII.V – APOSTOLIC ADORATIONS

1. *Apostolic Adorations* are forms of Adoration acknowledged and prescribed either by venerated members or by custom and tradition, not otherwise Plenary or Apostolic. Apostolic Adorations

Our Lady of Guadalupe

Our Lady of Guadalupe

Our Lady of Guadalupe, Mystical Rose,
May you intercede on behalf of the Universal Church,
And protect our Holy Father.
May you help all those who invoke you in their necessities,
And as you be the ever Virgin Mary,
And true Mother of all,
May you obtain for us from your most holy Son,
The grace of keeping our faith,
Of sweet hope in the midst of the bitterness of life,
Of burning charity and the precious gift of perseverance.
Amen.

LII.VI – EPISCOPAL ADORATIONS

1. *Episcopal Adoration* is a form of Adoration prescribed and reserved to the Office of Episcopal Bishop. Episcopal Adorations

Praise

Adoration

O Lord, open my lips,
and my mouth shall proclaim your praise

Title LIII – Prayers of Thanksgiving

LIII.I – PRAYERS OF THANKSGIVING

1. Thanksgiving is a type of Prayer of *Invocation* or *Meditation* for giving thanks and gratitude to a higher spiritual presence or a particular venerated being. Prayer of Thanksgiving

2. Prayers may be *formal*, according the norms of proper Divine Liturgy, or *informal*, according to the heart, mind and spirit of the one making such a prayer. When spoken, a prayer may be a form of invocation, or incantation. When not vocalised, a prayer is properly defined as a meditation. Form of Prayer

The proper formation and expression of prayer, whether invocation, or incantation or meditation is to be encouraged as a daily and regular occurrence of all people. Indeed, the innate right of every soul to communicate with the Divine is a fundamental pillar of the faith of the one true apostolic Universal Ecclesia of Christ. It was Christ himself that emphasised repeatedly that no academic or religious body may claim a monopoly upon others in respect of impeding, or permitting communication with Heaven.

3. Excluding specific forms pertaining to Sacramental Rites, all forms of valid Thanksgiving may be characterised as *Universal*, *Magisterial*, *Patriarchal*, *Apostolic*, *Episcopal* or *Ordinal*: Forms of Thanksgiving

(i) *Universal Thanksgiving* is a form of Thanksgiving as prescribed by Scriptural Revelation and/or ancient custom and tradition; and

(ii) *Magisterial Thanksgiving* is a form of Thanksgiving prescribed and reserved to the Office of Supreme Patriarch; and

(iii) *Patriarchal Thanksgiving* is a form of Thanksgiving prescribed and reserved to authentic Office of Patriarch of the Universal Ecclesia of Christ; and

(iv) *Apostolic Thanksgiving* is a form of Thanksgiving acknowledged and prescribed either by venerated members or by custom and tradition, not otherwise Plenary or Apostolic; and

(v) *Episcopal Thanksgiving* is a form of Thanksgiving prescribed and reserved to the Office of Episcopal Bishop; and

(vi) *Ordinal Thanksgiving* is a form of Thanksgiving as prescribed by the present sacred liturgy not otherwise Universal,

Magisterial, Patriarchal, Apostolic or Episcopal.

LIII.II – UNIVERSAL THANKSGIVINGS

1. *Universal Thanksgivings* are forms of Thanksgiving as prescribed by Scriptural Revelation and/or ancient custom and tradition. Universal Thanksgivings

Thanksgiving to God

Thanksgiving to God

Glory to God in the highest,
And peace to all people on Earth.
Merciful God, heavenly King,
Loving God and Father,
We worship you, we give you thanks,
We praise you for your glory.
Lord Jesus Christ, only son of the Father,
Lord God as the Lamb of God,
You did take away the transgressions of this world:
Have mercy then on us!
As the one seated at the right hand of the Father,
We humbly beg you receive our prayer.
For you alone are the Holy One,
You alone are the Lord,
You alone are the Most High, Jesus Christ,
With the Holy Spirit, in the glory of God the Father.
Amen.

Thanksgiving of Trinity

Thanksgiving of Trinity

Glory be to the Father,
And to the Son,
And to the Holy Spirit.
As it was in the beginning,
Is now, and ever shall be,
Our true Divine Creator without end.
Amen.

Thanksgiving of Trinity

Thanksgiving of Trinity

Sing unto the heavens a new song:
and unto the birds and the trees,
and all the beautiful life of the Earth.
Sing unto the angels and saints,
all to our departed ancestors, friends and companions.
Sing unto the Divine, and bless his name:
show forth his love and compassion every day.
Declare his mission of salvation and forgiveness,
unto all the peoples of this beautiful planet.
For the Divine is Absolute,

and the creator of all existence,
and all the wealth and money in the world,
and all the power of the richest nations,
be nothing compared to the priceless gift
of eternal life and wisdom,
granted to each and every man and woman.

Thanksgiving of Food

Thanksgiving of Food

For the gift of each morning of new light,
For the safety of shelter and rest at night,
For the sustenance and nutrition of food that we depend,
For love of friends and animal companions,
For everything your divine goodness sends,
We give thanks. Amen.

Thanksgiving

Thanksgiving of Food

For food that stays our hunger,
For rest that brings us ease,
For homes where memories linger,
We give our thanks for these. Amen.

Thanksgiving

Thanksgiving of Food

Lord, make us truly thankful for these and all other blessings.
I ask this in Jesus Christ's name, Amen.

Thanksgiving

Thanksgiving of Food

Thank you for the world so sweet,
Thank you for the food we eat.
Thank you for the birds that sing,
Thank you God for everything. Amen.

LIII.III – MAGISTERIAL THANKSGIVINGS

Magisterial Thanksgivings

1. *Magisterial Thanksgivings* are forms of Adoration prescribed and reserved to the Office of Supreme Patriarch.

Thanksgiving of Trinity

Thanksgiving of Trinity

Glory be to the Father,
And to the Son,
And to the Holy Spirit.
As it was in the beginning,
Is now, and ever shall be,
Our true Divine Creator without end.
Amen.

LIII.IV – PATRIARCHAL THANKSGIVINGS

1. *Patriarchal Thanksgivings* are forms of Adoration prescribed and reserved to authentic Office of Patriarch of the Universal Ecclesia of Christ. Patriarchal Thanksgivings

Thanksgiving of Trinity

Thanksgiving of Trinity

Glory be to the Father,
And to the Son,
And to the Holy Spirit.
As it was in the beginning,
Is now, and ever shall be,
Our true Divine Creator without end. Amen.

LIII.V – APOSTOLIC THANKSGIVINGS

1. *Apostolic Thanksgivings* are forms of Adoration acknowledged and prescribed either by venerated members or by custom and tradition, not otherwise Plenary or Apostolic. Apostolic Thanksgivings

Thanksgiving of Trinity

Thanksgiving of Trinity

Glory be to the Father,
And to the Son,
And to the Holy Spirit.
As it was in the beginning,
Is now, and ever shall be,
Our true Divine Creator without end. Amen.

LIII.VI – EPISCOPAL THANKSGIVINGS

1. *Episcopal Adoration* is a form of Adoration prescribed and reserved to the Office of Episcopal Bishop. Episcopal Thanksgivings

Thanksgiving of Trinity

Thanksgiving of Trinity

Glory be to the Father,
And to the Son,
And to the Holy Spirit.
As it was in the beginning,
Is now, and ever shall be,
Our true Divine Creator without end.
Amen.

Title LIV – Prayers of Promise

LIV.I – PRAYERS OF PROMISE

1. **Promise** is a type of Prayer of *Invocation* for pledging a solemn declaration to a higher spiritual presence or a particular venerated being to do or refrain from doing one or more actions. A Prayer of Promise must always be vocalised in the presence of at least one witness to have effect. Prayer of Promise

2. Excluding specific forms pertaining to Sacramental Rites, all forms of valid Promise may be characterized as *Universal, Magisterial, Patriarchal, Apostolic, Episcopal* or *Ordinal*: Forms of Promise

   (i) *Universal Promise* is a form of Promise as prescribed by Scriptural Revelation and/or ancient custom and tradition; and

   (ii) *Magisterial Promise* is a form of Promise prescribed and reserved to the Office of Supreme Patriarch; and

   (iii) *Patriarchal Promise* is a form of Promise prescribed and reserved to authentic Office of Patriarch of the Universal Ecclesia of Christ; and

   (iv) *Apostolic Promise* is a form of Promise acknowledged and prescribed either by venerated members or by custom and tradition, not otherwise Plenary or Apostolic; and

   (v) *Episcopal Promise* is a form of Promise prescribed and reserved to the Office of Episcopal Bishop; and

   (vi) *Ordinal Promise* is a form of Promise as prescribed by the present sacred liturgy not otherwise Universal, Magisterial, Patriarchal, Apostolic or Episcopal.

3. The formula and structure of Prayers of Promise shall be reserved to the formalities of liturgical rites as expressed within the Proper of Sacraments, Rites and Prayers in accord with the most sacred Covenants *Pactum De Singularis Caelum* and *Pactum De Singularis Christus*. Formula and Structure of Prayers of Promise

Title LV – Prayers of Blessing

LV.I – PRAYERS OF BLESSING

1. Blessing is a type of Prayer of *Invocation* in the name of a higher spiritual presence or a particular venerated being that another be consecrated or redeemed or protected or favoured or bestowed with good fortune. A Prayer of Blessing must always be vocalised in the presence of at least one witness as the beneficiary and recipient to have effect. Prayer of Blessings

2. Excluding specific forms pertaining to Sacramental Rites, all forms of valid Blessing may be characterised as *Universal, Magisterial, Patriarchal, Apostolic, Episcopal* or *Ordinal*: Forms of Blessing

    (i) *Universal Blessing* is a form of Blessing as prescribed by Scriptural Revelation and/or ancient custom and tradition; and

    (ii) *Magisterial Blessing* is a form of Blessing prescribed and reserved to the Office of Supreme Patriarch; and

    (iii) *Patriarchal Blessing* is a form of Blessing prescribed and reserved to authentic Office of Patriarch of the Universal Ecclesia of Christ; and

    (iv) *Apostolic Blessing* is a form of Blessing acknowledged and prescribed either by venerated members or by custom and tradition, not otherwise Plenary or Apostolic; and

    (v) *Episcopal Blessing* is a form of Blessing prescribed and reserved to the Office of Episcopal Bishop; and

    (vi) *Ordinal Blessing* is a form of Blessing as prescribed by the present sacred liturgy not otherwise Universal, Magisterial, Patriarchal, Apostolic or Episcopal.

LV.II – UNIVERSAL BLESSINGS

1. *Universal Blessings* are forms of Blessing as prescribed by Scriptural Revelation and/or ancient custom and tradition. Universal Blessings

Personal Blessing

Personal Blessing

Grant me your blessings oh God,
to discern in others,
the radiance of your own face.

General Blessing

General Blessing

Blessed Be all life.

Blessed Be this land.
Blessed be all peoples.
Blessed be our family.
Blessed be my life.
Blessed be. Amen

Blessing of the Earth

Blessing of the Earth

You are the wind and waves of a roaring sea,
and the first blooms of spring.
You are the thunderous flashes of a midsummer storm,
and the rains that break the harshest drought.
You are the torrent of a mountain river in spring,
and every new birth and form of life.
For I know who you are and what I am.
You blessed me with a soul that can never die.
I am a mind resolute in virtue that shall not break.
I am a body like stone that shall stand against ignorance.
And I shall not rest whilst injustice and perfidy reigns,
And that children and vulnerable go hungry and hurt,
Or that our streams and lands are poisoned for profits.
Amen.

Blessing for Peace

Blessing for Peace

So say that the elders may have wisdom
and speak with one voice.
Peace be with us.
So say that the country may have tranquillity.
Peace be with us.
And the people may continue to increase.
Peace be with us.
So say that the people and the flock
and the herds May prosper
and be free from illness.
Peace be with us.
So say that the fields may bear much fruit
And the land may continue to be fertile.
Peace be with us,
And May peace reign over earth. Amen

Blessing

Prayer to Christ

You are the peace of all things calm
You are the place to hide from harm
You are the light that shines in dark
You are the heart's eternal spark

You are the door that's open wide
You are the guest who waits inside
You are the stranger at the door
You are the calling of the poor
You are my Lord and with me still
You are my love, keep me from ill
You are the light, the truth, the way
You are my Saviour this very day. Amen

Blessing

Blessing of Children

Bless me Lord, this night I pray,
Keep me safe till dawn of day,
Bless my mother and my father,
Bless my sister and my brother,
Bless each little girl and boy,
Bless them all for heavenly joy.
Amen.

Blessing

Morning Prayer

You bless us Oh Sun,
Light of the plains and mountains
You bless us this new day
and call us to our cares
Watch over my family and the little ones
That no harm shall come to them.
I rejoice at your coming. Amen

Blessing

Morning Prayer

O Christ, our Morning Star,
Splendour of Light Eternal,
shining with the glory of the rainbow,
come and waken us
from the greyness of our apathy,
and renew in us your gift of hope. Amen.

Blessing

Evening Blessing

In your name, Lord,
I lay myself down
And in your name will I rise up...
O God, You art the first and before all others.
You are the last and final boundary
Beyond which nothing exists.
Waken me, I God, in the hour most pleasing to you.
And use me in the works most pleasing to you

That you may bring me closer to your glory

LV.III – MAGISTERIAL BLESSINGS

1. *Magisterial Blessings* are forms of Blessing prescribed and reserved to the Office of Supreme Patriarch. Magisterial Blessings

Blessing

May all beings be blessed with happiness,
and the wisdom to discern the root of true happiness;
May all be free from sorrow and the causes of sorrow;
And may all live in peace and equanimity.

Blessing

May you be filled with loving kindness.
May you be well.
May you be peaceful and at ease.
May you be happy.

LV.IV – PATRIARCHAL BLESSINGS

1. *Patriarchal Blessings* are forms of Blessing prescribed and reserved to authentic Office of Patriarch of the Universal Ecclesia of Christ. Patriarchal Blessings

Blessing

The Lord bless thee, and keep thee:
The Lord make his face shine upon thee,
and be gracious unto thee:
The Lord lift up his countenance upon thee,
and give you peace.

LV.V – APOSTOLIC BLESSINGS

1. *Apostolic Blessings* are forms of Blessing acknowledged and prescribed either by venerated members or by custom and tradition, not otherwise Plenary or Apostolic. Apostolic Blessings

Blessing

Peace be to this house And to all who dwell in it. Peace be to them that enter And to those that depart.

Title LVI – Prayers of Incantation

LVI.I – PRAYERS OF INCANTATION

1. Incantation is a type of Prayer of *Invocation* to a higher spiritual presence or a particular venerated being using a specific formula of words, often sung or spoken in the context of other rites. A Prayer of Incantation must always be vocalised in the presence of at least one other person as witness to have effect.

Prayer of Incantation

2. Excluding Incantations against Curses, the formula and structure of Prayers of Incantation shall be reserved to the formalities of liturgical rites as expressed within the Proper of Sacraments, Rites and Prayers in accord with the most sacred Covenants *Pactum De Singularis Caelum* and *Pactum De Singularis Christus*.

Formula and Structure of Prayers of Incantation

LVI.II – INCANTATIONS AGAINST CURSES

1. Episcopal Incantation is a form of Incantation prescribed and reserved to the Office of Episcopal Bishop.

Incantations against curses

Incantation

Let no man, or woman, or spirit, or being,
or elemental or consciousness,
Defy the laws of the Divine and cross the line,
Lest they be seized and bound to account. Amen

Incantation

That none may trespass against our soul
For any that call out to spirits to destroy life,
Let such words be returned to their maker ten fold
For any that calls out and summons spirits of destruction
To fill the minds of others with torture and pain
Let such words and actions be returned to their maker
So that they be held to account for their actions and negative intentions
For any that seek to conjure destruction and pain unto the lives of others
For the sake of hate or vengeance or power
Let such negative actions and spirit be returned to them a hundred fold
For none have the right nor the power to perform secret rituals against another
Nor invoke such acts without consequences. Amen

Incantation

For all ill will inflicted upon me, I forgive thee.
For I am not without blemish, nor a sharp tongue and wicked temper,
That I too have uttered words and thought against others.
Thus, to be free of the bonds imposed upon others against me,
I must free those whom I have bound by my own anger and negativity.
Verily, nothing can be undone,
unless one is prepared freely and willingly to sacrifice something in return.
No goods or trinkets are sufficient,
but the sacrifice and dedication to an authentic life
free of the base anger and negativity toward others.
Therefore, when one with a pure and open heart forgives those with ill intent,
having freed those with whom one has quarrelled,
no intent or words of ill will can harm. Amen

Title LVII – Prayers of Intercession

LVII.I – PRAYERS OF INTERCESSION

1. Intercession is a type of Prayer of *Invocation* or *Meditation* to a higher spiritual presence or a particular venerated being for some form of beneficial supernatural and spiritual intervention for another person.

Prayer of Intercession

2. A foundation of Christian faith is the confidence in the power and efficacy of prayer. Thus prayer is not only considered an obligation of respect to God and the Divine Creator, but a necessary means of communication and support.

Intercessions and Formula of Prayer and Networks

Christ himself awakened his disciples to the wider power of prayer beyond ritual praise and obligation, to cultivating a deep personal relation with God and the Divine Creator and Heaven. Yet, he was also clear that such prayers for intercession must be balanced with the right intention and approach.

In matters where a family or community for a pious and worthy cause seeks the merciful assistance of Divine Grace through prayers of intervention, the practice of group prayer through well formed and authorised prayer is encouraged.

In matters that are not for pious and worthy cause, or for selfish aims and desires, the use of prayer and in particular prayers of intercession are discouraged.

3. The formula and structure of Prayers of Intercession shall be reserved to the formalities of liturgical rites as expressed within the Proper of Sacraments, Rites and Prayers in accord with the most sacred Covenants *Pactum De Singularis Caelum* and *Pactum De Singularis Christus*.

Formula and Structure of Prayers of Intercession

Title LVIII – Prayers of Intervention

LVIII.I – PRAYERS OF INTERVENTION

1. Intervention is a type of Prayer of *Invocation* or *Meditation* to a higher spiritual presence or a particular venerated being for some form of personal beneficial supernatural and spiritual intervention. Prayer of Intervention

2. Whilst Christ himself awakened all who Trust in God and the Divine Creator to the power and efficacy of prayer, Christ specifically discouraged the general practice of individual prayers of intervention. Prayers of Intervention

   Such divine teachings were not to discourage individuals and groups of faithful in seeking the assistance of Heaven in earthly matters, rather it was because of the corrupt practices of prayers of intervention and the general history of misuse.

   The most notorious prayers of intervention are the strictly forbidden and wicked practice of cursing – that is seeking Divine intervention to cause harm to others. Even at the time of Christ, such prayers were frequently invoked, despite their abomination and contempt to the norms of Divine Law.

   Even throughout Christianity, there exists an unresolved history of prayers of intervention within hymns, songs and chants that are all openly and directly contrary to the teachings of Christ and God and the Divine Creator.

   Therefore, in the strictest sense, all prayers of intervention are reserved to proper liturgy to ensure their licit form and application.

3. The formula and structure of Prayers of Intervention shall be reserved to the formalities of liturgical rites as expressed within the Proper of Sacraments, Rites and Prayers in accord with the most sacred Covenants *Pactum De Singularis Caelum* and *Pactum De Singularis Christus*. Formula and Structure of Prayers of Intervention

Title LVIX – Prayers of Lamentation

LVIX.I – PRAYERS OF LAMENTATION

1. Lamentation is a type of Prayer of *Invocation* or *Meditation* expressing grief or sorrow or pain or anguish to a higher spiritual presence or a particular venerated being. — Prayer of Lamentation

2. Of all the forms of prayer that Christ revealed, Lamentation is unique in that its proper form is the personal words of the individual making such prayer; and that it is best accomplished as an individual and not in a group. — The Power of Prayer of Lamentation

A consequence of living are the experiences, senses and emotions of life. Pain is an integral part of the natural systems of a human body. Yet at times, the weight of life and of challenges seem to overpower us when faced with what seems overwhelming grief, anguish and suffering.

God and the Divine Creator revealed through Divine Revelation that the true nature of the Divine is Love, Compassion and Forgiveness. Contrary to false texts and teachers, God does not wish pain or suffering upon anyone. The effect of free will and the fundamental design of the Universe means there are natural limits. To break the laws that maintain existence is to jeopardise existence itself. It is why the greatest miracles are not necessary spectacular supernatural events, but the deeply personal and individual moments of compassion, love and healing between people and the Divine Creator.

So deeply does God and the Divine Creator want individual people to comprehend the extraordinary healing powers that come through sharing your grief and your anguish with the Divine, that he made certain in the form of Christ that everyone is given the gift to fully understands the true nature of Divine Love, Compassion and Healing.

The lamentations of Christ in being isolated and abandoned by so many people who publicly proclaimed their piety and awareness of God, demonstrates just how close God and the Divine Creator is to our own sufferings and pain. Christ freely chose his Mission during his singular physical presence upon the Earth, to help ease our suffering, pain and doubt, not to make it worse.

By personal example, Christ suffered many of the same emotions and pain and suffering that so many experience on a daily basis. Yet instead of turning his back on others or doubting his Heavenly Father, he demonstrated first hand the extraordinary healing power of prayer.

Thus in His ultimate sacrifice of his own life for others, Christ as the Son of God forged an unbreakable bond between Heaven and Earth. A bond that cannot be broken when we give in to self doubt and neglect our prayer, or choose not to share with the Divine our grief and anguish.

Title LX – Prayers of Confession

LX.I – PRAYERS OF CONFESSION

1. Confession is a type of Prayer of *Invocation* in the name of a higher spiritual presence or a particular venerated being as witness, to the truthful admission of one or more transgressions or offences. A Prayer of Confession must always be vocalised in the presence of at one other witness. Prayers of Confession

2. The formula and structure of Prayers of Confession shall be reserved to the formalities of liturgical rites as expressed within the Proper of Sacraments, Rites and Prayers in accord with the most sacred Covenants *Pactum De Singularis Caelum* and *Pactum De Singularis Christus*. Formula and Structure of Prayers of Confession

Title LXI – Prayers of Testification

LXI.I – PRAYERS OF TESTIFICATION

Prayers of Testification

1. Testification, is a type of Prayer concerning the act of vocalising and giving testimony or evidence; being a vocalised act involving not only at least one Invocation, but at least one promise and obligation in relation to the performance of a valid office. All valid offices are based upon truth and trust and so no office can be formed without a proper Testification.

All communication to the *Officium Systemata* (Offices Systems) of Heaven by living Members of One Heaven shall be by Testification of an Oath and at least one Vow in accord with the most sacred Covenant *Pactum De Singularis Caelum*. The methods, rules and standards of proper Testification shall be defined by the most sacred Covenant *Pactum De Singularis Caelum* and associated covenants and no other. All properly conferred Testification shall be received, recorded and acknowledged by the Officium Systemata (Offices Systems) of One Heaven.

Formula and Structure of Prayers of Testification

2. The formula and structure of Prayers of Testification shall be reserved to the formalities of liturgical rites as expressed within the Rite of Testification and the Proper of Sacraments, Rites and Prayers in accord with the most sacred Covenants *Pactum De Singularis Caelum* and *Pactum De Singularis Christus*.

Title LXII – Prayers of Unction

LXII.I – PRAYERS OF UNCTION

1. Unction, is a type of prayer seeking release, forgiveness, clemency, healing or redemption and are a formula of words knowingly and deliberately intended as a communication with the Divine. The word prayer itself originates from the Latin *precari* meaning "to ask earnestly; or beseech; or implore". Prayers of Unction

   As prayer is by definition a knowing and deliberate intention of communication with the Divine, prayer is a central and vital element of the life of the People of God and the Living Body of Christ.

2. Excluding specific forms pertaining to Sacramental Rites, all forms of valid Unction may be characterised as *Universal, Magisterial, Patriarchal, Apostolic, Episcopal* or *Ordinal*: Forms of Unction

   (i) *Universal Unction* is a form of Unction as prescribed by Scriptural Revelation and/or ancient custom and tradition; and

   (ii) *Magisterial Unction* is a form of Unction prescribed and reserved to the Office of Supreme Patriarch; and

   (iii) *Patriarchal Unction* is a form of Unction prescribed and reserved to authentic Office of Patriarch of the Universal Ecclesia of Christ; and

   (iv) *Apostolic Unction* is a form of Unction acknowledged and prescribed either by venerated members or by custom and tradition, not otherwise Plenary or Apostolic; and

   (v) *Episcopal Unction* is a form of Unction prescribed and reserved to the Office of Episcopal Bishop; and

   (vi) *Ordinal Unction* is a form of Unction as prescribed by the present sacred liturgy not otherwise Universal, Magisterial, Patriarchal, Apostolic or Episcopal.

3. The formula and structure of Prayers of Unction shall be reserved to the formalities of liturgical rites as expressed within the Proper of Sacraments, Rites and Prayers in accord with the most sacred Covenants *Pactum De Singularis Caelum* and *Pactum De Singularis Christus*. Formula and Structure of Prayers of Unction

Title LXIII – Prayers of Sanction

LXIII.I – PRAYERS OF SANCTION

1. Sanction, is a type of Prayer used for the expression of Obligations, Penalties or Condemnations. Sanction Prayers are an integral component of the issuance of writs, sentences, judgements and orders of enforcement or punishment by competent jurists possessing proper ecclesial authority. Prayers of Sanction

2. Excluding specific forms pertaining to Sacramental Rites, all forms of valid Sanction may be characterised as *Universal, Magisterial, Patriarchal, Apostolic, Episcopal* or *Ordinal*: Forms of Sanction

   (i) *Universal Sanction* is a form of Sanction as prescribed by Scriptural Revelation and/or ancient custom and tradition; and

   (ii) *Magisterial Sanction* is a form of Sanction prescribed and reserved to the Office of Supreme Patriarch; and

   (iii) *Patriarchal Sanction* is a form of Sanction prescribed and reserved to authentic Office of Patriarch of the Universal Ecclesia of Christ; and

   (iv) *Apostolic Sanction* is a form of Sanction acknowledged and prescribed either by venerated members or by custom and tradition, not otherwise Plenary or Apostolic; and

   (v) *Episcopal Sanction* is a form of Sanction prescribed and reserved to the Office of Episcopal Bishop; and

   (vi) *Ordinal Sanction* is a form of Sanction as prescribed by the present sacred liturgy not otherwise Universal, Magisterial, Patriarchal, Apostolic or Episcopal.

3. The formula and structure of Prayers of Sanction shall be reserved to the formalities of instruments, writs, decrees and procedures of competent forums in accord with the most sacred Covenants *Pactum De Singularis Caelum* and *Pactum De Singularis Christus*. Formula and Structure of Prayers of Sanction

Title LXIV – Notes

LXIV.I – NOTES

1. There are no Notes associated with the Official English First Edition of *Proper of Sacraments, Rites & Prayers* of *Missale Christus*. Notes

Title LXV – Forms

LXV.I – FORMS

1. There are no Forms included with the Official English First Edition of *Proper of Sacraments, Rites & Prayers* of *Missale Christus*. Forms

The design and procedures of all forms and instruments associated with the *Proper of Sacraments, Rites & Prayers* shall be subject to the rules issued by the proper authorities in accord with the sacred Covenant Pactum De Singularis Christus.

Title LXVI – Tables

LXVI.I – TABLES

1. There are no Tables associated with the Official English First Edition of *Proper of Sacraments, Rites & Prayers* of *Missale Christus*. Tables

Title CXI – The End and The New Beginning

GAIA E1:Y9:A1:S1:M8:D1 [21-Dec-2020]

CXI.I – DIVINE UNIVERSE

Divine Universe

1. On this day [Ucadia Space Day-Time GAIA E1:Y9:A1:S1:M8:D1 or Old time December 21st 2020], the world is witness to an extraordinary celestial event. For the first time in several thousand years, the Great Conjunction of the planets Jupiter and Saturn will appear at their closest proximity on the date of the Winter Solstice (Northern Hemisphere). It will be the closest that Jupiter and Saturn have appeared together for nearly four hundred years (since 1623) and the first time for nearly eight hundred years (since 1226 and the last year of the life of Saint Francis of Assisi) that the living world will be able to clearly witness this event with their own eyes.

The study and movement of the Celestial Sky has always held a fundamental role in human history. In ancient times, the most powerful leaders and empires often plotted the most significant events of their realms according the position of the planets and constellations relative to the fixed celestial houses. Births, marriages and even wars were calculated according to these signs of the Divine Universe in the sky.

The sacred scripture of the Holy Bible is no exception. Many of the most important events in scripture correspond to significant celestial events. As far back as the 17th Century, Johannes Kepler concluded that a Great Conjunction of Jupiter and Saturn occurring in the year 6 BC, during the mid of the old lunar calendar month of Nisan (Ides or 14th Mars to Romans) most likely heralded the Star of Bethlehem and why the Zoroastrian (Magi) Priests from Persia were able to confidently predict its precise arrival.

Yet from a celestial and historical perspective of the Divine Universe, the signs in the Heavens upon this day (21st December 2020) are every bit as significant as for the first time since human civilisation began, in the Sign of Capricorn on this Winter Solstice heralds not just Jupiter and Saturn, but the mysterious outer planet of Pluto, or Dis as it was known to the Romans. All these planets symbolise to the oldest civilisations of humanity the powers of death, finality and great change. From the perspective of Divine Celestial Events, December 21st 2020 signifies more than any other moment in history, since even before the time of the Sumerians and Egyptians, the definitive celestial equivalent of the *End of Days*, the *End of Time* and the beginning of a New Era.

CXI.II – DIVINE PROMISE

Divine Promise

1. To Christian Faith, trust in authentic scripture concerning the End Times and the Coming of Days is as fundamental a core belief as trust in the Resurrection of Christ. To Christians, the End Times and End of Days herald the final and definitive return of Jesus Christ, the Last Judgement and a new Covenant of unity between Heaven and Earth; and many more signs and beliefs both common and different between Christians around the world.

So important is the concept of the End Times and Coming of Days to Christianity, that most Christians are regularly called as a profession of faith to testify to their firm belief in the End Times and the Second Coming of Christ. However, unlike the volume and clarity of authentic scripture found in the New Testament concerning the Divine Word and Teachings of Christ, the authentic scripture that supports the Christian Eschatology (study of final events of history) rests in less than a handful of Biblical books – and with much of what is written enveloped in deep symbolism, allegory and mysticism. In fact, the most symbolic, allegorical and mystical passages of authentic Christian writing are largely found to be concentrated around Christian Eschatology, including such related epic works by poets Dante Alighieri, John Milton and even William Shakespeare. Consequently, Christian Eschatology is a discipline that has been hotly disputed and sometimes wildly speculated for many centuries.

Some Christian scholars and clerics have approached the passages within the few Biblical chapters and passages concerning Christian Eschatology in a superficial and literal sense as a kind of "Divine Checklist". Others have chosen to simply "cherry pick" sections of authentic Christian Eschatological writings to fit their given narrative. Others still have chosen the entirely novel approach of inventing their own claims and theories, loosely based on a few references of such authentic Christian writings.

Such divergence concerning the interpretation of End Times from a Christian perspective has not just been limited to theological and doctrinal differences, but in the application and use of such positions to advance various movements and claims concerning the End Times and the Return of Christ. Most notably, the greatest controversies and speculations have concerned both individuals seeking to "predict" the date of the "end of the world", whilst there have been many dozens of people who have proclaimed themselves "the Messiah" of the Old Testament or "Jesus Christ" returned.

All of this history and controversy and all of these differences of opinion and interpretation have made the clarity of any discussion concerning Christian Eschatology between the broader family of Christian faithful almost impossible, as the depth and complexity of the subject matter is troubling at best for many Christians. It is why a number would prefer to avert any detailed discussion all together, especially given the litany of lies and misrepresentations by so many over centuries, who saw the subject matter as an opportunity rather than a solemn and sacrosanct part of Christian faith.

Midst such division and confusion, there is still one thing that can cause all true Christians to unite, and at the same time expose those who hold less than honest motives concerning End Times Belief: Either you Trust in the Testament of Christ, that the End of Days and Judgement Day is both an End and a Beginning, or you do Not. It is that simple.

If you are a true Christian, then you trust in the Good News of Christ above the words of men and women that the nature of God and the Divine Creator is one of Divine Love, Forgiveness And Redemption and not condemnation and intentional destruction. You Trust in the Light of Christ that his return heralds a New Beginning and a New Age and a new Covenant of unity between Heaven and Earth.

Yet if you believe that the End of Days and the Final Judgement is the complete destruction of planet Earth and the Universe and the end of existence itself, then sadly you betray your lack of trust in the Divine Words and Message of Jesus Christ himself, that repudiated such fear mongering for profit and control among the people of his time. Christ not only rejected such false claims by the priests, scribes and scholars at the time, he made it a central pillar of faith among his disciples that personal responsibility and personal sacrifice is the true meaning of Divine Revelation concerning the end and a new beginning. In truth, the centrality of the most Holy Eucharist as the last blood sacrifice to save and redeem all humanity is a living rejection of the wickedly false and evil philosophy that God has doomed the world and will one day destroy it.

As cynical as it may sound, it has been powerful forces of nihilism, who hide as conservatives and liberals; and as clerics and judges; and as business and military leaders, that have promoted such blatant contradictions between the Divine Message of Christ himself and what some Christians are tricked to believe and follow. These people who believe in nothing but their own vanity, wealth and glory have always viewed the Divine Message of unity between Heaven and Earth and between Mind, Body and Soul as an existential threat to their power.

Frightened people are weaker than enlightened people. Ignorant people are more easily controlled than those whose eyes are open to the truth of the New Evangelisation of Christ. Above all, a people who believe in fear and division and doom are less likely to honour their solemn obligations to this planet and their communities, than those who remember and trust in the truth of the actual words of Jesus Christ.

Thus, the question that must be asked and answered by anyone reading *Missale Christus* concerning the End Times is: Do you Trust in Christ or not?

CXI.III – DIVINE FULFILMENT OF REVELATION

Divine Fulfilment of Revelation

1. At the time of Christ, knowledge of the existence, mind, nature and will of the Divine, as exemplified through Divine Law, was considered the foundation stone of human civilisation. The greater the knowledge, the greater its importance. In almost every case, such knowledge was divided into three distinct components: (a) the message; and (b) the true meaning; and (c) the authentic fulfilment of the true meaning.

In respect of the first part (the message), such knowledge was almost always transmitted in allegory via the techniques of short stories (parables) or prose (poetry). The use of such words or symbols to represent certain abstract and sometimes more complex principles enabled the dramatic compacting of what might otherwise be complex and confusing description. It also enabled the compressing of multiple meanings into the same combination of words – a hallmark of authentic Divine knowledge. Yet without the cipher (the true meaning), such allegory could be hidden in plain sight and still not understood. Thus, authentic Revelation has always been properly understood to be both (a) *the message*; and (b) *the true meaning*, even if (c) *the authentic fulfilment of the true meaning* has not yet occurred.

Many groups in power throughout history have considered such Divine knowledge and its interpretation should be kept hidden and secret from the wider community. In direct contrast, Christ revealed through his ministry that God the Divine Father of all Creation wills that all men and women be saved by coming to comprehend and discern the knowledge of the truth. Christ not only provided authentic Divine messages in the form of parables and prose, but also gave his disciples at least one cipher of meaning to understand at least one or more layer of true meaning.

Christ demonstrated that genuine Revelation is the self-evident manifestation of Divine Illumination, providing extraordinary enlightenment, clarity, perception, reason and knowledge, beyond the norm. It is its own witness, because its carries the living essence of the Divine within the unique character of the message. However, Christ did warn that there would be some in every generation who are tempted by the hope of riches and fame to deceive their community by confecting false claims of revelation. This is sadly a significant obstacle concerning Revelation and Christian Eschatology.

As it happens, virtually all the writings concerning Christian Eschatology come with only one part (the message) concerning authentic Revelation. Unlike the Divine Teachings of Christ, where He provided both the message and a key cipher of understanding to unlock at least one level of meaning, no ciphers appear to be widely accepted for the true deciphering of meaning and any fulfilment of such meaning in respect of Christian Eschatological writings.

CXI.IV – DIVINE MANDATE OF UNIVERSAL ECCLESIA

Divine Mandate of Universal Ecclesia

1. The most sacred Universal Ecclesia of One Christ, also known as the One Holy Apostolic Universal Ecclesia, also known as the *Sol Ecclesia*, also known as the *Authentic Body of Christ*, is the first, highest and supreme association, aggregate, fraternity, body, entity and society of Members sharing spiritual heritage associated with all forms of Christian and Jewish faiths, possessing a Divine Mandate for the next three thousand, two hundred and ten (3210) years.

   In accord with Article 4 (Authority and Power) of the sacred Covenant *Pactum De Singularis Christus* and Article 92 (One Christ) of the most sacred Covenant *Pactum De Singularis Caelum*, no Christian or Jewish person, association, aggregate, institute, body, entity or society may assert or claim higher jurisdiction or authority than the Universal Ecclesia of One Christ.

   All living Higher Life Forms who profess to be Christian or Jewish are *ipso facto* (as a matter of fact) subject first to the laws of One Heaven and second to the laws of the Universal Body of Christ above any other lesser society, association, aggregate, institute, fraternity, entity or body.

   Furthermore, every and all ordained, acknowledged, commissioned or certified clergy of any Christian or Jewish body are also officers of One Christ; and subject to the laws and obligations of One Christ first above any other lesser society, association, aggregate, institute, fraternity, entity or body.

The Divine Mandate of the most sacred Universal Ecclesia of One Christ comes in fulfilment of the true meaning of authentic Revelation and the End of Time, End of Days and Final Judgement; and the full and permanent presence of Christ in spirit, mind and body through the Living Word of Christ, the Living Liturgy of Christ and the Living Body of Christ as the awakening of all Christians to unite as one living body, consistent with Divine Revelation.

To deny the Divine Mandate of the most sacred Universal Ecclesia of One Christ is to openly deny Christ and the Divine Creator. Furthermore, to deny that the Divine Mandate is a manifest sign of the fulfilment of the true meaning of authentic Revelation and the End of Time, End of Days and Final Judgement is to openly deny the truth of the Promise of God and the Divine Creator as revealed by Christ. Anyone that chooses to openly defy and reject Christ and God therefore fulfils prophecy to themselves and their own Final Judgement.

CXI.V – THE LIVING WORD OF CHRIST

1. To all Christians, the Good News that is the Testament of Jesus Christ is the highest revelation and teaching of God the Divine Creator of all Existence and all Heaven and Earth. By the very definition of authentic Christian Revelation, the Good News of Christ has always retained his living spirit. It has never left. Christ himself even made this fact clear to his disciples and future generations, even if we sometimes fail to remember or fully comprehend. The Living Word of Christ

   The Divine Word of Christ *is* The Living Word of Christ and the permanent presence of His spirit upon this planet from the time of his first incarnation in flesh unto the present day and until the end of existence of planet Earth and the Solar System. The Spirit of Christ, through the Living Word of Christ never left us. Thus, much of the authentic revelation of meaning of genuine Christian Eschatology is the understanding that a time will come when we effectively "wake up to ourselves" and embrace once more the Good News of Christ and what it truly is. This is precisely the Mission of New Evangelisation.

CXI.VI – THE LIVING LITURGY OF CHRIST

1. When Christ first empowered his Disciples on a Divine Mission of Evangelisation through the Holy Spirit, it was an act of succession as an act of rebirth and renewal of a new apostolic generation. This understanding is in fact at the very heart and mission of bishops of the Universal Ecclesia as direct apostolic successors to the authority and The Living Liturgy of Christ

powers of the first disciples of Christ. Such rebirth and renewal can only exist as a continual Divine act of creation and life.

When Christ called upon his disciples and successors to bear witness to the Good News as His Living Spirit, it was to lead by example not only by deed but by words. With the inclusion of such words and teachings within a Living Liturgy, precisely to the instructions of Christ himself, the sacrifices of so many heroes of faith are manifestly more powerful and profound.

The Living Liturgy of Christ *is* The Living Mind of Christ. *Missale Christus* is a remembrance of this original Living Liturgy of Christ as the permanent presence of His Divine Intention and Mind upon this planet from the time of his first incarnation in flesh unto the present day and until the end of existence of planet Earth and the Solar System. The Mind of Christ, through the Living Liturgy of Christ never left us. Thus, the Living Liturgy of Christ must continue to evolve and adapt. It must recognise the need to be respectful and inclusive of different cultures and peoples, as well as the history of different denominations of the Universal Ecclesia now and forever more.

CXI.VII – THE LIVING BODY OF CHRIST

The Living Body of Christ

1. The Universal Ecclesia of One Christ as the Authentic Living Body of Christ is a Living and Universal entity registered and recognised in accord with the Great Ledger and Public Record of One Heaven as a True Person and *Universal True Trust* possessing certain Natural Rights of Use and Purpose. It is in essence both the personification and the embodiment of Christ on this planet and within this Stellar System.

The Authentic Living Body of Christ symbolises all Living Members as being incorporated into the true Living Body of Christ as one united family; and the fulfilment of Sacred Scripture in the return and permanent presence of Christ Redeemed.

As a Universal True Trust, the Universal Ecclesia of One Christ possesses a True Personality based upon its Divine Personality guided by its True Mind and Intent being the Covenant of One Christ. The Society of One Christ shall have mortal life for one (1) complete Era of three thousand two hundred ten (3210) years until its physical death. Upon its physical death, the people of the Earth may choose for the Society to be reborn for another Era, or for a new named Society to be created in accord with the canons and laws of One Heaven.

Christ himself expressed this truth at the time of the disciples when he spoke of himself being in them; and a critical purpose and significance of remembrance of the Holy Eucharist. The Last Supper was both literally and symbolically the creation of a new living body and a new living person of Christ. When imploring his disciples to remember the ceremony, it was in major part to remember and not forget this truth. Yet over time, the Christian family did sadly forget this command of Christ and the realisation that Christ had already transformed his living body and personality to the Universal Ecclesia beginning with the disciples. Christ has no need of being physically incarnated as flesh again, as this would completely undermine the purpose and meaning of his Divine Ministry. The Living Body and Living Person of Christ *is* already a permanent presence on Earth. We simply have to remember the signifiance of the message embedded within the ceremony of the Holy Eucharist.

www.ingramcontent.com/pod-product-compliance
Lightning Source LLC
LaVergne TN
LVHW060014210926
848481LV00013B/3709
* 9 7 8 1 6 4 4 1 9 0 6 8 5 *